A PROFILE OF
CORRECTIONAL EFFECTIVENESS AND
NEW DIRECTIONS FOR RESEARCH

SUNY SERIES, NEW DIRECTIONS IN CRIME
  AND JUSTICE STUDIES
AUSTIN T. TURK, EDITOR

A PROFILE OF
CORRECTIONAL EFFECTIVENESS AND
NEW DIRECTIONS FOR RESEARCH

BY
TED PALMER

STATE UNIVERSITY OF NEW YORK PRESS

Published by
State University of New York Press, Albany

©1994   State University of New York

All rights reserved

Printed in the United States of America

For information, address the State University of New York Press,
State University Plaza, Albany, NY 12246

Library of Congress Cataloging-in-Publication Data

Palmer, Ted,
 A profile of correctional effectiveness and new directions for
research / by Ted Palmer.
  p. cm. — (SUNY series, New directions in crime and justice
studies)
 Includes bibliographical references and index.
 ISBN 0-7914-1909-6 (alk. paper). — ISBN 0-7914-1910-X
(pbk. : alk. paper)
  1. Corrections—Evaluation. 2. Corrections—Research.
3. Corrections—United States. I. Title. II. Series.
HV9275.P347 1994
364.6'0973—dc20   93-24925
               CIP

10 9 8 7 6 5 4 3 2 1

To My Son, Clay
And My Daughter, Cara

Contents

Foreword

When policy scholars pronounced rehabilitation "dead" in the mid-1970s, much of the field was prepared to bury it. Critics of American sentencing practices blamed the idea of rehabilitation for everything from a rising crime rate to prison unrest. Nearly everything wrong with the correctional system, including both overly harsh prison terms (because of indeterminacy) and excessive leniency (because judges and parole officers coddled offenders), was traced to adoption of the rehabilitative ideal. Rehabilitation was said to cost too much and yield too little and to confuse the true punitive nature of corrections with social work. Even worse, some argued that under the guise of benevolence ("we're here to help you avoid a life of crime"), the state coercively intervened in the psychology of individuals whose only "crimes" were to be incorrigible or to have been declared "a delinquent."

Although a strong commitment to the rehabilitative ideal, was, even in the 1970s, disputable, the abandonment of the *possibility* of efficient and effective treatment fairly swept the field. Deterrence and incapacitation came into favor in policy circles and in the academy, with some arguing that it may be possible to save both money and innocent victims using incarceration programs that emphasized fear and isolation. Although treatment may be a noble idea, argued many policy scholars, it too often interfered with doing justice.

Consequently, when a few well-publicized literature reviews claimed to show, on the basis of the best available research, the ineffectiveness of treatment for delinquency and crime, it seemed almost possible to hear the field heave a collective sigh of relief. Doing good and doing justice did not really conflict if doing good was, after all, impossible. And the potential savings to the taxpayer were handsome. As one knowledgeable professor was fond of saying in those days, "if we can't save souls, at least we can save money!"

Well, from the perspective of the 1990s, the taxpayer most certainly would have been better off trying to save souls, because the policy shift to deterrence and incapacitation has certainly not been cheap. By almost any measure the situation subsequent to the adoption of policies favoring deterrence and incapacitation has become much worse. The crime rate, measured by police statistics, rose substantially during the 1980s and remains at very high levels. The number (and rates per 100,000) of individuals under some form of state supervision has skyrocketed. Nearly 500,000 more adults were incarcerated as of 1990 and 1991 than only ten years earlier. By 1990 more than 1,500 additional adults were incarcerated each week in the United States and the adults under parole or probation supervision was a staggering 3.2 million. The Bureau of Justice Statistics estimated that on any given day in 1990 in the United States about 1 in every 24 adult men was on some form of correctional supervision (all statistics from U.S. Department of Justice, 1992). As a result, correctional spending (principally for prisons) has been, during the decade of the 1990s, among the fastest growing part of state budgets, second only to health care.

It once was fashionable to deride rehabilitation programs by pointing out that, when pressed to account for the apparent lack of accomplishments, proponents of rehabilitation would claim "it has never really been tried." A little more money, better standards and training, and sufficient time will reveal that success is just around the corner. Today, proponents of the deterrent effectiveness of incarceration plead much the same: If we only have the courage to stick to harsh, mandatory prison terms for just about everyone convicted of a crime, if we only can show the will to apply incapacitation and deterrence to juveniles and first offenders, if we wait a bit longer so that the fear of imprisonment can trickle down to the street level, then we will begin to reap the benefits of this correctional spending spree. Well, if turnabout is fair play (and in this case it surely is not play), then just when, the beleaguered taxpayer might ask, will we begin to see some inkling of improvement from current policies, if not after a fourfold increase in incarceration and the highest per capita expenditure for criminal justice in history?

Policy currents are difficult to predict in criminal justice. It may well be that concern about crime and a short-term orientation, both of which may be said to characterize the American public, have forced legislators and other policy makers into a costly and lengthy tailspin. More criminal justice intervention may be the only politically feasible response to a failure to lower the criminal rate, and each proposal for harsher, more mandatory punishment must be approved for fear of appearing soft on crime.

In such an environment, the programmatic experimentation that Ted Palmer calls for, and that is necessary in order to improve our knowledge, provides a strong challenge to and a clear choice for the correctional system—a system whose present harsh realities would stifle learning or lead it to ignore such experimentation. But in today's environment, optimism may be as rational as pessimism; there is some reason to believe that the expansiveness of the incapacitation/deterrence movement will so encumber the state that a revival of experimentation in treatments will be forced on agencies struggling to cope with the burdens of ever-increasing caseloads.

Meanwhile, not everyone so readily condescended to the pronouncements of various policy scholars that a detailed review of the research literature called for pessimistic conclusions. In particular, careful scholars pointed out that some interventions did indeed seem to have some effectiveness for some individuals. Several social scientists, Ted Palmer perhaps being the first and among the most persistent, refused to allow the glib summaries to go unchallenged. If the requirement of effective treatment was the discovery of a panacea, then, sure enough, the policy scholars were correct. And, it was (remains) true that the perfectly controlled experiment with random assignment, complete integrity of treatment, high dosage, no sample attrition, and completely valid and indisputable outcome data were not reported. But, of course, threats to the validity of research (which, given sufficient creativity, should always be possible) are not dispositive evidence that the results are misleading. In fact, as revealed in *A Profile of Correctional Effectiveness and New Directions for Research*, the meta-analyses and literature reviews undertaken in recent years have shown that it has been the sweeping claims of *in*effectiveness that have most likely been misleading.

Ted Palmer has chosen in this book to focus attention on evaluations of programs for juveniles and adolescents. It is both ironic and unfortunate that so much of the policy debate about correctional effectiveness, the purposes of imprisonment, appropriate sentencing structures, and the like, has centered on the adult criminal justice system. Crime statistics have always suggested that we should be much more concerned with juvenile justice programs. For one thing, it has been reasonably well established that most of the crime problem is the responsibility of young people (teen and preteen years). Crime rates rise rapidly through the preteen years, peak in late adolescence and early adulthood, and then fall rapidly and consistently throughout life. Such a distribution focuses attention on juveniles, particularly young juveniles, as the point of maximum feasible impact on crime rates. Even modest success for programs with a juvenile focus could provide substantial returns relative to adult programs.

In addition, most research on delinquency causation now strongly suggests that early interventions are more likely to be effective over the life-course than are later interventions because there seems to be considerable stability of individual differences in crime rates over time. Thus, apart from our traditional instincts to help children and juveniles that derive from compassion, the evidence suggests a strong utilitarian rationale for a focus on juvenile correctional and intervention programs.

In this book Ted Palmer asks us to take a fresh approach to research on intervention programs. He shows it is no longer satisfactory to study individual programs in isolation, to ignore the complexity of programs in favor of simple descriptions of intended categories of treatment, or to ignore the real-life setting of action programs. Rather, what is now required is to carefully collect more useful information about programs, to attend to their many dimensions, to replicate successes and to seek their generalization to other populations, to cease simplistic assessments and to begin building systematic knowledge.

This book is the plea of a scientist to seek knowledge for the long term and to acknowledge complexities in our work larger than we have previously been prepared to accept. Ted Palmer provides a much-needed blueprint for the design of research studies that will make knowledge building more likely, a blueprint that offers a way to better conceptualize the difficult task ahead. He introduces and carefully describes new analytic strategies, specific procedures, and sets of specific variables that can be applied to future research studies to help us understand the nature of complex, often-multifaceted programs.

A Profile of Correctional Effectiveness and New Directions for Research shows us that we need to study programs in all their dimensions, to study process, to increase variations, and to document in detail what we do, in order to provide the information needed for the creation of a field of knowledge. By conceptualizing the task ahead and its specific goals, and by providing strategies, procedures, and analytic units that could help researchers achieve those goals, this book provides a major foundation for the creation of that knowledge, and it describes what should become the next decade of treatment research. It also identifies new ways in which the control programs that are part of experimental/control designs can directly add to knowledge. Although the book goes well beyond a review of treatment effectiveness, its early chapters provide a systematic review of many specific treatments that have been used to date. This review, which is based on the findings and conclusions of numerous meta-analyses and literature reviews, provides a careful and wide-ranging integration of what has been learned thus far about whether those specific treatments increase public protection.

The place of rehabilitation in juvenile and adult justice systems has always involved an interaction between fact and values. For some, rehabilitation will always be inappropriate as a justification for state intervention. For such people, the faintest indication of ineffectiveness is all that is required as an empirical refutation. For others, the very possibility of rehabilitation is an essential value for our society, and thus the dimmest glimmer of empirical hope is all that is required to maintain rehabilitation as a justification. But probably for most people, neither ready to believe in the magic bullet nor willing to concede defeat so early, the important questions are whether some programs work better than others for some offenders, whether there are less expensive and more humane methods of dealing with offenders that do not substantially increase risk to the community, and whether objective reviews of the research provide any clues for the future. These are the people who should read this book and learn the insights of an experienced researcher and careful scholar.

Michael R. Gottfredson
Professor of Management and Policy, Law, and Psychology
The University of Arizona at Tucson

Acknowledgments

I wish to thank Ms. Christine Lynch of SUNY Press for her excellent work in guiding the manuscript through all phases of its production. I also thank Ms. Carol Newhouse for her outstanding copy editing—easily the best I've ever seen.

Preface

For nearly two decades the question of whether correctional intervention is effective has generated interest, confusion, and controversy. Several articles have addressed this question, and more than two dozen literature reviews and meta-analyses have examined many effectiveness studies. Sometimes, a handful of reviews or analyses have been compared with each other, and when this has occurred their findings have sometimes been inconsistent. Yet, whether or not their outcomes agreed, seldom were more than a few such works examined together. Thus, the broad power of corrections' already available findings has remained untapped, since its many literature reviews and meta-analyses were never assembled and compared *en masse*—for instance, regarding the question, Does intervention reduce recidivism and thereby protect the public?

This book begins to tap that power. It does so by assembling thirty-two reviews and analyses and by examining their findings collectively. It determines—on a much larger scale than before—the extent to which results from numerous studies of intervention support and differ from each other, and whether consistent patterns exist. To achieve this result it examines the extent and areas of agreement and disagreement that exist across the many analyses and reviews.

The book mainly focuses on juvenile offenders in community and institutional settings. It targets twenty types of intervention, including confrontation, diversion, the behavioral, the cognitive, three types of counseling, and intensive probation supervision, among others. It addresses not only the effectiveness of those several interventions individually but also that of all such types together—thus, of intervention as a whole, or collectively.

This review of more than two dozen meta-analyses and literature reviews of numerous intervention approaches is, in effect, an overview and integration *of* corrections' overviews—each of which, individually, is both limited and somewhat different from others as to setting, offender sample, time period covered, and intervention approaches. The book is thus designed to help practitioners and policy makers, on the one hand, and researchers, academicians, and students, on the other, obtain a broader, more reliable, better balanced, and perhaps less confusing view of intervention's present utility and future potential than has been provided to date.

Based on this extensive review, several intervention approaches are identified that have been substantially less likely than others to reduce recidivism. In contrast, other approaches are identified that have been considerably more likely to succeed. A consistent picture of intervention's *overall* effectiveness emerges as well, as do definite limitations.

Taken as a whole, this overview and integration clearly indicates that although no all-purpose approaches exist, several "types" of intervention show considerable promise and many individual programs are effective. Equally clear, however, is the fact that corrections has a long way to go before it will contain many programs that are simultaneously very successful and widely applicable. Yet this goal, we believe, can be achieved.

To help achieve this and more modest goals, the book introduces and discusses the following view: In order to make continued and substantial progress in building knowledge about effective intervention, a broader research strategy is needed than has been used thus far. In the proposed strategy, correctional programs would be conceptualized and analyzed as the composites and complex wholes that they *are*—or very often are. They would no longer be described in over-simplified ways and mainly studied as little more than one-dimensional operations. To continue studying intervention in this manner would place major, unnecessary constraints on knowledge building.

Though the proposed strategy would be challenging and difficult to implement, it is clearly needed and could infuse intervention research with a new and deeper sense of direction. Moreover, it would increase this area's relevance. In the long run, the proposed multidimensional emphasis could provide corrections with a better understanding and more realistic portrayal of intervention than exists today and would otherwise exist tomorrow.

This book does not simply define or diagnose a current need, then point toward broad yet basic goals and leave the reader wondering, How does one get there? It does not just challenge or urge readers to work more systematically and vigorously toward such major goals as *(a)* better describing correctional approaches and the individual programs that comprise them, and *(b)* identifying key factors that contribute to success. That is, it does not just challenge without suggesting ways to proceed. Instead, the book provides guidance and directions, particularly by introducing and discussing strategies for achieving those goals. It specifies, for the first time, a set of interrelated concepts, tools, and analytic procedures that could help build the type of knowledge now needed.

We believe that if the proposed strategies, concepts, and procedures are given heavy emphasis, corrections—in the future—will be able to accurately and adequately describe effective programs and will understand the main factors and combinations of factors responsible for that success. Policy makers, practitioners, and others could then use this information and insight to develop new programs and improve existing ones. This ability would help corrections play an increasingly broad and valuable role.

Introduction

Beginning in the mid-1980s, several meta-analyses and literature reviews appeared that bore on two long-standing questions: Does correctional intervention—particularly rehabilitation—reduce recidivism and thus contribute to public protection? and, If and when intervention reduces offending, what kind of programs are involved?

The background for these questions is generally well known but far from simple. Briefly, from the 1960s to early 1970s there was a broad surge of confidence regarding rehabilitation's seeming ability to change and control offenders (President's Commission, 1967; Warren, 1971; Palmer, 1974; Glaser, 1975). This high optimism was quickly followed by widespread pessimism during the period 1975–81, a pessimism triggered by Martinson's mid-1970s critique of rehabilitation's presumed effectiveness (Martinson, 1974; Greenberg, 1977; Sechrest, White, and Brown, 1979). By 1983–84 evidence for Martinson's "relatively-little-works" view and for an alternative, "several-things-sometimes-work" view had been marshalled and became increasingly known (Palmer, 1978; Romig, 1978; Gendreau and Ross, 1979). As a result, a mixed and unsettled atmosphere emerged regarding effectiveness. More precisely, considerable confusion and uncertainty existed.

Yet one thing became clear: neither the deep pessimism of the middle and later 1970s nor the global optimism of the 1960s seemed justified. Instead, more moderate views took shape and soon became widely known, especially among researchers and academicians (Empey, 1978; Martin, Sechrest, and Redner, 1981; Palmer, 1983). This included a relatively open-minded skepticism on the one hand and a more cautious optimism on the other. Meanwhile, most practitioners believed programming was helpful, yet many wondered if that help was substantial. Other individuals were neutral but not uninvolved.

Since the mid-1970s more than twenty literature reviews have addressed correctional effectiveness; from the mid-1980s to the present, nine meta-analyses have done the same. Usually, these works examined an aggregate of forty-five to ninety individual studies each (the median is seventy-five); some focused on more than one hundred studies and one even had several hundred.[1] Based on the findings of these studies, each reviewer and analyst drew conclusions about the effectiveness of *(a)*

xxi

particular types of correctional intervention, for example, vocational training; *(b)* correctional intervention as a whole, that is, the several separate types collectively; or *(c)* both *(a)* and *(b)*. Several authors of these works, for example, Romig (1978), Gendreau and Ross (1979, 1987), and Andrews et al. (1990), expressed largely positive views about *(a)* and/or *(b)*. Others, for example, Martinson (1974), Greenberg (1977), and Whitehead and Lab (1989), expressed generally negative views. Still others—perhaps the majority (e.g., Rutter and Giller [1983], Gordon and Arbuthnot [1987], Gottschalk et al. [1987], and Lipsey [1992])—emphasized mixed results.

To date, this large body of individual literature reviews and meta-analyses has never been examined in the aggregate, that is, as a single group or collection. In particular, such an examination has not been conducted relative to the question, Does intervention reduce recidivism and thereby protect the public? Yet, an overview of these more than thirty reviews and analyses could be especially useful. It could determine if the overall findings from the respective works mainly support or largely differ and diverge from each other, and if general agreement exists regarding particular types of intervention. As such, it could provide timely information about correctional effectiveness that is more broadly based and reliable than before. Conclusions and generalizations from such an overview would not, of course, constitute the "final word." However, they would require fewer caveats than those associated with any one, two, or even handful of reviews or analyses.[2]

Caveats regarding individual literature reviews and meta-analyses that have been carried out to date either have reflected or should have reflected various limitations associated with those works. For example, they should have reflected the fact that many such works focused largely or entirely on one particular *setting*, such as the institutional or community. That limitation, in turn, interacted with *offender-representation*. For instance, because some "types" of offenders (e.g., the violent or previously violent) were strongly represented in given types of settings (e.g., the institutional), other categories of offenders (e.g., the nonviolent) were less likely to be found in those settings—and, thus, in analyses/reviews that centered on those settings. Though the degree of representation that existed for certain categories of offenders in given analyses/reviews may have been appropriate or unavoidable, this situation nevertheless limited or should have limited the conclusions and generalizations that were drawn in those analyses/reviews regarding intervention's effectiveness. That was the case because differing types of intervention may have been differentially effective with different types of offenders. (Despite this situation, a fairly wide *range* of offenders was included in most analyses and reviews, even though their representation may have been *unequal* within and across those works—and especially unequal in the individual studies that comprised the respective analyses/reviews.[3]) The above implies that interactions may have also existed by *type of intervention*— as, for example, with social casework, family intervention, or intensive probation supervision, which occurred more often in one type of setting (the community) than another.

Finally, another limitation related to *time*, and this applied to almost all meta-analyses and literature reviews. Specifically, although correctional interventions have been studied for thirty to thirty-five years at a moderately frequent and fairly steady rate, many analyses and reviews covered roughly six to twelve years each—and many of these periods, for example, 1960–72, 1974–80, or 1978–87 (and therefore the respective studies that were included in the analyses/reviews), did not necessarily or largely overlap. Though this truncated coverage was quite appropriate for specific purposes and although it was sometimes unavoidable (especially in earlier reviews/analyses), it nevertheless constituted a limitation regarding conclusions about intervention's overall effectiveness. It was a source of inconsistent findings from one analysis/review to the next, as well.

Even if the limitations associated with most individual literature reviews and meta-analyses had been small to moderate, an overview of those and remaining works *collectively* could provide added and more reliable information about the effectiveness of intervention overall. In addition, it could provide a more broadly based and perhaps a more objective or balanced composite profile of intervention's often-used, respective *approaches.* In particular, an overview could provide such a profile if the studies that are examined are—collectively—not just numerous but unselected and if they are—again, collectively—widely representative and inclusive as to settings, types of offenders, and time periods. Such an overview or integration of corrections' many individual meta-analyses and literature reviews could thus provide information—and a broader perspective—that might help practitioners, policy makers, researchers, and others better sort out and assess various conclusions that have been drawn regarding effectiveness.

Chapter 1 of this book describes the different ways that meta-analyses and literature reviews summarize or integrate information from a collection of individual studies, and how these respective methods shed light on somewhat differing as well as overlapping aspects of intervention. The chapter also describes the methods used in the present overview and integration of thirty-two meta-analyses and literature reviews, and how the authors of those works generally organized them by "type" of intervention.

Chapter 2 summarizes, one by one, ten of the thirty-two meta-analyses and literature reviews that have been among the best known, the most extensive, and/or the most recent. It focuses on the findings and conclusions of those works for correctional intervention *overall*. That is, it emphasizes not so much the separate types of intervention (though these are sometimes described as well) as the collective results for the several approaches taken together. The chapter also reviews key factors that contributed to the findings and conclusions of those separate meta-analyses and literature reviews, factors such as type of intervention approach and type of techniques used in the analysis.

Chapter 3 presents the results of the thirty-two meta-analyses and literature reviews for each of twenty subject-areas or intervention approaches *individually*. These areas or approaches include confrontation, diversion, the behavioral, the cognitive-behavioral or cognitive, life-skills methods, and intensive probation supervision, among others.

Chapter 4 describes the major trends regarding correctional effectiveness that emerge from the findings of the several analyses and reviews *collectively*. It then describes problem areas and underlying factors that contribute to those findings and that appear to limit them. The chapter also reviews the amount of recidivism reduction observed across the several approaches.

Drawing from the preceding chapters, chapter 5 discusses the absence of "all-purpose"—for example, very reliable yet widely applicable—intervention approaches. It examines several major factors related to this absence, such as limited program relevance, the level or adequacy of program implementation, and the adequacy of traditional (i.e., control or comparison) programs themselves. In this connection the chapter also describes the multidimensional nature of intervention approaches in particular—this being a factor seldom examined to date.

Chapter 6 proposes a new direction for intervention research: the study of *combinations* of features that comprise given programs. The chapter describes the nature, scope, and initial challenges involved in such research. It also discusses the need to examine interventions as composites of programmatic as well as nonprogrammatic factors, such as staff characteristics and staff/client interactions.

Chapter 7 discusses several needs and issues involved in increasing the quality, strength, and relevance of research studies. It introduces specific analytic units or features that can provide a foundation for more accurately describing and better understanding intervention than has been possible to date. It also discusses the general nature of process-features such as staff/client interactions and intervention strategies/techniques.

Chapters 8 and 9 describe ways of implementing the proposed new research on combinations or multiple features. They address the question, How might one determine which programmatic and nonprogrammatic features, combinations, and broad patterns contribute to successful programs? Using the analytic units described in the preceding chapter, chapter 8 presents a step-by-step "building-block" method designed to identify contributing features and combinations. Chapter 9 introduces a more holistic, yet also systematic, "global" approach for identifying key ingredients of effective programs, especially programs whose actual operations may be relatively complex and perhaps involve several interactions among components. Both chapters provide specific, logically simple procedures for addressing the above question.

Chapter 10 reviews the need for multiple-features research—a type and degree of investigation that would make it possible to adequately describe and understand the complexities of real-life interventions. The chapter points out the implications of single-feature analysis—that is, unidimensional or "salient-feature" analysis—for the results presented in chapters 3 and 4. It also discusses the priority that should be given to the global and building-block approaches through and beyond the 1990s and to studying *why* given interventions work.

The final chapters focus on particular technical and conceptual issues. Chapter 11 examines success criteria, a key aspect of intervention research. The discussion centers on criteria that can be useful when evaluating the efficacy of intervention in relation to specified goals and needs. The chapter also discusses the averaging of results from several positive-outcome studies. Both topics pertain to single- as well as multiple-features analyses. Chapter 12 describes the nature of "decisive" or "deciding" factors. This subject bears on multiple-features research in that, *(a)* although several of a program's components may contribute to its effectiveness whereas only relatively few of them may be sina qua nons, *(b)* only one or two of the latter components may actually put a program "over the top" with regard to success. The chapter also discusses formal dimensions of "change"—an important topic given the often-dynamic and phased nature of many real-life interventions.

Several appendices describe other aspects of intervention research that have received little attention to date and/or enlarge the discussion found in given chapters. Appendix F, for instance, focuses on rarely—if ever—examined issues involving control programs in experimental/control studies, and it illustrates the challenging implications of these issues, such as differential baselines, for past and future research. The appendix also discusses intra- and interjurisdiction changes through time in the nature and effectiveness of control programs, and it outlines new ways in which specific components of these programs—like experimentals themselves—may directly enhance knowledge.

Based on this book's review of twenty types of intervention that were examined in the above meta-analyses and literature reviews, several types of intervention—also called "approaches"—are identified that are substantially less likely than others to be associated with reduced recidivism; other approaches are identified that are considerably more likely. A consistent picture of intervention's *overall* effectiveness and present limitations emerges as well. In this connection the immediate message of this book is that meta-analyses and literature reviews clearly show that although no all-purpose approaches exist, several "types" of intervention show considerable promise, and numerous individual programs have proven effective. Yet, other types of intervention show relatively little promise and many individual programs are ineffective. Clearly, corrections has a long way to go before it will contain many highly successful and, at the same time, widely applicable approaches. But, of course, "successful" programs—in the sense of useful ones—need not always be *widely* applicable, for example, effective with almost all juveniles or adults and in nearly all settings.

In discussing and interpreting the findings from the above studies, the book identifies several factors that underlie inconsistencies which have existed across analyses and reviews, even for the more promising interventions. It suggests that these and related difficulties often reflect the fact that correctional programs, in general, have been narrowly conceptualized and, for understandable reasons, have often been analyzed on an artificially and overly simplified basis. Though this conceptual and analytic framework has produced important knowledge, continued emphasis upon it—certainly exclusive or nearly exclusive focus—could lead to rapidly diminishing returns in terms of critical knowledge building. In any case, such emphasis or focus would not tap the potential that exists for creative yet systematic research.

Therefore, the main long-range message of this book is that a major new emphasis or approach is needed in correctional effectiveness research. This approach must be broader and more integrative than that which has characterized meta-analyses and most literature reviews to date. It must ultimately be based on better, more detailed program descriptions than have existed thus far. In short, the book poses a difficult but important new challenge: In order to *(a)* more accurately identify effective and ineffective correctional approaches, *(b)* more adequately characterize correctional approaches and the individual programs that comprise them, and *(c)* identify key ingredients that contribute to success, intervention research must take greater account of correctional programs as composites and often-complex wholes, that is, greater account than it has done to date. This multidimensional approach could eventually provide corrections with a deeper understanding and more realistic portrayal of intervention.

Though such efforts would require many years and further technical development, the results would be worth it. They would help intervention play an increasingly useful and appropriate role in the spectrum of interactions and activities that range from delinquency prevention to institutionalization, and whose main aims are to protect society and assist offenders.

This book does not just define and discuss what is needed and simply urge readers to somehow accomplish the corresponding goals. Rather, it offers guidance and specific direction, particularly by describing strategies and methods for achieving those goals. By presenting a set of interrelated concepts, tools, and analytic procedures that can help build the type of knowledge base that is needed, the book offers several ways of moving intervention research in relevant directions into at least the next decade. We believe that if the proposed strategies, tools, and concepts are given high priority during the next several years, a great deal more will be known in ten or so years about the bases, the nature, and the limits of effective correctional intervention than is known today.

Part I
Profiling Correctional Effectiveness

Chapter 1

Background

This chapter describes the differing ways that meta-analyses and literature reviews summarize or integrate information from a collection of individual studies and how those respective methods shed light on somewhat different as well as overlapping aspects of intervention. The chapter also describes the methods used in this book's overview and integration of numerous meta-analyses and literature reviews, and how the authors of those works generally organized them by "type" of intervention. The chapter concludes by reviewing the main methods for measuring program effectiveness.

LITERATURE REVIEWS AND META-ANALYSES

Integrating Information

Literature reviews and meta-analyses provide different but complementary ways of integrating information and drawing conclusions. If one asks, Does intervention X work?, the conclusion that is usually drawn in a literature review has been largely based on an integration of all-or-none judgments about each of the several individual studies that comprise X. For example, say that ten separate family intervention programs have each been categorically judged to be effective or "working," based on their having reached the .05 level of statistical significance, and say that ten other such programs have been categorized as "not working" because they did not attain that level (even though several may have had a mildly positive outcome, such as $p < .20$). By then tallying—in this respect integrating—the categorical judgments regarding all twenty programs, it might reasonably be concluded that X yielded mixed results, that is, some positive and some negative, but did not reliably or even usually "work." (Throughout this volume "the .05 level" will usually be presented as "$p < .05$." In either case it will mean there were five or fewer chances in 100 that the results of a study could be accounted for by chance alone.)

In contrast, meta-analysis focuses more directly and primarily on the *group* or collection of studies. Its conclusion about the group's effectiveness is not derived from all-or-none judgments as to whether each individual study has reached a particular significance level; instead, it reflects the *degree* of difference that exists between each treatment or experimental program, on the one hand, and its control or comparison program, on the other (Light and Pillemer, 1984).

The statistic that is used to reflect this difference is called the "effect size" (ES). This statistic indicates the number of standard deviation units by which one program outperforms the other. (An ES of .10 corresponds to a difference of about 10 percent in the recidivism rates of the experimental as compared to the control/traditional programs, and ESs of .20 and .30 correspond to differences of approximately 20 percent and 30 percent respectively. This relatively straight-line relationship also exists whether one uses, as a *baseline*, a control/traditional-program recidivism rate that is 40 percent, 50 percent, or even 60 percent. However, the straight-line relationship disappears when, for example, one's control/traditional baseline drops well *below* 40 pecent, especially when one's ES is .40 or more [Cohen, 1988, p. 181].) An *average* ES can then be obtained for the group of individual programs that was studied collectively. As a result, by focusing on the same twenty studies mentioned above, meta-analysis could have possibly justified a conclusion that intervention X was moderately effective, that is, generally positive. This conclusion could have reflected the finding that X's programs, collectively, had reduced recidivism by, say, an average of 12 percent and that the variability across its studies was not very large (thereby reducing the likelihood that the difference was due to chance). Such a conclusion could have been drawn even if no individual study had reached the .05 level per se (Fiske, 1983; Glass, McGaw, and Smith, 1981; Hedges and Olkin, 1985; Leviton and Cook, 1981; Lipsey, 1992; Strube and Hartmann, 1983; Wolf, 1986). This outcome could have occurred independently of the fact that—not infrequently—individual studies miss the .05 level (a) mainly because the sample-sizes of their respective experimental and control/traditional programs are relatively small (e.g., 50 each), (b) despite the fact that a sizable difference may simultaneously exist between the recidivism rates of those experimental and control/traditional programs.

Meta-analysis proceeds from the valid premise that the significance level which is ordinarily obtained for any individual study is produced not only by differences that may *actually* exist between the experimental and control programs that have been compared (e.g., differences in recidivism), but by several extraneous factors as well. The latter—often called "noise" or "error variance"—includes both sampling and measurement error; together with other extraneous factors and with spin-offs from methodological shortcomings, they create erroneous variability among the studies being examined. Meta-analysis recognizes and tries to deal with the fact that results from individual studies, for instance, results which have traditionally been expressed as "significance levels," are probabilistically distributed and contain an unknown degree of error—therefore unreliability.

To increase reliability, meta-analysis depends essentially on across-study statistics—central tendency and variability—and then draws its conclusion directly from the entire set of studies. Though meta-analysis utilizes not only large but also relatively *small* differences or fluctuations that exist between given experimental programs and their controls (or other types of comparisons), the conclusion derived via this method is—overall—less influenced by the above-mentioned error variance than is the conclusion from a traditional literature review. In traditional reviews, this variance, especially if substantial, can sometimes make a program either reach or miss the .05 level when, in fact, the program should not—or not quite—have done so.

Presently, many researchers and academicians favor meta-analysis over literature reviews. Besides the above reasons, this preference especially reflects the fact that meta-analysis—via its "effect size" statistic—can more fully and directly reflect the *amount* of difference that exists between intervention programs and their respective controls, not just whether a statistically significant difference exists for a certain percentage of studies. In addition, meta-analysis can aggregate the findings from several individual studies on a quantitatively more refined basis.

Literature reviews, however, can more easily reveal and descriptively focus on particularly promising individual programs. This feature is important if one asks, not just *(a)* Does intervention X work? or How much, if any, does it improve performance? but *(b)* What elements and other factors characterize programs that seem to work? and, more specifically, What perhaps contributes to the latters' apparent success? Though meta-analysis can itself provide clues regarding this second set of questions, literature reviews are better-suited for discussing the set, including possible clues to success. (Of course, few widely recognized answers yet exist to the latter questions.) In any event, both types of questions are important today. Also, error variance notwithstanding, literature reviews, we believe, can probably provide a reasonably reliable, straightforward answer to the practical questions, Did specified *individual* programs improve offenders' performance? and, How often did certain *types* of programs, such as those emphasizing family intervention or vocational training, provide improvement?

In sum, the meta-analysis and literature review methods each shed light on somewhat different aspects or levels of correctional intervention; they may also cast somewhat different light on similar aspects. As a result, each has its advantages relative to integrating given information and addressing various questions about individual programs or groups of programs. In addition, some overlap exists as to what these methods can produce. For instance, both can address simple but important questions about public protection, for example, by indicating the average amount of recidivism reduction observed in specified types of programs. Meta-analysis can do this by statistically transforming its effect sizes into equivalent percent-reductions (Lipsey, 1991; Cohen, 1988), and literature reviews can usually generate such reductions directly.

Though neither meta-analysis nor literature review constitutes the only valid or complete approach to describing and assessing correctional intervention or the only promising road to knowledge, each one has considerable merit. In any event it seems unlikely that either method necessarily or commonly contains so much error or uncertainty that its results should, a priori, be considered seriously flawed and therefore of questionable validity. Both methods have made useful, complementary contributions to the evaluation of intervention; and insofar as their respective results suggest similar or substantially overlapping conclusions, those conclusions should probably be considered more reliable than if they were based on either method alone.

METHODS

To obtain a broad overview of correctional research findings we examined thirty-two meta-analyses and literature reviews—the two basic forms of study conducted to date. Specifically, we reviewed the results from all delinquency centered American and Canadian meta-analyses that have been published thus far, namely: Andrews et al., 1990; Davidson et al., 1984; Garrett, 1985; Gensheimer et al., 1986; Gottschalk et al., 1987; Izzo and Ross, 1990; Lipsey, 1992; Mayer et al., 1986; and Whitehead and Lab, 1989.[1] In addition, we examined the findings from some fifteen general, that is, multitopic, literature reviews. (Multitopic means that several types of intervention were covered.) These were: Gendreau and Ross, 1979, 1987; Genevie, Margolies, and Muhlin, 1986; Gordon and Arbuthnot, 1987; Greenberg, 1977; Johns and Wallach, 1981; Lab and Whitehead, 1988; Lipton, Martinson, and Wilks, 1975; Lundman, 1984;

Panizzon, Olson-Raymer, and Guerra, 1991; Romig, 1978; Rutter and Giller, 1983; Van Voorhis, 1987; Whitehead and Lab, 1989; and Wright and Dixon, 1977. (Martinson, 1974; and Palmer, 1975, 1978, 1983, 1984 were included, although their observations often related to the Lipton, Martinson, and Wilks study sample.)

While the sample of general literature reviews may or may not have included all or almost all multitopic yet large-scale works, it did, in the aggregate, encompass a very wide range of views and outcomes published from 1955 to the present—quite possibly the full range. Though the sample emphasized but was not limited to reviews that have been perhaps the most widely and often quoted, the general literature reviews were otherwise unselected and every effort was made to represent their full range of findings and conclusions—whether "positive," "neutral or mixed," or "negative." In any case, the sample of multitopic literature reviews was—when aggregated—very inclusive as to settings, types of offenders, and time periods.

Finally, we examined the results from eight special-topic reviews, that is, literature surveys that focused mainly or exclusively on a single approach or intervention (such as family intervention). These were: Altschuler and Armstrong, 1990; Armstrong, 1988; Brody, 1976; Geismar and Wood, 1986; Graziano and Mooney, 1984; Krisberg et al., 1989; Parent, 1989; Schneider, 1986; and Ervin and Schneider, 1990. Many of the above-mentioned, *general* literature reviews had included the single approach or intervention that was focused on in these respective, special-topic reviews. The general reviews, of course, each included several other approaches as well.

Individually, the above-mentioned meta-analyses and literature reviews focused entirely or primarily on adjudicated youths—individuals in institutional settings, in community settings, or both. Each analysis and review purposely selected and emphasized individual studies in which a treatment or experimental program—referred to as "E"—was compared with a traditional or control program, labeled "C." Each program's performance measure, that is, its outcome or effectiveness criterion with respect to recidivism (see "Measuring Effectiveness," which follows), typically involved a behavioral indicator such as arrests, convictions, detentions/incarcerations, or suspensions; however, revocation, unfavorable termination, or similar status criteria were not uncommon.

The authors of these meta-analyses and literature reviews generally organized them according to "type of intervention," "method," "general (or generic) approach," and so forth—these terms being synonymous. In this context, "type" refers to the program feature, for example, vocational training, that was used by an author (analyst or reviewer) to characterize the collection of experimental programs—that is, the treatments or interventions—that he or she had grouped together for purposes of analysis and discussion. For instance, a literature reviewer may have grouped fifteen separate studies that each emphasized vocational training and that differed from their control or comparison program in that respect. He or she may then have given those studies the generic label "vocational training" and may then have proceeded to determine whether—or, in the case of meta-analysts, to what degree—the various E programs within that group outperformed their respective C's, or vice versa.

The types of intervention, that is, the subject areas that are included in the present overview of meta-analyses and literature reviews, are as follows: confrontation; area-wide strategies of delinquency prevention; social casework, social agency, or societal institution approaches to delinquency prevention; diversion; physical challenge; restitution; group counseling/therapy; individual counseling/therapy; family intervention; vocational training; employment; educational training; behavioral; cognitive-behavioral or cognitive; life skills (skill oriented; skill development); multimodal; probation enhancement and parole enhancement; intensive probation supervision; intensive aftercare (parole) supervision; and, community-based approaches vs. institutional intervention.

Not all individual meta-analyses and literature reviews touched on every subject area; in fact, many addressed fewer than half. Nevertheless, whenever the findings, the conclusions, or even the basic data-displays from any analysis or review bore on any given subject-area (e.g., confrontation), those findings, and so on, are mentioned in the results summarized in chapter 3 for that subject-area, that is, approach. More precisely, they are referred to in connection with the given approach *unless* the overall research quality of the individual studies which comprised that approach was very questionable. This occurred, for example, when the percentage of random-assignment studies and/or quasi-experimental studies that comprised the approach was either known to be, or seemed likely to have been, other than high. This situation, however, was uncommon across the analyses and reviews collectively.

MEASURING EFFECTIVENESS

The main indices of a program's effectiveness should closely reflect the fact that intervention's primary goal is increased public protection against illegal behavior. Such protection is directly reflected in *recidivism*, defined as any form of repeat offending. Recidivism, as measured by arrests, parole revocation, incarceration, and so on, has long been used to assess the impact of rehabilitation, punishment, and incapacitation alike. Despite its complexities and the differing ways it is measured, this index is widely accepted by researchers, practitioners, policy makers, and the public itself, and it is usually considered a key element in any outcome evaluation (Maltz, 1984).

When evaluating rehabilitation in particular, additional measures are nevertheless common; sometimes, in fact, they appear instead of recidivism. These measures generally reflect intervention's secondary or offender-centered goal—one that involves attitude change, personality change, and skill development. Such indices often correlate with recidivism itself; beyond that, they are generally recognized as meaningful in their own right, even when the correlation is low. However, since intervention's primary goal—increased public protection—is society rather than offender centered, the main index of program effectiveness in this book will be considered the *reduction of recidivism*, especially as measured by arrests, convictions, and similar actions that reflect offender behavior. Without this index, program evaluation would not just be incomplete; it would miss the main point. This is independent of the fact that attitude change, skill development, and so on, doubtlessly contribute to recidivism reduction itself.

Chapter 2

Results from Individual Analyses and Reviews

This chapter summarizes several meta-analyses that have been among the best known, the most extensive, and/or the most recent. It focuses on the findings and conclusions of each analysis for intervention overall; that is, it emphasizes not so much the separate types of intervention, but each analysis' collective results for the several approaches *together*. The chapter also reviews key factors that contributed to the findings and conclusions of those separate meta-analyses and literature reviews, factors such as type of intervention approach and type of techniques used in the analysis.

FINDINGS FROM SPECIFIC META-ANALYSES

Garrett

Garrett analyzed 111 experimental studies, conducted during the period 1960–83, of adjudicated delinquents in institutions and, to a lesser extent, in community residential settings. Probation, parole, and diversion programs were excluded. Based on measures such as psychological and institutional adjustment, academic performance, and/or recidivism, the treatment groups, on average, outperformed their controls: "The change was modest in some cases, substantial in others, but overwhelmingly in a positive direction," that is, positive in most individual studies. "Across treatments, settings, offender types, and outcome measures, the treatment group performed, on the average . . . + .37 standard deviations above the level of the untreated group, [which] received only the regular institutional program" (Garrett, 1985, pp. 293, 306) (+ .37 translated to the sixty-fourth percentile, when regular programming equaled the fiftieth). For studies using *recidivism*, the results—including the effect-sizes—were also positive though "to a more modest extent than [with] other measures of success"; specifically, the average ES was .13.* As will be seen, effect sizes were higher than this in meta-analyses that were neither limited to nor mostly centered on institutional/residential settings.

The most powerful approaches were "cognitive-behavioral," "life skills," and "family therapy," though some of these findings reflected few studies. These approaches held up for studies involving recidivism, where they had substantial effect sizes: .24, .28, and .28, respectively ("Cognitive-behavioral" was a subcategory within a broader class labeled "behavioral," whose effect size was .18) (Garrett, 1985).[1]

Lipsey

Lipsey recently described his long-term, cumulative analysis of what are now some 400 published and unpublished experimental studies of juvenile delinquents (mostly through age eighteen) in institutional and noninstitutional programs, 86 percent of which were reported during the years 1970–88. Based on a range of behavioral outcome measures (one per study)–usually arrests/police contacts, and other justice system contacts—64 percent of the results favored the treatment group, 30 percent favored controls, and 6 percent favored neither. "Favored" meant "in the direction of," even if statistical significance was missed.

In further analyzing these results, and after adjusting for small sample-size within studies and for unequal sample-sizes across studies, Lipsey found *type of treatment* to be considerably more influential than any other generic factor, such as nature of outcome measures (e.g., length of follow-up) and "dosage" (e.g., duration) of treatment (Lipsey, 1992). However, he also found *offender characteristics* (e.g., first timers vs. repeaters; amenability; I-level) to be important (Lipsey, 1989). The overall influence of "type of treatment" remained substantial and statistically significant even after all "method" factors were accounted for in a stepwise hierarchical multiple regression. Among these method factors were *(a)* initial equivalence of E vs. C samples, especially on recidivism risk, *(b)* design quality (random vs. nonrandom assignment), *(c)* differential attrition in E vs. C samples, and *(d)* overall sample-size. Factor *(a)* was particularly important.

Within the type-of-treatment factor, *(a)* "multimodal," "behavioral," and "skill-oriented" approaches had the most impact; *(b)* "probation and parole enhancements" had no positive impact; and *(c)* "deterrence/shock" approaches were associated with worse outcomes for E's than C's.[2] For these approaches (which had been categorized in terms of their "primary intervention" whenever possible) and for the remaining approaches com-

---

*ES figures are positive unless preceded by a minus sign.

bined, there was a strong possibility that, on average, better implemented programs, that is, programs with more operational integrity, outperformed the rest. The findings regarding multimodal, behavioral, and skill-oriented approaches applied within justice and nonjustice system settings alike.

When all types of programs, all levels of program implementation, and all outcomes were combined, "recidivism" averaged 9–12 percent lower for E's than C's, depending on how many studies had been analyzed at the time. (For multimodal, behavioral, and skill-oriented approaches the recidivism reduction was 20–32 percent.) This included all positive and nonpositive outcome, justice as well as nonjustice system (e.g., diversion and school-based) studies combined. Lipsey's meta-analysis is certainly the broadest and most systematic to date (Lipsey, 1992).

Davidson, Gottschalk, Gensheimer,
and Mayer

Davidson et al. (1984) analyzed some ninety studies of juvenile offenders in institutional and community settings, mostly conducted during the years 1971–83. They found that when all types of approaches were added together, 60 percent of the treatment programs showed an overall advantage for E's vs. C's. However, when the actual effect-sizes were analyzed using a conservative "random effects" test, the E/C difference for the studies as a group, that is, analyzed collectively, did not reach conventional levels of statistical significance.[3] (Essentially the same results were reported by Gottschalk et al. in 1987, using in effect the same ninety studies.) Still, disaggregated analyses of those studies produced suggestive leads. For instance, when the various methods were reviewed individually, "behavioral interventions" were often associated with positive outcomes. In fact, when compared to several other approaches, such as vocational training, service brokerage, and transactional analysis, the behavioral interventions seemed to have stronger effects and/or may have been associated with positive outcomes more often. On the other hand, group therapy seemed to make little difference. Finally, positive outcomes were associated with program integrity as well as number of contact hours (Davidson et al., 1984; Gensheimer et al., 1986; Gottschalk et al., 1987; Mayer et al., 1986).

Whitehead and Lab (Meta-analysis)

In 1989, Whitehead and Lab analyzed fifty juvenile offender studies conducted during 1975–84 in institutional and community settings. Using stringent success criteria, they found that 24–32 percent of the studies evidenced what they called "program effectiveness" (success).

More specifically, to consider a program effective, Whitehead and Lab required phi coefficients (.20+ or .30+) that often reflected large recidivism reductions, not just *(a)* statistically significant E/C differences or even *(b) any* reduction, however small. Of the four major categories of studies analyzed, those most often successful were "system diversion" (40 percent of the studies in this category) and "community corrections"-oriented approaches (35 percent), for example, probation or parole. Least often successful were "non-system diversion" (17 percent), that is, diversion outside the justice system (sometimes involving programming or contact), and institutional/residential programs (14 percent).[4]

Using a more common but less stringent criterion—$p < .05$, chi-square—44 percent of the 50 programs had positive outcomes, that is, E's outperformed C's. (70 percent of the programs had outcomes in a positive direction, $p < .05$ or not. This compares with Lipsey's 64 percent and Davidson's 60 percent.) Nevertheless, by using only the stricter criteria, Whitehead and Lab concluded that the results, collectively, provided "little encouragement for advocates of correctional intervention. No single *type* of intervention displays *overwhelmingly positive* results on recidivism" (emphases added). Yet since several *individual* programs within given types evidenced substantial gains for E's vs. C's, Whitehead and Lab acknowledged that some (individual) programs, for example, some system diversion programs, "are able to reduce recidivism among experimental clients significantly" (1989, pp. 285, 289).

Whitehead and Lab's is the meta-analysis currently cited by individuals who believe intervention does not, in general, work. However, that conclusion—insofar as it would be attributed to that study—would have to rest on the following approach to meta-analysis: First, focus exclusively on *types* or categories of intervention (i.e., on generic approaches), viewed, respectively, as undifferentiated entities. In short, do not focus on, that is, do not separately emphasize and place independent value on, results from the *individual studies* which comprise those approaches. Next, require "overwhelmingly positive" results for each such, or most such, approaches, as Whitehead and Lab apparently did in drawing their overall conclusions about effectiveness. Finally, generalize from a set of studies that represent the main range of intervention approaches.

On this latter point the following might be noted. Of the fifty studies in this meta-analysis, thirty involved juvenile diversion alone. In this connection, when concluding that their results provide "little encouragement for advocates of correctional intervention," Whitehead and Lab were primarily (though not exclusively) generalizing from this one portion of the intervention spectrum to intervention as a whole. Moreover, prior reviews, and a forty-four-study meta-analysis, had largely shown that "juvenile diversion" (viewed collectively, e.g., without distinguishing between system and nonsystem diversion) was among the aspects of intervention that were least often successful when E's and C's were compared on behavioral measures, whatever success standard was used (Davidson et al., 1984; Dunford, Osgood, and Weischelbaum, 1981; Gendreau and Ross, 1987; Gensheimer et al., 1986; Gibbons and Blake, 1976; Klein, 1979; Romig, 1978; Selke, 1982; Whitehead and Lab, 1989). Related to these findings is the fact that, understandably, few such programs had focused on relatively serious offenders; and it is often recognized that E/C differences are relatively difficult to demonstrate with individuals who are nonserious—or, specifically, are fairly good-risk—offenders in the first place, and for whom less room for improvement on recidivism therefore exists.

Finally, given the substantially increased utilization and varieties of *behavioral intervention* (sometimes called "behavior therapy") in the 1980s, and given the related, often strongly positive reviews of this approach as well, the rather different conclusions of Whitehead and Lab should be noted: "Claims that behavioral interventions are the most powerful (Geismar and Wood, 1986 . . . Mayer et al., 1986) do not receive support in this analysis. A comparison of results for behavioral and nonbehavioral interventions reveals contradictory findings [—some being positive, and others negative]" (1989, p. 280).

Andrews, Zinger, Hoge, Bonta, Gendreau,
and Cullen

Andrews et al. (1990) reanalyzed and expanded on the analysis of forty-five of the fifty juvenile offender studies that Whitehead and Lab had meta-analyzed in 1989; they dropped most of the remaining five because of sample overlap with others among the forty-five. To "check on the generalizability" of possible findings from their analysis of Whitehead and Lab's sample they added thirty-five institutional and community studies, one-third of which focused on adults and almost all of which were themselves from the 1970s and 1980s. Besides obtaining approximately 65–70 percent positive outcomes (E > C, by any amount) and over 30 percent statistically significant outcomes (E > C, p < .05) in each sample, Andrews et al. had four main findings.

First, by content analyzing and categorizing each individual study (on the basis of three principles mentioned below) and by then meta-analyzing those studies collectively, Andrews et al. found that *"type of treat-ment"* (four types or "levels," collectively: "appropriate services," "inap-propriate services," "unspecified services," and "criminal sanctions") was much more strongly related to recidivism reduction than were any of the remaining factors: *(a)* juvenile versus adult target-sample; *(b)* weaker versus stronger research design; *(c)* community versus institutional/residential setting; *(d)* pre-1980 versus 1980s study; *(e)* Whitehead and Lab's sample versus Andrews et al.'s sample. Factors *(a)* and *(b)* were statistically unrelated to recidivism, while *(c)*, *(d)*, and *(e)* were moder-ately related to it (with *[c]* and *[d]*, this occurred only after covariance adjustments).

Second, within the "type of treatment" factor, *appropriate services* (see below) were more strongly ($p < .05$) related to recidivism reduction that were *(a)* inappropriate services, *(b)* unspecified services, and *(c)* criminal sanctions, respectively; in fact, *(a)* and *(c)* were statistically unrelated to recidivism, and *(b)* was only moderately related. More specifically, for programs categorized as appropriate services the average recidivism reduction was 53 percent (phi = .30); for inappropriate ser-vices and criminal sanctions it was nonexistent or slightly but not signifi-cantly negative; and, for unspecified services it was (based on Andrews et al.'s phi of .13) an estimated 12–15 percent. All in all, findings one and two, above, were similar for Whitehead and Lab's forty-five studies, on the one hand, and for Andrews et al.'s thirty-five, on the other.

The programs categorized as appropriate services were those which reflected three principles: "risk, need, and responsivity." (See Appendix A regarding these principles as well as the resulting definitions of appro-priate and inappropriate correctional services.) Ultimately, Andrews et al.'s views regarding these principles—and, as corollaries, regarding appropriate and inappropriate services—were derived from a combina-tion of *(a)* results from prior studies and literature reviews and *(b)* social/psychological theories of learning and delinquency causation. By using these prior results and existing theories, for example, they defined and then classified all programs that fell within certain *generic categories* as inappropriate; among these categories were "scared straight" (confronta-tional groups) and "non-directive relationship-dependent and/or unstruc-tured psychodynamic counseling" (Andrews et. al., 1990, p. 379). At the same time, those prior results and existing theories led Andrews et al. to classify programs that fell into various other categories as appropriate *or* inappropriate—depending primarily on their *individual-program* status with respect to risk, need, and responsivity, not on what those results and theories may have indicated or implied about the generic categories as such. This was evidently done because of the following: In Andrews et al.'s view, those results and theories, collectively, neither clearly demonstrated nor strongly implied that an overwhelming or even large majority of programs within those respective categories *were* (based on prior results)—and/or could be *expected to be* (based on prior results combined with theory, or primarily on theory)—either successful *or* unsuccessful and, in that respect, appropriate or inappropriate. Among those categories were academic and vocational training, and group as well as individual counseling.

Third, Andrews et al. also found that behavioral programs outperformed the nonbehavioral. This related to the fact that almost all behavioral programs and proportionately fewer nonbehavioral fell within the "type of treatment" category that was defined as appropriate.[5] In this connection, the behavioral versus nonbehavioral status of individual programs was less closely related to recidivism reduction than was those respective programs' categorization as either appropriate or inappropriate, itself.[6]

Fourth, stronger and weaker research designs were equally likely to reduce recidivism. The former generally involved random assignment; the latter, nonrandom. (Quality of research design differs from strength of program implementation, for example, operational integrity of program elements and techniques.)

Izzo and Ross

Izzo and Ross analyzed forty-six juvenile offender studies conducted during the period 1970–85 in institutional and community settings. They found that programs "based on an articulated theoretical conceptualization of antisocial behavior" had significantly lower recidivism rates—as reflected in effect sizes—than those which had "no particular theoretical basis." The conceptualizations were "social learning, behavior modification, modeling, systems theory, reality therapy, interpersonal maturity-level theory, general sociological theory, [or] other." Though no conceptual system had a significant recidivism-advantage over any other,[7] "programs that included a *cognitive* component were more than twice as effective as programs that did not"—again judging by effect sizes. Individually, cognitive programs used one or more of the following: "problem solving, negotiation skills training, interpersonal skills training, rational-emotive therapy, role-playing and modeling, or cognitive behavior modification." Moreover, "effective programs included as a target of their intervention not only the offender's . . . cognition, self-evaluation, expectations, understanding and appraisal of the world, and values" but his or her "behavior, feelings, and vocational or interpersonal skills" (Izzo and Ross, 1990, pp. 138–39). Thus, they were multitarget in nature.

Before proceeding to the literature reviews, which mainly examine separate intervention approaches in turn, please note the following point about intervention overall, that is, all approaches combined: though not all meta-analysts drew the same *conclusions* about intervention's overall effectiveness, virtually all obtained similar key *results*. Specifically, they found that for every study in which C's outperformed E's, approximately two were found in which E's outdid C's. (These results were commonly, but far from always, based on a behavioral outcome index, e.g., one form or another of recidivism.) In addition, and no less important, they found that the average effect-sizes (ES's)—that is, the unweighted, average ES's across the positive plus the negative studies collectively—were fairly similar to each other (Lipsey, 1992). (These similarities generally but not exclusively involved better-designed studies, such as those using random allocation.)

For example, as noted by Lipsey, fairly similar effect-sizes existed in the analyses by Garrett (1985), by Gottschalk et al. (1987) based on the Davidson et al. (1984) data set, and by Kaufman (1985)—studies in which the average effect size ranged from about .20 to .33—and in Lipsey's own analysis of some four hundred studies, where the ES was .17. (Lipsey's meta-analysis, which was by far the largest, was perhaps the least selective. Not unrelated, his effect size of .17 had been adjusted downward for the otherwise biasing effects of small-sample studies.) In addition, similarity was found in the analysis by Whitehead and Lab (1989), on the one hand, and Andrews et al. (1990), on the other—analyses that, nevertheless, produced mutually contrasting conclusions about intervention's overall effectiveness. More specifically, Lipsey, based on quantitative information about the studies that constituted these two analyses, determined that the average effect-sizes were .25 and .21, respectively. These ES's, of course, were also comparable to those mentioned above (Lipsey, 1992). Gensheimer et al. (1986) and Mayer et al. (1986) obtained an average effect-size of .26 and .33, respectively; this pertained to E/C rather than pre/post-only designs, and it was weighted for sample size.

Together, the similar percentages of positive-outcome studies and the relatively similar effect-sizes found across the various analyses suggest the following: Differing judgments that have been made about the effectiveness of correctional programming *overall* have sometimes reflected, to a substantial degree, differing global *success standards* that have been chosen by differing meta-analysts. For instance, some analysts seem to have believed that most E-programs which are examined collectively in a given meta-analysis should show the statistical equivalent of at least a 25–30 percent recidivism reduction or should perhaps obtain an average reduction of that degree, in order for intervention in general to be judged successful or even rather promising. Most analysts, however, have considered smaller average reductions a sign of intervention's promise, though certainly not of its striking success. Clearly, no a priori or otherwise widely agreed-upon standards exist as to when intervention— viewed as a totality—can or should be characterized as "effective," as "working," or even as "promising."

CONCLUSIONS FROM SPECIFIC LITERATURE REVIEWS

Van Voorhis

In 1987, Van Voorhis (pp. 56–57) presented various conclusions that she felt "represent[ed] a convergence of findings across numerous studies" but which had received little attention from policy makers since "the post-Martinson years," that is, from about 1981. One conclusion involved "social system" or "system-level" interventions, such as family therapy and peer-centered approaches, used as either a supplement or an alternative to individual therapies. Here, for instance, Van Voorhis indicated that, "according to several recent reviews of the evaluation research, family therapy has achieved a notable degree of success." The reviews included those by Olson, Russell, and Sprenkle, (1980), Masten (1979), and Gendreau and Ross (1979); singled out was work by Patterson and Fleischman (1979), Patterson (1986), and Alexander and Parsons (1982). Most family therapy programs associated with positive outcomes had not focused on juveniles with serious or multiple offense histories; many, for example, dealt largely with less-serious delinquents or with at-risk pre-teens and teens. Nevertheless, it was implied that these methods, individually and certainly collectively, would work—in terms of reducing recidivism, as well—for a sizable range of offenders. Van Voorhis (1987) considered the effectiveness of peer-centered approaches uncertain.

Whitehead and Lab (Literature Review)

In 1989, Whitehead and Lab preceded their meta-analysis by recapping main results from major reviews of diversion and family intervention, while focusing on the distinction between behavioral and other approaches:

Diversion Gensheimer et al. concluded, in 1986, that diversion overall, that is, all approaches combined and considered as an entity, had no effect on specified measures. However, they believed that "behavioral approaches (for example, token economy, modeling, and behavioral contracting) used outside the residential setting may have a positive impact" (Whitehead and Lab, 1989, p. 277).

Behavioral Approaches Mayer et al. (1986), who analyzed thirty-nine studies from 1971–82, concluded that there is "a high degree of effectiveness for behavioral interventions for the recidivism, behavior, and attitudinal outcomes, as well as the collapsed overall results" (Whitehead and Lab, 1989, p. 277). (The Gensheimer et al. and Mayer et al. analyses were based, respectively, on subsets of Davidson et al.'s ninety studies, about half of which involved diversion.) Graziano and Mooney (1984) believed that although behavioral interventions were promising, their impact was usually intraprogram and they had "only rarely and only very recently" shown "relatively long term" reductions in delinquent behavior (Whitehead and Lab, 1989, p. 278).

Family Treatment Geismar and Wood concluded, in 1986, that "*nonfocused* family interventions, that is, those that address themselves vaguely to encouraging communication in general or expression of feelings, are totally ineffective in the treatment of adolescent delinquency" (Whitehead and Lab, 1989, p. 278). However, they believed *behavioral*—thus, presumably, more focused—family intervention showed promise. Behavioral interventions with families were considered promising by Graziano and Mooney (1984) as well, though recidivism studies were uncommon (Geismar and Wood, 1986; Gensheimer et al., 1986; Graziano and Mooney, 1984; Whitehead and Lab, 1989).

Panizzon, Olson-Raymer, and Guerra

Panizzon, Olson-Raymer, and Guerra recently drew the following conclusions from their detailed review of numerous studies of community-based, nonresidential programs for adjudicated delinquents. These studies, conducted during the period 1960–88, used recidivism or other behavioral outcome measures.

Juvenile Diversion Several reviews, and Gensheimer et al.'s meta-analysis of forty-four programs, essentially agreed that few juvenile diversion programs made a difference on such measures. The programs were often nonspecific interventions that were applied by relatively untrained staff to low-risk youths with little history of delinquency. Nevertheless, an occasional program seemed effective, for example, if it provided a number of contact hours that was above or well above average and/or if it focused on other than low-risk youths (Panizzon, Olson-Raymer, and Guerra, 1991; Davidson et al., 1987).

Behavior Therapy Though behavior therapy programs have long and often reported improved adjustment, they were seldom carefully evaluated; moreover, most changes did not involve recidivism. Nevertheless, some improvements occurred for individuals with particular offense histories or problems, for example, for some sex offenders or alcohol abusers. These therapies included behavior modification, for instance, via direct reinforcement, contingency contracting, or modelling (Mayer et al., 1986).

Family Therapy Family therapy has often improved the adjustment of relatively aggressive children, "antisocial" and/or aggressive (though not necessarily adjudicated) adolescents, status offenders, and—less often—moderately delinquent youths. However, because most evaluation designs were relatively weak, no overall claim of effectiveness seemed warranted. Moreover, when family therapy was used with more serious delinquents, recidivism generally was not reduced. Nevertheless, some exceptions existed, for example, in work by Alexander and Parsons. (Family therapy programs were mainly categorized as "family system therapy," "behavioral-systems family therapy," and "parent management training" [Alexander and Parsons, 1982; Gordon and Arbuthnot, 1987; Patterson, 1986; Patterson and Fleischman, 1979]).

Social-cognitive Interventions Social-cognitive interventions described as "social skills training" and "social problem solving" reported positive outcomes in a few studies involving short-term follow-ups. However, those which tried to improve delinquents' "moral reasoning" usually achieved that goal but seldom reduced recidivism. Still other social-cognitive interventions, such as "cognitive self-control," were used mainly with nondelinquent, at least nonadjudicated, though often fairly aggressive children and adolescents (Camp and Bush, 1981; Collingwood and Genthner, 1980; Gibbs et al., 1984; Goldstein, 1986; Hazel et al., 1981; Ross and Fabiano, 1985).

Combined Therapeutic Approaches Several programs that combined two or more treatment modalities or were comparatively intensive and that seemed adequately researched, for example, Project CREST, reported positive outcomes for moderately to fairly serious delinquents. Positive outcomes were also observed for such combinations as restitution plus counseling plus recreation in particular, as compared, for instance, to either restitution or probation alone (Lee and Haynes, 1980; O'Donnell, Lydgate, and Fo, 1979; Schneider and Schneider, 1985; Shore and Massimo, 1979).

Therapy and Counseling Proportionately few individual "casework" programs reduced recidivism. However, one-to-one counseling by knowledgeable volunteers showed promise, and some multiple modality approaches that included individual therapy or counseling decreased recidivism for various offenders. As to group therapy or counseling, few comprehensive evaluations existed (Barkwell, 1980; Gottfredson, 1987; Palmer, 1974; Shore and Massimo, 1979; Wright and Dixon, 1977).

Restitution Despite this approach's frequent use, few controlled evaluations were found. Gendreau and Ross, whose review appears below, observed that even those few reported little difference between restitution and control groups. One exception (Schneider and Schneider, 1985), reviewed by Panizzon, Olson-Raymer, and Guerra, is referred to under "Combined therapeutic approaches," above. (For other exceptions, see Panizzon, Olson-Raymer, and Guerra, 1991, p. 32.)

Physical Challenge Physical challenge programs, for example, wilderness experiences such as Vision Quest and Outward Bound, have often improved self-esteem but seldom shown clear recidivism reductions (Winterdyk and Roesch, 1982).

Largely based on the above reviews, Panizzon, Olson-Raymer, and Guerra also concluded that *(a)* programs which used intensive, theoretically well grounded treatment and planning were among the most effective or those most often effective, *(b)* offender/program matching should occur whenever possible, and *(c)* longer-term programming is generally appropriate, even though each program may have an optimal length for its typical participants.

Gendreau and Ross

In 1987, Gendreau and Ross reviewed some 150 studies (mainly of juveniles) conducted since 1979, thereby updating their earlier review of 1973–78 studies. With respect to juveniles, their conclusions regarding *diversion, family intervention, restitution, physical challenge* (e.g., Outward Bound), *intensive programming*, and *offender/program matching* closely resembled those later presented by Panizzon, Olson-Raymer, and Guerra; partial agreement was found regarding *social-cognitive* approaches. Though both reviews also agreed that some sex offender and substance abuse programs showed promise, Gendreau and Ross cautioned that few controlled studies existed. Regarding *probation/parole enhancements* and *deterrence/shock* approaches, respectively, their conclusions were largely paralleled by those of Lipsey's (1992) meta-analysis: fairly small recidivism reductions were likely to be found in the first area and very few improvements were likely in the second.

Another conclusion concerned intervention (e.g., "stress inoculation training") with violent offenders: No strong assertions regarding effectiveness were warranted, since almost no controlled studies existed. And while interventions (e.g., "psychological skills training") with aggressive but not necessarily adjudicated youths *have* often involved controlled studies, outcome measures in those instances have focused almost exclusively on intraprogram change (e.g., less school aggression, not on illegal behavior in the community) (Gendreau and Ross, 1979, 1987).

Chapter 3

Results from Analyses and Reviews Collectively

In this chapter we present the aggregated, that is, the assembled results from thirty-two meta-analyses and literature reviews with respect to twenty subject areas or intervention approaches taken *individually*. These areas include confrontation, diversion, the behavioral approach, and intensive probation supervision, among others.

RESULTS FOR SPECIFIED APPROACHES

Together, the six meta-analyses and four literature reviews summarized in chapter 2 illustrate all analyses/reviews but are not exhaustive. However, our overall collection of nine meta-analyses and twenty-three literature reviews (with those including the six and four from chapter 2) *is* fairly exhaustive of all major and sizable reviews since the mid-1970s, or at least it reflects essentially the full range of conclusions that have been drawn to date. This overall collection includes not only the early reviews and findings of Lipton, Martinson, and Wilks; 1975, Brody, 1976; Greenberg, 1977; Wright and Dixon, 1977; Romig, 1978; and Gendreau and Ross, 1979; instead, it also includes the 1980s reviews by Johns and Wallach, 1981; Rutter and Giller, 1983; Palmer, 1983, 1984; Graziano and Mooney, 1984; Lundman, 1984; Geismar and Wood, 1986; Genevie, Margolies, and Muhlin, 1986; Gensheimer et al., 1986; Mayer et al., 1986; Schneider, 1986; Gordon and Arbuthnot, 1987; Gottschalk et al., 1987; Armstrong, 1988; Lab and Whitehead, 1988; Krisberg et al., 1989; Parent, 1989; and Altschuler and Armstrong, 1990. When this overall collection of reviews and findings (including those in chapter 2) is examined, the following emerges.[1]

Confrontation

Confrontation, for instance, direct deterrence efforts such as Scared Straight and shock probation, has been rather consistently considered unsuccessful.[2] Specifically, Gendreau and Ross, 1987; Lab and Whitehead, 1988; Parent, 1989; Whitehead and Lab, 1989; Andrews et al., 1990; and Panizzon, Olson-Raymer, and Guerra, 1991 found this approach made no difference in recidivism; Lundman, 1984 concluded its results were mixed at best; and Lipsey, 1992, based on the largest sample-size of all, found it had the weakest—in fact, the most negative—results of the approximately twenty approaches he studied (ES = −.24); a minus sign in front of an effect size means the treatment/experimental group performed worse than its control. No reviewer or analyst reported positive results for confrontation as a whole or even for several of its individual studies.

Delinquency Prevention

Area-wide Strategies of Delinquency Prevention   Such strategies, for example, (1) community organization efforts encompassing entire neighborhoods or other sizable portions of large urban settings and (2) efforts by street corner gang workers, have uniformly been judged unsuccessful in reducing crime and delinquency (Wright and Dixon, 1977; Romig, 1978; Rutter and Giller, 1983; Lundman, 1984).

Social Casework, Social Agency, or Societal Institution Approaches to Delinquency Prevention   Such approaches, for instance, child guidance clinic and public agency referrals/services, have generally been considered either unsuccessful—with little qualification (Wright and Dixon, 1977; Romig, 1978; Rutter and Giller, 1983; Gordon and Arbuthnot, 1987; Panizzon, Olson-Raymer, and Guerra, 1991)—or else *usually* unsuccessful (Gottschalk et al., 1987). However, Gendreau and Ross, 1987, while in general accord with those conclusions, also described positive outcomes for early intervention efforts that involved *(a)* the Perry preschool component of Head Start, *(b)* specified family techniques, and *(c)* cognitive problem-solving. In addition, Lipsey, 1992, found that casework services which occurred outside the justice system substantially impacted delinquency (ES = .16).

Diversion

While diversion has often been viewed as having little effect on recidivism (Greenberg, 1977; Romig, 1978; Gensheimer et al., 1986; Whitehead and Lab, 1989, relative to nonsystem diversion), some reviewers have added that a modest percentage of such programs comprise clear exceptions to the rule (Gendreau and Ross, 1987; Panizzon, Olson-Raymer, and Guerra, 1991). Other reviewers have listed a number of positive-outcome programs or differentially positive programs (Gendreau and Ross, 1979; Johns and Wallach, 1981; Andrews et al., 1990, with "service oriented" efforts). Still others have either listed as many positive as nonpositive programs (Lab and Whitehead, 1988) or concluded that diversion is probably *as* effective (Rutter and Giller, 1983) or *at least* as effective (Lundman, 1984) as further penetration into the justice system. Finally, Whitehead and Lab (1989) have indicated that—collectively—diversion programs which occur within the justice system have a higher percentage of positive outcomes than do programs categorized as any of the following: "nonsystem diversion," "probation/parole/community corrections," or "institutional/residential." Diversion, of course, encompasses a wide range of program components and general interventions—from recreation, advocacy, and resource-brokerage, to vocational or educational training and group or individual counseling; moreover, its frequency as well as duration of client contacts varies considerably (Gensheimer et al., 1986), and differing meta-analyses and literature reviews have emphasized somewhat different components and general interventions.

Physical Challenge

Evaluations of physical challenge, for example, Outward Bound and Vision Quest, have been mixed and wide ranging. In some analyses/ reviews, the studies—collectively—showed little if any impact on recidivism (Romig, 1978; Gendreau and Ross, 1987; Panizzon, Olson-Raymer, and Guerra 1991); in others, conflicting outcomes appeared (Greenberg, 1977). In still other analyses, either positive outcomes were reported (Garrett, 1985, under "Life Skills") or such programs were presented as part of a broader category that was itself positive (Lipsey, 1992, under "Skill Oriented"). However, across all analyses/reviews, these programs are few in number, and often the same ones are discussed.

Restitution

Restitution has been systematically studied and discussed by relatively few analysts/reviewers. Though Lipsey (1992) found that thirteen such programs—collectively—had an average effect size of only .08 and a mean recidivism reduction of about 8 percent, other researchers described a number of successful ($p < .05$) individual programs in well-controlled E/C studies conducted during the mid-1980s (Ervin and Schneider, 1990; Galaway, 1988; Schneider and Ervin, 1990; Schneider, 1986). A few successful restitution programs were observed in the 1970s as well (Heinz, Galaway, and Hudson, 1976; Wax, 1977).

Group Counseling/Therapy

The group counseling/therapy approach presents an especially mixed but, on the whole, somewhat negative picture. While only one analyst/reviewer found it almost entirely unsuccessful (Romig, 1978), most concluded it was *(a)* usually unsuccessful, *(b)* successful under certain conditions only (presumably somewhat limited conditions), or *(c)* simply unclear as to its promise (Lipton, Martinson, and Wilks, 1975; Wright and Dixon, 1977; Garrett, 1985; Gordon and Arbuthnot, 1987; Van Voorhis, 1987). When judged unclear, this was partly because few good evaluations were thought to exist (Panizzon, Olson-Raymer, and Guerra, 1991). Other analysts/reviewers focused on individual instances of success, or else concluded—or presented data that either implied or directly indicated—that group counseling/therapy might be as often successful as unsuccessful (Gendreau and Ross, 1979; Greenberg, 1977; Genevie, Margolies, and Muhlin, 1986; Gottschalk et al., 1987). Finally, Andrews et al.'s (1990) data display suggested that group approaches can be successful if they are carefully focused and, in general, other than "nonbehavioral"; and Lipsey (1992) found that whereas group approaches which operated within the justice system showed fairly modest recidivism reductions on average (ES = .07), those outside the system had substantial reductions (ES = .18).

Individual Counseling/Therapy

Individual counseling/therapy had somewhat similar—namely, mixed—results, though its studies were less often considered qualitatively questionable. For instance, Romig (1978), Genevie, Margolies, and Muhlin (1986), Gordon and Arbuthnot (1987), and Gottschalk et al. (1987) concluded that few—perhaps 20 percent—of these programs reduced recidivism; in fact, Gottschalk et al. found this generic approach (though not "client centered therapy" in particular) the least successful of the several they studied. At the same time, the data display in Andrews et al. (1990) indicated—possibly in contrast to Gottschalk et al.'s finding—that "non-directive client-centered/psychodynamic counseling" did not reduce recidivism. Others, however, concluded that individual counseling/therapy sometimes did work in institutional (Lipton, Martinson, and Wilks, 1975) or community (Panizzon, Olson-Raymer, and Guerra, 1991) settings, though perhaps under particular conditions or for certain types of offenders (Rutter and Giller, 1983) only. Still others pointed to specific instances of success (Gendreau and Ross, 1979, 1987); and although Lipsey (1992) found no overall impact in nonjustice system settings (ES = −.01), this approach seemed to reduce recidivism to a modest degree when implemented in justice system settings (ES = .08)—again, on average.

Family Intervention

Family intervention presented a more promising but still somewhat mixed picture. For instance, positive or very promising overall assessments were made by Van Voorhis (1987) and Garrett (1985); and, Gendreau and Ross (1979), Johns and Wallach (1981), and Gordon and Arbuthnot (1987) either highlighted or noted specific studies that showed promise. Similarly, Graziano and Mooney (1984) concluded that—although several research shortcomings and few experimental studies involving recidivism existed—family intervention was "the most promising approach" of all, at least when behavioral programming was used. Other analyses and reviews stressed that although success sometimes occurred, it seemed even more conditional. For instance, Geismar and Wood (1986), Andrews et al. (1990), and (somewhat earlier) Romig (1978) each concluded—or suggested via their data displays—that although nonfocused family interventions do not ordinarily reduce recidivism, those which are carefully structured and/or focused according to family problems or client needs often do succeed. Still, Rutter and Giller (1983) and Panizzon, Olson-Raymer, and Guerra (1991) highlighted the frequent existence of research shortcomings and other deficiencies; and although they collectively mentioned instances of short- and longer-term success, they believed definite conclusions about family intervention's effectiveness were premature. Finally, Lipsey (1992) found that, on average, such interventions within the justice system produced or were associated with essentially no recidivism reductions (ES = .02), while those outside the system had moderate impact (ES = .10).

Vocational Training

Analyses/reviews of vocational training routinely found this approach associated with lower recidivism in about one of every three studies (Lipton, Martinson, and Wilks, 1975; Wright and Dixon, 1977; Romig, 1978; Gottschalk et al., 1987 [in the last, 50 percent of all outcomes were positive when vocational and educational training were reported as a single unit]). However, the influence of vocational training alone was difficult to assess, since the studies in which it appeared generally included one or more employment components as well, for instance, job referral/placement/experience, and they sometimes contained an educational training feature, too. Genevie, Margolies, and Muhlin (1986) found "inconsistent" results for vocational training, that is, some positive and some negative outcomes. Lipsey (1992), on the other hand, found a sizable negative impact on recidivism (ES = −.18) when such programs were operated within the justice system. For nonjustice system programs, however, he analyzed vocational and employment studies together and observed essentially no net impact (ES = −.02).

Employment

Work experience programs were associated with positive outcomes in about one of every three such operations found in the data displays of Lab and Whitehead (1988) and Andrews et al. (1990); and Genevie, Margolies, and Muhlin (1986) considered work-study among the few promising/successful approaches. In addition, Lipsey (1992) found employment the single most powerful justice system intervention (ES = .37), though his sample of studies was quite small in this instance. At the same time, employment (analyzed together with vocational studies, as mentioned above) had no apparent effect on recidivism in the case of *non*justice system programs (ES = −.02)—the sample being much larger in this instance.

Educational Training

Educational training, which usually consists of standard or special academic programming, remedial education, and/or individual tutoring, was associated with positive outcome in some two of every three studies discussed by or listed in Lipton, Martinson, and Wilks, 1975, Romig, 1978, and Andrews et al., 1990, respectively. Gottschalk et al., 1987 reported a positive outcome for one-third of all programs in which educational training was a component, though not necessarily the "primary intervention." Nevertheless, Lipsey (1992) found no net impact of this approach on recidivism (ES = .00) for all studies combined (only nonjustice system programs were reported), and Genevie, Margolies, and Muhlin (1986) described their results as "inconsistent."

Behavioral

The behavioral approach, for example, contingency contracting and token economies, was the one most widely recognized as having many positive results, and it was among the strongest of all. Lipsey (1992), who analyzed this approach separately from the "skill oriented" (see later section of this chapter), found its average effect sizes to be .25 and .20 for justice and nonjustice system programs, respectively; Garrett (1985) obtained an ES of .18 for institutional and community residential settings combined; Mayer et al. (1986) found effect sizes of .50 and .33 (unweighted, and weighted, for sample size) for settings that also included community nonresidential programs; Gottschalk et al. (1987) obtained positive outcomes for 64 percent of all studies in which the behavioral approach was the primary intervention; Andrews et al. (1990) found this approach to have a significantly higher effect size (.29) than the nonbehavioral (.04); Geismar and Wood (1986) concluded that the behavioral approach outperformed the nonbehavioral on family intervention (the focus of their review); and, Gendreau and Ross (1979, 1987) as well as Rutter and Giller (1983) noted several instances of success. The 1983 reviewers nevertheless found few high quality designs and believed long-term effects on recidivism were unclear. Johns and Wallach's (1981) relatively few studies involved more successful than unsuccessful outcomes. Though Graziano and Mooney (1984) found a small but increasing number of long-term reductions for behavioral interventions, they described this approach as promising.

The above findings centered on recidivism reduction, and, collectively, they included predelinquents as well as adjudicated. Only Romig (1978) and Panizzon, Olson-Raymer, and Guerra (1991, focusing on community settings alone) concluded that the behavioral approach had shown relatively few positive effects on recidivism; and Whitehead and Lab's meta-analysis (1989) suggested that the overall results for this approach were only mildly positive, though 31 percent of all behavioral programs had a phi coefficient of +.20 or more.

Despite these differences among some meta-analysts/reviewers, the positive and often strong findings for the behavioral approach seem clear. It might be noted that this method (for instance, contingency management, behavior contracting, and token economies) has commonly been used to help implement each of several *other* categories, such as family intervention and vocational or educational training, not just to encourage and reinforce socially acceptable behaviors per se or to discourage specific unwanted behaviors. As a result, the behavioral approach has perhaps been as much or as often a generic technique as a general approach per se. This applies to the cognitive-behavioral approach as well, though to a much lesser degree.

Cognitive-behavioral or Cognitive

The cognitive-behavioral or cognitive approach has sometimes been analyzed as a subset of the behavioral and sometimes as separate from it;

in both cases it has been considered positive and promising (Garrett, 1985; Gordon and Arbuthnot, 1987; Izzo and Ross, 1990, based on numerous programs with recidivism as an outcome). However, Panizzon, Olson-Raymer, and Guerra (1991) indicated it has had relatively few reported instances of success with regard to recidivism (these authors called this approach "social-cognitive interventions"). Though Gottschalk et al. (1987) and Andrews et al. (1990) singled out too few "cognitive therapy" and "cognitive-behavioral" approaches for meaningful quantitative analysis, Gottschalk et al. separately reported a successful outcome for 45 percent of the twenty studies in which "modeling/role playing" was included. This particular feature appeared to constitute a sizable part of Panizzon, Olson-Raymer, and Guerra's and Izzo and Ross's earlier-mentioned, broader categories of "social-cognitive interventions" and "cognitive programs," respectively. (The latter categories, in turn, sometimes appeared under other labels, e.g., "social skill training," "social perspective taking," "negotiation skill training," "interpersonal skills training," and "role-playing and modeling.") More broadly, several of these categories might be considered *interpersonal skills training*, whether or not the latter is placed in the *(a)* cognitive-behavioral or cognitive category or, for that matter, is classified under *(b)* "skill oriented" per se (see "Life Skills," below). Obviously, some category-boundaries are still somewhat fluid in this relatively new research area.

Life Skills

The approach called "life skills" (Garrett), "skill oriented" (Lipsey), or "skill development" (Lipton, Martinson, and Wilks) is a mixture or group of categories that individually consist of approaches already discussed; collectively, that is, from one analysis/review to the next, the groups in question partly overlap each other. Specifically, in Garrett, 1985, "life skills" consisted of academic training, vocational training, outdoor experience (Outward Bound), and drug programs; in Lipsey, 1992, "skill oriented" contained not only "academic educational/tutoring" (other than that which was "school based") and outdoor experience ("wilderness/outward bound; survival training") but interpersonal "social skills" training (e.g., via role playing); and in Lipton, Martinson, and Wilks, 1975, "skill development" referred exclusively to educational training, vocational training, and to a lesser extent, work exposure and job placement. This substantively diverse yet conceptually coherent (albeit broad) category was among the more successful approaches—or, perhaps, dimensions—observed by Lipsey (1992) in the case of justice system programs (ES = .20). Within the nonjustice area it was the most successful one by far (ES = .32). (Lipsey separated the skill-oriented approach from that which he analyzed as "behavioral.") Garrett (1985) found "life skills" not just successful (ES = .28 on recidivism) but even more so than the behavioral approach (ES = .18). Finally, Lipton, Martinson, and Wilks (1975) reported positive outcomes for skill development approaches that were "specialized" rather than "standard" in nature, especially regarding educational programs.

Multimodal

The multimodal approach (for instance, such combinations as [hypothetically] work-study plus counseling plus restitution) was found, in general, to be the second strongest category analyzed by Lipsey (1992): effect sizes were .25 and .21 for justice and non-justice system programs, respectively. Panizzon, Olson-Raymer, and Guerra (1991) presented some positive findings regarding this approach (called "combined therapeutic" intervention), as well—specifically for community settings. Palmer, in earlier reviews, suggested the apparent or at least probable importance of multimodal programming (first called the "combined-modalities approach" [1978, pp. 48–49] and later called broad-based or "extensive"—but not necessarily intensive—intervention [1983]). Nevertheless, relatively few analysts/reviewers have focused specifically, let alone systematically, on this aspect of programming—programming which reflects the idea that certain combinations of elements may have considerably more relevance to clients, and in that sense more power, than any of those elements alone. This general absence of focus reflects most analysts' emphasis to date on what might be called "single-feature" or "salient-feature" analysis.

Probation Enhancement and Parole
Enhancement

Probation enhancement and parole enhancement have generally been described as involving *(a)* more contacts than in standard supervision (often made possible by reduced caseloads) and/or *(b)* the addition, to standard supervision, of one or two service or control elements, for example, family and collateral contacts, or, in recent years, electronic monitoring. Before the early 1980s these enhancements received somewhat mixed reviews. On the one hand, Greenberg (1977), Wright and Dixon (1977), and Romig (1978) suggested that enhancements, including reduced caseloads, made little difference; on the other, Martinson (1974) considered special probation programs possibly the only promising intervention. In addition, Lipton, Martinson, and Wilks (1975) furnished several examples of positive or promising outcome, and Palmer (1978), after examining all recidivism studies reviewed by Lipton, Martinson, and Wilks, observed that 50 percent of those in probation and 71 percent in parole had outcomes in which E's outperformed C's by 15 percent or more. In the 1980s, Gendreau and Ross (1987) suggested that although an increased amount of supervision produced fairly small recidivism reductions by itself, improvement could be substantial if well-selected, *new* program elements were added. At the same time, however, the three meta-analysts who reviewed this area obtained—collectively—a range of results: Lipsey (1992) found that reduced caseloads and other enhancement made only modest differences (ES = .08 and .07, respectively);[3] Whitehead and Lab (1989) found that 35 percent of their "probation/parole/community corrections" programs had satisfied their standard of success (phi = .20 or more); yet Gottschalk et al. (1987) found that 60 percent of the programs in which probation played a role had positive (E > C) though not necessarily statistically reliable ($p < .05$) outcomes. Thus, as before, reviews were mixed and sometimes mutually inconsistent.

Intensive Supervision

"Intensive Probation Supervision"   Programs using "intensive probation supervision" during the 1980s were reviewed by Armstrong (1988) and Krisberg et al. (1989). In many such programs the control/surveillance component and/or the service-provision component was emphasized or augmented considerably more than in the enhancements of the 1970s. Both reviews found that no clear conclusions could be drawn about effectiveness because too few well designed studies—including adequate, not necessarily excellent studies—had been conducted. (A review of intensive probation supervision was conducted by Byrne, Lurigio, and Baird [1989], but this focused solely on adults.)

"Intensive Aftercare (Parole) Supervision"   A detailed review of "intensive aftercare (parole) supervision" was conducted by Altschuler and Armstrong (1990), who found that too few acceptable studies existed to allow for reliable conclusions. Nevertheless, well-designed experiments by Barton and Butts (1990), Gruenewald, Laurence, and West (1985), and Fagan, Forst, and Vivona (1988) suggested, collectively, that multicomponent probation and aftercare interventions which are carefully conceptualized and relatively intensive can be at least as effective as standard approaches. The 1985 and 1988 experiments involved high-risk, violence-prone, or violent youths who were perhaps otherwise institution-bound or else already sentenced to, but not actually sent to, an institution.

Community-based Approaches versus
Institutional Intervention

Since the mid-1970s, literature reviewers and—later—meta-analysts have variously considered community-based approaches *(a)* no *less* effective than institutions (Greenberg, 1977; Lundman, 1984), *(b)* possibly (Wright and Dixon, 1977) or probably (Rutter and Giller, 1983; Van Voorhis, 1987) more effective or slightly more effective, and *(c) more* effective or more often effective, with respect to reducing recidivism. Regarding *(c)*, Lipsey (1992) found that community-based programs had larger effect sizes than those implemented in institutions; Andrews et al. (1990) found that "appropriate treatment" programs in the community had a substantially higher ES (.35) than similarly categorized programs conducted in institutions (.20); Whitehead and Lab (1989) obtained a 2.5:1 ratio of successful community programs to successful institutional ones; and Izzo and Ross (1990) found that proportionately more effective programs had occurred in community settings. No reviewers/analysts considered the institutional approach better than the community-based in terms of recidivism, at least not for unselected, heterogeneous offender-populations. This was independent of Brody's (1976) view that institutional programs are largely unsuccessful in themselves (Sechrest, White, and Brown, 1979)—a conclusion that not all reviewers shared. Moreover, the above-mentioned findings and conclusions from meta-analyses and literature reviews do not ipso facto mean that institutional programs and/or settings have had little or no positive effects, in themselves.

Chapter 4

Trends and Problem Areas

This chapter describes the major trends regarding correctional effectiveness that emerged from the findings of the several analyses and reviews *collectively*. It then describes problem areas and underlying factors that contributed to those findings and seemed to limit them. The chapter also reviews the amount of recidivism reduction that was observed across the several approaches.

MAJOR TRENDS AND CONSISTENCIES

Combined with the earlier summaries of ten individual analyses and reviews, chapter 3's overview of findings suggests four interrelated points:

Less Effective Approaches

When individual programs were grouped together and analyzed according to their distinguishing program feature—one that they shared in common, such as group counseling—several such groups or analytic entities were substantially less likely than others to have been associated with reduced recidivism. (When analyzed this way, each of these groups was, in effect, treated as an entity, i.e., a homogeneous or undifferentiated conceptual unit. The distinguishing program feature was—if only by implication—often the quantitatively most "salient" feature as well.)

   More specifically, each of the former groups, when compared to each of the latter, had a considerably lower percentage of programs that showed *(a)* statistically superior performance ($p < .05$) for E's vs. C's or *(b)* E's outperforming C's by any amount, even without $p < .05$. Moreover, such groups, respectively, have often been called ineffective or unsuccessful because *(c)* their E-programs, collectively, did not outperform their respective C-programs fairly often (for example, in at least two-thirds of the individual programs that comprised the respective groups); that is, they did not outperform them to that degree in terms of criterion *(a)* or *(b)* above. In short, since several programs within a given group had a positive outcome in terms of *(a)* or *(b)* whereas several others had a negative outcome (e.g., E = C, or even E < C), the overall results for that group, collectively, were sometimes characterized as "inconsistent"—and frequent inconsistency was often equated, implicitly or explicitly, with lack of success for the overall group. (Success criteria are further discussed in chapter 11.)

At any rate, the following were the *groups* or generic approaches whose individual studies either had—collectively (within each approach)—the lowest percentage of recidivism reduction (i.e., of "successful outcomes") or had, in some cases, an average effect size that was relatively low: *confrontation; area-wide strategies of delinquency prevention; diversion (at least "nonsystem"); group counseling/therapy; individual counseling/therapy.* Conceivably, if some of these generic approaches had been combined with others and analyzed together, outcomes—including average effect size—might have differed. Also, as indicated in "Effectiveness of Individual Programs," below, the results for most of these approaches, especially the last three, were far from entirely negative. In fact, these particular results were basically mixed—with modest-to-moderate overall recidivism reductions being the rule and partially counterbalancing the various negative findings. At any rate, these three approaches could not, in toto, be described as "successful," whether in comparison to other approaches or on their own.

Some of these approaches (for instance, diversion and both forms of therapy/counseling) were studied much more often than others (namely, confrontation and area-wide strategies of delinquency prevention). In addition, the last three approaches listed above, which contain dozens of studies each, were much more likely than the first two to contain numerous studies that were methodologically adequate and even some that were excellent. Given these interrelated reasons—even that of numerical differences alone—the finding or conclusion regarding a generally lower or low success for each of those three approaches can be considered more definitive or reliable than that for confrontation and for area-wide strategies of delinquency prevention; this principle would apply to other small-sample-size approaches as well (for instance, physical challenge and restitution). Nevertheless, since even some of the small sample-size approaches did not just contain a handful of studies each (e.g., eleven confrontation studies were analyzed by Lipsey), and since *some* of these studies (though, for obvious reasons, not a *large* absolute quantity of them [i.e., "numerous" such studies]) were methodologically adequate, the findings for such groups, though by no means strong, may be considered clearly suggestive. At any rate, they are not largely unfounded, as would have been true if the evidence, collectively, were essentially insufficient and therefore highly inconclusive.

The generally *negative* findings (i.e., "little or no E/C difference") for *confrontation* were based on three meta-analyses and three literature reviews; those for *diversion* mainly reflected two analyses and four reviews. Similarly, the often negative results for *individual counseling/ therapy* mainly came from two meta-analyses and three literature reviews. On the other hand, the negative results for *group counseling/ therapy* came almost entirely from six literature reviews (there was one meta-analysis as well), and those for *area-wide strategies of delinquency prevention* came from that method alone (four such reviews)—no meta-analyses having yet focused specifically on this approach. In any event, these overlapping meta-analyses and literature reviews partly complemented each other's findings regarding the main trends that were observed for given approaches, and in that respect (and to the degree described in footnote 1) these two *methods* reinforced each other.[1] More specifically, such reinforcement (involving "method-overlap") occurred in four of the five approaches individually, and—when one generalizes— across the five collectively.

(For any one approach, method-overlap existed when some authors assessed the approach by means of one method, whereas the rest evaluated it via another. Thus, no such overlap would have existed if that approach had been evaluated—by the authors *collectively*—via either meta-analysis or literature review only, but not via the two combined. Each author, of course, used only one method.)

Whether or not method-overlap existed for any approach, or for even two or more, the following question would arise regarding *study*-overlap. (This question would arise whenever two or more authors had evaluated an approach. It centers on the extent to which identical *studies* are co-present across those authors. Such studies are also called "overlapping evidence" or "repetitive evidence.") Were the respective authors' evaluations of the approach based mainly on *repetitive* ("overlapping") evidence or mainly on *converging* ("nonoverlapping") evidence—"evidence" being the individual studies that comprised the approach? In other words, did one author who had examined/evaluated the approach—for instance, had provided conclusions or inferences about it—do so by utilizing most of the same studies that were used by another author who had examined/ evaluated it, or did the two (or more) authors generally use differing studies? (In the present discussion we will focus not on *all* authors who had evaluated a given approach—e.g., not on the ten who assessed individual counseling/therapy—but only on those who concluded, implied, or otherwise suggested that that approach had shown little or no success/promise thus far. For individual counseling/therapy [ICT], this involved five of the ten authors.)

(Two points before continuing. First, the term "authors, collectively"—or its equivalent—will basically refer to an aggregation or total group of authors, whatever their number may be. In addition, it will functionally resemble the term "across authors" in referring to all such individuals in question. [The same would apply to the terms "studies, collectively" and "across studies."] Both terms can be used not only in relation to one approach alone but also to two or more. Second, "authors" will refer either to the *single* author—the examiner/evaluator—or to the *joint* authors of any meta-analysis or literature review.)

To address the question of study-overlap, one would determine if the conclusions, inferences, or data-displays that were provided by the specified authors—for instance, the five authors for ICT—had been based largely on the same individual studies or mainly on different ones. Thus, in the present case, one would determine if the authors who directly or indirectly indicated that ICT had shown little or no success/promise had utilized much the same studies or else generally different ones—that is, the same or different from one author to the next. This question would apply whether the respective authors had used either meta-analysis or literature review. (As indicated above, in the case of individual counseling/therapy the authors, collectively, happen to have used meta-analyses *and* literature reviews—two of the former and three of the latter. However, with other approaches, such as area-wide delinquency prevention, no method-overlap occurred.)

The answer to the question of whether there was more identity than difference—more study-overlap than nonoverlap across authors—is as follows: The authors mainly used what turned out to be converging evidence, that is, nonoverlapping (nonidentical) individual studies. More precisely, differing rather than identical studies clearly dominated across the authors collectively; at least they did so with four of the five generic approaches (the fifth being confrontation). For details, discussion, and quantities, see Appendix B, especially the section titled "Less Promising and More Promising Approaches."

This finding does not mean *few* overlapping—that is, identical—studies existed within any given approach; in fact, for three of the five approaches, a substantial minority of all studies were identical from one author to the next. Nevertheless, the finding indicates that the authors had not based their respective conclusions/inferences on evidence which—when examined across those authors—turned out to involve mostly the same studies. This, in turn, means that the generalization which was made regarding the five above-mentioned approaches—namely, that they constitute (collectively) those which were "less effective" among the 20 that were examined in chapter 3—can be considered stronger (better anchored or more broadly based) than it would have been if the evaluations of those approaches, by the various authors, had reflected mainly repetitive evidence.

Effectiveness of Individual Programs

Although the individual E-programs which comprised some generic groups (e.g., those listed in the preceding section) did not—*collectively*—outperform their C-programs fairly often (this being criterion *(c)*, above), a substantial percentage of E-programs that comprised those and/or other categories did—*individually*—outperform their C's in terms of criterion *(a)* or *(b)*, above. For instance, using a $p < .05$ criterion, individual E programs outperformed their C's in approximately 25–35 percent of all programs across the several generic groups combined, while C's led E's in less than 10 percent. (This applied to all twenty generic approaches combined, not just the five "less effective" ones. The specific figures—33 percent and 7 percent, respectively—were the unweighted averages of all 270 separate juvenile delinquency studies that were reported, collectively, in fourteen of the thirty-two meta-analyses and literature reviews. These constituted all analyses/reviews in which the level of significance either was routinely reported or was derivable from the numbers presented e.g., from sample sizes and recidivism rates. See Appendix C.) In addition, using *any* degree of recidivism reduction ($p < .05$ or not), E's led C's in about 65 percent of all programs while C's were ahead in some 30 percent—again, for all groups (all twenty generic categories) combined. (Even in Whitehead and Lab's meta-analysis, E's had lower recidivism rates than did C's in 70 percent of the individual studies, though $p < .05$ was much less frequent. With rare exceptions, these E/C outcome-differences involved the respective study-samples as a whole, not simply, e.g., particular offender *subgroups* [e.g., "higher-risks" and/or specified personality-types] *within* the overall E versus C samples.) These percentages differed considerably from one grouping or category to another.

At this level of analysis it did not matter if, or how, an individual program had been generically typed, that is, grouped or categorized. This was because the program's "success" or "nonsuccess" depended entirely on its own performance, not that of "its" category as a whole—that is, not on all its category's individual programs combined (as in the discussion of less effective approaches, above), several of which may have missed the $p < .05$ criterion. As a result, hypothetical program A was not in effect penalized or ignored because of program B's performance—a situation which would otherwise have been possible simply because A and B fell within the same generic category.

Thus, for example, even if a researcher did happen to categorize all programs but also reviewed them individually, he or she would have found statistically successful ($p < .05$) individual programs in almost every category, including diversion, group counseling/therapy, and individual therapy/counseling—even though some of those *categories* may have been considered unsuccessful, and perhaps dismissed wholesale, because of frequent *inconsistencies* across individual-program outcomes and/or due to low average effect size. (The successful or at least positive [E > C] outcomes for individual programs that comprised the diversion, group counseling/therapy, and individual counseling/therapy categories, were found in meta-analyses and literature reviews alike.)

In short, individual programs would have been found that would *not* have emerged as "successful" if they had originally been grouped—and, in a sense, submerged—within an overall category (e.g., "diversion") and had then been counted as part of (and perhaps subsequently dismissed together with) that category alone, as seen in the discussion of less effective approaches above.

(As chapter 11 will show, the "success" or "failure" of a given program is not a cut-and-dried matter, that is, a condition or fact that can be determined with absolute certainty and 100 percent precision by simply knowing if the program's performance, for example, its E/C difference in recidivism rates, has satisfied a preestablished criterion, such as $p < .05$. As indicated earlier, some degree of uncertainty and inexactness always exists.[2] Nevertheless, such criteria, or cutoffs, can indicate the amount of confidence that may be placed in the results, for instance, in the stability of any such E/C difference, after taking account of such uncertainty generators as chance and measurement error. $P < .05$, in particular, suggests considerable confidence.)

Equally Effective Approaches

Many or even most generic approaches (vs. individual programs) had been or could have been judged unsuccessful from an E-*better-than*-C perspective, this being the framework used in the discussion of less effective approaches above. In general, this judgment in effect reflected or could have reflected the approach's failure to meet a criterion of two successes out of every three programs, especially if success, for each individual program that comprised the approach, required $p < .05$. Nevertheless, although some broad strategies and interventions did not satisfy a "better-than" criterion—whether "two out of every three" or higher— they may have been associated with an essentially *equal* outcome. For instance, community-based and institutional programs frequently seemed to yield comparable recidivism rates; and often the former, but never the latter, seemed better. In addition, under various conditions, even diversion's rates seemed to equal those of further justice system processing, whether or not the latter involved institutionalization per se. (The findings regarding community-based programs reflected four meta-analyses and six literature reviews; those concerning diversion's *equality or near equality* involved one such analysis and three such reviews.)

This point is significant not so much because *(a)* the percentage of programs that might be called "successful" would increase if a criterion of "equal-rates" or even "equal percentage of positive outcomes" were used ($p < .05$ or not), but mainly because of *(b)* the often-expressed view that E-programs need not provide *more* public protection than C's in order to justify their existence via positive contributions. Specifically, it is often felt that E-programs can constitute valuable alternatives or supplements to C-programs if—while providing essentially *equal* protection— they achieve or contribute to some of the following (especially the final two): reduce penetration into the justice system; reduce official as well as self-labeling; increase humaneness; and, reduce costs, whether per youth/ per day, per youth/per program, or capital outlay (Bartollas, 1985; Clear and Cole, 1990; Cullen and Gilbert, 1982; Empey and Stafford, 1991; Lillyquist, 1980; McDonald, 1989; Siegal and Senna, 1985).

More Effective Approaches

Again at the generic level, as in the discussion of less effective approaches above, the following interventions were those most often or proportionately most often considered successful or promising from an E-better-than-C perspective (whether or not one used $p < .05$) and/or those which seemed, on balance, to have the strongest positive results (e.g., the largest average effect sizes or recidivism reductions): *behavioral; cognitive-behavioral or cognitive; life skills or skill oriented; multimodal;* and *family intervention.*[3] The largely *positive* results obtained for these approaches were from meta-analyses and literature reviews alike. Specifically, positive findings for the *behavioral* approach were based on five analyses and two reviews, while those for the *cognitive-behavioral or cognitive* related to three analyses and one review. Similarly, positive findings for the *life skills* approach came from two meta-analyses and one literature review, and those for *multimodal* reflected one analysis and two reviews. Finally, the successful or promising outcomes for *family intervention* were based on two analyses and seven reviews.[4]

As seen in Appendix B (section titled "Less Promising and More Promising Approaches"), judgments regarding the success, promise, and/ or relative success or promise of these approaches were (except for the behavioral approach) largely based on converging (nonoverlapping) rather than repetitive (overlapping) evidence. This finding is essentially the same—in terms of direction and degree—as that for the "less effective approaches," discussed earlier in this chapter.

PROBLEM-AREAS AND UNDERLYING FACTORS

Nevertheless, a number of meta-analyses and/or literature reviews did not find some of these approaches, for example, "behavioral" and "family intervention," to be successful, let alone among the most successful. Differing assessments occurred for several other generic approaches as well; for instance, physical challenge, group counseling/therapy, individual counseling/therapy, and probation/parole enhancements.

These differences and even inconsistencies as to whether given approaches were judged successful—or just how successful/promising they were—partly resulted from differences in the *samples, definitions,* and/or *success criteria* that were used. (Chapter 5 reviews other factors.)

Samples

Studies that comprised any given approach, for example, the behavioral, were not—collectively—entirely the same from one analysis to the next; that is, some analyses/reviews (a/r's) contained a sizable percentage of studies that were not included in other a/r's, and vice versa. This difference in sample composition partly reflected the respective analysis/ review's somewhat different *time periods*, their rather different *range of settings*, and/or—within given settings—their emphasis on differing *system levels*. Other factors substantially affected the respective samples' composition as well.

Time periods For instance, as seen in the following, less than a perfect correspondence—often much less—existed from one study to the next in terms of the time-periods covered. Garrett's, Davidson et al's, and Whitehead and Lab's samples extended through 1983–84, whereas Lipsey's and Panizzon et al.'s went through 1988 and thereby contained many different programs. Although moderate differences existed in the extent to which the above analysts/reviewers covered pre-*1970* (or pre-1975) studies, these studies, collectively, usually constituted a small percentage of the total sample. Nevertheless, much larger differences existed between the sample composition of *(a)* a/r's that included the period prior to 1970–75 and which were summarized above, and *(b)* a/r's that were not summarized above but emphasized the 1960s and/or 1970s or were entirely limited to them. The latter included the works of Lipton, Martinson, and Wilks (1975), Palmer (1975, 1983), Greenberg (1977), Wright and Dixon (1977), Romig (1978), Gendreau and Ross (1979), and Sechrest, White, and Brown (1979), among others.

Settings In addition, though two different analysts/reviewers may have emphasized essentially the same time period, their samples might have involved somewhat different settings. For example, while Garrett (1985) centered on institutions (81 percent of her studies) and excluded all community *non*residential programs (diversion/probation/parole), Davidson et al. (1984) and Whitehead and Lab (1989) focused on institutional and community settings alike, with Whitehead and Lab emphasizing diversion. Similarly, though the bulk of Lipsey's (1992) and Panizzon, Olson-Raymer, and Guerra's (1991) respective study-samples fell within a similar time period, the former's included institutional and community programs while the latter's covered community nonresidentials alone. At the same time, Gottschalk et al. (1987) studied residential and nonresidential community programs, but not institutional ones.

System levels The system level or legal status of the client also affected sample composition. For instance, whereas *(a)* Izzo and Ross (1990), Panizzon, Olson-Raymer, and Guerra (1991), and Garrett (1985) studied adjudicated youths only, and while *(b)* Davidson et al. (1984) and Gottschalk et al. (1987) examined youngsters referred for official delinquency ("officially labeled delinquents")—only *some* of whom, however, were adjudicated—*(c)* Whitehead and Lab (1989), Andrews et al. (1990), Van Voorhis (1987), Gendreau and Ross (1979, 1987), and Lipsey (1992) included studies that involved not only "official delinquents" but youths who seemed "maladjusted, antisocial," and so on—in short, "at-risk" or delinquency-prevention clientele. "At-risk," group *(c)* clientele would probably have lower average arrest rates on post-program follow-up than would either *(a)* or *(b)* clientele.

Other factors One additional factor centered on the scope of the literature search—thus, on the potential degree of inclusiveness of the group of studies that might comprise any given approach. Here, the analysts/reviewers had generally examined a wide range of sociological and psychological abstracts and refereed or nonrefereed journals as well. Yet they differed considerably regarding the inclusion of not only unpublished, nonrefereed studies and reports by local and state agencies or departments but also dissertations, theses, and, to a lesser extent, books. Another factor involved design quality. Here, although most analysts/ reviewers required at least a quasi-experimental approach, a few included substantially less rigorous studies as well. Among the latter were Davidson et al. (1984), Gottschalk et al. (1987), and—somewhat earlier—Lipton, Martinson, and Wilks (1975).

Definitions

Varying and Nonexclusive Definitions   The approaches (e.g., "behavioral" and "cognitive-behavioral") were generally defined somewhat differently in a number of meta-analyses and literature reviews. This complicated both the basic picture and the overall assessment of the given approach. More generally, by causing presumably *different* approaches to partly *correspond* to each other from one analysis or review to the next— that is, to *seemingly* correspond conceptually—these varying yet partly overlapping definitions opened the door to apparent interpretation problems that would have existed even if time period, program setting, and inclusion criteria had been identical across all analyses/reviews.

A few examples serve to illustrate this definitional/partial-correspondence issue. In some analyses/reviews "behavioral" intervention was defined in ways that substantively overlapped with the definitions of "vocational training" and/or "cognitive" (but not necessarily behaviorally oriented) in some *other* a/r's. Similarly, "vocational training," as defined in one or more a/r's, included aspects defined in others as "social skills" or "skill development." Finally, in some analyses/reviews, "family intervention" included certain programs which, in other a/r's, appeared under "behavioral." This apparently occurred because some behavioral principles and techniques were considered integral to the family interventions in question. More broadly, one or more a/r's singled out and focused upon family interventions (despite various *programs'* utilization of behavioral techniques), while others focused on the behavioral techniques themselves, even though these had occurred in the context of family interventions. Along related lines, life skills training sometimes included vocational and educational programs and was used as an analytic category itself; yet elsewhere, vocational training was analyzed on its own, and the otherwise broader life-skills category did not appear as such.

Thus, varying and nonexclusive definitions of given interventions sometimes reflected not only differing levels of abstraction or analysis. Such differences, by themselves, can make it difficult for researchers to reliably identify and track given interventions from one analysis/review to the next; this problem involves not only generic categories (approaches) but individual programs that comprise those categories. That, in turn, can make it difficult to establish a *set* of generic intervention categories to use for reliably and systematically assessing the intervention outcomes (for particular categories and for one category vs. another) by compiling and comparing all the separate results obtained from each respective meta-analysis and literature review. (The set of categories in question might include, e.g., carefully defined, mutually exclusive analytic units such as educational/vocational training plus counseling plus survival/interpersonal-skills training, etc.; or, it might break these down more finely.)

Inadequate Data   Definitional problems sometimes reflect another, perhaps more basic issue. This centers on the *primary literature* and can exist even without the above-mentioned emphasis/framework/level (EFL) problem (in turn, EFL can exist without the primary literature issue): Reports and articles often lack critical details about various aspects of the intervention programs on which they focus, and this sometimes makes it difficult for meta-analysts and literature reviewers to reliably label those programs as "belonging" within one or another generic category. As with the EFL issue, insufficient detail can also complicate researchers' efforts to establish a set of generic analytic units—more specifically, a set of categories that *(a)* are mutually exclusive, *(b)* involve consistent definitions across analyses/reviews, and *(c)* are essentially exhaustive (collectively). Though the present issue centers on the primary literature as such, it partly reflects and is exacerbated by the current absence of any widely accepted, relatively standardized, preexisting intervention taxonomy. Yet, like the emphasis/framework/level problem itself, that of insufficient detail or otherwise inadequate data could exist even if such a taxonomy or classification system were present.

At any rate, varying and nonexclusive definitions complicated and rendered somewhat ambiguous the conceptualization and assessment of even various approaches that several meta-analysts and reviewers considered generally successful or at least among the most promising.

Success Criteria

When evaluating the results from any individual study, the vast majority of meta-analysts and literature reviewers considered $p < .05$ or its equivalent a statistically defensible and/or pragmatically useful criterion—one that, in those respects, represented a reasonably reliable, prudent, or otherwise meaningful sign of success or at least promise. However, a few analysts/reviewers employed a different criterion, and this difference contributed to inconsistent interpretations and conclusions across those individuals.

For instance, Whitehead and Lab (1989) believed individual outcomes should have a phi coefficient of at least .20—preferably .30—to be considered effective. The latter phi was usually much stricter than $p < .01$, and its equivalent effect size was larger than that used in other meta-analyses; this directly contributed to Whitehead and Lab's generally as well as comparatively pessimistic conclusions about effectiveness. Similarly, when evaluating each individual *approach*—that is, each analytic grouping of several individual studies—other analysts/reviewers used a framework whose strictness exceeded even a criterion of "two successes out of every three studies." For example, Martinson (1974) required that almost every individual study that comprised a given approach be successful (basically, using $p < .05$) in order for that approach to be considered effective. That is, if even a modest fraction—say, 20 percent—of all individual studies were unsuccessful (at $p < .05$), that naturally meant that "inconsistencies" existed and the overall approach could not be recommended as "a sure way of reducing recidivism" (Martinson, 1974, p. 49). Martinson then equated this lack of near certainty, that is, the absence of a virtual guarantee, with "not working" (Palmer, 1975, 1978). The fact that Martinson later (1979) softened this position remained generally unknown or overlooked, and it only modestly impacted the treatment-evaluation literature of the 1980s.

Despite the several differences mentioned above, many meta-analyses and literature reviews reached similar or substantially overlapping conclusions. In some cases and to some extent they probably did so because many of the individual studies they examined were identical and because, simultaneously, many interpretations of the findings from those studies were not based on widely differing success criteria. Other analyses and reviews, however, drew similar conclusions, even when many or most of the individual studies—and, in some cases, virtually all such studies—were different, as, for example, when the respective analyses and/or reviews emphasized differing time periods or program settings. This occurred not just when two or more meta-analyses were involved; it also happened when two or more literature reviews were involved and when at least one meta-analysis plus one literature review (i.e., an equal percentage of each method) was involved.

AMOUNT OF RECIDIVISM REDUCTION

It has been claimed that although E-programs "occasionally" have less recidivism than C's, the difference is generally small (Martinson, 1974, 1976). In contrast, some have said it is often large (Andrews et al., 1990). Based on the collective results from several hundred recidivism studies conducted during the past three decades, what *is* the difference in rates?

As indicated earlier, if one averages all such studies, E's rates are about 10–12 percent lower than C's. (E/C differences presented in this section are actual percentage differences, not percentage-point differences.) This is consistent with the E/C percentage difference that is reflected in Lipsey's *(a) median* effect size of .100 for all positive-outcome plus negative-outcome studies combined, corrected for small sample-size, and in his *(b) mean* effect size of .103 for all such studies when they are jointly corrected for small sample-size and E/C sample-size differences.

Before continuing, we should also consider the following: As seen in Lipsey's massive analysis, E's had lower rates than C's ($p < .05$ or not) in 64 percent of all studies. C's outperformed E's in 30 percent, and the remainder were ties. The 64 percent are called positive-outcome studies (POS's), and these studies are central to the question, What size are E/C differences in programs that *reduce recidivism?*[5] If one examines only these studies, that is, positive-outcome studies, E's recidivism rates are about 17–22 percent lower than C's.[6] Approximately one of every four POS's have rather sizable reductions, that is, 25 percent or more, and roughly one in five have reductions of less than 10 percent. (See chapter 11 regarding the validity of averaging positive-outcome studies.)

Finally, and naturally, when programs are selected on other or more specific grounds, including theoretical reasons and leads from prior research, reductions can be unusually large. For instance, when focusing on a subsample of thirty-six studies (involving fifty-four statistical comparisons) that were described as "appropriate correctional services," Andrews et al. (1990) found an average reduction of 53 percent. Most of their findings were probably independent of the fact that very large recidivism reductions may sometimes occur when, for example, above-average or even excellent E-programs are compared with well *below* average C's. (It might be noted that half of the selected programs were from Whitehead and Lab's meta-analysis, mentioned earlier.)

Thus "reductions" or differences obviously range from modest to large, and the E/C difference a meta-analyst obtains depends on how his or her study pool has been constructed. The latter, in turn, reflects the analyst's goals, questions, design requirements, and resulting exclusions. Given such factors and variations, the following nevertheless summarizes the situation for programs which, to date, reduce recidivism, that is, reduce it for all positive-outcome programs combined, without their being otherwise or further selected: 17-22 percent reductions are average, and larger as well as smaller ones are not uncommon. Such differences, it might be added, are generally nonchance in nature. For instance, when examining all studies for which Lipton, Martinson, and Wilks (1975) not only indicated at least a 15 percent recidivism reduction but also reported a significance test, Palmer (1978) found that 81 percent involved a statistically significant ($p < .05$) difference between E's and C's and that 88 percent at least tended to be significant ($p < .10$).

Chapter 5

The Absence of All-purpose Approaches

This chapter discusses the absence of "all-purpose" intervention approaches. It examines several major factors related to this absence, such as limited program relevance, the level or adequacy of program implementation, and the adequacy of traditional programs themselves. It also describes the multidimensional nature of intervention approaches in particular—a factor seldom examined to date. The chapter concludes by discussing likely contributors to today's increased acceptance of correctional effectiveness.

THE ABSENCE OF PANACEAS

Though meta-analyses and literature reviews indicate that many individual programs reduce recidivism, the following is clear: As of 1990–91, no *categories* existed that usually, say, in two-thirds or more of their individual programs, produced large recidivism reductions with their total offender population.[1] Moreover, such reductions did not even occur in one-third of the programs, though moderate reductions were common. ("Large reduction" means 25 percent or more; "moderate" is about 10–12 percent. In both cases this is apart from whether $p < .05$ has been reached, since that significance level can be attained when a sample size is very large, even if the percentage reduction is less than moderate.) Since a total population may involve a broad range of offenders and may, in the aggregate, be average or common in terms of its characteristics, it can be considered a typical, heterogeneous client-group. "Category" or "type" again refers to a program's distinguishing or, in some cases, rather salient (even seemingly dominant) component or approach.

This absence of even a few such approaches means it is presently impossible to offer any all-purpose methods or "magic bullets," for instance, to recommend any categories of programs to policy makers as being—reliably—far better than standard or traditional programs for clients overall. Stated differently, one cannot claim that any randomly selected individual program which falls within a given category will probably produce a large E/C reduction with a typical, unselected client-group.

Types of Partial Success

Despite this limitation, one can reasonably expect that certain categories of programs *(a)* will often produce *moderate* reductions with their unselected—that is, overall, heterogeneous—populations, *(b)* will be no *less* effective than standard programs with those populations, and *(c)* may produce above-average E/C reductions with *some offender-subgroups*. In addition, one may describe *individual* programs that have produced moderate or even large reductions, for example, with specialized populations such as substance abusers, with particular offender-subgroups such as the "higher maturity," and perhaps even with more heterogeneous, unselected populations.

Some studies of offender-subgroups can serve to illustrate such partial successes. For instance, experimental programs that have reduced recidivism *(a)* for one or more subgroups within an E-program more than for other subgroups in that same program, and/or *(b)* for a particular subgroup only (within an E-program compared to the same subgroup in its *C*-program), have long been known. Three brief examples follow.

1. In the Fricot Ranch study, "neurotic or emotionally disturbed delin-quents" (E's) who were assigned to an interpersonally supportive, small living-unit program, had a twenty-four-month recidivism rate of 48 percent; for "non-neurotics," that is, the remaining E's in that program, the rate was 75 percent ($p < .05$, E vs. E). The rate for neurotic *C's* (standard program) was 77 percent ($p < .05$, E vs. C); and for non neurotic C's it was 73 percent (not statistically significant [NS], E vs. C) (Jesness, 1971–72). "Neurotics" are often called "higher maturity" as well as "conflicted." Both the neurotics and non-neurotics in this sample would probably have been considered high risks, using present-day scales.

2. In Project IMPACT (Intensive Matched Probation and After-care Treatment), the twelve-month recidivism rate for "cases [E's] who have both high problem totals and low criminal tendencies" was 27 percent; however, for E's "who have both medium or low problem totals and moderate or high criminal tendencies" it was 45 percent ($p < .07$, E vs. E). Rates for those subgroups' respective *C's* were 50 percent ($p < .08$, recalculated; favoring *E's*) and 25 percent ($p < .01$;

favoring *C's*). Thus, "[a] differential treatment effect for differing types of offender[s] was apparently demonstrated" by the joint, E/C comparisons. E's received "intensive situational treatment"; C's received "normal probation supervision" (Folkard, Smith, and Smith, 1976, pp. 21, 23).
3. A study of Project Outward Bound "showed that program to be [more] effective with those delinquents who were 'reacting to an adolescent growth crisis' [than] with the more immature, emotionally disturbed, or characterologically deficient boys" (Warren, 1972, p. 7; Kelly and Baer, 1971).

Some of these programs, like others that will be summarized shortly, were included in various meta-analyses and/or literature reviews mentioned earlier. These programs, however, were not the main focus of those works; and offender-subgroup analyses other than those involving risk-level distinctions remain relatively infrequent today.

FACTORS RELATED TO THE ABSENCE OF PANACEAS

Program Relevance

One possible contributor to the absence of categories that are highly and usually effective with unselected populations springs from the fact that individual programs which comprise any given category often differ considerably from each other in their components, operations, setting, or structure (Klockars, 1975; Palmer, 1975). Because of these differences, some such programs may also differ considerably from others in their relevance to and influence on one or more sizable offender-subgroups that are common in each of their populations. These subgroups may consist, for instance, of passive or aggressive individuals, of confused-insecure or self-assured persons, and, in any case, of those who are younger or older. If such programs are differentially relevant to given subgroups, they may also differ from each other in their ability to reduce the recidivism of those subgroups and, thus, of the overall populations. Still other programs— again depending on which subgroups comprise most of their populations and on the programs' relevance to those individuals—may not reduce recidivism at all; yet with rather different offenders they might well produce reductions. Some of these issues, for example, "differential relevance" and "implications of subgroup mix," are reflected in the following four examples:

1. In the Pilot Intensive Counseling Organization (PICO) project, which featured an individual-centered approach (ICA), "treated amenables" outperformed "treated non-amenables" (E vs. E).[2] In addition, al-

though the treated amenables, all of whom received ICA, outperformed their "control amenables" (all of whom received the standard institutional approach [SIA]), the treated *non*-amenables performed *worse* than their "control amenables" (all of whom received SIA) (Adams, 1961). Amenables probably had much in common with individuals elsewhere labeled "higher maturity" (cf. "conflicted" or "neurotic"). Nonamenables probably resembled those often called "middle maturity" or "lower maturity," many of whom were also called "power oriented."

2. In the Canadian Volunteers in Corrections (CaVIC) program, "relationship oriented counseling (the worker's use of nondirective, empathic messages) correlated with decreased crime rates among the clients who had above average empathy scores but [it] increased criminal behavior of those with less empathic skills, especially when the clients were also low on the Gough Socialization Scale" (Kiessling and Andrews, 1980, p. 420).

3. Alcohol and drug abusers with a "negative [low] self-image and low interpersonal warmth" had higher recidivism rates, after an intensive group treatment program, than similar individuals who received the regular institutional program. In contrast, persons with a high self-image and low interpersonal trust had lower rates following the group program than after the institutional. Thus, "there was evidence of a significant differential treatment effect of offender type on recidivism" (Annis and Chan, 1983, p. 170).

4. Conflicted youths in California's Community Treatment Project (CTP)—that is, experimental subjects (E's)—averaged 34 arrests per thousand months on parole; power-oriented youths in CTP averaged 55. In addition, during a four-year *post-parole* (i.e., post-discharge) follow-up, the arrest rates were 32 and 68 for those same E-subgroups, respectively (Palmer, 1978).

However, although *(a)* conflicted E's also outperformed their *C's* (standard institutional plus parole program) during as well as post-parole, and given that *(b)* power-oriented C's outperformed their *E's* during the post-parole period, the post-parole findings mentioned next suggest the following: A different mix of these two youth-subgroups would have produced different post-parole results for the *overall* program, that is, for all subgroups combined (conflicted plus power-oriented youths comprised some 80 percent of the total sample; passive conformists plus all others were the remainder). The slightly better performance by favorably discharged C's, that is, by *post*-parole follow-up C's (all subgroups combined) than by their favorably discharged E's (all subgroups combined), "seemed to largely reflect the comparatively good performance which was chalked up by what amounted to a relatively large number of *Power Oriented* individuals among the favorable-dischargee control-subsample, when compared with the performance of the relatively smaller number of control *Neurotics* [Conflicted youths] who had also received a favorable discharge. (As seen [elsewhere], Neurotic *experimental* boys, taken by themselves, performed better than their controls after having left the CYA [California Youth Authority] on the basis of a favorable discharge. [But v]ery much the opposite was found in the case of Power Oriented experimentals.) In short, the Power Oriented individuals contributed enough points to have tipped the postdischarge balance [for the overall sample] in favor of the control group—i.e., when all [subgroups were not simply] counted at the same time [but] when the performance of the Power Oriented youths was weighted according to the number of such individuals who were present in this subsample of favorable dischargees. [Unfavorable dischargees, a much smaller group, had not yet been analyzed due to their longer average lockup-time.]" (Palmer, 1974, p. 6. These results involve "Phase 1" and "Phase 2" of CTP, combined [1961–69])

CTP emphasized counseling—mainly individual and secondarily group—though it drew from other features as well (see chapter 6). Other programs that illustrate differential relevance within the broad category of counseling included those mentioned above, for instance, PICO and CaVIC. Though such programs also shared certain other features with each other and with CTP, for example, relative frequency of contact, some also differed in particular ways, such as in the use of *group* vs. *individual* counseling.

Setting and structure   The above studies showed interactions between client subgroups and program content, not program *setting*. However, examples of interactions with setting have long been known and have been summarized by Warren (1971). These include the Weeks (Highfields), the Reiss, and the Mueller studies, respectively, and the Mannheim and Wilkins (early Borstal) studies as well. Other examples were presented by Palmer (1974), in connection with CTP-Phase 3 (1969–74), by Sealy and Banks (1971), again with Borstal boys, and by Brill (1978), with respect to Shawbridge (Quebec) Youth Centres males.[3]

Yet, it is very possible that substantially different types and/or amounts of programming (i.e., program content)—and of staff/client interactions as well—often occur in connection with different types of settings themselves, for example open versus closed institutions, or institutions versus community. Insofar as these further interactions exist, setting per se is neither the sole nor necessarily even the principal factor in accounting for differential impact on clients. Further complicating the situation, the above interactions may be distinguished from those involving program-*structure*. For instance, in the Fricot Ranch study, differential outcome was associated with some but not other client-subgroups, depending on their placement in relatively small versus standard-sized living-units (Jesness, 1971–72). In any event, we would hypothesize that—with many or most individuals—not only positive outcome but perhaps differential outcome is more a function of "what" transpires in a given program than of "where" and within what "structure" those inputs occur. To be sure, setting and structure can undoubtedly support and sustain key interventions ("whats") themselves, and they can perhaps help make them possible or likely in the first place.

Additional factors that may bear on the absence of all-purpose approaches are risk level, level of implementation, and adequacy of standard programs. These will now be discussed in turn.

Risk Level

A substantial portion of the studies that comprised any given category, for example, vocational training, may have had E's and C's who were *inadequately matched* with each other on average risk level; and, simultaneously, the direction of this mismatch may have varied among the studies that comprised the given categories. For instance, while some of these "unmatched" studies (the set x subsample) may have contained, say, approximately 45 percent higher-, 35 percent middle-, and 20 percent lower-risk E's., they may have had roughly 33 percent of each such risk level among their respective C's. Simultaneously, however, the remaining "unmatched" studies (the set y subsample) within that same generic category may have contained roughly the reverse percentages of higher-, middle-, and lower-risk E's and C's, respectively (i.e., the set y E's may have had about 33 percent of each risk level; and so on). Other things being equal, E-programs from set x would have been less likely to reduce recidivism than those from set y, and the same would have applied to C-programs from set y as compared to set x. For this reason alone the overall category in question could have had a sizable percentage of positive (E > C) as well as negative (C > E) results—thus, substantial "inconsistency"—even if E's and C's from all remaining studies (set z) within the category were well matched.

This situation could have contributed to the absence of all-purpose categories despite the following facts. First, some individual programs are more effective with higher risks than with middle risks and with middle than with lower-risks as well (Palmer and Wedge, 1989a). This suggests that the influence of certain program/offender matches can outweigh that of a priori risk, even in the case of relatively *standard* programs. Second, "amenables"—individuals who may have been comparable to what are currently called "middle risks" or "lower risks" (at least *within* any given sample)—have sometimes performed neither better nor worse than "nonamendables," even in *special* programs (Adams, 1959; Guttman, 1963; Andrews, Bonta, and Hoge, 1990). This is despite the fact that amenables—essentially by definition—have been considered more open to change than "nonamenables" (Glaser, 1975; Lipton, Martinson, and Wilks, 1975; Wilson, 1980), and it may be reflected in the fact that this openness has also been considered conditional (Palmer, 1983).

Even if E's and C's in each of a category's studies had been adequately matched on risk, that is, on likelihood of future offending, some E-programs within that category may have been more *relevant* than other E-programs to offenders of a particular risk-level and may therefore have produced better results than the latter programs. As a consequence, inconsistencies may once again have occurred in the given category's collective outcomes. Support for this possibility is found, for instance, in results from several individual programs that suggested the following: Regarding the reduction of recidivism, the specific content of a program (and possibly its intensity as well) can be more important with *higher risks* (and perhaps middle risks) than with lower risks (Andrews et al., 1986; Andrews, Robinson, and Balla, 1986; Andrews, Bonta, and Hoge, 1990; Jeffrey and Woolpert, 1974; Lerner, Arling, and Baird, 1986; Palmer and Lewis, 1980). These findings are reflected, for example, in Andrews, Bonta, and Hoge's (1990) and Andrews et al.'s (1990) "risk principle" and in the hypothesized interaction between that and the "responsivity principle" (see Appendix A).[4]

To be sure, the situation regarding risk is quite complex (Gottfredson and Gottfredson, 1986). For instance, in special as well as standard programs, *middle risks* have often been considered more amenable to change than higher risks and have sometimes been the only group—that is, including lower and higher risks—to show a significant reduction in recidivism when E's are compared to C's (Harrison and Mueller, 1964; Havel and Sulka, 1962; Glaser, 1975). In any event, the relationship between risk level and outcome seems neither clear-cut nor strong. This at least has been the case when a broad range of programs has been examined, collectively—including, presumably, those which are more as well as less relevant to their offender samples (whatever the latter's risk levels may be). For example, Lipsey, in his massive meta-analysis, "test[ed] the possibility that certain juveniles were especially responsive to treatment, whatever its nature . . . [and found that w]hile there was a slight tendency for studies of juveniles with higher risk levels, that is, greater involvement with delinquency, to show larger effect sizes, the overall influence of this cluster was small and statistically nonsignificant" (1992, p. 121).

Level of Implementation

Other possible contributors to today's absence of reliably powerful while widely applicable programs are well known. Mediocre implementation is one such possibility, even in programs that might conceivably have met those specifications. Still other programs, even when well implemented, may be only powerful enough to produce moderate but not major reductions for most individuals they serve.

Thus, regarding *implementation*, Lipsey's analysis (1992) suggested that programs with greater operational integrity outperformed the rest. Similar results were obtained by Davidson et al. (1984) and—using essentially the same studies—by Gottschalk et al. (1987). Related findings were also obtained by Gensheimer et al. (1986), using a diversion-focused subsample from Davidson et al.'s (1984) set. No meta-analysts have reported contrary results with respect to implementation. Collectively, the above findings therefore support the National Academy of Science's earlier view regarding the importance of program integrity (Sechrest, White, and Brown, 1979).

As to *power* one possible component involves quantity of intervention and is sometimes called "amount" or "dosage" of treatment. Here, Davidson et al. (1984), Gensheimer et al. (1986), and Gottschalk et al. (1987) found that a larger effect size—thus, more recidivism reduction—was associated with more hours of contact or treatment. Similarly, Lipsey (1992) found that higher dosage, for example, greater amount and longer duration of intervention, was related to larger effect size. Quantity of intervention, of course, differs from *type*—a dimension that can specifically involve relevance (as discussed above) and, therein, another aspect of power. Further, type and amount may interact. For instance, some types of programs, such as the relatively complex and especially the multimodal, may take longer to implement and may entail more overall input.[5]

Adequacy of Standard Programs

A further possibility is equally obvious, yet rarely mentioned: Though many programs, which may be called "nontraditionals" (E's), may have been effective themselves, the particular programs with which they were compared—that is, the standard or traditional programs (C's)—may have been quite good as well. This is a reasonable possibility given the assumption that some standard programs, like some nontraditionals, had a number of particularly competent or unusually talented staff and that such individuals had some—often considerable—effect on implementation and outcome.[6] In this scenario E and C staff would have made comparable, important contributions, whether or not differentially effective *program* differences existed between the nontraditional and traditional operations. (Whether staff, programming per se, or both made comparable contributions across those programs, the result in any case could still have been an absence of any E/C recidivism differences, however effective E itself may have been.)

Regarding this possibility, Lipsey found that for studies in which control clients received *some* degree of intervention, for instance, "treatment as usual in a juvenile justice setting," the difference in effect sizes—thus, in recidivism rates—between those individuals and the experimental clients tended to be smaller (but still in favor of experimentals) than in studies in which controls "receiv[ed] no treatment at all" (1992, p. 121). On the other hand, Gottschalk et al. (1987) observed essentially no such difference regarding type of control.

The issue of standard programs—which are also called "traditional" programs or controls—is further discussed in chapter 7.

UNIMODAL AND COMBINATION APPROACHES

Though inadequacies in available program descriptions prevent one from determining this systematically and with certainty, it is very likely that the individual programs which comprised any given generic category were not, in most cases, literally unimodal; that is, they were probably not single-feature approaches, even though their generic label may have suggested they were and even though one feature may sometimes have seemed quantitatively and/or operationally dominant. Instead, the actual situation seems to have been as follows (and its implications will soon be indicated):

First, generic categories often functioned as—and essentially were—abstractions for conceptualizing and more easily describing what were actually multielement programs or for analyzing those programs more manageably and reliably. Toward this end, the generic label that was used, for example, to represent or analytically distinguish a group of E-programs from its controls, intentionally reflected only one program component, one that consistently differentiated the E's from the C's and seemed to reflect the E's distinguishing—and, in that sense, salient—feature. Sometimes, in fact, in order to operationally create an E-program, that component was simply substituted for, added to, or "beefed up" from one in the traditional program. At any rate, the name of a major category/ method (e.g., vocational training) that was used in an *individual program* and which distinguished that program from its control or comparison could have been later used as the label that characterized the *category* into which several programs—each of which contained that same feature— were grouped. Such usage directly accounted for the unimodal, that is, the single-component, descriptions that have characterized meta-analyses and most literature reviews to date. In any event, as Lipsey pointed out, "treatment modality [was] often described rather crudely in the source studies upon which [his analysis of some 400 studies] relie[d], often by no more than a label or phrase" (1992, p. 123). (*Unimodal, one-dimensional,* and *single component* are synonymous.)

Second, the fact that one component usefully distinguished E's from C's did not mean that E's—or, for that matter, C's—therefore *contained* only one component or feature. (*Component, feature,* and *element* are used synonymously.) For example, in some cases traditional (C) programs may have lacked the distinguishing component entirely; in other instances their difference from E's on that component may only have been one of degree—albeit a substantial degree—as in many probation enhancement programs. Yet, whether the difference involved type or degree, many E's and C's each contained still *other* elements; and, considered one by one, those elements may also have distinguished E's from C's as to type or degree (e.g., an element existed in E but not C, or it was used to a greater extent). Unfortunately, some such elements, for instance, recreation or occasional counseling in institutional programs, may often have been considered too routine or else part of "normal operations" to have been focused on in various program descriptions. For whatever reasons, descriptions were often sketchy at best, and not just for control programs.

The point is that E-programs which have been explicitly or implicitly described or analyzed as unimodal approaches, that is, as "single-modality" programs, have often been combinations of components; and even in any such program, the components may have cut across generic categories. For instance, some institutional programs for juveniles—though usefully labeled "educational training," since they might have contained much of it and perhaps purposely emphasized it (and, in any event, were distinguished in terms of it—may have simultaneously or successively utilized the following supplementary or complementary components with most individuals in their respective target-populations: a moderate amount of routine recreation; a small amount of group counseling; and, perhaps, one other element, again in moderation.[7] Whether the setting was institutional or community, similar, additional elements may have been used in programs labeled "counseling" or "vocational training." This may also have occurred not only in programs labeled "behavioral" or "cognitive-behavioral"—whatever their primary focus and/or vehicles may have been, for example, educational achievement or discussion group—but in "probation enhancements" and "intensive probation" as well. The latter pair may have contained, for instance, not just an increased amount of contact and reporting, but such requirements as substance abuse counseling and/or participation in a life-skills/social-survival course. Thus, rather than the respective categories/programs being unimodal, a one-dimensional *label* was used to describe or analyze them as such.

At any rate, though experimental programs may often have been thought of as unimodal, partly because their labels focused on one program element alone, it was *combinations* of that element plus others which actually existed in many—very likely most—of those programs.[8] (Appendix D indicates how the latter situation could have made it unlikely that no *actual* unimodal E-programs would emerge as successful.) (This conclusion is consistent with Lipsey's observation that "the categories" he used in his large-scale study—categories such as behavioral, skill oriented, individual counseling, group counseling, employment, and education ["school class/tutor"]—"overlap considerably for those *many treatments with multiple elements*" [1992, p. 123; emphasis added].) This situation probably existed with most generic categories that were reviewed and analyzed in recent decades.

Thus, we believe that many experimental programs that have been conducted to date can and should be thought of—individually—as combinations of various components—combinations, as mentioned earlier, that have often differed from one E-program to the next. (Simultaneously, of course, the programs may have contained a combination of any two or more techniques—including modes of staff/client interaction—that were used to implement those components.) In addition, meta-analyses and literature reviews have already indicated that many individual programs were successful or promising, whereas many others were not. Given this situation, we hypothesize the following: For any "generic" category, such as counseling, *only some combinations of features were effective* with a large portion of the offenders who were involved in the category's respective programs. (This does not preclude effectiveness for any unimodal programs.[9]) The remaining combinations—in effect, the remaining individual E-programs (with *their* particular sets of components)—were insufficiently relevant, inadequately applied, or perhaps even effective, but with only a small portion of offenders.[10] For these reasons alone, no category could probably have emerged as being highly reliable in terms of effectiveness, even if time period, settings, system levels, and other factors had been quite similar across given meta-analyses and literature reviews. (An example that illustrates and supports the above hypothesis appears in Appendix E. There, it is seen that some E-program combinations which existed within a given generic category outperformed others in that same category.) Please note that this discussion centers on comparisons between some E-program combinations, on the one hand, and other *E*-program combinations, on the other. In contrast, chapter 6 will emphasize E- versus C-combinations, though it will also bear on the E versus E.

Which particular combinations of E-program features have commonly yielded positive results with large portions of their populations—and which ones have not—has seldom been systematically explored and remains largely unknown.[11] Discovering these combinations is one of corrections' most important challenges. (See chapter 6 for related clues.) Of course, to help corrections clearly and reliably delineate *any* combinations in the first place, and to help it then generate sets of studies in which various such combinations are systematically compared with each other to determine which ones are more effective, researchers and others should first develop relatively standardized descriptions of or definitions for the several features that may comprise any given combination, that is, for the combination's components.

At any rate, the above hypothesis implies that if a large proportion of the combinations which existed within a generic category were not especially effective, that overall category might well have been considered only moderately effective, since it was basically a direct reflection of its individual programs. (The fact that the category was a direct reflection of those programs—though not necessarily a simple aggregation or an "averaging" of them—applied to meta-analyses and literature reviews alike. This was true even though these analyses and reviews used differing techniques for integrating the results from any one group of individual studies.) By the same token, however, the hypothesis implies that generic categories which were described as the most promising were those which contained a large or larger proportion of effective combinations. Yet even here, a category's *distinguishing* feature would not, by itself, have necessarily or entirely accounted for that category's relative promise, even though the feature may indeed have often exerted more influence than others that were present.

With respect to promising programs that were grouped within a given category, we thus hypothesize the following: The programs' salient (distinguishing) feature operated in concert with other features; and together, this group of features, that is, the overall combination,[12] adequately or fairly adequately addressed delinquency related needs of the respective offender samples. At least, it did so to a greater extent than did *(a)* the control programs' combinations and *(b)* the combinations that existed in less-promising E-programs. In any event, each category's salient feature operated not alone, but in a context. For promising programs, this context was more relevant or more often relevant to offenders than that which operated for nonpromising programs that had the same salient feature. This is apart from the fact that nonprogrammatic features, such as staff characteristics and various types of staff/offender interaction, were part of the context and probably contributed to program outcome themselves.

Finally, studies of combinations would be complicated by the following (which is another hypothesis): What sometimes contributed to the *absence* of an E/C recidivism-difference was the fact that certain features which are important or essential to an E-program either were absent or, when present, were insufficiently or inadequately used in addressing critical though not always obvious needs. This could have occurred even in otherwise sophisticated and well-implemented programs (Palmer, 1991b).

As a general point, of course, the absence of an E/C recidivism difference could also have occurred if E and C were equally strong or weak, whether they were uni- or multimodal. In addition, regarding E itself, well-implemented programs that contain several components are, theoretically, better able to reduce recidivism than those with very few, since they may pertain to a wider range of offenders. This would apply unless only a very few *specific combinations* of components are critical with most clients, whereas the sheer *number* of components that comprise those combinations are not. Of course, an underlying relationship necessarily exists between combination and number, since any combination requires at least two parts, and most complex ones require more. Yet, once a program contains three or four components, any that are added may conceivably provide diminishing returns in terms of recidivism—except, perhaps, as follows: *(a)* with particular types of offenders who would otherwise be inadequately served or even entirely excluded (by the original components); *(b)* if and as the added components would increase operational flexibility with individuals who, in the main, are already adequately served by the original combination of components.

Whether most positive-outcome programs do in fact function mainly as *(a)* a combination of interrelated components, such as skills training, counseling, and external controls or else as *(b)* a unimodal operation after all, with one component truly dominating, the following remains true for intervention's many "types" of programs combined, that is, for intervention *overall:* The large number of positive outcomes that have been found in the past three decades with studies whose designs and analyses were at least adequate leaves little doubt that many programs "work," and not just with one or two types of offenders and programs. Moreover, the contribution of these programs, individually and especially collectively, is far from minor. For instance, among those which reduced recidivism by any amount, the average drop was about 20 percent. Thus, for every one thousand potential offenses during the programs' follow-up periods, two hundred were avoided. Though most of the latter would probably have been run-of-the-mill yet not ipso facto trivial, many would have been violent and unusually costly in several respects.

CONTRIBUTORS TO INCREASED ACCEPTANCE OF EFFECTIVENESS

Despite the lack of categories that are reliably powerful while widely applicable, and whatever the actual reasons for this may be, the following seems clear: Various meta-analyses and literature reviews conducted since the mid-1980s (and even earlier) have left a fairly strong impression that several programs or approaches *have* very likely impacted recidivism, and not just for "amenable" and/or low-risk offenders. This impression, which currently is more widely and perhaps more strongly held than it was in the early and mid-eighties, is seldom challenged on empirical grounds. This relative absence of challenge exists despite the obvious fact that the research designs of most studies which comprised the meta-analyses and literature reviews themselves were by no means excellent and were therefore potentially vulnerable. Given this potential vulnerability, what might explain the increased acceptance of positive outcomes, and, perhaps, the relative lack of serious questioning itself?

Attitudes Regarding Designs and Analyses

Increased acceptance of what were reported as positive outcomes did not seem to result from a sudden, first-time awareness of such findings, since many were well-known before 1985. Nor did it mainly reflect the fact that it was largely *meta-analysis*—a quantitative, seemingly objective, though not entirely bias-proof technique—that had further focused people's awareness on those findings and had made them better known; to be sure, this focus provided considerable help.

Above all, increased acceptance implicitly reflected the fact that, since the mid-eighties, few researchers and academicians had suggested that only those studies which have *excellent* or near-perfect designs and analyses should be considered when evaluating intervention and that all others should in effect be discounted. (The view that only the former studies should be seriously considered had been implied by a national panel several years earlier, and had exerted substantial influence in the early eighties [Sechrest, White, and Brown, 1979].) More specifically, there was a combination of increased acquiescence and acceptance regarding studies which, while neither excellent nor near perfect, seemed to meet long-established standards of scientific *adequacy* (e.g., regarding the use of randomized or quasi-experimental designs, and as to the equivalence of E's and C's on a number of relevant preprogram variables). Falling short of the ideal was, in itself, no longer considered grounds for dismissal, as long as a study's flaws were far from fatal with regard to negating the thrust and direction of its main findings.

Nevertheless, though adequately designed studies comprised a sizable portion of meta-analyses and literature reviews, many borderline and even poorly designed studies existed. It is especially because of such weaker studies and not mainly due to an absence of routine *excellence,* that strong claims regarding given categories of programs are indeed open to question. For instance, wide-ranging statements about the effectiveness of family counseling, cognitive-behavioral intervention, and even behavioral approaches should be carefully qualified, since a sizable portion of the individual studies that comprised those categories were in fact less than adequately designed. This is apart from the fact that not all their *adequately* designed studies proved successful and that—nevertheless—those types of programs, on balance, were among the most promising. It is also aside from the fact that, in the early 1980s, critics of intervention commonly focused on borderline and poorly designed studies and downplayed the more adequate—for instance, those with a fairly well matched E/C sample in the context of a quasi-experimental design—whatever the category.

It should be noted that, in general, borderline or questionable studies were probably not associated with overblown results. For instance, several meta-analysts and reviewers found that recidivism reductions which occurred in borderline/questionable studies were, collectively, essentially the same size as those in better-designed studies or else were slightly smaller (Andrews et al., 1990; Bailey, 1966; Davidson et al., 1984; Gensheimer et al., 1986; Gottschalk et al., 1987; Lipsey, 1992; Palmer, 1978 [regarding Lipton, Martinson, and Wilks's (1975) review]). That is, the presence of borderline or questionable studies in samples that were analyzed or reviewed may not, ipso facto, have produced an exaggerated picture regarding intervention's likelihood or extent of effectiveness, and it may not have thereby invited unduly optimistic conclusions. Yet, some meta-analysts reported that borderline/questionable designs, compared to adequate or strong ones, *were* associated with slightly (Whitehead and Lab, 1989) or considerably (Garrett, 1985) larger recidivism reductions.

The "last word" on this to date—or at least the most weight—should perhaps go to Lipsey (1992). This is mainly because of the wider-ranging, far larger, and probably more fully representative nature of his study sample— combined with a no less sophisticated analysis. Basically, Lipsey found that "the nature of subject assignment to groups (random vs. nonrandom), often viewed as synonymous with design quality, had little relationship to effect size" (p. 120). That conclusion, which involved all intervention approaches combined, does not preclude the possibility that effect sizes which are substantially larger (or smaller) in borderline/questionable studies may have occurred for *particular* intervention approaches within the overall sample; this, in fact, was observed by Garrett (1985) with regard to behavioral programs. Similarly, the conclusion in question is independent of further findings by Lipsey and others (e.g., Davidson et al., 1984; Andrews et al., 1990), which suggest that additional method factors (see chapter 2) can produce "distorted" results, that is, those which—by comparison—seem inflated or deflated. This applies regardless of design quality.

Number of Positive Studies

Despite today's valid questions about individual categories, another reason for today's more sanguine view of intervention as a whole is probably the sheer number of positive-outcome studies, that is, studies in which E's had lower recidivism rates than C's. By the period 1985–87 at least several dozen such studies were also statistically significant using the $p < .05$ criterion, and many of these latter studies were scientifically adequate in terms of supporting those nonchance, E/C differences.[13] (Of the 270 separate juvenile delinquency studies reported in Appendix C, 89 had a positive outcome at or beyond $p < .05$.) The large number of positive-outcome studies for all categories combined were made apparent by the meta-analyses and literature reviews.

Convergence of Evidence

Finally, another contributor to the more sanguine view may have been the apparent convergence of positive outcomes across different generic categories; these outcomes involved individual studies that were often good to excellent, whether or not they reached the $p < .05$ level. Such convergence occurred in positive-outcome studies within and across various approaches, and it was found across as well as within given analyses/ reviews: This evidence was observed in studies that resembled each other not just in name alone (e.g., "behavioral" programs) but on various offender, setting, structural, and program dimensions. As such, the studies in effect constituted—collectively—unplanned, partial replications of each other, and their resulting, mutual reinforcement increased the contributions of all (Palmer, 1983, 1984).

In sum, one or more of the factors discussed in this section may have tacitly reassured many individuals that studies—collectively, or on average—need not be excellent in order to help one decide if intervention often "works." Nor need they be excellent or near perfect individually before they can make any contribution at all to correctional knowledge. Here, "works" includes moderate, not just major, E/C reductions, whether for overall target-populations or particular subgroups alone. It extends beyond outcomes in which E's simply perform as well as C's and beyond pre/post reductions among E's themselves, a type of outcome that is fairly common (and often occurs among C's as well). Studies that are adequate can contribute to knowledge.

Whether or not the preceding factors largely explain today's increased acceptance of positive outcomes and the growing impression that several programs or approaches have very likely impacted recidivism, the fact remains that findings from the several meta-analyses and literature reviews have helped to change or modify many individuals' assumptions about intervention. All in all it seems fair to say that, by the close of the eighties, the emerging picture regarding intervention's effectiveness with juvenile offenders was as follows: "something" (that is, some individual programs) apparently works, but no generic method or approach especially shines. Alternatively stated, and with different emphasis, several methods seem promising, but none have been shown to usually produce major reductions while also applying widely, that is, to typical composite populations. In addition, other methods have shown largely mixed results, while still others have demonstrated relatively little promise or only scattered success.

Part II
New Directions for Research

Chapter 6
Conceptualizing Combinations Research

This chapter proposes a new direction for intervention research: the study of *combinations* of features that comprise given programs. The chapter describes the nature, scope, and initial challenges involved in such research. It then discusses several "nonprogrammatic" factors, that is, factors such as staff characteristics and staff/client interactions, which are not programmatic. The chapter provides experimental evidence regarding the possible importance of those factors, and it concludes with a general discussion of the need for research that would examine programs as composites of programmatic as well as nonprogrammatic factors.

As indicated earlier, many successful E-programs were undoubtedly combinations of features, not unimodal operations. Since many C-programs they outperformed were doubtlessly combinations themselves, this means that many combinations, that is, those in successful E-programs, were more effective than others—those in corresponding C's. (This is independent of chapter 5's hypothesis that some E-combinations were more effective than other *E's,* within any generic category.)

In one recent example, restitution, counseling, and recreation were combined in the E-program, while restitution and standard probation characterized the C (Schneider and Schneider, 1985; Panizzon, Olson-Raymer, and Guerra, 1991). Combinations found in other successful E-programs for juveniles include the following (these studies, too, involved random assignment to E and C conditions, and they may be characterized as multimodal): *(a)* job placement and job counseling, individual counseling, and (if needed) remedial education (Shore and Massimo, 1979); *(b)* individual counseling, pragmatically oriented discussions, routine supervision, family counseling if needed, and academic training as well as individual tutoring if needed (Lee and Haynes, 1980); and *(c)* counseling, pragmatically oriented discussions, limit-setting and control-centered

67

discussions, recreation and socializing experiences, and (if needed) academic training as well as individual tutoring (Palmer, 1974; Barkwell, 1980).[1]

Though successful instances have therefore occurred, what is unknown is whether any given combinations—combinations that were effective in individual E-programs—were fairly *reliably* effective. Specifically, it is not known if they were associated with recidivism reduction in the preponderance or at least large majority of the studies in which they appeared. Moreover, it is not even known if those or any other combinations really *did* appear in several studies, even though it is clear that some combinations or portions of large combinations occurred in more than one. The absence of such information generally reflects the broader fact that clearly delineated combinations have hardly been focused on in the first place and have rarely even been hypothesized as such for purposes of systematic research.

RESEARCH ON COMBINATIONS

General Considerations, and Scope

To identify combinations that may be reliably effective, one would need a multistudy research effort in which the outcomes of similar or identical combinations from individual E-programs would be compared across studies. These studies need not have occurred only within the same generic category, for example either in group counseling/therapy or vocational training. In this research effort, the first or broadest task would center not on the question, Which E-program combination (EPC) is the *most* effective? or even on, "Which EPCs are more effective than others?" Instead, it would focus on the question, Which EPCs are effective at all, particularly across most (or at least a sizable portion) of their studies? that is, What constitutes those combinations?

Given this task, initial efforts would not center on comparing the outcomes of two or more EPCs with one another—combinations that would each have been effective relative to their respective C's (in individual studies) and differentially effective relative to each other (across studies). Instead, they would focus on comparing the outcomes of various E's, on the one hand, with those of their respective C's, on the other, to determine if those EPCs, when aggregated across the individual studies, commonly outperformed the C's, also aggregated. The E's whose outcomes would be compared with those of C's would be a preestablished set of similar or identical EPCs, for example, counseling, routine limit-setting supervision, pragmatically oriented discussions, restitution if and as feasible, academic training and individual tutoring if needed, and job placement plus job-centered discussions if needed.

Combinations of Program Components

To date, research on combinations has hardly existed; rarely has it been discussed in detail. Instead, researchers have centered their analyses of intervention-effectiveness around single program features or components, that is, around a distinguishing or salient feature of given programs. These features have often been "programmatic," as, for example, in the case of counseling or educational training. Often, however, they have involved "approaches," as, for instance, with the "behavioral," "cognitive-behavioral," and "confrontation"—not that these lacked specific content or subject-matter focus.

In analyzing the given program component or approach, researchers have used that feature as the equivalent of an independent variable and have, we believe, produced much knowledge and many important leads. However, while occupied with that already large and complex task, they have not tried to also take on the following challenge (as already implied and as will be clearer below, the basic information needed to seriously address this challenge was generally absent in individual studies; this in itself would have made the third and fourth steps of the challenge impossible to adequately implement):

> 1. based on prior research—and/or, to a slightly lesser extent, on theory—delineate one or two combinations of features, for example, combinations of "program components" (see description, below), which one hypothesizes to be effective across various E-programs;[2]
> 2. analytically use each of those combinations, that is, each one in turn, as the equivalent of a single, independent variable;
> 3. determine, via systematic comparisons across various E/C studies in which a given, hypothesized E-combination appears, if that combination is in fact successful in many (or most) of those studies; or,
> 4. at least determine, via the same type of systematic, cross-study comparisons, not only which particular program components—that is, which subset of features or factors within the total combination—appear most often in the programs that are successful (see n. 1), but also, if possible, their degree of success as well, for instance, their effect size.

At any rate, researchers have not yet hypothesized and utilized any specific combinations of program components for the purpose of systematically studying them *as* combinations. Certainly, no such combinations have been widely discussed, let alone generally accepted as prime candidates for such research.

Necessary and Sufficient Conditions   If one focuses on program components alone—these being the individual features, that is, the generic categories or approaches, that have served as the main analytic units in meta-analyses and literature reviews to date—the following emerge as examples of what might be called "hypothetically effective combinations": *(a)* life skills plus cognitive-behavioral approaches and *(b)* family intervention plus educational training (or employment). More precisely, these and other combinations of program components may provide either necessary or sufficient conditions for positive outcomes (success).

For instance, regarding necessary conditions, one might hypothesize that some combinations are essential for success, and in fact contribute to it, but that those combinations—by themselves—are not strong enough to produce statistically significant E/C differences for their overall samples. On the other hand, one might hypothesize that those same combinations *are* sufficient for success; at least, one might justifiably do so if there is no substantial evidence to the contrary, that is, few if any negative results and certainly none that are strong.

Moreover, both the necessary- and the sufficient-conditions hypotheses could be considered plausible even if no specific *positive* results yet exist regarding the given combinations' effectiveness. For example, both hypotheses may be considered plausible simply on grounds that if each individual component included in the combinations in question has shown promise in several studies and if those separate components are relatively promising overall, a *combination* of them should itself be as effective as or even more effective than the individual components.

Yet, hypotheses that are plausible on those particular grounds or on other empirically weak or even untested grounds may or may not be supported in actual operation.[3] An absence of support might, for instance, reflect the fact that still *other* factors may be actively operating and may oppose or otherwise weaken the individual and/or collective components that were believed to be effective. These factors may be inputs and conditions that were perhaps unknown or not considered when the hypotheses were formulated. Alternatively, as suggested below, such inputs and conditions may be essential themselves—say, essential as operational supports to the hypothesized components; yet even they may not have been sufficiently present or adequately/appropriately used, and the E/C difference may therefore have been less than significant.

At any rate, plausibility, by itself, is just a starting point in knowledge building, one that requires little or no prior empirical verification with respect to hypotheses. Specifically, a hypothesis—like a conclusion itself—is logically plausible if it is not seriously contradicted by known, relevant facts (assuming some exist), if it is neither fallacious nor far-fetched relative to its premises, and if it is internally consistent overall. It is empirically, not just logically, plausible if it is also supported by at least one relevant finding. This applies whether one's hypothesis relates to necessary or sufficient conditions.

In sum, whatever the logical/empirical grounds of one's hypothesis may be—more specifically, whether or not they involve more than the simplest levels of plausibility and perhaps even reflect substantial prob-ability—the following, by-no-means remote possibility remains: Pro-gram components, viewed as generic inputs such as educational training, life-skills training, restitution, or cognitive-behavioral approaches, may not actually produce positive outcomes by themselves. That is, even if those components are essential for success, they might still be insufficient on their own. More to the point, they may be insufficient even if—and regardless of how—they are combined with each other.

Thus, an equally reasonable or no less plausible possibility arises: To achieve successful outcomes—say, statistically significant E/C differ-ences—additional types of inputs and/or supportive conditions may have to be involved, again individually or in combination. For purposes of contrast these inputs/conditions may be called "nonprogrammatic" com-ponents; as might be inferred, they, too, can be considered either neces-sary or sufficient with respect to positive outcomes.

Combinations of Nonprogrammatic
Components

Staff and Implementation Factors   A modest amount of experimental evidence already exists regarding the possible importance of non-programmatic components, that is, inputs which are other than program-matic in the sense of counseling approaches, educational approaches, and so on. Some of the earliest but particularly relevant evidence centers on what might be called "staff" and "implementation" factors. For instance, based on extensive observations and analyses of a large, multiphase, multiyear, well-implemented-and-matched, random assignment study of serious repeat offenders in an intensive, rehabilitation-centered, in-lieu-of-institutionalization program that operated in one large urban and two medium-sized California cities, the following were identified as "signifi-cant contributors" to the success of that program: "a. matching of specific types of clients [offenders] with certain types of workers [agents]; b. level of ability and perceptiveness of workers; c. intensive and/or extensive intervention by workers with regard to several areas of the client's life—

made possible by low caseload assignments; [and] d. emphasis upon the working through of the worker/ward relationship as a major vehicle of treatment" (Palmer et al., 1968, p. viii). More precisely, it was a series of interrelated substudies that had successively teased out the individual and combined role of those factors. These substudies had built on each other and were, in that connection, partial replications as well as systematic variations. Together, this series of substudies (or this single, large study) was known as the Community Treatment Project (CTP).

In another example along related lines, Canadian and American researchers subsequently concluded that the following—especially in combination—were key ingredients of successful intervention (this conclusion was based on studies—especially the CaVIC study [see below]— in which no particular category of offenders, for instance, the serious or repeat, was emphasized; most individuals were older adolescents and young adults):

1. use of authority by correctional worker;
2. anticriminal modeling and reinforcement, by worker;
3. a problem-solving strategy;
4. use of [appropriate] community resources; and,
5. a particular quality in the worker/offender relationship (Andrews and Kiessling, 1980; Andrews et al., 1990; Cullen and Gendreau, 1989).

Also related was the offender's risk level (Andrews et al., 1986; Andrews, Robinson, and Balla, 1986). The hypothesized relationship between risk level, on the one hand, and appropriate level of service, on the other, is indicated in Appendix A.[4]

Leads such as these directly imply that effective combinations involve more than program components, that is, programmatic features, alone. For instance, positive outcomes that were probably contributed to by "level of ability and perceptiveness of workers" and by "anticriminal modeling and reinforcement, by worker," indicate that *staff characteristics* (e.g., personality features, including modeling qualities; professional orientations) and various aspects of *staff/client interaction* (e.g., matching; particular qualities in the relationship) may often be important. Examples of individual programs and types of outcomes that reflect these nonprogrammatic, generic factors are as follows:

First, in the CaVIC (Canadian Volunteers in Corrections) program,

> probation officers, [whether] volunteers or professionals, who were interpersonally sensitive to conventional rules of conduct (above average on the Socialization Scale) were the most effective one-to-one supervisors according to [various reports, to] the officers' actual behavior during audio-taped sessions

with probationers, the attitudinal gains exhibited by probationers, and recidivism rates. (Andrews and Kiessling, 1980, p. 454).

Regarding client subgroups,

among low risk probationers, [e.g.,] those who were older (20 . . . or older) and/or who scored above the median on Gough Socialization, the professional status of officers was unrelated to recidivism. [However, a]mong the higher risk probationers, [e.g.,] the young and the unsocialized, volunteer supervision was significantly more effective than professional supervision, particularly so among those young unsocialized probationers who scored above the median on Hogan Empathy. (p. 453)

Nevertheless, matching effects seemed to exist for even

the indigenous [volunteer] workers . . . only [when they] possess[ed] the preferred personality dispositions, [e.g.,] high empathy/socialization. (p. 455)

Second, in the Youth Center Research Project,

the non-specific factor of client positive regard for staff potentiated whatever specific treatment effects were present and contributed about as much to outcome as did type of treatment . . . [W]here specific overt behaviors are targeted in a behavioral [i.e., behavior modification] program, greater changes can be made when the client feels positively toward staff; similarly in a transactional analysis program, greater changes on attitudinal and self-report measures can be obtained where good relationships exist. (Jesness, 1975, pp. 759, 777)

Third, related, though somewhat different, results were obtained in the Cooperative Behavior Demonstration Project. There, the

violation rate for clients more highly regarded by their workers was 10%; for the low-positive-regard group the rate was 33%. There was also a small difference in problem-remission rates favoring those clients who felt high-positive-regard for their officers . . . [Also,] where there was high mutual regard or high mutual dislike between client and caseworker, the differences in recidivism were great. Only 10% of those showing high mutual regard failed; 40% of those showing high mutual dislike failed . . . [T]he association between positive regard and recidivism was more likely a consequence of differences in the caseworker's behavior toward the client than of common client characteristics. (Jesness et al., 1975, pp. 153–54)

Fourth, in the Camp Elliot study,

the interaction between the maturity level of the subjects and the supervisor characteristics significantly affected later success rate of subjects. Not only were the treatment methods of some internally-oriented supervisory teams effective in increasing the success rates of high maturity offenders, but also, the treatment methods [of those teams] were markedly detrimental to the success chances of low maturity offenders. Furthermore, the externally-oriented supervisory team had the reverse effect on high and low maturity subjects. (Warren, 1971, p. 245)

Fifth, in the Community Treatment Project, for all subgroups combined,

> boys who were closely matched with their CTP worker had a failure rate . . . of 23 percent over a fifteen-month parole follow-up. Those not closely matched had a failure rate of 49 percent (p < .01) . . . After twenty-four months, the failure rates were 34 and 57 percent, respectively (p < .05). (Palmer, 1973, p. 101)

Also, with regard to particular subgroups within CTP's overall sample:

> Among "conflicted" youths, those described as "neurotic, acting-out" (with little felt-anxiety) performed better when assigned to matched parole agents [those specifically matched with the "acting-out" youths, not just matched, skilled, and/or sensitive in general] than to all remaining agents, combined [the latter being skilled, sensitive, etc., but only matched to one or more *other* subgroups and not specifically matched to "neurotic, acting-out" youths] . . . Similarly, among "power oriented" youths, those described as "manipulators" performed better with matched agents [i.e., with agents specifically matched to power oriented youths, vs. those not matched to that subgroup—even though matched with other individuals] while those called "subcultural conformists" [e.g., gang-involved youths who *want* to consider themselves delinquent] did not. (Palmer, 1975, p. 148)

Sixth, in the Santa Monica study,

> *"Relationship/Self-expression"* officers [change agents] achieved their best results with youths who were Communicative-alert, Impulsive-anxious, or Verbally hostile-defensive; they did less well with those who were Dependent-anxious. *"Surveillance/Self-control"* officers had their greatest difficulties with individuals who were Verbally hostile-defensive or Defiant-indifferent; they did considerably better with those who were Dependent-anxious. *"Surveillance/Self-expression"* officers seemed uniquely matched with probationers who Wanted to be Helped and Liked. (Palmer, 1965, pp. 19–20)

An additional type of factor that may contribute substantially to reduced recidivism might involve given *strategies* (steps; phases) and *specific techniques* for implementing overall plans. Individually and collectively, these staff and implementation inputs may help establish and maintain a general atmosphere plus other conditions and dynamics that not only *(a)* help program components themselves function well in general, but also *(b)* encourage or convince particular clients to give those components, for example, educational training, counseling, or cognitive-behavioral intervention, a serious try, whether or not those components are combined with each other. The atmosphere, conditions, and dynamics in question may include, for instance, clear and open communication by staff, frequent and ready availability of staff, and a generally positive working relationship, say, one that involves considerable respect, trust, and reliability. These are among the "process" factors that merit careful study. The existence of implementation inputs and process factors is reflected, for example, in the earlier list of "significant contributors" to CTP outcomes and of "key ingredients" in the CaVIC studies.

Many staff who are adept at establishing such an atmosphere and conditions may also have skills and features that include the following—perhaps more so with some types of clients than with others:

1. An above-average ability to identify clients' main "criminogenic needs," for example, delinquency-related (causal) factors suggested by Andrews et al. (1990), and to detect other current or long-standing factors, for example, strengths, desires, and fears, that positively or negatively influence most clients or, at least, particular types of clients. (Palmer, 1992)

2. An added sensitivity to methods of addressing those needs and factors and to ways of utilizing given strengths and constructive desires on the part of clients; thus, for example, an above-average ability to effectively interact with and motivate various types of clients and to otherwise implement the "responsivity principle" described by the above authors. To help reach and motivate those clients, particular personality features of staff may be important as well. (Palmer, 1967, 1973)

Insofar as these staff and implementation inputs matter, intervention that is to be effective would require more than simply linking together various well known and/or promising *program components* and then making those linked components available to clients regardless of how and by whom. This need would probably exist even if those program components were linked to each other in a dynamic, operationally well coordinated, and theoretically well conceptualized way, not just in a loose, building-block, or somewhat mechanical and perhaps only moderately integrated fashion. In addition, it might exist whether or not those components were made available to clients on a relatively individualized basis, for instance, as a result of careful diagnostic testing and subsequent tailoring of program content to the clients' main interests, needs, and circumstances.

PROGRAMS AS COMPOSITES

The need to link up programmatic and other types of features not only suggests but reflects the view that programs should be regarded and studied as composites and often-complex wholes. More specifically, wherever feasible all four types of factors—program components, staff characteristics, staff/client interactions, and intervention strategies/techniques—should probably be part of any combination that is hypothesized and adopted for future systematic study, since each factor may make a necessary contribution, and no single one may suffice.[5]

For instance, staff characteristics and particular intervention strategies/techniques may not, by themselves, provide sufficient direction or engender enough change to produce significant improvement. Instead, only the actual program components may allow staff and clients to directly focus on and concretely address various adjustment needs, problems, and issues that may trigger or help sustain illegal behavior. These needs, and so on, may include practical and social-skill deficiencies, personal conflicts or fears, restrictive or dangerous environmental conditions, and negative relationships or affiliations.

Yet, at the same time, the following might apply: Though staff and intervention factors may not, for instance, provide practical skills or alleviate certain environmental conditions by themselves, and although particular program components may be essential regardless of how pertinent staff's characteristics and skills may be and however appropriate their strategies/techniques, those same staff and intervention factors may, for example, nevertheless provide conditions that are needed to support those program components and to otherwise promote positive change. Thus, combinations research should almost certainly include more than any one generic factor alone. In so doing, it would reflect the view or assumption that important and often crucial interactions may occur among the four types of input.

Further complicating the research task is the fact that important differences may exist across differing types of clients.[6] For instance, not only might the specific *content* of hypothesized effective combinations differ a good deal across such clients—for example, vary for highly dependent or perhaps submissive/vulnerable clients, on the one hand, and highly independent or perhaps defiant/self-reliant individuals, on the other—but the *relative strength or ranking* of the four generic factors may differ as well, as may the specific strength of their interactions. These differences may exist despite the presence of considerable commonality across many or all of those same clients, that is, commonality regarding content, ranking, and specific strength. At any rate, though possible client-differences would further complicate matters, they should be carefully examined along with the rest—and with type of setting or structure as well. Unfortunately, there is no escaping complexity, at least not if one is to untangle the realities of intervention—especially, but not only, the multimodal.

In this chapter we discussed four broad types of factors: program components, staff characteristics, staff/client interactions, and intervention strategies/techniques (the final three being termed "nonprogrammatic" components). In chapter 7 we will present specific "data items" that comprise those and other factors. First, however, we will review several general needs that bear on corrections' upcoming challenges with respect to knowledge building. This review will provide a framework for understanding the role of data items and various ways of integrating them.

Chapter 7

Further Challenges in Knowledge Building

This chapter discusses general needs and issues involved in improving the quality of research studies, in strengthening and expanding their findings, and in increasing their relevance. It also presents and discusses specific analytic units—called "data items" or "features"—that can provide a foundation for more accurately describing and better understanding correctional intervention. The chapter next discusses the general nature of process features such as staff/client interactions and intervention strategies/techniques. It concludes by reviewing the preceding as well as the present chapter and by setting the stage for subsequent chapters, ones that introduce specific methods for conducting "combinations research" designed to address the question, How might one determine which features and combinations of features are related to successful programs?

GENERAL NEEDS AND ISSUES

Better Designed Studies

Several critical challenges for intervention research extend beyond the scope of meta-analysis and literature reviews per se. For one thing, a larger number and higher proportion of well-designed studies is needed in order to raise the percentage of solid findings within and across categories and to reduce the need to heavily qualify various generalizations about the effectiveness of those categories. Thus, for example, random assignment is more often needed, and even if this occurs, E/C matching on several crucial variables should, if possible, be assured rather than simply be assumed to invariably accompany this procedure.[1] At any rate, though many designs have thus far ranged from mediocre to acceptable or good, far too many have been borderline or poor, and the percentage of studies that are good to excellent is too low.

In some respects it is just as important to substantially reduce the percentage of borderline or poor studies as to increase that of excellent ones. For instance, though many studies that comprised the meta-analyses and literature reviews were adequate or good, the mere presence of many weak or clearly questionable ones necessarily reduced the strength of certain conclusions regarding effectiveness. (Findings and conclusions about effectiveness are, of course, only one aspect of knowledge building.) It especially calls for caution and qualification at the level of individual generic approaches, such as group counseling and variants thereof, for example, guided group interaction and milieu therapy. This is because far fewer studies are usually present in an individual generic approach than in most meta-analyses or nonspecialized literature reviews overall, that is, when all individual approaches are aggregated and analyzed as an entity.

Also needed are studies that analyze, not only *(a)* the effectiveness (e.g., the recidivism) of E versus C programs during a given *post*program follow-up (say, two years) but also *(b)* the amount of change in both E and C from a *pre*program period—for instance, the two years immediately preceding program entry—*to* a postprogram period. By itself, an examination of postprogram rates (i.e., analysis—*(a)*) could, for example, determine if E had a significantly lower recidivism rate than C during the postprogram period itself. However, unless it is combined with analysis-*(b)*, it could not determine if the pre/post change for E and/or C in fact reflected *improvement*, that is, involved a lower recidivism rate. It is possible, for instance, that E and C both became worse from pre to post, but that C did so to a greater degree than E—thus making E less *un*successful than C, but not successful in terms of recidivism reduction per se. Most studies that comprised the meta-analyses and literature reviews provided E versus C information about arrests, convictions, and so forth, for the postprogram period only and may not have collected similar preprogram data—say, rate-of-arrest data—in the first place.

See Appendix F for additional, major issues regarding control programs per se.

More Replication Studies

In the future, a much higher percentage of studies should be purposely designed as replications or partial replications than was the case from 1960 to 1990. Replicated (cross-validated) results could give theorists as well as practitioners more confidence in particular programs or given approaches. The first such studies might be planned repeats or partial repeats of programs that seemed promising, feasible, and relevant—for instance, those associated with sizable recidivism reductions, whose designs were at least adequate, which were implemented appropriately, and whose settings or (especially) client sample seemed common. Since 1965, many unplanned or minimally planned partial replications have been conducted. Collectively, they have often provided converging or mutually reinforcing evidence—sometimes even opposing evidence— regarding the effectiveness of given interventions. If those studies had been specifically developed as replications designed with several major areas of correspondence and few of known or assumed critical difference, their contributions to knowledge building would have been larger and more precise. The contextual value of the earlier (replicated) studies might have been larger as well.

More Purposive Variations

Purposive variations of earlier studies should be conducted more often than they have been in the past. This could be done especially, but not only, if the earlier (varied) studies have yielded significant and sizable positive results. For instance, a purposive-variation study could test— with setting and/or population Y (say, urban males aged sixteen to eighteen)—results from a previously promising program that dealt with X (rural males aged thirteen to fifteen). Also, variations of earlier studies could be conducted regardless of whether, but particularly if, those earlier studies have been at least partly replicated. Once a replication or planned replication helped confirm, qualify, or even challenge findings that related to a previously studied program, a purposive variation could address the latter's generalizability or broader applicability, for example, its relevance to other settings or populations. Thus, the key issue in purposive variations is expanded relevance, not operational transferability. Combined with each other and implemented in the context of adequate or strong designs, planned replications and purposive variations could constitute a powerful and efficient tool for knowledge building and practical action. This goes beyond the assessment of intervention's overall effectiveness.

To maximize the value of purposive replications and purposive variations, one should carefully describe not only the general nature and key features of the setting and sample but also as many of the following as possible: *program* goals, philosophy, atmosphere, staff, staff roles, resources, relations with community and outside agencies, and general procedures and activities; and, *organizational or agency* structure, relationships between components, and key policies and procedures. These descriptions could help practitioners and others more accurately decide if a given replication or variation is relevant to, and can perhaps be adapted to, their own situation. They could enhance the study of theoretical issues as well. There have been too few of these descriptions—descriptions which can be useful without purposive replications and purposive variations, that is, useful based on the original programs themselves.

Frequent Subgroup Analyses

Wherever possible, each study should describe the main offender (client) subgroups that comprise the overall target sample, and separate outcome analyses should be conducted for each subgroup whose number of cases is not too small to yield statistically reliable results or otherwise useful clues. These "differentiated analyses" could be valuable whether or not— but especially if—differing interventions have been used with those subgroups. For one thing, in any given study they could efficiently help identify one or more techniques that may be particularly successful or unsuccessful with some but not other offenders. They could thereby accelerate knowledge building by allowing, in effect, for several simultaneous substudies—one per offender subgroup—rather than separate studies for one or two subgroups in turn (Palmer, 1978).

Of course, some form of offender classification is needed in order to delineate the respective subgroups, and classifying requires added resources. But the added effort and expense may sometimes be useful (Van Voorhis, 1994). For instance, given certain classification-based distinctions among offenders and given the setting/organization/program descriptions mentioned above, differentiated analyses could identify significant relationships that may exist among certain offender subgroups, on the one hand, and setting/organization/program factors or activities, on the other. Besides reducing or avoiding overgeneralizations about what is and is not effective with offenders (presumably all offenders, under any or all program conditions), and besides reducing the masking of positive outcomes (see chapter 7, note 2, regarding masking), results from differentiated analyses or analyses of interactions could give practitioners and policy makers more precise and accurate suggestions not only about how to organize and operate particular programs, but also about the types of offenders for whom those programs, or different parts thereof, might be most and least useful. Such findings could also advance correctional theory.

The more differentiated one's analysis is to be, the more precise one's study design should be in terms of pre- and postprogram equivalence of E versus C offender characteristics. This equivalence applies not just to the sample as a whole—that is, to all offenders combined, separately for E's and C's—but to each of its major subgroups, including its respective offender-types. Also, the more differentiated one's analysis, the larger the sample size should be. To be sure, the above equivalence can partly compensate for a small sample-size, and it is, as implied, very important in any event. Nevertheless, other factors being equal, larger samples would increase reliability—and this, too, is quite important.

More Studies of Process

Intervention processes (e.g., specific techniques, strategies, and program features) should be examined closely and described more often and more fully than before. When such examination occurs in the context of well-designed studies in which positive outcomes ($p < .05$) are found, researchers may obtain clues or strong evidence as to which of those factors—and which combinations—substantially contribute to intervention. Although many intervention processes may contribute to positive outcomes, fewer such factors are probably *major* contributors and/or essential ingredients. If, in the 1990s and beyond, studies of process help identify several such contributors or ingredients (collectively called "key elements"), correctional knowledge and practice could advance on firmer grounds and perhaps more rapidly than by any other means (Andrews and Kiessling, 1980; Andrews et al., 1990; Empey, 1978; Gendreau and Andrews, 1989; Glaser, 1975; Palmer, 1978).

Process or "black-box" descriptions should obviously include much more than names of particular approaches, such as behavioral or group counseling, and more than brief or perhaps standard accounts of their main features or variants, such as contingency contracting or guided group interaction. Though detailed descriptions could be especially useful if provided separately by offender subgroup, they could be helpful without them.[2] In addition, whether or not subgroups are delineated, key elements may be identified without meta-analyses, or, for that matter, literature reviews.[3]

DESCRIBING PROGRAM COMPONENTS AND OPERATIONS

Data Items: Background and Examples

Especially important to knowledge building are careful descriptions of the components and operations of programs that are evaluated. As indicated, correctional programs often contain several components, for instance, educational training, group counseling, and recreation or restitution. Some of these components or features may be found in other programs as well—those which, however, meta-analysts and literature reviewers may sometimes place in different program (intervention) categories, often because each program's respective, seemingly dominant feature is different. But regardless of what an intervention's dominant or salient feature, that is, component, may be, that and other interventions also involve staff characteristics, intervention strategies/techniques, and so on. For purposes of program description and analysis, such components, staff characteristics, and so forth, can be thought of as types of variables and factors, or—more generally—types of *data items.* A detailed set of specific data items will be presented shortly, for these as well as other types. First, however, the role and function of such items with respect to knowledge building will be briefly reviewed. (Specific items will simply be called "data items" or "data elements.")

Data items, or data elements, supply the content basis of systematic knowledge, the *what* of "what do we know, in objective terms." Other things being equal, the more items one can work with, the greater the chance of developing a comprehensive picture of any given phenomenon, say, a particular intervention program. By the same token, if only a few data items have been singled out, for example, few variables that describe the client population or particular strategies associated with the program, basic limitations will soon appear. For instance, the program will be difficult or impossible to describe in a detailed, systematic way. In addition, numerous similarities and differences that exist between that program and others may be impossible to pin down or scientifically validate. Finally, differentiated analyses may be impossible to carry out, depending on which specific items *have* been singled out. These limitations are not without practical and theoretical significance, and they probably cannot be fully overcome.

The first limitation, for example, can make it difficult to replicate the given program in other than a fairly general way. This can represent a substantial loss if, for instance, the results for that program are quite positive in terms of recidivism rate. Subjective impressions and personal recollections that bear on possible replication of a program cannot provide a reliable substitute for the data items in question—specifically, for the detailed accounts that can be derived from preestablished, systematically presented data items.

The second limitation bears on the identification of reliable leads. Impressionistic reports that focus on the apparent similarities and differences among given programs cannot provide an adequate basis for the identification of such leads. This is because such reports often involve *(a)* large amounts of selective recall, halo effect, and wishful thinking; and *(b)* a possible trend toward overly broad generalizations. Reports that are often subject to such a wide margin of error should not be used as substitutes for systematic observations—those based on preestablished data items and, for example, objective rating scales. (Use of these items and scales cannot guarantee an absence of overly broad generalizations. However, by reducing the amount of selective recall, wishful thinking, and so on, it can markedly lower their chance of occurring.) This applies despite the valuable contributions sometimes made by *impressionistic* reports that draw direct comparisons among small numbers of well-observed programs. At any rate, whether few or many programs are involved, such reports can provide a supplement to, but not an adequate substitute for, *systematic* observations. The latter are a necessary ingredient in the development of reliable leads.

Limitations associated with an absence of differentiated analyses can be inferred from earlier remarks, and they need not be further reviewed.

To avoid or reduce such limitations and to help advance correctional knowledge, researchers should, insofar as is feasible, collect and report information on a large number of data items in connection with programs being studied. This applies especially, but not exclusively, to E (vs. C) programs. Researchers should do this even if, as individuals, they themselves may be unable to fully utilize their data, say, to systematically compare their outcome results with those of other researchers in connection with particular items. As to researchers and academicians who *are* in a position to make these comparisons or to further analyze single programs, it is almost certain that their efforts will be hampered or possibly abandoned if the desired information is not close at hand, for instance, if it has been collected but is either unreported or difficult to obtain.

Apart from the sheer number of data items, researchers should increasingly attend to a core of standard or benchmark items, each of which may bear on various aspects of client adjustment. These items would include not only *operations* (which involves program components, staff/client interactions, and intervention strategies/techniques) but *staff* (e.g., staff characteristics) as well. In addition, the items would include *offenders* (offender characteristics) and *setting* (setting or structure). Within each area, namely, operations, staff, offender, and setting—and whenever opportunity allows—researchers would gather and analyze information on items such as those illustrated below. (Please note: Each area contains two or more subdivisions, e.g., Area I [operations], subdivisions A, B, and C. Across the four areas, there are ten subdivisions in all. In areas I-A, II-A, III-A, and IV-A, all items are mutually exclusive. Within these areas, separate information would therefore be needed on all items. In other areas, say, I-B and the first section of IV-B, all items comprise a single set of alternate choices. Within these areas, information would be recorded on only the particular item(s) describing the program or setting in question. Still other areas are discussed in a footnote.[4])

I. *Operations*

A. *Formal aspects:* basis of assignment (geographic, available case opening or living-unit space, person match, program match, other); offender/staff ratio or caseload size; living-unit size; extent of initial diagnostic workup; direct intervention-centered contacts (frequency, number, total hours, total duration); collateral contacts (frequency, number, total hours, etc.); number of intervention approaches/modalities; quantitatively salient or dominant intervention(s)/combination (e.g., individual counseling and educational training); programmatically/operationally/dynamically central or dominant intervention(s)/combination; supervision of staff (type, amount); postprogram or postdischarge contacts.

B. *General features:*

1. *Approaches/modalities and intervention patterns:* confrontation; area-wide strategy of delinquency prevention; social casework, social agency, or societal institution approach to delinquency prevention; diversion; physical challenge; restitution; group counseling/therapy; individual counseling/therapy; family intervention; vocational training; employment; educational training; behavioral; cognitive-behavioral or cognitive; life skills (skill oriented; skill development); multimodal; probation and parole enhancement; intensive probation supervision; intensive aftercare (parole) supervision; standard probation supervision; standard aftercare (parole) supervision; milieu intervention; work release; recreation and cultural enrichment; involvement in community activities; advocacy and legal assistance; crisis intervention; medical approaches (specified); imprisonment/institutionalization; coeducational or noncoeducational; other components or activities (family assistance, referral to other agencies, work assignments, day passes, furloughs, other).

2. *Orientations and schools:* eclectic; rational-emotive; reality therapy; existential; transactional analysis; gestalt; behavior modification; analytic (neo-Freudian); I-level; conceptual level; differential association; general theory; habilitation/developmental; integrated theory; social bonding; social learning; subcultural deviance; subcultural strain (blocked opportunity); other (specified).

C. *Specific features:*

1. *Goals and areas of focus:* enhancing/promoting a nondelinquent or noncriminal self-image; modifying attitudes toward adults/establish-

ment; teaching values and controls; increasing self-awareness/self-acceptance; reducing illegal behavior; reducing apathy/indifference; improving/altering family/parental relationships; altering peer influence/pressure; everyday practical adjustment; client/worker relationship; other.

2. *Process and lines of approach:* gaining client's confidence in worker as understanding/capable; expressing personal concern for and acceptance of client; exposure to masculine (and/or feminine) adult models; "programming"/rehearsing client for specific life situations; ego bolstering via success experiences; using positive peer influence; using authority (legitimate power or force); using internal stress as stimulus/motivator; doing the unexpected; client's participation in case planning and decision making; concreteness versus abstractness of verbalizations and interpretations; other.

II. *Staff*

A. *Background characteristics:* age; gender; ethnicity; amount of training; type of training; amount of experience; type of experience; work status (professional, paraprofessional, volunteer, other).

B. *Personal characteristics:*[5] strength of feelings, expressions, and opinions; sharpness-alertness; criticalness; past personal difficulties, felt as such; satisfaction with own work and accomplishments; socially desired qualities; socially undesirable qualities; aggression-hostility; other.

C. *Treatment orientations:* A type versus B type; instrumental versus expressive; relationship/self-expression or surveillance/self-expression or surveillance/self-control; I_2 or Cfm or Mp-Cfc or Na or Nx worker (I-level system); other classifications; general factors (orientation toward change and activity; use of own past experiences as primary basis for working with others; other).

III. *Offenders*

A. *Background characteristics:* age; gender; offense history;[6] base expectancy (or standardized risk-score/level); IQ; grade level attained; school status at intake; work history; work status at intake; marital status; parental status (client's parents; client as parent); residence (urban, semiurban, rural); neighborhood (high, medium, low delinquency); socioeconomic status; ethnicity.

B. *Personal characteristics:* developmental level (interpersonal, psychosocial, moral, ego, conceptual, and/or other[7]); classification or personality type (Warren, Quay, Schrag, Megargee, and/or other); trait clusters: communicative-alert, passive-uncertain, defiant-indifferent-alienated, dependent, independent, other (Palmer); specific factors or generic variables (cognitive complexity, locus of control, internalized standards, affect awareness, impulse control, planfulness/foresight, persistence, rigidity/inflexibility, social consciousness, other) (Quay, 1984; Schrag, 1971; Megargee, Bohn, and Sink, 1979; Warren, 1971; Kohlberg, 1976; Gibbons, 1965; Palmer, 1965; Hunt, 1971).

IV. *Setting*

A. *Formal aspects:* jurisdiction and sponsorship (justice system; nonjustice system, public; nonjustice system, private; other); size (offender population); physical condition (age, upkeep, space); adequacy of services (food, clothes, medical, other); level of physical security; accessibility to community.

B. *Type:* adult prison or youth institution; jail; camp/ranch/farm; halfway house; day care center; other community center (specified); group home; free community (natural setting, e.g., family, relatives, independent placement); management and decision-making styles; social climate dimensions (Moos); homogeneous offender grouping (e.g., by Quay types) versus nonhomogeneous grouping; coeducational versus noncoeducational (Moos, 1975; Quay, 1984).

In most studies, individual researchers would be unable to gather information on most items from all ten subdivisions of this list (collectively). However, they might often be able to do so with many subdivisions (individually). This applies even though the list is not exhaustive, particularly in areas I-C, II-B, and II-C.

Whatever information they may gather and analyze, researchers, as individuals, might bear the following in mind. First, the more data items they can study, the faster correctional knowledge can advance. This does not mean progress will probably be swift in an absolute sense. It means that progress can be accelerated by the exploration of many rather than few items, within and across the areas listed above. Second, studies that involve a sizable number of data items are likely to call for considerable effort and analysis.[8]

To help corrections obtain maximum payoff from any given item, researchers, collectively, should increasingly utilize identical or virtually identical categories when describing that item. For instance, on age of client, they could better compare their respective findings if each researcher were to subdivide the item into standard groupings, say, 0–12, 13–15, 16–18, and so on, than if some were to use those groupings while others were to use 0–11, 12–14, 15–17, 18–21, and still others were to use 0–13, 14–16, 17–20, and so forth. To be sure, in many studies or for specific reporting purposes, some categories would be more appropriate than proposed standard categories and would naturally be used. However, this need not preclude the use of standard categories in connection with additional analyses and reporting, either by the original researchers or by others with whom raw data are shared.

The concept of 'standardized categories' bears on the broader need to develop uniform definitions of data items and uniform methods, for instance, specific rating scales, for assessing those items. With most items, this need can probably be met without great difficulty. In cases where complete uniformity seems neither possible nor desirable, any movement in this direction would still constitute a gain. Standardization, together with uniformity or at least similarity of definitions, is a prerequisite for meaningful communication and efficient knowledge building in every science.

Data Items and Program/Nonprogrammatic
Components

Of the four areas in which examples of data items have just been listed, areas I and II—operations and staff—encompass the "program components" and the three "nonprogrammatic components" discussed in chapter 6.

First, *operations* includes program components and various nonprogrammatic components alike: On the one hand, section B(1) of operations ("general features: Approaches/modalities, and intervention patterns") contains, among its data items, all *program* components described in chapter 6. These components are the generic approaches, for example, group counseling, discussed throughout this book, and some components divide into more specific features, such as guided group interaction. On the other hand, sections C(1) and C(2) ("specific features: goals, and areas of focus" and "specific features: processes and lines of approach") include but do not exhaust two of the three *nonprogrammatic* components, namely, staff/client interactions (SCIs) and intervention strategies/techniques (ISTs).

Next, *staff* contains the third nonprogrammatic component. Specifically, section B ("personal characteristics") includes several aspects of staff characteristics, for example, "sharpness-alertness," and section C ("treatment orientations") contains still others, for instance, "instrumental versus expressive." Staff also includes some SCIs and ISTs.

Finally, as indicated, neither operations nor staff individually exhausts the first two nonprogrammatic components, namely, SCIs and ISTs: Though C(1) and C(2) of operations contain some staff/client interactions and some intervention strategies/techniques, section B of staff ("personal characteristics") implies several others and section C ("treatment orientations") directly reflects even more.

Data Items and General Needs

Replications   As implied earlier, replications can be facilitated by all four types of data items: operations, staff, offenders, and setting. Other things being equal, the more items (thus, the more details) one uses from any such area and the wider the range of items from across those areas, the stronger one's replication or partial replication can be—also, the better one can assess the quality, and specify the implications, of replications already completed.

When preparing to replicate an already completed program, practitioners, policy makers, and researchers should, if possible, require at least the following items (for all three items, the program to be replicated, i.e., the one already completed, would serve as the basis of comparison; in addition, since the first item—operations—would largely *define* the *new* program, i.e., the replication program, it would be especially important): The replication program should *(a)* use rather similar operations—certainly very similar components, including several specific dimensions; *(b)* contain most of the same types of offenders—at least the one or two most common—and preferably in similar relative proportions; and *(c)* be implemented in a similar type of setting. Utilization of a data-item list that specifies various operations, offenders, and settings can help operationalize "similarity," can thus facilitate and increase cross-study comparability, and can thereby accelerate progress. (See Appendix K for a related discussion.)

Fortunately, knowledge building via replications does not rest entirely on the presence of high levels of comparability across programs and—in support of such comparability—on a mass of details that have first described those programs. Instead, even moderately comparable, moderately described studies can contribute. Nevertheless, the greater the comparability and the better the description, the more confidence one can have in results from the original program—if, indeed, the replication program supports those results.

Purposive variations   By systematically using data items when describing and implementing a purposive variation, one can more reasonably and reliably decide if a program's findings may be validly generalized, and, if so, *how*. Here, offender and setting items would be especially relevant, whether one's main emphasis is practical or theoretical.

For instance, the following might apply to practical issues that involve department-wide planning, interagency coordination, reports to funding or regulatory bodies, and so forth: Most practitioners and policy makers who may wish to assess a program's possible generalizability would probably feel a greater need to obtain broad information about offenders and settings than, say, about staff. Regarding offenders, their particular or initial interest might well involve gender and age; as to setting, it would perhaps center on type. Other information, for instance, offense history and risk level, might also be desired.

In response to just the first set of interests, researchers might therefore suggest various studies that would each target a specified combination of gender, age, and setting. Typical combinations might be as follows (practically speaking, the first study that is conducted would be considered the original one, and the rest would therefore be variations; analytically, however, any study could serve as a basis for comparison, and in that sense could function as an "original"):

Males, aged 13 to 15, on intensive probation

Males, aged 13 to 15, in probation camps

Males, aged 16 to 18, on intensive probation

Males, aged 16 to 18, in probation camps

. . . .

Males, aged 22 to 29, *(a)* on intensive probation or *(b)* in prison [two studies]

Females, aged 16 to 18, *(a)* on intensive probation or *(b)* in probation camps [two studies]

Females, . . .

Together, studies that involve such target-combinations not only could provide decision makers with policy relevant information about the scope of an original program's applicability but also might supply researchers, academicians, and others with theory-relevant findings. Such findings could be obtained whether or not any of the above combinations happened to be found in the same specific programs as the combinations of socioeconomic status, ethnicity, and so on, that are discussed next, in connection with theories of causation.[9]

While selection of the preceding combinations may have been largely influenced by practical issues, that of other targets can be guided by theories of causation. Each such theory would not only emphasize a particular kind of offender population or populations but would also describe those individuals in relation to presumed causes of or contributors to illegal behavior. These causes could include high-delinquency neighborhoods, major educational deficiencies, psychological vulnerabilities, alienation, and so on (Aichorn, 1935; Akers, 1977; Becker, 1974; Cloward and Ohlin, 1960; Cohen, 1966; Elliot, Ageton, and Canter, 1979; Glaser, 1971; Gottfredson and Hirschi, 1990; Hirschi, 1972; Lemert, 1972; Matza, 1964; McCord, 1968; Merton, 1968; Miller, 1958; Nye, 1958; Palmer, 1991b; Quinney, 1977; Reckless, 1967; Shaw and McKay, 1972; Sutherland and Cressey, 1970; Sykes, 1974; Warren, 1971; West and Farrington, 1977). Since some theories would emphasize a given gender, a main age-range, and so on, these and other practical-issue-centered data items could be combined with theory-guided items within a given target-combination, and the two types of items would be neither mutually exclusive nor contradictory. Finally, such theories would suggest or imply ways of changing illegal behavior (see "Examining Process," below).

Regarding causes and contributors, theories that mainly emphasize social, structural, or historical factors may single out data items such as offenders' residence (e.g., urban or nonurban), type of neighborhood, socioeconomic status (SES), ethnicity, and minority/nonminority status. In contrast, those which emphasize the "inner person" more often point to developmental level, personality type, specified psychological features (e.g., impulse control), and/or particular experiences (e.g., child abuse). In both types of theories other factors, such as gender, age, school status, and work status, may receive moderate-to-considerable weight; however, they are not likely to be viewed as decisive contributors to most offenders' illegal behavior.[10] Finally, these or other theories may postulate critical interactions between sociological and psychological factors. ("Item" and "factor" are used synonymously. In addition, specific items or types of items that have been singled out or emphasized by one or more theories may be selected for use in a given E/C study; and once selected, they can be called "targets.")

Given the above, then, the differing theories may suggest or imply various *combinations of data items* (thus, "target-combinations"), such as the following (sociological theories would emphasize the first two; social-psychological, the remainder):

Lower socioeconomic status, black or Hispanic, urban males

Unemployed, below-average-in-grade-level males, from high-delinquency neighborhoods

Young, middle-level-of-interpersonal-development conformists, from high-delinquency neighborhoods

Indifferent or alienated, higher-maturity, middle-socioeconomic-status Caucasians

These *particular* four combinations do not jointly comprise a unified series, say, a set of permutations to be used in a sequence of interrelated studies—specifically, in a purposive-variation sequence. Rather, any one of the combinations (target-combinations) could be used entirely on its own, and this would include being used in connection with an original study alone. In that situation it could be used as the starting point for an independent, that is, a separate and self-contained, series of variation studies.

In implementing a series of studies, one's original target-combination, that is, one's set of theory-derived data items, would be followed by a number of other combinations. Each combination would be associated with a separate E/C study. In each of the latter combinations, one or more individual data items would be varied from one or more that appeared in the original target-combination; thus, each of these new combinations of data items—and especially the study with which it is associated—would be a purposive variation. Compared to an "original," theory-derived data item, any modified item would—analytically—consist of a different point, or even the opposite end, of a scale (e.g., "middle" vs. the original *"lower"* SES, or "higher" vs . . . *"lower"* SES). Or, it could be a categorically different factor, such as employment rather than the original *un*employment, or Caucasian rather than *black*.[11]

Thus, for example, whereas "lower socioeconomic status, black or Hispanic, urban males" may be the principal target of an original E/C study, *(a)* "lower SES, *Caucasians* who are urban (or nonurban) males (or females)" and *(b)* "*middle* SES, black or Hispanic, urban males" may, respectively, be the dominant targets of each of two subsequent studies. Similarly, although "indifferent or alienated, higher-maturity, middle-SES Caucasians" may be the dominant target-combination of a different original study, the purposive variation strategy may focus, in subsequent studies, on the "responsive, communicative, or engaged," the "middle maturity," and/or the "non-Caucasian," respectively, or on various mixes of one or more such items, on the one hand, with one or more from the original combination, on the other.

Since most theories have a particular focus and scope with respect to target-populations as well as causal/contributing factors, there is a danger of overlooking or excluding numerous factors of both types when using those theories as the sole or predominant basis for selecting items. Purposive variations would reduce this theory-based content-limitation. Yet, even without purposive variations it could be reduced by using *(a)* a combination of reasonably compatible or mutually complementary theories or *(b)* an unusually broad theory, in the first place.

Despite such limitations, the theory-guided approach could help direct attention to specific factors (data items) and combinations of factors that might receive little or no emphasis based on various practical issues alone (for instance, those centered on system maintenance). This would apply even apart from the fact that theory-guided approaches could be combined with ones that are centered on practical issues (or immediate needs). At any rate, by postulating given offender items (background as well as personal characteristics) as causal or contributing factors to illegal behavior, and—as will be seen—by postulating various operations and staff factors as contributors to positive outcome, the theory-guided approach could suggest relationships that might not have been considered before, at least not explicitly, and it could, in effect, provide hypotheses for testing.

Subgroup analyses   Here, offender items would be particularly relevant, whether they consisted of background features or personal characteristics. Such items, say, those involving specified age categories or personality types, would provide the content basis for differentiated analyses, those in which an overall offender sample or a descriptive dimension is first divided into various subgroups or segments, which are then examined separately.

Whether or not offender items are part of an integrated conceptual system, (e.g., Kohlberg's classifications or Quay's typology), a differentiated analysis of each offender item could help achieve practical as well as theoretical goals (Van Voorhis, 1994). This would apply, for instance, not only to separate examinations of each Quay personality type but also to the analysis of each age group, each offense history category, or each socioeconomic level that is distinguished. (Differentiated analyses that focus on offender items—mainly on developmental classifications and personality typologies—have generally been called "subgroup analyses." As will be seen, this term could apply to staff groupings as well. In any event, because of their structural and often-substantive overlap, the terms *differentiated analyses* and *subgroup analyses* are often used interchangeably, even though the former is broader than the latter.)

Regarding practical goals, a differentiated or subgroup analysis could promote better-targeted programming—thus, presumably, more effective/efficient intervention. Concerning the theoretical, such an analysis could involve better delineated and targeted hypotheses—specifically, more theory-relevant hypotheses—with respect to two broad questions: Which factors or conditions substantially contribute to or even largely trigger illegal behavior?[12] and Which interventions forestall, check, reduce, or eliminate that behavior? *"Which"* questions—for example, Which factors substantially *contribute to . . .* ? Which ones *are . . .* ? and Which ones *have . . .* ?—are central to practical and theoretical progress alike and are the hallmark of differentiated/subgroup analyses.

Differentiated/subgroup analyses are not associated just with offender items; they pertain to staff as well. This is true whether the staff items involve personality characteristics, treatment orientations, or both, and whether they are used in replication studies, purposive variations, or neither. Moreover, the practical and theoretical progress that is associated with differentiated/subgroup analyses can probably be promoted *whatever* the content and focus of one's study may be. This follows from three interrelated facts: *(a)* such analyses are possible with setting and operations items, not just with the above; *(b)* together, the four areas— offender, staff, setting, and operations—may cover essentially all relevant content; and *(c)* both types of progress can occur relative to any one area—probably regardless of the specific items which may represent that area. (However, see later chapters regarding organizational/administrative factors.) The above view also reflects the findings mentioned in previous chapters, findings which—although quantitatively modest with respect to staff and setting—suggest that factors from all four areas can influence outcome.[13] (For further information about operations, see "Examining Process," below.) Finally, utilization of a detailed data-item list for differentiated/subgroup analyses may help one better conceptualize and more systematically examine or refine hypotheses regarding interactions among and within the above areas.

Examining Process   Studies of process involve operations and staff items. Together, these include three major types of factors described in chapter 6:

1. Staff/client interactions
2. Intervention strategies/techniques
3. Staff characteristics

To date, many practitioners and others have viewed process as consisting largely of type 1. Type 2 has also been included, but to a lesser degree. Type 3 has been even less common, and never primary. (*Type, factor,* and *process-factor* will be used synonymously.)

Type 1, we hypothesize, indeed constitutes a major part of process. This reflects its direct, action/interaction component, a self-evident and essential element in any account of process. Yet this factor—regarded as a force that affects outcome—should not automatically be viewed as any of the following (this would also apply to each remaining process-factor, taken individually): *(a)* prepotent, that is, far outdistancing or virtually eclipsing the remaining process-factors, individually or combined; *(b)* decisive, that is, the deciding factor, whether or not it is the strongest single one, overall (see chapter 12 regarding "deciding factor"); *(c)* independent, that is, operating entirely apart from the remaining factors.

As to content, factors 1, 2, and 3, collectively, include not just the actions/interactions found in factor 1, but a wide range of inputs, conditions, features, and events, any of which may affect outcome. Moreover, we hypothesize that all three factors usually operate together, that their influence may be direct or indirect, and that their respective impacts may vary by type of client, goal, setting, and perhaps program phase.

Though fairly complex, this view of process seems more realistic than an alternative framework that, say, might involve any one or two factors alone, with or without interactions. Insofar as it *would* prove more realistic, that is, more accurate, this view would likely have greater practical utility and be more theoretically fruitful than its alternative. This would apply even if the first view did not provide a fairly complete account of process (and it might not), and although it might take longer and be more difficult to test. (Adequate testing would require a sizable series of experiments, with emphasis on systematic variations.)

How do the three process-factors formally and substantively relate to program components—these being the generic approaches (for instance, educational training and individual counseling) emphasized in earlier chapters? Formally, factors 1, 2, and 3 operate *on, in conjunction with,* and/or *through* those components, depending on the particular context. Substantively, or more concretely, they operate as moment-by-moment activities, or meeting-by-meeting conditions and events, that *(a)* directly facilitate the implementation of those components;[14] *(b)* indirectly support those components, for example, provide background conditions that allow component-implementation to occur (whether or not it occurs adequately); and/or, *(c)* utilize the components in order to influence client-behavior mainly by themselves, that is, mainly via factors 1, 2, and 3. Process-factors may perform those functions individually or collectively. As indicated below, they may also make a *separate* contribution to outcome, one that is distinct from influencing it by working on, with, or through the program components per se, as in *(a)*, *(b)*, and *(c)* above. Finally, many specific items that comprise factors 1, 2, and 3 can probably carry out the above functions in relation to several of the components described thus far, and can probably do so at various phases of the program. In that respect or to that degree they are neither component specific nor phase specific.

We hypothesize that process-factors may affect not just relatively specific areas but also ones that are more general, and that, in either case, the subsequent long-term effects may often be far reaching. For instance, while facilitating, supporting, or utilizing given program components, a factor, say, factor 1, might help clients recognize the possible or actual relevance of those components to their lives. In that relatively specific way, such factors may help involve those individuals in the overall program to a greater degree than before, or perhaps more actively and rapidly than might otherwise have been the case.[15] Alternatively, and sometimes more basically, the process-factors might *themselves* reduce the individuals' initial and subsequent confusion or anxiety about the program and, perhaps, their simultaneous ambivalence about and resistance to it. This may help them better understand it and may motivate them to seriously consider it for the first time. Available program components, per se, might not have done that.

Process-factors' areas of impact may also be fairly general. For instance, such factors may help establish a largely positive, sufficiently comfortable, yet appropriately serious and businesslike *atmosphere* (which, e.g., might include clear goals/subgoals/expectations and reliable followup as well). This relatively broad or contextual influence may have considerable bearing on the clients' overall response to the program and on his/her reactions to specific yet potentially pivotal events such as personal crises and atypical, client/worker misunderstandings regarding goals and expectations.

We will now briefly review and summarize each factor.

Items that comprise type 1, *staff/client interactions,* are probably those most often associated with process. This especially applies when process is mainly viewed as a collection of particular actions or events that comprise a "black box" and which may make key contributions to outcome. At any rate, this view emphasizes relatively detailed aspects of working with clients. (For examples of these actions/interactions/events, see "processes and lines of approach"—i.e., I.C.(2) of the data-item list.) These and additional such items appear in Appendix G; there, each item is accompanied by further details which collectively constitute an operational definition of the item.

We hypothesize that type 1 items—singly or grouped—directly or indirectly produce or otherwise contribute to client change. Also, like types 2 and 3, with which they interact, type 1 items usually generate or help produce that change by working on, with, or through program components such as those already described.

Type 2 items, *intervention strategies/techniques*, also contribute to change. (These items constitute I.C.(1) of the item list, where they are called "goals and areas of focus.") They and other type 2 items are found in Appendix G. ISTs thus involve the more directional and topical aspects of process, that is their objectives and general thrust, overall scope, and main content-areas. In general, ISTs are therefore less specific and more—as well as more often—abstract than staff/client interactions (SCIs); still, they too can be systematically studied.

Compared to SCIs, intervention strategies/techniques have been less often viewed as forces or conditions that *(a)* "stir within" the figurative black-box and, more particularly, *(b)* may make large contributions to outcome or may make them often. Yet, although *(a)* might be a fair, that is, valid, comparison, ISTs may still make sizable contributions and may do so as often as SCIs.

Stated differently, although intervention strategies/techniques may—compared to SCIs—be likened to certain outward features (e.g., to the box's "size," "perimeter," and "design") more than to any inward features, they may still have considerable absolute and relative impact. This would also apply if ISTs were instead likened to the box's "compartments" or structure or even to its "address," that is, its intended use(s).[16] More generally, one factor may be no less and no less often influential than another, even though the former is, in a sense, situated "without" more than "within," and whether or not the former is less specific and more as well as more often abstract.

Finally, as with many staff/client interactions themselves, the following can apply to individual intervention strategies/techniques, that is, to given goals or areas of focus: ISTs can each exist in the context of *several* program components rather than being limited to one or two alone (this applies both within and across overall programs). In this regard—and, switching perspectives—more than one such *component* can therefore serve as a context in which, or a vehicle through which, practitioners may work toward the given goals or subgoals (these being the ISTs themselves), for instance, toward "modifying [the client's] attitudes toward adults" (see section [I-C[1]). In pursuing those type 2 ends, practitioners may focus on type 2 *areas* that substantively relate to those ends;[17] in this example they may, among other things, emphasize the "client/worker relationship" (again see I-C[1]). Rounding things out, the particular *means* by which practitioners may actively and directly address those goals, subgoals, and areas would likely include one or more of the above-mentioned staff/client interactions, that is, type *1* items; and as suggested next, other items may bear on those goals, subgoals, and areas as well.

Type 3 items, *staff characteristics,* involve two further aspects of process. These constitute the "personal characteristics" and "treatment orientations" in II-B and II-C of the data item list. (Further details regarding these aspects appear in Appendix H.)

Some such features probably operate more or more often passively than many type 1 items (i.e., staff/client interactions). More specifically, they often "draw" or attract clients more than "push" or force them. For instance, when certain staff characteristics exist and are perceived as such or are otherwise felt by clients, this situation may make it easier for some of those individuals to accept given requirements and to act or respond more consistently in those respects. Or, the characteristics may help various clients generate more interest in or enthusiasm about pursuing given goals.

Both sets of responses may, for example, partly reflect the following: *(a)* the "type of person" those clients consider the staff member to be; *(b)* the staff member's general attitude toward the clients; *(c)* the client's knowledge of or enthusiasm about given goals and subjects; and, *(d)* the client's wish to gain that staff member's approval. In addition, or instead, the responses might partly reflect the client's possible wish to emulate, or to some extent acquire, certain apparent staff characteristics or qualities (also including achievements and particular social values). Included, for instance, may be those which either suggest or directly express interpersonal competence, self-confidence, self-control, persistence, job satisfaction, general well-being, respectful/honest/straightforward treatment of others, and consistency.[18] Given this client motivation—though it may vary through time—relatively forceful efforts by the staff member (whether or not the efforts are threat dominated) may be less often in the picture in connection with various requirements, areas, or goals.

Nevertheless, other personal features that staff may express *do* involve as much activity and effort by those individuals as type 1 items. These type 3 features might, for example, reflect the substantial level of energy that staff often need and express in order to implement given interventions (including specific program components), particularly on a long-term basis or during periods of above-average confusion, anxiety, or resistance on the part of clients.

Similar considerations apply to the "treatment orientation" dimension of staff characteristics.

REVIEW

In chapter 6 we described the first task of combinations research as that of addressing the question, Which E-program combinations are effective at all, particularly across most of their studies? "Combinations" referred to any group of two or more features, and in this context "features" involved only the following, broad categories: *(a)* generic program approaches, say, educational training or individual counseling; *(b)* staff/client interactions; *(c)* intervention strategies/techniques; *(d)* staff characteristics. (In any given program, the content of *(b)*, *(c)*, and *(d)* can vary independently of the particular category *(a)* approach that is used.) This usage of "features" differs from that found in the next chapter, a usage which centers on specific items rather than the four broad categories.

Though chapter 6 discussed the relevance of categories (b), (c), and (d) to combinations research, it did not describe specific items that comprised them. Therefore, it also did not describe methods of systematically *identifying* specific items that may often be associated with programs considered successful or promising. ("Specific items" will now be called "specific features," or "data items," whether or not they are found to be associated with successful programs.)

The present chapter listed several specific features that comprise categories *(a)* through *(d)*. These data items are examples of the basic details or particulars that, at the same time, comprise four wide-ranging content areas. These basic areas are operations, staff, offenders, and setting; collectively, the first two areas contain all the program approaches, staff/client interactions, intervention strategies/techniques, and staff characteristics mentioned above. Use of data items that comprise any of the four content areas can help researchers and others systematically develop empirical knowledge about intervention—knowledge that can be more specific, reliable, and objective than if such items were unavailable or unused.

After briefly reviewing the need for better designed studies for replication studies, the present chapter discussed two bases for determining offender and setting targets that could be useful in purposive-variation studies.[19] These bases were practical need and theories of causation. Since this discussion mainly involved the question of whether specific features that worked with one target would also work with others, it did not address the issue of studying programs (or large portions of them) as integrated entities, that is, totalities. Nor did it suggest ways of identifying specific features that *(a)* may often be associated with programs which have positive outcomes and that *(b)* might substantially contribute to those results.

The present chapter also reviewed subgroup analyses—in effect, the question, For whom is a given program, setting, and so on (and/or parts thereof) more and less appropriate? Finally, it discussed the general nature of process features such as the above-mentioned staff/client interactions, intervention strategies/techniques, and so forth. Yet here, too, it did not ask, How might one determine which specific features—which data items—are related to successful programs?

The next chapter addresses the latter question in a broad but concrete way, one that involves simple, first-cut, exploratory paradigms. The chapter points out several issues and difficulties involved in such research, and it then begins to discuss the following: the need to examine programs not just on a feature-by-feature basis but as totalities and in their overall context. (Chapter 9 continues the discussion. The need in question would exist even if one studied more than *one* specific feature at a time and more than one *type* of specific feature as well, say, categories *(b)*, *(c)*, and *(d)* above. In this respect the study of overall programs or large portions thereof can be considered a particular form or aspect of combinations research.)

The latter, more global studies would bear on program utilization, for instance, on its operational transferability. They would also help deal with complications that result not only from *(a)* interactions among known, examined features but also from *(b)* unknown, unexamined, and/or even counterproductive ("negative") features, regardless of possible and likely interactions. In this context, "features" refers to specific items, not to the four broad categories per se, that is, those which themselves comprise the specific items and which were emphasized in chapter 6.

Chapter 8

Identifying Promising Features, and Overall Programs

This chapter will introduce an approach designed to identify specific features and combinations of features associated with successful or promising programs. It will also suggest the need to focus on programs more broadly or holistically, and this need will then be discussed in chapter 9. These approaches or strategies will be called the "building-block" and "global" methods, respectively, and they can each contribute to practical as well as theoretical knowledge. Though first articulated in the late seventies these methods have been neither systematically nor frequently used, whether in connection with specific data items or, of course, combinations research (Palmer, 1978). For present purposes they can therefore be considered new.

AN ANALYTIC FRAMEWORK

Characteristics and Goals

In each method a group of individual programs would be analyzed together. This group would typically contain programs that—collectively—cover a range of generic approaches, say, vocational training, educational training, and group counseling. However, any *one* program would involve only *one* such approach, say, group counseling. In any event, a building block or global analysis would contain not just programs which, *collectively*, all have the same—that is, one and the same—salient or quantitatively dominant program feature (e.g., group counseling) and which, in that respect, all "belong" to the same program category. At least, it *need* not just include such programs, and it probably would seldom do so.

Since the building-block and global methods need not be limited in scope to programs that fall, collectively, within only one generic program-category, and since they are not analytically organized around any one or more such categories, they involve what might be called a "generically unrestricted, across-categories" framework. This GU-AC framework focuses on individual programs and ignores the fact that any program, say, one which highlights vocational training (VT), simultaneously falls within a *broad program category* (always the highlighted one)—in this case, the generic approach called "VT." *Broad program category, generic approach, generic program approach,* and *generic program category* are synonymous.[1]

"Focuses on individual programs" means, more precisely, that one studies each program's specific features, for instance, process-factors such as the staff/client interactions or the interaction strategies/techniques found in the data-item list (chapter 7). In any event, one does not examine any *grouping* of studies *as* a grouping—for instance, any collection of VT studies, as an entity.[2] Thus, in the building-block approach one would focus on individual programs by examining, program by program, the relationship between one or more of each program's *specific features* (data items, viewed as inputs), on the one hand, and that same program's *performance* (outcome, or output), on the other. One would focus on these features regardless of which generic category—say, VT, educational training (ET), or group counseling (GC)—might be used to describe the program or programs in which those features are found. In fact, one would emphasize *only (a)* the program's specific features, never *(b)* the generic approach within which that program falls or even *(c)* the generic approaches that characterize other programs in the analysis.

Emphasis (a) reflects the fact that the GU-AC framework is not designed to determine how effective or ineffective any generic program approach may be. More specifically, it is not structured to assess the overall level of performance (e.g., the average recidivism rate or effect size) of programs that may all have the same salient programmatic feature, say, vocational training or some other generic program approach (GPA). Though GPAs are part of the data-item list, and although they may be of interest in a given analysis, the study of these characteristics is neither a special nor a signal concern of the GU-AC framework, let alone its *raison d' être.*

Category Boundaries

The fact that GU-AC is generically "unrestricted" and operates "across categories" indicates that programmatic category-boundaries do not, in effect, exist with respect to GU-AC analyses. Since these boundaries do not exist, they cannot affect the analyses' results. For example, they cannot serve as channelers, subdividers, and focusers (lenses), and they cannot otherwise direct the analyses and help organize the results.

Indeed, even the possibility of such influence is absent; that is, it is structurally and logically nonexistent. This springs from the fact that the generically unrestricted, across-categories framework contains no pro- grammatic categories and, therefore, no program boundaries in the first place. In effect, the framework establishes no "cast of players"—in this context, no lineup of mutually distinct "compartments" or "boxes" (with "lineup . . . of 'boxes' " referring to the generic program approaches such as vocational training, educational training, and group counseling.) In sum, absent those analytic structures or categories, there can be no channeling, focusing, or other forms of directing, organizing, or even restricting by—and in terms of—generic program approaches.

Moreover, without categories and their boundaries, the analysis of a program's specific features cannot be restricted to any given category, namely, the generic category to which the program may be said to belong because of its salient or quantitatively dominant program characteristic. In short, the analysis of such features cannot be limited in scope or even type, in the sense of being bound to just one program category. When program categories exist, an individual *program* can be viewed as belong- ing to only *one* such category, based on its salient or dominant feature. As a result, any feature which is part of that program cannot be added to and then analyzed together with a similar or identical feature—one which, however, belongs to a program that is part of a *different* generic category because of the latter program's salient/dominant feature. Under these conditions, a given program's specific features would, in effect, be unable to cross the latter program's category boundaries or "walls," and the respective programs would thus be incapable of jointly contributing to knowledge.

In contrast, because the generically unrestricted, across-categories framework lacks such boundaries it allows one to examine features that may be (and often do appear to be) found in programs which, collectively, cut across two or more generic program categories, that is, even though those categories do not participate *as* categories. In effect, the features can cross that which—in some frameworks other than GU-AC—would have been barriers that prevented those features from being examined collectively and from then having their respective results aggregated. (At a broader level, this could happen to entire programs. That is, even if no effort were made to analyze specific features, the results obtained for an overall program, for instance, results on recidivism, might not be added to or otherwise integrated with those of another program. This could occur simply because the two programs fell within differing generic categories, by virtue of having different salient/dominant features.)

In any event, GU-AC makes it possible for the building-block and global methods to single out and examine one or more of any program's features entirely aside from the issue of generic program categories, or, say, as if that issue could be studied separately. In that respect, specific features or data items are analogous to basic chemical elements, that is, to distinctive atoms which, within limits, may be examined as such— *across* the differing types of molecules in which they are embedded or with which they are otherwise associated. Though this analogy, like many others, is fairly limited, the following remains the case: Because the GU-AC framework does not center on broad categories or groupings of programs and because it involves no constraints with regard to category-boundaries, its resulting analyses can place as well as maintain emphasis on individual programs and their specific features.

Independent Contributions

Given the above, each program independently and directly contributes to knowledge. This applies with respect to the building-block and global methods alike, and it occurs because the individual program's contribution is neither modified (enhanced or diminished) nor mediated by that of other programs.[3] This is true *(a)* whether or not the individual program and the latter programs have the same salient/dominant programmatic features and, therefore, identical or similar program labels; *(b)* whatever the programs' respective performance levels may be; and *(c)* whether few or many programs and types of programs are involved. At any rate, the individual program's contribution to knowledge reflects *its own* results, particularly the direction and degree of relationship between its specific features and its level of performance.

Inclusion and Exclusion

For a program to contribute, it must first have an opportunity to do so; and to have this chance, it must be in the sample. A program should be in the sample, and should be analyzed, if it meets preestablished sampling requirements and satisfies standards of scientific adequacy.[4] However, it should also be included and analyzed regardless of its salient programmatic feature, its relationship to other programs, and specific aspects of those programs.

In particular, no program should be barred because of its generic (categorical) affinity to other programs and because of how those identically or similarly labeled programs have performed. For instance, if one learns—when assembling studies in order to construct a sample—that some 65 percent of all vocational training programs had not reduced recidivism, that knowledge should not prevent any of the remaining 35 percent—programs that seemed more successful but also emphasized VT—from being included.[5] Nor should that knowledge exclude the 65 percent themselves.

Once a program enters into a generically unrestricted, across-categories analysis, it can be examined on is own merit and can contribute to knowledge in the same way and to the same degree as any other program. More precisely, and particularly important, the GU-AC framework allows *specific features* from each included program to be analyzed regardless of the generic categorization of the programs in which they are found.

The major dimensions and complexity of this analysis can be illustrated in the following overview: The analysis may indicate that *(a)* most of the successful 35 percent of all vocational training programs have a specific feature in common and that *(b)* this feature may distinguish the 35 percent from most of the 65 percent. (The opposite can occur instead, in both cases.) In addition, *(c)* a *beyond-chance* proportion of the 35 percent may contain the common feature—a finding that could be useful regardless of how the 35 percent and 65 percent compare. Moreover, and independent of *(a)*, *(b)*, and *(c)*, the analysis may indicate that (d) the 35 percent of vocational training programs (not to mention the 65 percent) may or may not share that feature with most of the successful programs in educational training, group counseling, and so forth, that are also part of the overall analysis. Finally, *(a)*, *(b)*, and *(c)* can each apply to more than one feature—one data item—at a time. Such dimensions and issues are further discussed below.

Both the building block and global methods—especially the former—call for a more systematic and uniform recording of specific features than has ordinarily occurred to date—within and across programs and regardless of their generic category. In fact, as will be seen, the building-block (or "bottom-up") approach places central and exclusive reliance on those specific data items and combinations thereof; in those respects it literally requires the presence of such features. This approach therefore differs somewhat from the global ("top-down") strategy, even though the latter, while far less features centered than the former, itself calls for the specification of individual data items. The top-down method also relies less on strict, statistical analysis (testing) of such items.

Nevertheless, in each method the first step that might be taken before starting to analyze a possibly important feature is to decide on a target, that is, on specified offenders and/or settings. (Say that the target is chosen *after* a feature has been selected—a sequence that is not, however, essential.) This step would reflect such questions as, For whom might this feature be effective? and, Do target-offenders X—in, perhaps, target-setting Y—respond positively to programs in which the possibly important feature appears?

THE BUILDING-BLOCK METHOD

Once a target is established—say, minority males, 22–29 years old, who are participating in community-based programs—one then assembles the available information regarding all programs that meet sampling and design requirements and have focused heavily or at least quite substantially on that target. (These might be called "primary" and "secondary" target-programs, respectively.)[6] Insofar as the main immediate goal is to identify specific features associated with successful or promising—that is, positive—outcome in programs that address the target, any such items that are found will be called "positive features" or "identified positive features."

Procedure 1

Step A To address the question, What features are associated with successful outcome? we would first divide all target programs into two groups, successful and unsuccessful. For any program, we could define success or promise as a recidivism reduction of at least 15 percent, relative to a comparison or control. Alternatively, we might use an ES of at least + .15 or + .20. Whichever we choose, we might also use a $p < .05$ significance level;[7] however, although this criterion can be quite valuable and is recommended for use when available, it can be considered a supplement and not a sina qua non. Thus, a reduction of 15 percent or more or an equivalent ES would remain the principal criterion—one that, by itself, would directly reflect a difference of substantial practical import. (For related issues involving *sample size*, see Appendix I. In the following, *feature*, *item*, and *data item* are interchangeable and are the same as *specific feature*.)

　　Step B Next, for all successful programs we would examine certain features on which requisite information exists. In particular, we would analyze items hypothesized to bear on success—items called "potentially positive features." This step would determine if successful programs are more likely to receive one type rather than another type of rating on the potentially positive features in question, or one level rather than another level or score.

　　(Three points before proceeding. First, at this point we will consider only one item at a time, even though the above-mentioned steps can also apply to combinations. Second, for purposes of illustration, we will assume that all target programs contain the needed information about the given item. To be sure, more than a decade will probably pass before this condition will even approach being an achieved goal, at least in terms of any large-scale data-item list. Finally, regarding the 15 percent criterion and any equivalent ES, it should be recognized that these numbers are neither exact nor inviolable, since they each jointly reflect not only true variance but error—for instance, measurement error in independent variables, and unreliability in dependent variables. Even $p < .05$, which directly addresses the issue of error, is by no means noise-free. Yet, this estimate at least indicates how prone the obtained E/C difference is to major error, not just slight to substantial noise; that is, it conveys the extent to which chance might have produced the *entire* difference.)

To illustrate steps A and B, say there exists a separate rating on each of several data items that appear in each of 40 target programs, half of which are successful.[8] Next, say we focus on the following item in particular (from section *I-C*(2) of the data-item list): *"programming"/ rehearsing client for specific life-situations*, for example, via role-playing or sensitization sessions. Now, instead of using a null-hypothesis framework we will—to facilitate the presentation—simply hypothesize that the presence of this intervention approach is positively related to outcome, for the given target. (We will assume the intervention approach is adequately implemented.) To test this view, we would focus on each program's status with respect to the presence or absence of programming/ rehearsing.[9] Specifically, to determine if a statistically significant, and in that sense reasonably reliable, relationship exists between the intervention approach, on the one hand, and program success, on the other, we would undertake a two-step process.

First, we would ask if the 20 successful programs are just as likely to have a "present" as an "absent" rating on programming/rehearsing. Had we hypothesized that such programs are equally likely to be associated with its presence as its absence, we would have expected a "present" rating in about 10 of the 20 programs and an "absent" rating in the remaining 10. This would represent roughly a fifty-fifty, or even-chance, distribution. However, since we in effect hypothesized that such programs are more likely to be associated with the presence than the absence of programming/rehearsing, we would expect a distribution distinctively different than chance.

To see how the ratings actually fall, we would next tabulate the results from all 20 programs. Say we find the following: 15 of the 20 are rated "present" and the remaining 5 are "absent." Whereas chance alone would have produced a present:absent distribution of approximately 10:10 (or even 12:8 or 8:12), the 15:5 represents a reasonably reliable, that is, a $p < .05$, difference (The Staff of the Computation Laboratory, 1955). This E/C difference indicates that programs *(a)* whose clients are minority males who are 22–29 years old and are participating in community-based interventions and that *(b)* reduce recidivism by at least 15 percent, or have an equivalent ES, are *(c)* more likely to have used than not used the intervention approach of "programming"/rehearsing client for specific life-situations. Though this finding does not necessarily mean programming/rehearsing *caused* the 15 percent reduction, it raises the chances that this approach or activity did contribute, perhaps substantially.

The procedure just described could also be used with any remaining programs, in this case the 20 unsuccessful ones. Here, the question would be, What features are associated with unsuccessful outcome?

Four points should be noted before continuing. First, procedure 1 can be called a "dichotomized-variables" approach. This involves a two-part independent variable, say, presence versus absence of a feature, such as programming/rehearsing. It also involves a bipartite dependent variable, for instance, successful versus unsuccessful programs. Though dichotomization is structurally simple, it is appropriate in many situations; moreover, it is sometimes the only feasible approach, given the way data have been collected or the type of variables themselves.

Still, wherever possible and appropriate, one's analytic approach should subdivide the variables into more than dichotomies. For instance, an independent variable could perhaps involve several degrees of *presence*, say, four levels of programming/rehearsing, rather than two. Similarly, a dependent variable may involve various categories, for example, 45 percent or more, 35–44 percent, 25–34 percent, and 15–24 percent recidivism reduction among the successful programs, and even some distinctions among the unsuccessful. Such refinements in the independent variable, the dependent variable, or both could increase the sensitivity or power of one's statistical analysis, sometimes more than moderately.

To raise sensitivity, one would, where appropriate, also use statistics other than chi-square or even the basic sign-test. Under these circumstances, one's statistical results could directly indicate the degree of relationship between the independent and dependent variables, not just whether that relationship is, say, statistically significant and perhaps not only the categorized extent of that significance, say, $p < .05$, .01, or .001. Thus, the degree of relationship could be expressed as a specific correlation or multiple correlation.

These more sensitive analyses could be conducted with variables, that is, features, such as those on the data-item list. However, like dichotomous-variable analyses themselves, they must await a time when information about the variables has been recorded much more often than at present—since, without that information, various individual programs cannot be meaningfully included in the analysis in the first place.[10] At any rate, the more sensitive analyses could be used in connection with *(a)* all successful programs alone, *(b)* all unsuccessful's alone, and/or *(c)* all programs combined, whether classified as successful or unsuccessful;[11] and analyses *(a)*, *(b)*, and *(c)* would apply whether or not one's statistical results are expressed as correlation indices per se.

Second, whether or not one's analysis is dichotomous, the generalizability of its findings can be assessed in the usual way, namely, by comparing results for the original target with those for other, often subsequent, targets. Thus, if one's original findings on programming/rehearsing (P/R) for minority males aged 22 to 29 who participate in community-based programs are largely replicated for individuals aged 16 to 18 and possibly even 19 to 21, this would suggest that P/Rs relevance is rather widespread. At least, the earlier findings would be generalizable to that extent, whether or not they later extend beyond community-based programs, and so on.

Third, generalizability aside, further relevant information can be developed via differentiated analyses. For instance, by subdividing the original group of programs according to most of their clients' level of interpersonal development (section III–B of the item list), one might find that the 15:5 result which was obtained for the 20 successful programs breaks down as follows: programs emphasizing lower- and middle-level clients (combined): 10:0; programs focusing on higher-level clients: 5:5.[12] Thus, the original, undifferentiated findings for P/R may be largely accounted for by the lower- and middle-level clients, and the feature in question might not be associated with successful outcome for those at the higher level.[13]

Fourth, in procedure 1, all studies are weighted equally; this reflects their having satisfied minimum research standards.[14] However, if one wishes to distinguish between acceptable and excellent studies or between those and any borderlines, one might develop a differential-weighting scale that reflects the extent to which such standards are met.[15]

Procedure 2

To broaden the information provided by procedure 1 we might ask, Does a significant difference exist between the type of ratings or the level of scores that are obtained for specified features in successful (S) versus unsuccessful (U) programs? To address this question we would compare S and U rather than focus on either one alone.

To specifically implement this comparison in a dichotomized-variables framework we might ask, for example, if the following judgment (rating)—namely, programming/rehearsing is *present*—is more often associated with S than U; and, as before, we would use the 15 percent criterion to define success. (Alternatively, but using the same framework, we might focus on larger versus smaller effect-sizes, not percentage of reduction per se.) If the answer is *yes*, this would heighten the importance of the feature in question—in this case, programming/rehearsing. Though such heightening would occur with larger effect-size programs as well, it would have practical import only if "larger" meant more than slightly greater. In both cases the heightened importance could exist even though the original finding could also stand on its own and could remain important without a comparison.

In table 1, we use a dichotomized-variables approach and present a set of hypothetical findings in order to address the above question, namely, Do successful and unsuccessful programs differ from each other on the given feature? Here, for programming/rehearsing, we first observe that 15 of the 20 successful programs are associated with "presence" and that 5 are not; these figures are just a carryover of the earlier results. However, we also notice that 8 of the 20 *un*successfuls involve "presence," whereas the remaining 12 do not. Using chi-square we find that this difference—15:5 for S programs, compared to 8:12 for U's—cannot be attributed to chance ($p < .05$).[16] Thus, the analysis suggests that P/R is more likely to be found in successful than unsuccessful programs. In this example, the difference is almost twofold: 75 percent versus 40 percent of the time.

Table 1

Number of Successful and Unsuccessful Programs Associated with Presence or Absence of Programming/Rehearsing for Specified Life-situations

| | Programs and Presence or Absence | | | |
| | Successful Programs[a] | | Unsuccessful Programs[b] | |
Feature	Present	Absent	Present	Absent
Programming/Rehearsing	15	5	8	12

[a]N = 20.
[b]N = 20.

Sometimes, neither a significant nor a substantial difference may exist between the successful and unsuccessful with regard to a given feature. For instance, though *presence* of P/R may indeed be significantly associated with S (while *absence* is not), this feature may also be found in the U, and to much the same degree. Specifically, the following might be observed regarding the 40 target programs: *(a)* 15 of the 20 successfuls involve P/R, and the remaining 5 do not; *(b)* 15 of the 20 unsuccessfuls themselves involve P/R, and the remaining 5 do not. (Points *[a]* and *[b]*, of course, might have instead applied in the context of effect sizes that reached and did not reach the "effective-program" cutoff, respectively.)

In short, besides indicating that programming/rehearsing does not characterize successful programs alone—an important fact itself—points *(a)* and *(b)* jointly show that this activity is no less likely to exist in the unsuccessful (or perhaps the lower effect-size). Yet, although P/R or any other feature may not distinguish successfuls from unsuccessfuls, the scientific validity of the finding for S and the one for U is not thereby compromised, let alone eliminated. Nor is its practical significance eroded. Reasons for this can be seen in the following examples, in which successful programs are described in connection with validity and significance:

Regarding scientific validity, findings observed in connection with successful programs acquire their standing apart from that of unsuccessful ones; they retain it independently as well. This is evident when one considers successful programs apart from the unsuccessful. There, for example, a 15:5 finding for S-programs would be neither strengthened nor weakened if U-programs *(a)* did not exist, *(b)* existed but were not analyzed, or *(c)* were analyzed and yielded any given results, whether oppositional, neutral, or supportive. In short, whatever situation and outcome may exist for *un*successful programs, the 15:5 indicates that the presence of P/R is, and would remain, significantly associated with successfuls, and that an absence of that feature would not.

As to practical significance, this would exist even if the given feature were usually found in successful and unsuccessful programs alike, and if it were found to the same relative degree in both sets of programs (say, 15:5 in S and U alike). In other words, if one wished to increase the chance of *establishing a successful program,* one would use existing findings regarding the researched programs irrespective of the findings for unsuccessful ones, or for those with lower effect-sizes. To be sure, if one knew, for instance, that programming/rehearsing was rather likely to exist in successful programs and generally did not exist in unsuccessfuls, one would have even more reason to utilize that finding. But sufficient reason would exist in any event. Such practical considerations, judgments, and resulting decision-making may sometimes be needed, even though one might not know if the feature in question is absolutely essential—rather than, say, "simply" *important* yet amenable to substitution. This difficulty is compounded by the following situation, one whose implications are not just practical.

Though a feature may not by itself significantly contribute to successful programs, it may do so when combined with others. Moreover, it may successfully distinguish S- from *U*-programs under those conditions, but—as before—not by itself. For instance, regarding the latter situation, a combination of P/R and above-average physical condition of setting may exist more often in successful than unsuccessful programs—something not true for either feature alone. These joint relationships, however, can be demonstrated only through a direct analysis of the features in combination (see table 2 for a hypothetical example, i.e., a data display). They would be indirectly supported but still not empirically established or validly deduced even if *each* such feature were independently associated with successful programs, or with S's more than U's (see table 3).

CHALLENGES AND LIMITATIONS

Specific Challenges

Within corrections, as in several fields, it is difficult to determine with considerable certainty which combination of features is making an *important*—a major—contribution to outcome. Identifying those features will

Table 2

Number of Successful and Unsuccessful Programs Associated with Presence or Absence and with Specified Scores for a Combination of Features

| | Programs and Presence or Absence and Scores | | | |
| | Successful Programs[a] | | Unsuccessful Programs[b] | |
Combination of Features	P/R Present PCS above Average	All Other Combinations of P/R and PCS	P/R Present, PCS above Average	All Other Combinations of P/R and PCS
Programming/Rehearsing[c] and Physical Condition of Setting[d]	13	7	6	14

[a]N = 20. [c]P/R.
[b]N = 20. [d]PCS.

Table 3

Number of Successful and Unsuccessful Programs Associated with Presence or Absence or with Specified Scores for Selected Individual Features

Individual Features	Programs and Presence or Absence or Scores			
	Successful Programs[a]		Unsuccessful Programs[b]	
	Present	Absent	Present	Absent
Programming/Rehearsing	15	5	15	5
	Above Average	Below Average	Above Average	Below Average
Physical Condition of Setting	16	4	8	12

[a]N = 20.
[b]N = 20.

be called "challenge 1." Here, "considerable certainty," for instance, hardly a shadow of doubt, is a more stringent standard than "substantial probability," say, a convergence or even preponderance of evidence. In corrections, this difference partly reflects the fact that considerable certainty requires a larger number or higher proportion of excellent-quality studies than does substantial probability. The latter can be achieved—theoretically—not only with fewer studies but also with those which, in most cases, are adequate.

As if challenge 1 were not enough, it would be far harder to determine which combination of features makes an *absolutely essential* contribution to outcome, that is, which combination has no substitute. (Indispensability includes but goes beyond making an important contribution—the latter being the focus of challenge 1.) This second challenge, namely, determining which combination is absolutely essential, would be greater than the first even if one's knowledge-level standard in challenge 2 were substantial probability rather than considerable certainty—the latter being the standard in challenge 1. (Challenge 2 would still be more difficult than 1 if the standard in *1* became substantial probability.) Moreover, both challenges would remain formidable even if one typically used nondichotomous variables and conducted differentiated analyses.

Yet, the difficulties involved in meeting the above challenges—challenges that are reflected in the three general goals mentioned below—would not just relate to the number and quality of studies that are needed. Nor would they reflect only the presence of a stringent knowledge-level standard, such as considerable certainty. The general goals are as follows:

1. Identify important, that is, major, contributors
2. Identify essential contributors (these are also major contributors, and more)
3. Distinguish essential contributors from major ones

In short, the earlier-mentioned difficulties—especially challenge 2—would exist whether or not many excellent studies were involved and even if— (though to a considerably lesser degree)—the standard of knowledge were substantial probability rather than considerable certainty. These difficulties would exist because of at least two fundamental limitations, described below. Both limitations would be prominent with regard to all three goals, especially the second and third, and they center on the identification of combinations. These limitations are basically logical and/or methodological in nature, rather than pragmatic and resource centered.

Logical/methodological Limitations

Limitation 1 Regarding any combination of features that is analyzed in connection with a sample of programs, it is difficult to know if the overall program-outcome, for instance, recidivism reduction, would have differed substantially if one or more of those features had *not* been present.[17] This, in other words, involves the question of whether any features are superfluous. As a result, the following would apply unless one were to conduct or otherwise analyze additional studies—studies that, individually or at least collectively—did *not* contain the various individual features that comprised those combinations: It would be difficult to know if the program outcome was produced by (i.e., was very largely—or, almost entirely—produced by) the entire combination or by only part of it, that is, by certain features alone.

Yet, even with such analyses—ones that, in effect, could be purposive variations or even partial replications—the following would be the case: One could not settle, with absolute certainty, the question of whether the "whole" or something other than that specified whole (e.g., a specified "part") produced the outcome. Basically, this is because unidentified and/ or unanalyzed factors may have substantially contributed (see limitation 2). Moreover, even if the question were settled with substantial probability—and perhaps even considerable though not absolute certainty—the further question of whether the combination was essential to the outcome (specifically, whether it could not be substituted for) would remain very difficult to answer with anything approaching certainty. Basically, this reflects limitation 2, and it would also apply to the question of whether only *some* of the combination's features were essential, instead. ("Overall program-outcome" would be measured, for example, in terms of the average recidivism-reduction or effect-size for all such programs combined. Regarding the term *combinations*, descriptors such as *entire* and *overall* will now be synonymous.)

(Before continuing, a few corollaries and related points might be kept in mind: Whatever studies may be used, if it is determined that only *part* of the entire combination was responsible for the total outcome it follows that the combination—in its *entirety*, that is, as an entity or totality— could not have been indispensable to that entire outcome, except in the formal sense that it encompassed the part. Nor could the combination have been a sina qua non, that is, *essential*—again in its entirety. This fact, in turn, is independent of the following: *(a)* the entire combination, not just a part, might have been essential to only a *portion* of the total outcome; *(b)* on the other hand, that same part, namely, one or more features, might—by itself—have been essential to that same portion or some other portion, but not necessarily to the total outcome.[18] See Appendix J for related discussion of parts and wholes.)

At any rate, since one cannot be completely certain if an entire combination (a whole) or only part of it accounts for a given program-outcome—that is, for either a total or partial outcome—it is impossible to definitely (as distinct from probabilistically) determine whether the whole or the part—or, for that matter, either one—is *essential* to that outcome (cf. goal 2). As a corollary, it would also be impossible to distinguish an essential from a major contribution (cf. goal 3) with complete certainty. This is because—under the above condition—it is not absolutely known, in the first place, if the entire combination is anything other than a major contributor itself. Nevertheless, as implied, *purposive variations* as well as *partial replications* could help one distinguish *(a)* between the contributions of the whole as compared to those of the part and also *(b)* between essential contributions and important ones. More specifically, they could do so at the level of substantial probability and, under some circumstances, perhaps also considerable certainty.

Limitation 2   The second limitation centers on the fact that any individual features or any overall combinations of those features which have been analyzed are undoubtedly not the only ones that *could* be analyzed. (See "Unidentified positive factors," below. These differ from the presumed excess or superfluous factors that produced the first limitation.) This reflects the fact that the sample of studies which has been analyzed as of a given point doubtlessly contains additional features—

and, therefore, further possible combinations—that were not analyzed. As a result, the original features or combinations—the ones already analyzed—were not the only ones that could have contributed.

Thus, for example, although feature or combination X may cause or partly cause outcome Y, X may not be Ys only possible cause or contributor. To be sure, of all the features/combinations (F/Cs) that are *examined* as part of a study, X's contribution may indeed be essential in the following, joint respect (this situation applies independently of the fact that—within the particular program which is studied—more F/Cs may exist than have been examined): (a) outcome Y would not be produced without input from F/C X, and (b) F/C X cannot be adequately substituted for by any other F/Cs that have been *examined* in the study. Nevertheless, in a broader sense, one cannot defensibly maintain—whether based on logic or observation—that X is absolutely and unconditionally essential. This is because it always remains conceivable, and it is never implausible, that one or more presently unknown or *unexamined* F/Cs might adequately substitute for those which have been examined and may seem essential within that limited context.

MAIN PRODUCTS

Despite these limitations and complexities, procedures 1 and 2 can eventually produce three lists of *individual features* and *combinations of features* that are statistically associated with successful or unsuccessful programs:

> 1. A list of *(a)* individual features associated with successful programs for particular targets, and of *(b)* individual features associated with unsuccessful programs for those same targets
> 2. A list of *(a)* individual features more often associated with successful than unsuccessful programs and of *(b)* individual features that are less often associated with such programs
> 3. A list of individual features that, when combined with each other, *(a)* are often associated with successful programs and/or *(b)* are more often associated with successful than unsuccessful ones, for particular targets. (A [3c] and [3d] set of combined features would center on the unsuccessful programs and would be part of the same list. They would parallel, with respect to combined features, the *individual-features* lists 1*(b)* and 2*(b)*.)

Though a feature or combination is statistically associated with outcome, its contribution to that outcome is not ipso facto essential. Nor is it necessarily major, say, in terms of its accounting for at least 25 percent of the variance (r = .50+). Nevertheless, since the feature's or combination's relationship to outcome *is* statistically significant, the contribution in question *may* in fact be major and essential. At any rate, the relationship constitutes an important practical and theoretical lead.

Each list could be continuously strengthened and developed via replication and partial replication studies and through careful exploration of new targets and previously untested features. Such efforts would result in additions, deletions, and refinements, as appropriate. For instance, in the offender area, lists 1 and 2 might be modified by adding or deleting various targets, such as specified age groups or risk levels. As to settings, one or both lists might be refined by differentiating particular conditions within community and institutional programs. Similarly, in the staff area, a list may be expanded to include treatment personnel whose professional orientation is more "instrumental" than "expressive" (section II-C of data-item list)—and vice versa—depending perhaps on the type of client. This expansion might create or even augment a given *combination* of features that is significantly associated with successful programs (list 3[a]).

Regarding operations, such intervention areas as "everyday practical adjustment" or "family/parental relationships" (section I-C [1] of data items) might be added. To be sure, they may later be deleted, say, because of substantial contrary evidence and a resulting loss of p < .05. Alternatively, they may be retained, but only for some of their original targets. Likewise, an operations-centered list of features or combined features may eventually include such lines of approach as "exposure to . . . adult models" or "[use of] positive peer influence" (I-C [2]), again for specified targets. Or, it might include several previously unlisted features.

This process of testing, strengthening, and/or modifying could thus constitute a direct, step-by-step approach to knowledge building. Its main products would consist of aggregated and, in varying degrees, integrated findings regarding individual features and combinations thereof, for specified targets. ("Aggregated" findings refers to the successful or promising individual features, taken one at a time. "Integrated" findings means the combinations as such—any two or more of which may in turn either remain aggregated or become functionally integrated themselves. For instance, the combinations may become mutually interrelated and capable of jointly operating as a broader entity, one that might be stronger or more flexible than either one alone.)

Lists resulting from this building-block method could help guide not only the modification of existing programs but also the establishment of new ones, some of which might be relatively unusual or even original.

Such lists might assist in general correctional planning as well, for instance, regarding broad priorities, resource allocation, and possible new directions.

In sum, the test/strengthen/modify process would help one examine targets and potentially positive features that were spotlighted mainly for practical reasons, theoretical reasons, or both. By carefully choosing the hypotheses one tests regarding offender, staff, setting, and/or operations features, one could promote continuity with past research efforts and could thereby better accumulate various empirical findings and reduce fragmentation of effort.[19] Continuity would be especially promoted if one systematically utilized a data-item list.

Interest in continuity need not preclude, seriously curtail, or otherwise diminish one's support for new directions, different emphases, and fresh perspectives. Depending largely on the correctional climate, on related staff and material resources, and on individual interest and initiative, efforts involving new directions and emphases may be no less feasible than those which promote or emphasize continuity. The former efforts, and any resulting progress, may be no less important as well. In any case, the scientific results of such efforts could be incorporated into the above listings, and this could be done on the same basis as those of other efforts, say, the continuity-centered ones. Such results could augment the basic item-list, as well.

Thus, by building on practical experience, on theory, and on direct research, one could expand the areas and levels of knowledge reflected in lists 1, 2, and 3. This knowledge could be useful whether or not those lists reflected more than statistical association alone, that is, more than correlation (irrespective of causation) only. Though causation-centered lists would be important to work toward, they need not be required products of the building-block method. Thus, lists 1, 2, and 3 could be useful even if they just indicated which features and combinations of features were reliably associated with given outcomes, for example, at $p < .05$. This utility would exist whether or not those features/combinations were essential contributors to the outcomes, and thus, were definite causes of those results. Finally, each list in turn (starting, say, with list 1) could be organized in terms of—that is, subdivided into—a modest number of broad targets (e.g., males under age 18, females under age 18, males 18 to 29, etc.).

FURTHER COMPLICATIONS

The building-block method, described above, mainly tries to identify, in a step-by-step manner, individual features and combinations of features associated with positive outcome in numerous programs. Though this method is conceptually coherent and has a worthwhile goal, it would take much effort to implement and many years to accomplish. But energy, persistence, and patience are needed in any complex field, whatever methods are available and even if ample resources exist. Although this especially applies if step-by-step methods predominant while no major alternatives exist, it does not mean important advances can never occur rapidly—whether via step-by-step methods or alternative means.

Even if the goal of producing scientifically sound lists were quickly and easily reached, a major issue, we believe, would remain: For many or most targets, the building-block method would not provide a picture that is complete enough for practitioners to develop effective new programs, even though it could generally help improve existing ones.[20] (As before, effectiveness would mainly involve recidivism reduction, though other outcomes would also be meaningful.) As a result, more information would be needed before one could make a new program "gel"—and, in some cases, before one could improve existing ones—via the results of step-by-step research.

In particular, if one wished to develop an effective new program, information beyond that which would ordinarily be generated via the building-block method would be needed in order to obtain an overall set of appropriate ingredients, not just more ingredients.[21] These appropriate ingredients (features and combinations) would have to not only *(a)* eventually function together in an actual program, namely, a program one wished to develop, but also *(b)* jointly make a difference in producing and/or maintaining behavior change—that is, they would have to be strong or flexible enough to do so.

It is not necessarily easy to satisfy requirements *(a)* and *(b)* in a "real-life," new program. In particular, it is one thing to have identified various ingredients that are *each* significantly related to recidivism reduction or to other outcomes—and the building-block method may have helped one do this with regard to prior programs. However, it is something else to identify a set of ingredients that can not only function *together* in the first place but can also be *complete and strong enough* to reduce recidivism when operating as, or in the context of, an actual functioning program (i.e., when operating as, or in the context of, a directed entity or totality). It is also something else to identify ingredients that can jointly reduce recidivism within one's available operational resources and in acceptable program and evaluation time-frames.

Time and resource limitations are not the only factors that may prevent the building-block method and its resulting lists of identified ingredients from providing a sufficiently complete picture of effective intervention for given targets. That is, even if those practical limits were gone, other limits or problems would remain. Basically, these further limits would involve the fact that various important ingredients or factors would still be missing. As will be seen from the types of factors in question, the reasons for this absence can be methodologically and logically deep-seated.

The following examples involve two classes of factors that, for such reasons, would be quite difficult to pin down via the building-block method. These will be referred to as unidentified positive and negative factors. To facilitate matters, we will discuss these factors given the assumption that the building-block method was previously applied and already yielded lists of significant features and combinations of features. The assumption that those features, and so on, were listed, allows one to describe them as "*identified*"—specifically, as having been *set forth* and in that respect "made known" (not merely uncovered or discovered). Thus, by definition, all features/combinations (F/Cs) that are "identified" *appear*, that is, are made known, on a given list; and these F/Cs are the sole constituents of that list.

Unidentified Positive Factors

As already indicated, identified positive features and combinations were important contributors to recidivism reduction, and some were doubtlessly even essential. Sometimes, however, these F/Cs, we hypothesize, would not be enough to constitute an effective *new* program or to substantially improve existing ones to which they may be added. That is, they would not be enough individually and collectively.

More specifically, identified positive F/Cs may *help* build new programs and/or improve existing ones; and without them, or some of them, little or nothing might move forward in that regard. However, those same features and combinations may not be able to do "the whole job" by themselves—the "job," or at least the primary one, being the reduction of recidivism relative to a comparison/control group. (Regarding the improvement of *existing* programs, one could speak of doing the *rest* of the job.) Moreover, apart from their possible role in new programs, those same identified F/Cs may not, individually and collectively, have done "the whole job" by themselves in programs that already *were* studied. This is despite their important or essential contributions, and even though such programs reached .05. Finally, some F/Cs that helped reduce recidivism or achieve other desired goals might not have even been studied. In this case, of course, they could not possibly have been listed (identified) as important or perhaps essential contributors in the first place; and being unlisted, they would, by definition, be unidentified.

At any rate, the *identified*—listed—features/combinations sometimes have too little power or flexibility to produce, by themselves, a new program that will reduce recidivism (E > C; $p < .05$); and the same applies to the augmentation of existing programs.[22] That, at least, is our premise.

To achieve or closely approach the goal of recidivism reduction in the programs to be developed/improved, the already-identified positive F/Cs, we hypothesize, therefore have to be supplemented by other ingredients. The latter, however, may often be unknown—thus, missing. Obviously, missing or unknown factors are also unlisted; and both the unknown and unlisted can be called "unidentified." (As used here, "unidentified" specifically means not present, that is, not set forth or "identified," on any lists of statistically significant items. Also, "unknown" means either of the following: *[a]* There is essentially no awareness of these factors, that is, their existence or presence has not been recognized; or *[b]* the factors have not been differentiated from any other factors, namely, from those which *are* recognized. In *[b]*, there is no analytic reflection of their separateness; as a result, they do not functionally exist in the given analyses, and they are instead automatically subsumed under some other feature or features. Our later discussion of "unknowns" will emphasize meaning *[a]*.)

Though mentioned above as "supplementary" to identified and listed features and combinations, unidentified ones are not necessarily less important than the identified ones, in the programs to be developed/ improved. In fact, insofar as E/C recidivism reduction can be neither achieved nor closely approached without their presence in those programs, some unidentified F/Cs can be essential. The possibility that these F/Cs may play a crucial role in given programs is independent of whether they may eventually be *substituted for* by still other, also unidentified F/Cs. In short, the first F/Cs need not be sina qua nons in the sense of lacking any possible substitutes; yet if they are missing, E/C recidivism reduction might not occur unless a workable substitution takes place.

Assuming those "supplementary" (not substitute) features and/or combinations do actually exist and can somehow be found, two broad, mutually complementary hypotheses arise as to why they are unidentified. *Hypothesis 1:* Some features/combinations were analyzed in the prior studies but did not satisfy a preestablished statistical requirement for inclusion in any list of identified positive features. For instance, they did not reach .05, did not attain a certain degree of recidivism reduction, or did not have at least a given effect size. (Thus far, we have regarded .05 as the only requirement. To facilitate the discussion—while acknowledging the role of "noise" and the potential value of alternative criteria—we will continue to use .05.) In short, the F/Cs were not reliably associated with the given target. *Hypothesis 2:* Some F/Cs were *not analyzed* in the first place, and without being analyzed they could satisfy no requirement and appear on no list. (To readily distinguish unidentified from identified features and/or combinations in this discussion, the *unidentified* will now be called *"factors"* or *"factors and conditions."*)

When identified supplementary factors are *analyzed*, as in hypothesis 1, they need not invariably miss .05. For example, in hypothetical scenario A, below, they *would* often fail to reach that level; however, in scenario B they would commonly attain it. These scenarios or contexts suggest broad reasons why .05 may be either missed or attained by such factors.

Scenario A Here, the unidentified (unlisted) factors are analyzed *by themselves*, and for that particular reason they routinely miss the required level—sometimes by little, at other times by much.[23] (The factors are analyzed "by themselves" in the sense that they are not analyzed in combination, whether with previously listed features/combinations or with other known F/Cs.) Though these unidentified factors routinely miss the required level when analyzed on their own, this does not imply they would reach .05 or even attain a preestablished effect-size level whenever they are analyzed *together with* various features/combinations.[24] However, they sometimes would reach that level under those circumstances; and this brings us to the next scenario.

Scenario B Here, the unidentified factors are not analyzed by themselves. Instead, they are examined in conjunction with others—specifically, with previously identified features/combinations.[25] In this context, the unidentified factors may commonly reach .05 and thus help fill a gap with regard to outcome.[26] This could apply to any individual factor as well. (If some unidentified factors are *not* analyzed together with previously identified F/Cs, that could have occurred because the unidentified factors did not reach .05 when analyzed *individually*—this, say, being the only way they were examined to date. Thus, having missed .05—or, say, having had a relatively small effect-size—those factors may have been dropped from various further analyses, including those which involved previously identified features/combinations.)

Scenarios A and B specifically involve analyses; they thus differ from any context in which unidentified factors are not analyzed in the first place, as in hypothesis 2, above. All unanalyzed factors are, by definition, "unexplored"; and they are sometimes unexplored because they are unknown. Had they been known and explored, some might have helped various known but perhaps *unlisted* features/combinations reach .05. Moreover, if an F/C with which an otherwise unanalyzed (but now known and analyzed) factor was combined *had* already reached .05—(that F/C was therefore already listed)—the addition of the otherwise unexplored factor would have resulted in a new, broader combination. The latter combination might have had an even stronger and possibly sufficient overall impact on program effectiveness.[27]

Unidentified Negative Factors

The preceding discussion involved positive factors that were *missing* but presumably *needed*. For instance, those unidentified factors were needed in order to give already-identified positive features and combinations (IPFCs) enough power to help practitioners create effective, actual programs. Yet, those and/or other IPFCs, we further hypothesize, substantially contribute to positive outcomes only if certain *other* current unidentified factors are *minimal or absent*. This situation exists because the net influence of these other unidentified factors on the IPFCs either is or would have been negative. ("Is" applies if the unidentified factors are minimally present; "would have been" applies if they are absent.) Thus, to avoid making a negative contribution to IPFCs, these unidentified factors should either be entirely absent or—if and when appropriately present—they should operate to only a minor degree. In any event, they are neither superfluous nor neutral.

Sometimes, the *content* of these factors may be clearly recognized (see hypothetical examples, below). However, their negative *impact* on particular targets may not be recognized as such. This absence of recognition could have occurred, for instance, if the factors had never been statistically identified as detrimental to the given targets—say, never tagged at .05. This situation is called "case 1." Alternatively, the impact of those factors may have been unrecognized because the factors themselves were entirely unknown; that is, their existence itself was unrecognized in the first place, and the factors in question were not analyzed at all. This is called "case 2." Whether case 1 or 2 was involved, these factors were unidentified in the sense of being unlisted; and their actual, albeit unrecognized, influence was negative.

We hypothesize that, for certain targets, unidentified negative factors may include, for example, high frequencies or intensities of external control of clients and perhaps certain types or intensities of counseling as well as confrontation.[28] Yet, with other targets, or with different intensities, those same factors might have had mixed, neutral, or even positive impact, even though their respective impacts were not actually measured.[29] But the point remains: For certain targets, unidentified (unlisted) negative factors may restrict, weaken, or undo the influence of various features and combinations.[30] Those negatives, if present at the outset and if sufficiently strong, may prevent otherwise positive factors from "getting off the ground" or getting very far, say, during a program's early or middle stage. Alternatively, if negatives are only later introduced to a program that did start off well, they may *then* begin to weaken various beneficial effects that positive features helped produce or maintain.[31] In either case they may prevent a program from reaching $p < .05$.

The preceding hypothesis is independent of the following: Even if one *had* statistically identified various negative features as such—say, via separate analyses of unsuccessful target studies—one might not have isolated still other possible negatives. Like the former (the "basic") negatives, and like unidentified positives as well, the latter may involve the operations, staff, offender, or setting areas, singly or combined. Both groups of negatives may also include broader factors or conditions, for instance, the administrative/organizational. Even if these additional negatives did not exist or could be ignored, the areas in which the "basic" ones may exist are multiple, and the circumstances under which they operate are probably diverse. Given this multiplicity and diversity, the nature and impact of the "basic" negatives may often be difficult to uncover, statistically or otherwise;[32] and if factors are not identified they may be impossible to avoid or remove.

REVIEW OF BUILDING BLOCK ISSUES

In sum, a program may contain many more features than have been statistically analyzed—in this case, analyzed via the building-block method. Of the features that have been analyzed, many have been accurately identified (at $p < .05$) as either positive or negative in their contributions to program effectiveness. Features identified as positive (or negative) may exert their influence either by themselves or in certain combinations; in fact, some may reach .05 only when combined with others. In either case, however, those features may often have too little power or flexibility to generate an effective *new* program by themselves, or to substantially improve various existing ones. Instead, they may only have that ability when joined by still *other* features. However, many of the latter features may be unknown, either as to their existence or content. Alternatively, although their existence and content may be recognized, the significance of their contributions may be unrecognized. Negative features whose existence and/or influence has not been recognized as such may hamper, eclipse, or eliminate various positives and may otherwise prevent a new program from progressing very far or from remaining effective.

In the building-block method, if positive and negative features have not been statistically identified as such, one has no quantitative empirical basis for adding the positives to a prospective program or to one that is to be improved. Nor is there such a basis for subtracting the negatives. Yet, each type of feature may be important or perhaps critical to the program's success or improvement. Thus, given these unidentified positive and negative factors, the building-block approach, by itself, may often produce too little information for the construction of new programs or the substantial improvement of existing ones.

Even if sizable resources existed, the task of statistically uncovering otherwise unidentified positive and negative factors via the building-block or any other step-by-step method would be quite difficult and time-consuming. Even if the task could be accomplished more easily and quickly, it would require at least the following: *(a)* the use of very detailed and extensive data-item lists; *(b)* a higher percentage of above-average experimental designs than has existed to date and *(c)* complex statistical analyses. These, of course, can be valuable by themselves, entirely apart from unidentified factors.

With or without ample time and resources, and even with *(a)*, *(b)*, and *(c)*, the question remains, Are there alternative ways of addressing the major analytic difficulties and possible gaps in knowledge discussed above, including ways of reducing or partly avoiding them? As suggested next, the answer is *yes*—although there is a "price," and though the single approach that is presented need not ignore step-by-step methods.

Chapter 9
The Global Approach

This chapter presents a holistic yet systematic approach to identifying key features of effective programs, particularly those whose actual operations may be relatively complex. The chapter describes specific procedures for implementing this "global" approach, and it concludes by discussing issues of reliability and generalizability as well as the value of a logical-inductive framework in developing accurate insights through long-term efforts at knowledge building.

GENERAL CONSIDERATIONS

To help address, reduce, and in some respects obviate the analytic difficulties and complexities mentioned in chapter 8, one could utilize a more global or holistic approach. This would involve examining programs mainly as entities or totalities, not primarily on a feature-by-feature or combination-by-combination basis. In contrast to the building-block method, no feature/combination would be examined largely on an individual and quantitative basis for the purpose of evaluating its utility. For instance, in the more global or holistic approach, the statistical significance of the relationship between that F/C and a given outcome measure would not be examined. As a result, information about that relationship would not exist and obviously could not be used as a principal or exclusive basis for assessing the F/C's value, for instance, its contribution to an outcome such as recidivism reduction. This would also apply to effect sizes, and so on.

In short, whatever test or measure might be available, the program's features/combinations would still not be statistically assessed one by one as the major or sole way of determining their utility, whether in general or for specified targets. Consequently, the more holistic approach would not produce the types of lists described in connection with the building-

126

block method. The latter lists contained only F/Cs that had each—one by one—been found to have a statistically significant ($p < .05$) relationship to the given outcome. Moreover, that characteristic of the building-block lists was independent of the fact that a sizable portion of the features or combinations which were listed may not have existed together in many actual programs. (The relevance of this point to the global approach will soon be clear. *Parts*, *components*, and *ingredients* will now be used synonymously, and they can also substitute for features or combinations.) That is, many or most of those parts may not have operated together in many "real-life" programs, even though several others may well have done so.

The analysis of programs' jointly present (and presumably operating) parts will be called the "global" approach. Though global, this approach does not end up reflecting every ingredient the program contains; instead, as with the building-block method, it describes only some. However, unlike that method, it *begins* by considering all that are known—at least recorded. (For present purposes, only successful programs need be considered.)

The global approach mainly attempts to identify key features of programs viewed as totalities. In particular, it tries to present shared— therefore more generalizable and more reliable—components of actual programs. Here, components are considered "major"—with regard to programs collectively—*insofar as* they are shared. ("Totality" and "shared" are clarified below. Other things being equal, shared components are probably more likely than unshared to have particularly important implications.) The present approach's emphasis on cross-program sharing does not negate the idea that a feature may make an important or essential contribution within an individual program, yet not be present in most or all other programs under study.

At any rate, the global approach attempts to focus on certain individual components and/or combinations of components that existed in actual operational contexts, that is, in real-life programs. These components or ingredients can be any variables or factors, such as the operations, staff, offender, and setting features on the data-item list. If—for all programs collectively—one assembled each feature that had been identified via the *building-block* method as having made an important contribution to each program *individually*, a relatively large number of features might well be involved. That is because many programs are structurally complex and may contain—among their several features—one or more important ones that may be present in a sizable portion (but not necessarily the majority) of the other programs with which they are studied.

Nevertheless, the final descriptive product of the *global* approach would not contain this potentially large or at least larger number of features, mainly because it would include or at least emphasize only those features that seemed to be *shared* by specified programs. By utilizing shared features or ingredients under conditions described below, one would raise reliability above what would otherwise be an unacceptably risky level. One could increase practical utility as well.

The global approach does not require ingredients to pass a standard statistical test, for instance, to reach .05, in order to be considered "shared" and to thereby be included among its products. It uses a more general, convergence-of-evidence criterion. This criterion involves an ingredient's presence across a majority of the programs being studied. (Under certain conditions this may instead be a sizable minority.) This degree of presence, or repetition, provides sufficient sharing for present purposes: It can alert researchers, practitioners, and others to the existence of ingredients that are probably important across specified programs or types of programs—ingredients that can be seriously considered as bases for developing new programs and perhaps improving existing ones. In any event, "repetition" operationally refers to the documented copresence—in that respect, the sharing—of ingredients, across specified programs. When an ingredient is to be present across most such programs, the global approach is using what might be called a "likely-success" standard.

The global approach's determination of likely success is not based on the relatively large quantity of programs that is utilized in the building-block method—a quantity that facilitates standard significance testing. Though it studies fewer programs at any one time, the global approach uses a substantially stricter criterion than does the building-block method with respect to the *types* of programs examined. This criterion, described shortly, enhances practical utility and, in any event, helps compensate for the reduced quantity of programs.

The global approach proceeds in a "top-down" manner: It moves from the whole (the overall program) to the parts (the program's ingredients). More precisely, it begins with all the recorded ingredients (that being "the whole," at least the analytically operationalized whole) from each of several programs, and it then tries to identify ingredients that are common among those programs. Though mutually shared, these ingredients substantively differ from ones that are not shared or are seldom shared. That is, their content differs. In that specific sense they are not just "common" or shared among themselves, they are simultaneously "distinct" from others, in a cross-programs context. For a concrete example, see "Guide Programs" (the next section).

In contrast, the building-block method proceeds from the "bottom up": It first tries to identify statistically significant *individual features or combinations*, and it then tries to construct successful *programs* or improve existing ones by assembling those features/combinations which are found to be significant. In that respect the building-block process, unlike the global, does not begin with intact programs whose ingredients are already presumed to have worked—worked at least collectively— judging by the programs' apparent success.[1] "Intact programs"—the already existing operations with which the global approach begins—were not constructed (assembled) on the basis of statistical findings regarding individual ingredients. At least, they did not necessarily consist—whether entirely, largely, or at all—of ingredients that were *each* previously shown to have a statistically significant relationship to outcome, whether individually or in combination.

The "top-down" direction reflects the global approach's premise that each program is a synthesis of all or essentially all its ingredients. These ingredients or parts are seen as operating more or less as a unit (efficiently or not), and in that sense they are considered—collectively—a "totality."[2] In implementing the global approach one therefore begins by excluding no known parts of the programs under consideration and by regarding each such ingredient as having made a possibly important contribution to outcome.[3] In that respect one starts with the whole program.

This "unitary-operation, initially inclusive" framework is used despite the following. Some ingredients—if they had been analyzed via the building-block approach (i.e., had been statistically examined together with like ingredients from many other programs)—might well have been found to contribute either substantially more than or less than other ingredients, but not the same as them.[4] Some ingredients might even have made a statistically *significant* (.05) contribution, while the others— again, analyzed separately—may have appeared nonsignificant. At any rate, though the global approach "starts with the whole program" (as analytically operationalized), it does not assume that all or even most ingredients make an essentially equal contribution to outcome. It assumes they *may* make an important one and should therefore be considered at the start. None of the above eliminates the possibility of eventually uncovering neutral, superfluous, or even negative factors that may operate in generally successful programs. Programs can function more or less as units—and can succeed—despite such factors. To be sure, they would undoubtedly perform better without the negatives and be more efficient absent the superfluous.

As indicated, the global approach does not try to statistically determine if individual ingredients are significantly related to outcome in numerous targeted programs, analyzed collectively. In particular, it does not try to do so for the purpose of subsequently constructing effective new programs or improving existing ones by combining, sequencing, and otherwise assembling those ingredients—say, the "identified positive features or combinations" (IPFCs). Underlying this stance regarding the assembling of individual ingredients is the fact that the global approach rejects or seriously questions the following joint position: First, an effective new program can be constructed (routinely, or at least in most cases) by assembling IPFCs; secondly, those features/combinations can achieve that goal by themselves.[5] More specifically, the global approach challenges the view that such a program can generally be developed simply by using those ingredients, and neither more nor less than those ingredients, which have been individually and/or in given combinations associated with positive outcomes either at $p < .05$ or in terms of some related criterion, across a given collection of programs. This does not mean successful programs may never or only seldom be developed on that basis. Indeed, such results might not be infrequent with given features or at least combinations thereof, and this may not just apply to "easier" targets or goals.

In any event, two key assumptions or hypotheses underlie the above challenge:

1.   Though several different individual features may have been found effective in numerous programs, those features—if then assembled to form a *new* program—would not necessarily function well together in that program. (Note: Each of the assembled features need not have been found effective in *all* those programs, and those features which were found to be effective—say, at .05—need not all have been effective in the *same* specific programs.)
2.   Even if those assembled features did prove operationally compatible in the new program, they might not be jointly strong enough to often reduce recidivism ($E > C$) or achieve some other goal. (Here, "often" would mean even one-third of the time. However, it would not mean usually, let alone regularly.)[6]

As suggested by the discussion of unidentified positive and negative features, the difficulty of identifying a set of features that is strong enough to reduce recidivism may reflect deep-seated methodological issues and logical limitations of the building-block approach. If so, the difficulty would go well beyond the working-out of various operational "bugs," for instance, tactical/logistical program-issues, and even beyond routine issues and requirements of research design, data handling, and statistical analysis. It would apply whether the tactical/logistical issues involve staff, offenders, and settings, not just program content and processes.[7]

To see whether and how the above-mentioned issues may be addressed, we next examine various facets involved in implementing the global approach.

GUIDE PROGRAMS

Programs used in the global approach must satisfy the same criteria for inclusion in a study sample that are used in the building-block method: they must meet preestablished sampling requirements, satisfy standards of scientific adequacy, and so on. However, to increase the strength and utility of this approach, not all programs that meet those criteria are included. Instead, one selects all programs that have not only met the above inclusion criteria but also have shown unusual promise; in particular, those which have shown a substantial level of success with their principal or exclusive target—success in terms of recidivism reduction, effect size, or some other measure. The level in question is specified later in this discussion.

Judging from its considerable success, each selected program—called a "guide program"—consists of features that apparently were compatible in their real-life context. More specifically, given the fact that those features—collectively—were associated with the level of success in question, it is reasonable to believe they actively and/or passively "got along" with each other anywhere from sufficiently to very well. This would apply to all the program's features, to most of them, or to a smaller portion that—collectively—was nevertheless critical to success. Moreover, this compatibility apparently prevailed despite any negative or otherwise detrimental features that may have coexisted with the positive. More precisely, it existed even though some features, combinations, and general conditions may have actively or passively and strongly or mildly opposed the achievement of intermediate and/or final objectives.[8] (*Programs* and *operations* will now be used synonymously.)

At any rate, in the guide-programs procedure, the global approach is focused on selected programs, especially those whose respective recidivism reductions or effect sizes are quite sizable and can hardly have resulted from chance. This procedure helps one directly examine—and compare across programs—the known components and workings of what seem to be the most quantitatively promising individual operations available. Judging from their quantitative results, it seems reasonable to say that if any programs or operations should be examined, it is they.

By studying guide programs as totalities—provided one does so collectively, especially in ways described below—one may obtain a better integrated and perhaps fuller picture of successful operations than that which is derived from the building-block method. Moreover, because it examines only the most quantitatively successful programs, the guide-programs procedure can increase not only the face validity of the results but also one's actual ability to discriminate between E and C programs. (The basis of comparison with respect to these increases or improvements is the level of face validity and discriminating ability that would have resulted if one had instead used *every* successful [E > C] program, not just "guides.") Regardless of how it compares with the building-block method or performs under contrasting conditions, the guide-programs procedure, in itself, can provide important leads in identifying features and combinations that are central to success.

Scope and Focus

Guide programs can involve any generic approach, such as group counseling (GC), vocational training (VT), and restitution. Beyond this programmatic content and other operations features they can involve setting, staff, and offender variables, not to mention organizational/administrative factors. As a result, these programs may be used to examine any particular *target*, such as the males aged twenty-two to twenty-nine years old who were mentioned earlier. Guide or "lead" programs can therefore be found, for instance, within the previously mentioned sample of 40 hypothetical programs that was discussed in connection with the building-block approach. More specifically, since those 40 included all known programs that focused on a given target—here, on the males mentioned above—all guide programs that focused on that same target would be part of that same sample. This follows because all guide programs were among the "known" ones.

As used here, the global approach centers on the joint analysis of several guide programs. To more easily describe the method for analyzing these programs—in effect, the guide-programs procedure—we will use an example in which *(a)* the building-block method has already been applied to a group of 40 E > C programs whose main target we wish to examine and in which *(b)* all the guide programs that are jointly analyzed can be found among those 40. As will become clear, guide programs could have been examined even if building-block analyses had never occurred.

Presently, "guides" probably comprise a small portion, for example, 15 percent of *all* experimental studies (the "totality" of relevant studies) whose E's outperformed their C's, even when the performance difference of some studies within that totality missed .05.[9] This estimated portion is an overall average, and different percentages—some higher, some lower— would undoubtedly exist for the various categories of programs (e.g., cognitive-behavioral and confrontation), which, together, might comprise an overall sample.

Before we proceed, three points might be kept in mind (see chapter 4 regarding each point):

> 1. Together, the results from various meta-analyses indicated that some 65 percent of all E/C studies favored the E-program over the C by any amount (not necessarily $p < .05$). This means that about 26 of the previously mentioned 40 target programs could probably be described as E > C.
>
> 2. The present author's review of 270 E/C studies indicated that the results favored the E-program over the C by at least $p < .05$ some 33 percent of the time. Out of 40 programs, this would yield 12 such results.
>
> 3. The overall review of meta-analyses indicated that, of all studies in which E outperformed C by any amount (i.e., of all E > C programs), some one-fourth involved a recidivism reduction of 25 percent or more. Of the 26 E > C programs mentioned in point 1 above, this would yield about 6 such E-programs.

Procedures and Issues

Our first step in the guide-program procedure for implementing the global approach would be to identify all programs that—as part of the building-block analysis—were particularly successful with the given target. These would be the selected programs—the guides or leads—mentioned above. We might define, as particularly successful operations (therefore as guides), those programs which each reduced recidivism by at least 40 percent or had an equivalent effect size, preferably after some twelve or more months of follow-up. (For an alternative approach, see Appendix F—section titled, "Using Absolute Rates.") Given a sample of 26 E > C target programs and a guide-program incidence within that sample of, say, 15 percent, this selection process would yield a guide sample of four programs for the particular target. Again, this is just an example. In reality, there may be more or fewer "guides" for any given target. (Mainly for ease of presentation, but also more or less in line with points 2 and 3 above, we will use six rather than four guide programs.)

The main question in the analysis would be, Which features, if any, do these guide programs *share* with each other? A supplementary one would be, Which guide-program features *differ* from features already identified as positive for the overall study-pool (here, the pool of 26 programs minus its "6" guide programs)? The latter question can be addressed only if a building-block or other separate analysis has occurred. In this question, "guide-program features" emphasizes items that are mutually shared by a sizable portion of the guide sample. In both questions, "features" can involve operations, staff, offender, and setting items alike.

A specific, positive answer to the *shared*-features question can perform a function similar to that performed by results from a set of partial replication studies: By indicating that certain features are shared by various guide programs and by specifying which features they are, this answer can increase the reliability of one's findings (observations) from any one program, and it can thereby increase the confidence one may justifiably place in those results. For instance, say that a total of eight features (A through H) were known to comprise guide program one. If three of those features (A through C) were also observed in guide program two and were then seen in programs three and four as well, those results, collectively, would substantially increase the reliability of the findings from program one—and, for that matter, from two through four, respectively.

When one identifies shared features, such as A, B, and C, among a number of guide programs—especially among a majority (recall there were six)—this outcome can strengthen one's basis for believing the following: Those features, individually and collectively, may be important or possibly essential in constructing new programs and perhaps in improving current ones. Such an outcome can also strengthen the view that various program features, particularly those most often shared, may well be mutually compatible in a newly constructed program. Both beliefs would apply even if one, two, or all three of the above-mentioned features (namely, A, B, and C, which were shared across programs one through four) did *not* appear in—were not shared by—one or both of the remaining guide programs (five and six) that comprised the guide sample. The beliefs would apply even if some of the first four guide programs (say, one and two) shared a few other of their respective *remaining* features (say,

D and/or E, but perhaps not F, G, and H) with one or more other guide programs (say, three and four, or four and six).[10]

Certain answers to the *differing*-features question could strengthen and broaden findings obtained from the shared-features analysis. For instance, if none of the first three features (A, B, and/or C) that were shared by the first four of the six guide programs were also found in a sizable majority of the overall sample's 20 *remaining* programs (i.e., 20 nonguide programs [26 minus 6 guides], each of which had the same main target as the guides), this finding would substantially increase the practical and theoretical significance of the original, shared-features results: In conjunction with those original results, the added finding would suggest not only that A, B, and C may indeed have been especially important in programs that were among the strongest and presumably most likely to succeed, that is, in guide programs, but also that an absence of those three features would be associated with considerably less program strength for the given target. This is because they had less strength in those 20 remaining programs. A comparable conclusion could be proposed in connection with the absence of any one or two such features. Here, however, the "weakness" would be less than if all three features were absent. The above suggestion would probably be even stronger if all 40 target studies had been used rather than the E > C subsample of 26.

(In this and the following discussion, "features" refers especially but not exclusively to combinations of single items, not just to any group of them analyzed individually. Placing top priority on combinations reflects the relatively global, integrative framework underlying the guide-program procedure.)

When using the global approach—more specifically, its guide-programs procedure—a $p < .05$ relationship to outcome need not be demonstrated for any shared feature or shared combination. For instance, it need not be shown for any of the three features that were shared by programs #1 through #4 above, in connection with their main target. In fact, .05 simply is not used as the basis or standard—certainly not as the sole or principal standard—for identifying promising features and combinations, even if enough guide programs exist to permit such a test.

In order to perform such a test, simple binomial probability tables can be used (The Staff of the Computation Laboratory, 1955). Thus, if six programs are involved as in the above example, .05 would be reached (given a one-tail context) for each feature that is shared by at least five programs. However, in our view, the use of .05 as a touchstone for including or excluding *any single* feature has a serious practical shortcoming. In the present case, for example, such usage does not reflect the fact that any feature which occurs in, say, *four* (even three) of the six programs still warrants very close attention—even though .05 has been missed. This position applies even more strongly if there happens to be *a number of* shared features, as in A, B, and C. These features would be the same ones, or mostly the same, in most or all programs across which they were shared, for instance, in programs one through four or in one through three.[11]

In our view, the repeated appearance of one or more features in a group of guide programs—specifically, programs whose performance is unusually positive in the first place—should ipso facto be considered a particularly valuable lead in the search for features that may help construct effective new programs. This situation, it should be kept in mind, differs—obviously differs in degree—from that in which those same features were simply repeated in a group of more ordinary, that is, nonguide, programs. (Even among nonguides, .05 would not *have* to be the final or principal determiner of inclusion/exclusion. Nor would an equivalent effect size.)

Thus, going back to the start, all features would first be considered "*potentially* important," simply because they are part of a guide program. This, at least, would seem to be a plausible view and working assumption. Next, however, those features that are shared by *most* such guide programs—here, by four of the six—would merit what could be called "very close attention" as to their possible use in developing new programs for the given target. (With larger numbers of guides, say, ten or more, sharing among even 40–50 percent of the programs would warrant much attention.) This status, in effect, would be earned rather than simply plausible, assumed, or acquired, in contrast to the above. Finally, any features that were shared by most guide programs would remain very important even if they were simultaneously found in a moderate proportion of *non*guide E-programs that outperformed their respective C's. To be sure, such features would be less salient or simply less outstanding or unique than those which might have sharply contrasted with nonguide features in that respect.[12]

Negative, neutral, and superfluous features   The guide-programs procedure, which purposely culls out and focuses on shared features only, may tend to filter out or greatly reduce any negative features that were perhaps operating in given guides. This might occur largely for the following reason, one that—again—especially involves the fact that *guide* programs, that is, rather successful operations, are involved: Any particular type of negative feature that is operating in a given guide program is probably less likely to subsequently appear in some other guide program than is any particular positive feature which is part of that same, first program. That is, the negative feature is probably less likely to be repeated in one or more *different* guide programs. (This is independent of the fact that some *other* type of negative feature may be operating in a different guide program. Though the latter feature might be observed, it would not be a repeat of the first one.) This might apply to superfluous and even neutral features as well, though to a lesser degree. In any event, features that are repeated across a number of guide programs and in that sense are shared by them are probably much more likely to be positive than negative, and so on.[13] This would especially apply if *several* guide programs are involved, and it should increasingly apply as the number of programs further increases.

(Features identified via the *building-block* approach do not include neutral and superfluous items, since building block's "positive features" are, by definition, only those which have contributed significantly.[14] As to the global approach, since its guide programs obviously work—error variance almost certainly notwithstanding—any excess baggage that the neutral and superfluous features might individually or collectively contribute to the total would not decisively undermine the program's overall value with respect to providing public protection. To be sure, such excess could reduce efficiency and increase costs, and the latter could itself be decisive to many policy makers.)

GLOBAL APPROACH COMPARED TO BUILDING-BLOCK APPROACH

At this point in correctional knowledge-building, one cannot readily estimate the relative powers of the global and building-block approaches. Specifically, one cannot—without oversimplifying—make a definitive overall judgment that reflects and summarizes the two approaches' respective abilities to achieve the following goals: (1) identify effective features; (2) help develop effective new programs and perhaps improve existing ones[15] (achievement of goal 2 is largely built on 1). Still, several comparisons are possible regarding key abilities, advantages, and limitations.

First, the global approach is direct and can probably have considerable early "payoff" with respect to goals 1 and 2. There should be little doubt that its results would reflect programs that are relevant to given targets and have in fact worked. This does not imply that the building-block method emphasizes the irrelevant and cannot provide important information about goals 1 and 2. Instead, it suggests the global approach may provide *more* key information; in any event, it means this approach could probably supply information that is critical to goal 2 (certainly regarding new programs) more quickly and directly. Whether the building-block method would eventually "catch up" is unclear; but, in the long run, it could, theoretically, approach the global.

Second, results from the building-block method can be more reliable than those from the global approach, mainly because the former are based on more programs—usually many more. This advantage applies to results involving individual features and combinations in particular, not necessarily to programs as a whole. Given this advantage, the building-block method can better help one justifiably believe its individual findings—for example, its list of "identified positive features"—are statistically sound. That is, it can provide a quantitatively stronger basis for believing the given results occurred neither by chance nor, say, under somewhat extreme or unusual and therefore perhaps questionably transferable or minimally reproducible and adaptable conditions.

This conclusion would hold even though individual features that are shared across *several* guide programs may be rather reliable themselves. (Such sharing can occur even though the guide-programs procedure may usually involve fairly small samples, as in the earlier example of six programs.) In any event, features that are individually and especially collectively shared by a number of guide programs are not likely to be chance events. Nor, for that matter, are the *programs* from which those particular features spring likely to be extreme. Both points—the one involving chance and the other centering on extremes—apply whether or not, but especially if, the shared features are also singled out in building-block analyses.

Given the above, the building-block's higher reliability does not mean one should automatically consider the global approach's findings of questionable transferability, let alone reliability. (This, of course, does not mean the latter's findings should go unquestioned, even if more than very few guide programs are involved.) Nor, on the other hand, does it mean the *building-block's* results *would* be automatically or even fairly easily transferable—in particular, translatable (by themselves) into actual new programs.

The latter caution regarding transferability partly reflects the following: The findings that the building block method can produce concerning any given target may involve individual features/combinations which, collectively, might not be mutually compatible in real-life operations; in fact, the F/Cs may not even be copresent. In contrast, the features identified by the global approach's guide-programs procedure would more likely be characterized by compatibility.

Third, the global approach may have more to contribute than the building-block method to the development of effective *new* programs, particularly in the short run. However, in both the short and the long run, findings from the building-block method may be better able to help improve *existing* operations, basically by modifying them (e.g., by being added to and/or substituted for the existing features). Or, their ability to improve such operations may be at least equal. The former situation (the global-approach advantage) occurs independently of the fact that any or all features identified via the global approach may sometimes be found among those identified by the building-block method itself. The latter situation (the building-block advantage) occurs apart from the fact that the features identified via the building-block method may, collectively, sometimes include many or all that are found by the global approach—and may even include few other features.

Fourth, other things being equal, building-block results would be more generalizable to different situations and targets than would the global, since the former's results would almost always be based on a wider range of programs and potential targets. This does not imply that the global approach's program/target-base is usually *narrow*—only that it is narrower than the building block's. Other factors being equal, narrower program/target-bases would produce results whose practical and theoretical value is more restricted. However, as implied above and below, those "other factors" may not generally be equal in various important respects. These considerations are apart from the fact that various *principles* of successful intervention which may be derived from or inferred via the global approach may be quite generalizable.

Fifth, though results from the building-block method may be more reliable and generalizable than those from the global, new programs based on the former's results may often prove less successful than those developed from the latter's.[16] However, this difference in success does not imply that the building-block method offers *little* by way of relevance and possible success with regard to new programs—only that it may generally offer less. Nor does the difference diminish this method's likely ability to improve existing operations, or to provide generalizable clues regarding principles of successful intervention.

Reliability, when present, can help establish the relative stability of given findings: In a sense, it can empirically create a "status" for, or description of, the relationship observed between particular features (collectively) and any given outcome. Thus, for example, reliability estimates can provide direct and sufficient evidence as to the relative stability and/or reproducibility of that relationship and of those features. This applies even though differing views exist as to exactly how much reliability—stability, and so on—is needed for various purposes. Generalizability can then expand the value of that which "reliability" helped establish. However, by themselves, neither reliability nor generalizability can generate *relevant* and *positive* results in the first place. To generate such findings in the context of new programs, the global approach seems more promising than the building-block. At the same time, the building-block method may be better able—or at least *as* able—to improve ongoing programs, whether or not these were considered successful.

Together, these five points suggest that the global and building-block approaches need not be considered largely irreconcilable or even mutually exclusive. For instance, it seems likely, not just plausible, that results from the global approach could add pragmatically and theoretically relevant information to those from the building block. Moreover, this could probably occur even if the building block's findings turned out to be *no* less discriminating than the global's with regard to specific E/C outcome differences and no less able to develop real-life programs as well. At any rate, a supplementary and in some respects complementary relationship could probably exist between the global and building-block approaches. If such a relationship existed, and if time and resources allowed, one might neither wish nor need to utilize only one such approach, despite the important contributions it might make.

Several final points and issues will be briefly mentioned regarding the global approach.

Convergence and Priority

Of the features identified via this approach, many or most may be singled out as positive via a building-block analysis as well, assuming one is conducted. More specifically, shared features derived via the global approach's guide-programs procedure may often be observed among the generally larger group of features that could emerge as successful anyway, via a *building block* analysis of many more programs.[17] Though such a convergence of findings from the global and building-block analyses is a reasonable possibility, its probability of actually occurring cannot be presently determined. Nor can the specific degree of convergence yet be determined.

If considerable convergence or overlap occurs—thus, if the global approach's findings are supported by the building block's—this would suggest that the global's main findings, namely, the shared features, may often be among the most reliable and perhaps generalizable after all.[18]

(The specific degree of reliability and generalizability would, of course, depend on the precise similarities and differences between the programs that comprise the global and building-block samples, respectively.) Yet, it is possible that overlap between the two approaches does not exist or is rather limited—a situation which would not, however, automatically mean the global approach's findings are unreliable or nongeneralizable. Presently, this second possibility is as plausible as the first, though we consider it less likely.

Convergence or nonconvergence aside, one who relies on the building-block method alone can find it difficult to single out those features—from among the method's several identified-positives—which might be more important than others. This is because the method, by itself, is not designed to help one prioritize among the items within each of its product lists. In rough contrast, the global approach's often-shared features are already considered high priority, and those which are shared most often might be viewed as the highest.

Thus, if one uses *both* the building-block method and the global approach, and if substantial convergence occurs across their respective findings, the following would be implied: *(a)* the priority that would otherwise be associated with the global approach's main findings alone, that is, with its often-shared features, would receive further support;[19] and *(b)* the reliability and generalizability of the global approach's main findings could probably be considered higher and broader than otherwise. Implication *(b)* would apply equally and simultaneously to the building-block findings that overlapped the global, that is, applied to identified-positive features. In other words, the second point regarding convergence would apply both ways.

Individual Programs and Replication

Any given guide program—say, any of the six in the earlier example—may, by itself, provide valuable descriptions and distinctive insights, assuming considerable information was recorded and analyzed. The program's contribution to theory and practice may be substantial, and the possibility that its findings may trigger or comprise a sizable advance should be recognized. Such progress may especially occur if the program incorporates, for perhaps the first time, knowledge and experience accumulated in several earlier programs. (Though these points especially apply to guide programs, as defined earlier, they need not be limited to them.)

Thus, one should keep alert for especially unusual programs, particularly those which perform very well. ("Unusual" refers to content and operations.) If possible, one should describe the features of any such programs separately from, that is, in addition to, those of the entire program-sample collectively. (This sample would include the unusual program plus all remaining programs combined.) Yet, when drawing conclusions about features that might be used to develop new programs or to improve existing ones, one must remain cautious and systematic, and—insofar as is feasible—should not rely primarily on any such unusual one.

Specifically, however promising and useful a program and its features may seem—and may in fact *be*, under specified conditions—other programs should also be utilized and given considerable weight. Thus, per normal procedure, those "other" programs should be studied collectively and the unusual program should be included among them. The main reason for conducting these "joint analyses" rather than relying largely on any "single-program description" is as follows: When focusing on only one program, however unusual or even novel, one would necessarily forego the advantages of possible replication and of using comparative, that is, cross-program, findings. (In this discussion, replication will focus on cross-program analyses involving *guide* programs.)

For instance, absent at least some partial replications, each of the following would be the case:

1. One would have no empirical basis for believing that results from any one program might be reproducible at all and, in that respect, even minimally reliable. (For results to support the conclusion that even *moderate* reliability exists for any given program, in this case the unusual one, they would have to be at least fairly common within the study sample, that is, be repeated at least a few times.)
2. One would have no convergence of varied clues, especially independent ones, as to which of the single program's features may be more important than others.[20] ("Independent clues" are those which come from a program other than the "unusual" program itself.)
3. Aside from the first two implications, which involve reliability and priority, the findings from any single program could be generalized with less confidence than those from a group of programs. (This assumes that differences exist within that group, and that the group—collectively—covers a broader range of targets and/or program-components than does the single program—here, the "unusual" one.)[21]

In the context of the global approach, there are at least two broad ways to study an unusual individual program *in conjunction with* other programs—ones that are not necessarily unusual—and to thereby retain important advantages of partial replication. In the first method, the individual program is given extra emphasis compared to every other program. In the second, it starts on the same footing as any other program, exactly as in any basic guide-programs procedure.

Specifically, in method one, the researcher would ask if *(a)* any of the unusual individual program's features are repeated in the remaining programs that comprise the study sample and, if so, *(b)* how often and what proportion of the time. By asking question *(a)*, one in effect gives the unusual program extra emphasis or influence, that is, analytic priority. More specifically, by using that program's features and *only* its features to determine the content and focus of the analysis, one allows that program not only to "set the terms" of the analysis and to conceptually "lead the way," but, in so doing, also to exclude various other dimensions. Thus, for example, the first method would make it impossible to examine, and to thereby possibly replicate, various features that are *not* found within the unusual program but which nevertheless exist in some, many, or most remaining programs.

Method two is essentially the basic guide-programs procedure itself. Here, all features would have an equal chance of being examined, and no one program would lead the way in the sense of setting the terms and excluding features it did not itself contain. Though the main question would be, Which features, if any, are shared across one or more programs? this would apply regardless of the program those features are part of, including the unusual one. In those respects, all programs would be analytically equal and weighted the same.

The mere existence of these two methods implies that a program which seems unusual or perhaps novel when examined alone may, when studied jointly with others, be found to share certain individual features with many or most of them. If any or all of those shared features from the various programs (including the unusual one) can be operationally linked with each other, they—collectively—might form a core or nucleus for developing successful new programs, especially if most such features are mutually compatible.[22] At any rate, as further discussed below, unusual programs may not be entirely unique.

The preceding involves individual features. Besides sharing such features, some of those jointly studied programs—say, a moderate to sizable proportion of them—may share some *(a) combinations of features*. Moreover, they and/or other programs may share certain types of *(b) interactions among features* and/or various *(c) general operating or background conditions*. Individually and collectively, these three factors may be at least as important as the individual features themselves, say, with respect to developing new programs. Ideally, and where feasible, all such factors should therefore be examined, preferably together.

Such a joint-factors analysis would usually be challenging, analytically and especially pragmatically. Yet even if these challenges were somehow diminished, this analysis could not be adequately implemented by focusing on any single program alone; more specifically, it could not be adequately implemented with respect to addressing the earlier replication issues. This is because those issues, for instance, reliability and generalizability, must be addressed on a cross-program basis, since they center on the question of how much sharing, if any, occurs. This applies however unusual, outstanding, or novel the individual program may be and however well its parts and processes may have been described.

Despite the various limitations mentioned above, unusual individual programs can, by themselves, *(a)* constitute a valuable starting point or even a later check-point in the identification of useful individual features. They may also *(b)* supply reasonable hypotheses and/or serve as possible checks regarding the identification of important combinations, interactions, and general conditions. Contribution *(a)* assumes those programs were originally well documented and at least fairly well described. Contribution *(b)* would ideally call for their being systematically or otherwise very carefully examined and described—as via chapter 7's data items. ("Starting point" in contribution [a] means the programs would be used either on their own, that is, apart from methods one and two, or to "lead the way," as in method one.)

This discussion of individual programs and replication is neither contradicted nor diminished by the fact that any given program, when viewed as a totality, may well be substantively and perhaps dynamically unique. At the very least, the program's particular combinations, interactions, and general conditions, when taken together, may distinguish it in no small way from every other program in the sample, even though several individual features may be shared by each program. In sum, an individual program—however it happens to perform—can be justifiably considered unique as a totality, though perhaps not in all its separate parts. But whether the program is unique at the former or even latter level, or whether it is just *unusual* in terms of degree, it may still provide clues and directions for improving intervention.[23]

Prominent-programs Procedure

When a target has very few guide programs, one may want to increase the sample size in order to raise the reliability and expand the empirical base for generalizing one's results. To do so, one might modify the basic guide-programs procedure, by using a "prominent-programs procedure." Here, one would still focus on the more successful or notable programs but no longer be limited to those considered topmost or "guides," for example, those with at least a 40 percent recidivism reduction. In short, one would moderately relax the selection criterion.

For instance, one might define, as "prominent," the upper 25 percent of all programs in which E outperformed C by any amount for the target of interest. Given this "any amount" standard, slightly more than two-thirds of the E/C outcome differences in the *sample-base*, that is, in all such programs combined, would probably miss .05. However, the preponderance of differences in the upper 25 percent, that is, in the prominent-programs sample itself, probably *would* reach that level.[24] As a result, when using this modified approach, one would not seriously erode the advantage that is associated with the large difference in performance between E- and C-programs, that is, the advantage which characterizes the basic guide-programs procedure. As with the latter procedure, performance in the modified approach can be measured in terms of recidivism reduction or effect size.

If one used the modified standard, the resulting prominent programs would generally fall about halfway between *(a)* the average E-program that currently outperforms its C at or beyond .05, on the one hand, and *(b)* most guide programs, on the other. As a result, for any given target that is examined via a sample of guide programs, one could reasonably expect the modified procedure to expand that sample by some 30–50 percent; in any event, one could aim for that increase. The prominent-programs sample would of course contain all the previous guide programs as well. That is, the latter would be carried over into the new, expanded sample.

One would ask the same principal and supplementary questions about prominent programs that were asked for guides: Which features, if any, do these programs share with each other? and, Which prominent-programs features differ from features already identified as positive for the overall study pool? that is, for all programs combined. If the prominent-programs sample largely consists of the *same* types of programs as the guide-programs sample, albeit more of them and no longer just the topmost ones, this will mainly increase reliability.[25] However, if the prominent-programs sample emphasizes *different* types of programs (and/or adjacent targets), or if it at least contains a number of them, the modified procedure can substantially increase generalizability as well.

FURTHER ISSUES

Increasing Reliability

Background and Terminology By increasing the reliability of findings, say, those from a sample of previously analyzed programs ("original programs"), one can increase confidence in the results. One way to raise reliability is to expand the sample size by adding new programs. Using the global approach this can be done by including all newly observed guide programs which, individually, are similar in some way(s) to one or more of the original programs and which, in that respect, repeat ("replicate") them. When examining these "replication programs" one would use the guide-programs procedure and could focus on the following: *(a)* individual features or combinations of features that are similar to various F/Cs derived from the original programs and/or *(b)* programs as a whole ("overall operations"), that is, all individual features/combinations together. Consistent with the guide-programs procedure, the replication-programs sample would be analyzed collectively; that is, all observations regarding individual programs would be integrated at that level.

We will now mention selected issues relating to the improvement of reliability. In so doing we will first focus on overall operations rather than individual F/Cs, that is, on item *(b)* instead of *(a)*, above. We will also emphasize similar rather than literally identical operations, since the latter are probably rare at the level of overall programs. Finally, since similarity rather than complete identity is involved, the term *replication*—whenever used—will actually mean "partial replication."

Adjacent Targets versus Similar Programs As suggested earlier, the number of guide programs available for an original target, say, males aged 22 to 29, will often be limited, in fact severely limited. If, indeed, no more guide programs exist for that particular target, that is, if none exist besides those which comprise the original programs, other steps could be taken to increase sample size.[26] One might choose to examine all additional guide programs whose content is similar in various respects to that of the original programs but which focus on *adjacent targets*. The targets that might be focused on by this added group, that is, by these replication programs, could involve, say, males aged 19 to 21 or 30 to 39 rather than the original programs' age range of 22 to 29. Using the guide-programs procedure, these added programs would, per routine, then be analyzed collectively—not as a group of their own, but as part of an overall sample that includes both them and the original sample.

(Although the adjacent-target categories used in the above example are contiguous with the original target, such contiguity, that is, actual boundary contact, is not required in order to qualify as adjacent. Nor, of course, is partial overlap. Thus, for example, though they do not quite contact each other, subjects aged 22 to 24 might be considered "adjacent" to those aged *26 to 30*, as may those aged 32 to 35. In short, one can use "adjacent" in the broader sense of "fairly close," since this can still be considered similar.)

Though adjacent targets would help raise reliability by increasing the sample size, they would not, by themselves, provide a relatively strong substantive base for doing so. This is essentially because they *are* adjacent rather than, say, partly identical in the sense of being specifically and substantively related or mutually overlapping.[27] (Restated, this partial identity simply means that these respective targets have some specific characteristics or specific areas in common with each other.) Overlapping or partly identical targets would, generally, be more alike than adjacent ones, even if the latter were contiguous rather than fairly close.

We now turn to *similar programs*—operations that resemble the original ones in a number of substantive ways. Similar programs would provide a stronger content-base than adjacent targets for raising reliability via an increase in sample size. In fact, generally speaking, replication that centers on the use of similar programs, that is, somewhat comparable operations, would probably provide a larger increase in reliability than would replication based on adjacent targets.[28] This likely difference in the degree of increased reliability may well reflect the fact that similar programs probably would, or at least readily could, have more by way of content overlap with the original programs than would adjacent targets. That is, similar programs, collectively, would probably have more points or areas of specific similarity or partial identity.[29] The higher degree of content overlap between the similar programs and the originals does not mean there would be a near or virtual *identity* between these respective groups of programs viewed as *wholes*, for example, as integrated totalities. This is despite the fact that these respective groups may share several identical or almost identical individual features with each other and may, in that regard, share several "specific similarities."

The degree to which the reliability of original programs can be increased is a function of various factors, a situation that applies to adjacent targets and similar programs alike. For instance, in partial replications that involve the use of *adjacent targets*, the amount of increase can vary depending on such conditions as the following: *(a)* the narrowness or breadth (say, in years) of the adjacent target-categories and the original target-category, individually and comparatively; and *(b)* the closeness or distance of those adjacent categories from the original target-category (again in years, and on average). At the same time, the ability of *similar programs* to increase reliability by partly replicating the original programs could depend, as suggested above, on *(c)* how closely they resemble those originals. (Definitional issues regarding "similarity" are noted in Appendix K.)

Moreover, depending on the amount of increased reliability associated with the above-mentioned adjacent-target situation *as compared to* the amount associated with the similar-programs situation—that is, depending on the specific increase involved in conditions *(a)* and *(b)*, on the one hand, as compared to that involved in condition *(c)*, on the other—the following may be the case: The *difference* in increased reliability that could result from using adjacent targets rather than similar programs may, in the end, turn out to be large, small, or even nonexistent. Under most conditions, however, programs that are relatively similar will probably outdistance those which are indeed adjacent, even if, say, the adjacent-target categories are relatively narrow and fairly close to the original.

Global Approach versus Building-Block Approach The preceding discussion and examples focused on the goal of improving *overall-program* reliability via specified applications of the global approach's guide-programs procedure. If additional guide-programs are available, the global approach can probably achieve that reliability-centered goal better than the building-block method, whether via the use of adjacent targets or similar programs. However, as to improving the reliability of *individual features/combinations*, the building-block method may usually outdistance the global. This mainly reflects the fact that, for any given F/Cs, the former method would almost always involve more studies that bear on a target of interest than would the latter, and it would never involve fewer. For these same quantitative reasons, the building-block method is also likely to have produced higher reliability in the first place, that is, with the respective individual features/combinations that were derived from the original programs.

However, these likely building-block advantages do not mean that an overall program which might be constructed from selected individual F/Cs that were derived via the building-block method will probably be more *relevant and effective*[30] than an overall program developed via the global approach; in fact, the opposite may well—indeed, would probably—apply. This is because results from the global approach may be as important as or even more critical than those from the building-block method with respect to the goal of developing effective new programs. The global's likelier relevance to this overall-program goal would exist despite the following characteristics of building-block results, that is, results which were derived from the original programs, collectively: first, the building block's *individual features/combinations*—specifically, its identified-positive F/Cs, taken separately—are probably more numerous than comparable features that were identified via the global approach (cf. the latter's "shared features"), based on its own original programs (guide programs); second, those identified-positive F/Cs may constitute important contributions in their own right, even beyond improving the effectiveness of existing overall programs.

Factors Relating to Generalization

Terms and Approach   We will now examine some logical, empirical, and content-related factors involved in appropriately generalizing the outcomes (findings) obtained for an *original* target to a different target—specifically, to an *adjacent* or more distant one. As used here, generalizations regarding this outcome-relationship between these targets take the following form: The finding obtained for X (the original target) is applicable to Y (the adjacent target). Thus, for example: The finding for males aged 18 to 21 can be validly applied to males aged 22 to 29. The finding or findings for the original target can be based on one or more studies. Those resulting from adjacent-target studies are explained below. To facilitate the presentation we will focus on "positive" generalizations only; here, the original target's finding *applies* (rather than not applies) to the adjacent target.

The generalizations discussed below focus on results that already exist and those which are predicted. In the first case, one largely summarizes or abstracts; in the second, one often projects or hypothesizes. When *summarizing*, one generalizes from the original target's findings to those from the adjacent or more distant target—with "distant" simply meaning less adjacent. (See case A, below.) In effect, one asserts that the results obtained for the adjacent target largely correspond to, or otherwise match or are similar to, that observed for the original target. (Results may involve behavioral outcomes, such as recidivism.)

This assertion, and any accompanying content, is a form of inductive generalization: It is either *(a)* a summary or "reduction" of, *(b)* a "best fit" for, or *(c)* an "abstraction" based upon particular instances—the last being the separate findings from individual studies. Such generalizations are a variation of standard induction, since such induction usually focuses on all findings collectively, not on the relationship between originals and adjacents.

When *projecting*, one is either entirely extrapolating or is doing so to some extent. (The latter instance does involve generalizing, but to a quantitatively minimal base. See case B, below.) Specifically, one is either extrapolating from the original target's findings to an adjacent or more distant target for which no findings yet exist, or one is generalizing to a target for which no more than one finding exists.

To facilitate the discussion, the term *generalization* will cover summaries as well as projections—and their related, respective case A and case B situations. Though generalization will include extrapolation, extrapolation will sometimes be specified as such.

In case A, an adjacent target has been the subject of at least two studies, each of which yielded results similar to those associated with the original target. These results will be called "supportive findings"—ones that support/strengthen those from the original target.[31] (In our examples, both the supportive and original findings will be *positive*. That is, they will involve a positive relationship between the program and its outcome. Preferably, both the supportive and original findings would be based on guide programs.) We will later mention case B, in which one generalizes or wishes to generalize from an original target to an adjacent or more distant one for which either *no* studies or no more than *one* was conducted.

Regarding case A, the supportive findings one obtains for adjacent targets are, by definition, essential for the empirical portion of what might be called an "appropriate" generalization, that is, one which is logically and empirically justifiable. ("Appropriate" characterizes the product, not the process; and the generalization need not be indisputable.) We hypothesize that supportive findings associated with adjacent targets may have more influence on generalizability than on reliability. This reflects the assumption that such findings, which by definition only occur in connection with adjacent and more distant target-studies, have more intrinsic relevance to generalizability than to reliability. That, in turn, rests on the following: generalizability, by definition, logically requires some type or degree of *difference*; and "adjacence" (as in "adjacent targets") intrinsically involves difference—here, difference from the original target. In some contrast, reliability—which emphasizes stability, sameness, or repetition—focuses more on *similarity or identity*. Since the latter qualities tilt away from difference or change—and, therefore, from adjacence— supportive findings associated with adjacent targets are more intrinsic to generalizability than to reliability; and that which is more intrinsic may have more influence, or presumably could have more.

(The above distinctions do not mean that [1] adjacent targets can share nothing with the original one—in particular, that the former and latter can have no content overlap in real-life operations. Nor do the distinctions imply that [2] findings associated with adjacent targets hardly affect reliability itself. Instead, [1] and [2]—especially [2]—largely involve differing degrees and emphases, not either/or's and complete contrasts.)

Logic and Statistics   Given the above, if *(a)* a target exists that differs from an original one, say, from the males aged 18 to 21, and if *(b)* that adjacent target is associated with studies whose findings are similar or identical to those of the original, the following could be the case: Logical/ analytical preconditions would exist, as would empirical findings, for generalizing the original target's findings to those of the adjacent target. Restated, a conceptual/analytical base for generalizing would exist, as would a substantive connection: Regarding the base, see the differing targets in *(a)*; as to the connection, see the similar—thus, supportive— outcomes in *(b)*.[32] The adjacent-target findings could provide empirical support and in that sense could help justify the specific generalization; prior to that, however, the basic conceptual/analytical structure would have made generalization itself logically possible. Under these conditions, then, a relevant connection would exist between the original and adjacent targets, and one's generalization would, in principle, be justifiable and supportable.

Though logical support can establish conditions needed for generalizing, it cannot guarantee that a valid generalization will occur. In particular, it cannot by itself preclude or greatly reduce the risk of making generalizations that are inappropriate (in the sense of inaccurate). Such risk partly reflects the widespread presence of "noise" or error variance, which often centers on unreliable independent and/or dependent measures.[33] Inappropriate generalizations, in the above sense, can be distinguished from generalizations that are empirically unsupported or minimally supported but which may or may not be *inaccurate*. The latter generalizations involve the case B situation—in which either no study or one study has been conducted (thus, "unsupported" and "minimally supported," respectively). As indicated, these generalizations/extrapolations may sometimes be "on track," that is, accurate or partly correct; they should not ipso facto be considered invalid/inappropriate. Nevertheless, logical support cannot, by itself, guarantee the appropriateness of these generalizations, either.

To sharply reduce the risk of making inappropriate generalizations, one must move beyond the logical foundation and establish a sufficient statistical base. The latter would involve findings from a number of adjacent-target programs, not just one. Although the presence of *one* supportive finding[34] would mean that one's generalization is no longer entirely unsupported, and though this itself would *substantially reduce* the risk of making an inappropriate generalization, this one finding (namely, the *only* finding associated with the one adjacent-target program) would by no means minimize or markedly reduce that risk. That is, a substantial risk of drawing an erroneous conclusion would remain, and one would not be able to fairly confidently generalize one's findings from the original target to the adjacent one. Again, this is apart from the fact that the supportive finding from the adjacent target—a finding which, in fact, is a partial replication—would make an important quantitative and qualitative difference compared to having no such finding at all. This is especially true if the adjacent-target's program were a "guide," or "prominent" (as described earlier), and, in any event, if no separate findings were nonsupportive or oppositional.

Content-related Factors Critical though numbers can be in markedly reducing risk, content-related factors can independently influence this dimension and thereby affect the accuracy of any generalization. For instance, as explained below, the extent to which a generalization can be supported may be influenced by such factors as the following, ones that may also affect the chance of obtaining any support in the first place:

1. the particular analytic category that comprises or dominates the original target
2. the direction of the generalization

(Depending on the adjacent target's sample-size, the influence of these factors would rapidly escalate and then—also rapidly—would theoretically taper off.)

Thus, for example, regarding *particular analytic categories*, one's generalization from subjects aged 13 to 15 (the original target) to those aged 16 to 18 (the adjacent target), on the one hand, may be more accurate than that from those aged 16 to 18 to those aged 19 to 21, on the other. It may be more accurate because it might be easier to make. For instance, other factors (e.g., number of adjacent-target studies) being equal, this differential accuracy could reflect differences in the respective sets of individuals' sociopsychological make-up and in their overall situation within contemporary American society.[35] More precisely, it could reflect *differential* degrees and/or types of complexity that exist between them. In short, the chances of accurately generalizing could be different for one set of individuals than for the other, if, say, the type and/or amount of difference that exists across the categories that comprise the first set (i.e., the difference between those aged 13 to 15 and those aged 16 to 18 and those 19 to 21). Thus, there could be either more or less content overlap in one set than in the other.

Also, as suggested, the chances that an original target will obtain *any support* from its adjacent-target studies may be different for one set of individuals than for another, even if the sets' respective sample-sizes are identical in all regards. This situation focuses, for instance, not on differential complexity, but on differences in the extent to which the respective adjacent targets are simply *the same as* their respective "originals." Thus, we would hypothesize that if the individuals within a given set of *adjacent*-target studies (ATSs) are more similar to each other than are the persons in a second set of ATSs, the studies that comprise the first set of adjacent targets are, collectively, more likely to support the *original* target-study's results than are those from the second-set. This, again, involves the likelihood of support, not accuracy of the generalization itself.

As to *direction of the generalization*, the same considerations apply. Thus, for example, one could perhaps generalize more accurately when moving from an original target comprising subjects aged *13 to 15* "up to" an adjacent target consisting mostly of those aged 16 to 18 than from an original group of subjects aged *19 to 21* "down to" adjacents aged 16 to 18. Also, as before, one might be more likely to obtain supportive results in the first place—or a higher ratio of support to nonsupport—when moving in one direction rather than another.

The above discussion suggests that the accuracy of a generalization may vary depending on "what" one started with and "where" one is going, that is, on the nature of the original and adjacent targets and on specified relationships between them. The following suggests that distance, that is, "how far" one generalizes, may matter as well. This situation may reflect not distance per se but various content differences that exist between the studies that comprise an original target-sample, on the one hand, and those comprising either their more distant or their less distant adjacent-targets, on the other.

Though the preceding would apply regardless of sample size, let us say—for purposes of illustration—that *no* studies had been conducted in an adjacent target-area to which one might wish to generalize (extrapolate) an original set of findings.[36] Under this condition, the risk of making an erroneous generalization would probably increase quite rapidly the further one generalizes from the original target.[37] (Moreover, any such error might be larger than one that could occur with a less distant target, however likely or unlikely the error itself might be.) For instance, the chance of making such an error might be considerably larger if one generalized from a group aged 16 to 18 to one aged *25 to 29* than from that younger group to one aged *20 to 23*. The same type of risk would exist even if *one* study had been conducted in the adjacent target-area and if that study yielded a supportive finding. However, the degree of risk—particularly of substantial error—would probably be considerably less than if no study existed.

Implicit in these considerations is the following: If a number of studies had been conducted in a relatively "distant" target area and if supportive findings were obtained for that area, empirical grounds would exist for generalizing *more broadly* than if such findings existed for less distant targets only or for one that was literally adjacent.[38] Of course, without those grounds, one would—by the same token, be taking a larger risk when generalizing from the original to the more distant targets.

Summative and Ampliative Generalizations   Thus far we have only focused on the task of generalizing from one target area to another—from an original to an adjacent. This is different than focusing on a general statement which, in effect, summarizes the main results from several particular studies that were all found within a *single* target area, namely, the "original" area (e.g., persons aged 18 to 21). The latter type of generalization involves induction in its more typical sense: the derivation of general conclusions from several specific instances. In the present context, this would involve a statement which reflected the fact that the findings from programs that all fall within an original target area largely support an overall conclusion about those same, original target programs collectively. This statement would thus convey the main thrust of the individual findings. As such, it would be more a summary or abstraction than an extension or amplification.

Such statements, or generalizations within a single area, have not been focused on in the present discussion. Instead, the presentation has involved statements regarding the relationship between findings for an original target's studies and those for an adjacent target. Statements, that is, generalizations, regarding this relationship expand upon or amplify the original target's findings in the sense of asserting (or else challenging) their possible broader applicability. As a result, they can be called "across-target" or "ampliative" generalizations, rather than "within-target," that is, single-target, or summative ones (von Wright, 1972).

Ideally, these generalizations from an original target-area to an adjacent one would be based on at least one partial replication, that is, on some empirical support from at least one study found in other than the original area itself. Yet, it is scientifically and pragmatically appropriate as well as important to suggest hypotheses—here, to suggest extrapolations—that as yet *lack* such support. Specifically, such hypothesizing is no less legitimate and important within corrections than in other fields. But the hypotheses should be specified as such and their risks should be recognized—as, in fact, might those of *not* hypothesizing.[39] (At any rate, such extrapolations involve the case B situation in which *no* studies exist within the adjacent or more distant target-area; they are thus a form of prediction. Regarding distinctions within case B, see the subsection titled "Terms and Approach," earlier in the present section ["Factors Relating to Generalization"].)

Quantity and Quality By increasing the number of studies even moderately, one would probably increase the number of content similarities—that is, the average number of similarities per program—that exist between programs associated with an "original" target, on the one hand, and those associated with an "adjacent," on the other.[40] This applies whether or not the adjacent target is literally contiguous with the original and whether—if not contiguous—the former is close to or distant from the latter.

Increased sample size and greater similarity (content overlap) can do more than substantially broaden the logical base for an ampliative generalization: They can increase reliability—statistical/empirical strength—as well, since they pave the way for, and/or may directly involve, partial replication itself.[41] The prominent-programs procedure or other approach could be used to carefully increase sample size and thereby initiate this process. To be sure, programs that are added via procedures which differ from those such as prominent programs may conceivably yield a sizable proportion of *non*supportive or even specifically oppositional findings and might thereby weaken or undo any current generalization, or may preclude an otherwise expected one. Yet even if such findings appeared, the added programs from which they sprang could have improved reliability; and—most important—the findings would have increased overall accuracy and broadened knowledge.

Whatever the quantity of added studies—and regardless of their portion that may be partial replications—the *quality* of information available in the original and adjacent target-areas will sometimes be too poor to justify ampliative generalizations or any related cross-target conclusions at the time. However, even this quality shortfall should not by itself prevent one from hypothesizing and extrapolating, particularly when no immediate alternatives to knowledge building present themselves and provided one's conclusions or generalizations are carefully qualified. Hypothesis testing is scientifically justified whenever a need for increased knowledge exists. As to the plausibility and relevance of a given hypothesis, that is a separate matter.

Knowledge Building as Process

Generalizations and conclusions that are justified and strong can increasingly appear if and as well-designed studies accumulate in the given adjacent target area and as they are analyzed collectively. In a small-sample context, that is, when few studies exist, this increasing strength may be more noticeable and rapid if one has emphasized and/or continues to emphasize guide and prominent programs, particularly if these are well described. Thus, to warrant continued exploration, ampliative generations or conclusions, and the individual findings on which they are based, need not be virtually unambiguous from early on; indeed, they are not likely to be, if they involve few studies at that time. Whether these generalizations do in fact end up stronger and clearer in the long run, and whether they—in any event—support or oppose given predictions, they can, in the meantime, be considered reasonable steps, in fact necessary steps, in knowledge building.

Accurate Insights   Strong, resilient insights about the nature of effective intervention will seldom emerge full-blown, swiftly, and/or from very few studies—unless, perhaps, the quality and depth of these studies are outstanding. Nor, on the other hand, will such insights almost automatically "fall into place" once a large and presumably critical mass of studies has accumulated (especially if the design quality of those accumulated studies is, on the average, mediocre). Instead, accurate insights about effective intervention for given targets often emerge and take shape progressively—as sound individual studies and their findings keep accumulating. These step-by-step gains pertain to ampliative and summative generalizations alike. They involve specific *content*, that is, a discovery of such content, not the relationship between one target's findings and another target. That is, the gains bear on an increasing knowledge of relevant content, not on whether an original target's findings *(a)* are either similar or not similar to those of an adjacent target (case A) or *(b)* either can or cannot be extrapolated to an adjacent target (case B).

Sometimes, the development of such knowledge could be greatly assisted by a series of analytically coordinated studies, including, for example, the systematic variations mentioned earlier. Yet, other studies, ones that are not specifically or purposely coordinated by and across various researchers, could also contribute substantially. Studies of this type are generated and implemented rather independently of each other and are the most common ones to date. Yet, although accurate insights could be and sometimes have been developed independent of analytic coordination, such knowledge would almost certainly be sharpened and often accelerated by such interstudy efforts.

The development of strong, relevant insights depends on more than analytic coordination, important though this strategy may be. In particular, individual E-programs should contain a range of information, by means of which one can descriptively reflect their various parts, especially any parts found relevant in terms of outcome. Such information would include details regarding program operations, staff, clients, and setting, among others—these being the main content-bases for differentiated analyses and related, subsequent syntheses. This would apply whether or not but especially if the average complexity of future programs were to increase. Where possible, administrative and organizational factors should be examined as well, since they, like the broader sociopolitical setting and climate itself, can help clarify a program's dynamics, impact, and prospects.

The preceding discussion applies to the global and building-block approaches alike. Yet, even if these were to meet various qualitative and quantitative conditions and requirements that have been discussed, and whether or not a long-term, coordinated search-strategy were to be used, their respective contributions might differ in important ways. For one thing, it might well turn out, as suggested earlier, that only the global approach would uncover and adequately reflect certain key patterns and interactions underlying many effective programs. Yet even if this were true (as we believe it is), the building-block method could provide accurate and relevant insights of its own, especially if long-term, coordinated efforts *were* to be involved. All in all, progress could occur simultaneously at differing levels; both it and any eventual strong conclusions could take various forms as well. These differing aspects of reality could be addressed, approached, and reflected via complementary means, such as the global and building-block approaches.

Inductive Logic One can safely assume that some risk of error will always exist when generalizing or predicting from one category or target to another and even when drawing a general conclusion about results from various individual studies within just one category or target. Yet standard, relatively uncomplicated logic, operating in the context of commonsense induction, can often substantially reduce those risks. Operating jointly, these basic tools for hypothesis testing and knowledge building might be called the "logical-inductive" approach. At any given point this approach could help one determine approximately when, where, and how far one might justifiably generalize, whether in the sense of summarizing or amplifying. In these roles, the logical-inductive approach could be particularly important when the potential for sizable error is largest. This would probably occur *(a)* when it is applied to relatively small samples (as in, but not limited to, the guide-programs procedure) and, in any event, *(b)* especially during early stages of knowledge building. Whatever the context, this approach would not be used simply or mainly because statistical tests may be absent.

Whether in ampliative or summative contexts, utilization of the logical-inductive approach does not guarantee strong or even sharply delineated results. Moreover, the knowledge-building process that draws on this approach is not cut and dried and devoid of uncertainty, judgment calls, and/or subjectivity, let alone room for improvement. Nevertheless, the logical-inductive approach is a framework for drawing reasonable and properly qualified conclusions; at least, it provides an opportunity to do so.

Continued Realities and Needs

In short, progress in evaluating and improving correctional intervention can be made by using a logical-inductive framework plus various innovations or adjustments. This is true even though *(a)* error variance and its consequences will persist at various levels and although *(b)* some— perhaps considerable—ambiguity and uncertainty will remain, even if larger samples exist and statistical tests are used. Yet progress can be made despite risks and limitations; and advances in recent decades— certainly during the eighties—support this view.

Thus, although the preceding indicates there are unavoidable limits to knowledge and suggests these may sometimes be substantial, it also indicates that significant progress is possible, and it implies that this continues to be so. The possibility that progress can occur—indeed, the fact that some knowledge about correctional intervention *has* been continuously gained during recent decades—this, in itself, has undoubtedly provided and can continue to provide a scientific incentive for research. Another type of incentive would derive from the fact that many practitioners, policy makers, and others believe that numerous interventions should be and *need* to be improved and that this can occur via increased knowledge. In particular, relatively few *practitioners*—seasoned and otherwise— seem to believe that existing programs, collectively, are of high enough quality to adequately address today's and tomorrow's need for effective intervention.[42] This view appears to be held by many researchers and policy makers as well, and it is not inconsistent with the growing belief that many individual programs and some *types* of programs have shown promise—though even more have not—with a fair proportion of clients (Palmer, 1992).

At any rate, few individuals would probably dispute the need for improvement, whether they consider this need widespread or otherwise strong. Obviously, the basic alternative to change and possible improvement is to largely maintain the status quo. The latter choice, however, probably has limited appeal to many persons in corrections; and, today, it is perhaps considered increasingly untenable given the apparent need for improved programming. (At any rate, maintenance of the status quo would be unnecessary, given the fact that improved research methods and strategies can better identify effective programs and their ingredients.) This limited appeal probably exists independently of whether the individuals in question believe that *enough* progress, or even considerable progress, is likely to occur during the next several years.[43] In any event, most practitioners and, quite possibly, most policy makers, recognize and accept the idea that change which is based on carefully tested information is more likely to succeed than that which stems form hunch and hurry, or even from practical experience alone (without much hurry). This recognition, and so on, is likely to further stimulate scientific and other careful testing. At any rate, the above feelings and views, taken together, are likely to support continued research, though not necessarily at the pace and scale many individuals would desire.

Relevant Information   Though the logical-inductive approach can guide analyses and interpretations along justified lines and can thus make scientific progress formally possible, only relevant information can give this process practical and/or theoretical value. Absent such information—in particular, without data regarding variables that may predict positive outcome—there can be little meaningful knowledge to build and little empirical or systematically tested basis for program development or improvement. Even adequate designs, samples, and sampling cannot, by themselves, meet this specific content-need—in essence, a need for relevance regarding desired outcomes.

To begin addressing this need, a wide range of variables, such as those illustrated in chapter 7, must first be delineated. These variables would involve program operations, staff, setting, and so on, and their relationship to desired outcomes would be explored via the building-block method, the global approach, and/or others. To develop insights into what makes programs work, the ability of these and other variables to predict positive outcomes would best be studied across lines that have traditionally separated program domains from each other. In particular, such variables (features, characteristics) would best be examined together with other such features that may also be found in other "types" of programs. Thus, for example, variables found in VT programs would be studied together with those found in GC and/or "cognitive-behavioral" programs. Moreover, these variables would have to be studied in combinations, not just as one variable at a time.

Innovations   Finally, when planning and implementing future intervention and research, unusual or possibly original approaches should be encouraged in principle and explored whenever feasible. Such efforts would complement or at least supplement those which focus on already existing ideas and programs. The new or innovative approaches would include concepts as well as programs and services. They could involve, for instance, not only *(a)* programs whose techniques, underlying assumptions, and/or main areas of focus are relatively unusual or even novel but also *(b)* alternative operating principles and organizational/interagency/intergovernmental (even state/local and public/private) arrangements. The *(b)* factors could occur in the context of new *or* existing programs, structures, and services.

These different arrangements, perspectives, emphases, and applications may in some cases directly improve or otherwise bolster existing operations, ones that are not necessarily failing. In other instances they may help bypass or obviate what could otherwise be, or what already are, substantial obstacles or impasses in real-life program implementation. Equally important, but not always related to this situation, the innovative concepts, programs, and/or services may revitalize many practitioners' efforts; and—especially—they may improve many programs that have long "run on automatic" but have either lost some of their original relevance and power or never fully realized their potential (Duffee and McGarrell, 1990; McShane and Williams, 1989).

Though even innovative approaches are not guaranteed to work, they, like basic replications and systematic-variation studies themselves, should be implemented whenever possible. Regarding innovations, this is particularly true if existing operations seem inadequate and if programs that appear promising in related settings nevertheless seem unavailable, unacceptable (e.g., politically or philosophically), or otherwise unfeasible at the time. In any event, innovations that are implemented and experimentally studied can then be added to programs which are already part of one's regular analysis; and they can be examined separately as well.

Implementing the Global Approach: Summary of Main Steps   1. Select a principal target of study—say, a category of offenders (e.g., urban males, aged 16 to 19) who have been focused on in many programs conducted within a given type of setting (e.g., an institution). 2. From among the many programs identified in step 1, select only those in which the E-program clearly outperformed its C—using, say, the guide- or prominent-programs performance-standard. 3. For each program selected in step 2, record descriptive information on as many of its specific operations, staff, offender, and setting features/combinations (F/Cs) as possible. 4. Compare step 3's F/Cs with each other, to see which ones were commonly shared by the respective, step 2 programs. 5. Utilize commonly shared F/Cs as major or central elements in the creation of new programs.

Chapter 10

Complexities, Tools, and Priorities

This chapter first reviews the need for multiple-features analysis—combinations research— in order to adequately describe and understand the complexities of real-life interventions. The chapter points out the implications of single-feature analysis for the findings and conclusions presented in chapters 3 and 4, and it suggests that although complete or absolute knowledge may be unattainable regardless of one's approach, multiple-features analysis may still produce reasonable insights. The chapter then describes recent advances in meta-analysis, and it concludes that research, in the coming decade or so, should nevertheless give top priority to the global and building-block approaches and, in any event, to examining *why*, not whether, given interventions work.

STUDYING COMPLEXITY

A program's effects on outcome may be called "complex" if *(a)* a number of program features contribute to that outcome or if *(b)* the effects of any feature vary across targets. Here, we will focus on item *(a)*, and we hypothesize that programs—interventions—are often complex in that two or more programs inputs (together called "multiple features") contribute to outcome. We further assume the contributions of those features may be substantial and may involve staff, setting, clients, organizational factors, and so on. However, to simplify the presentation we will emphasize only program features—the characteristics most often studied to date.

 To better examine this presumed complexity, researchers, in the future, should de-emphasize the type of analysis that has been typical to date—one that chiefly or exclusively focuses on a salient, most salient, or seemingly dominant E-program feature.[1] This feature—for example, "educational training" or "counseling"—has been used to analytically distinguish the E-program from its more traditional C, and it has ordinarily been studied to the exclusion or near exclusion of all others that may have existed in the E-program. Accordingly, this feature, or input, has implicitly or explicitly been assumed to account for *(a)* whatever E/C outcome-difference emerged, *(b)* whatever such E/C difference "really mattered," or at least *(c)* enough of whatever mattered. However, insofar as the E/C outcome-difference was actually produced by two or more features, this account has oversimplified reality.

Multiple-features Analysis

To examine intervention's complexity with respect to outcome—to even recognize and perhaps records its multiple features in the first place—the research strategy that predominated in the eighties and earlier will not suffice. There, effectiveness analyses were mainly organized around single-feature or unimodal questions such as, Does educational training work? or—separately—Does counseling work? To be sure, such questions were relevant and can remain relevant in the nineties and beyond, especially if they are better focused—for instance, Which *kinds* of counseling work? Yet, better-focused questions can be explored only if detailed information exists, in this case multiple-feature information.[2]

To examine complexity, information about a program's multiple features is, by definition, essential; however, it is not necessarily enough: Such information would not, by itself, virtually ensure the occurrence of proportionately fewer single-feature or unimodal analyses, even if they involved better-focused questions. What is needed in order to essentially guarantee fewer such analyses and to also move in a new direction is a different scope and focus for research—together, of course, with appropriate tools. (Here, we will discuss scope and focus only, i.e., content.) More specifically, to de-emphasize single-feature analyses and to examine hypothesized multiple contributors instead, researchers would have to increasingly ask such questions as, What *combinations* of educational training, counseling, and additional program components/techniques substantially contribute to effectiveness?[3] To further increase scope, other *types* of contributors, such as staff and setting, would be explored as well, preferably in interaction with the above.

We believe a strong, first-time emphasis on multiple-features analysis is now in order, within and across the various types of contributors; at least, such analyses should soon begin and should rapidly increase in proportion to the total. These analyses would reflect such assumptions as the following: *(a)* an "educational training" program is not *just* educational training and a "counseling" program involves more than counseling; *(b)* *who* implements a program and the conditions under which it occurs also matter; and *(c)* the added factors involved in *(a)* and *(b)* can often affect outcome substantially, not just slightly. The building-block and global approaches are tools for accommodating such assumptions and thereby examining multiple inputs. Based on multifeatures analyses carried out via such tools, outcomes associated with groups of studies may thus be shown to reflect the contributions of two or more features.

Analyses that focus on multiple inputs and on combinations of features per se could, we believe, better represent the frequent complexities of real-life operations. At the very least, results from such analyses could provide an empirical basis for reducing or eliminating possible blanket responses to the above-mentioned questions—responses such as "educational training works," "counseling does not work," "behavioral approaches work (or do not work)," and "probation enhancements do not work."[4] Using the first example, an empirical basis would, of course, exist only if the results clearly suggest that "educational training" *is*, in fact, not the sole component. That is, the results would have to contradict or otherwise not support a blanket response.

Complete Versus Partial Knowledge

Whatever results are obtained, they, like other scientific findings, would constitute a packet of information from which logically acceptable and probabilistically supportable conclusions could and should be drawn. However, they could neither "force" such conclusions to be drawn nor prevent unwarranted ones from appearing. Moreover, even if *(a)* proper reasoning were used, *(b)* supportable conclusions were drawn, and *(c)* multiple-features analyses were involved, those steps, collectively, could not guarantee that the conclusions in question would constitute *complete* knowledge. Specifically, even if one's conclusions were supportable and detailed, and, say, even if they consisted of relevant content alone, this would not necessarily mean they constituted or otherwise provided a complete rather than partial insight regarding such questions as, What *combinations . . .* contribute substantially to effectiveness?

Basically, this limitation exists because one can never be sure that all factors are present and accounted for and that "noise" has hardly entered the picture. Indeed, this ultimate uncertainty—in effect, a lack of "absolute" (apodictic) knowledge—exists in all sciences. This is despite the fact that considerable confidence—and a confidence that is empirically justified—can exist as well. At any rate, some factors might not have been included in the analysis—and may therefore not have been reflected in one's conclusions—even though the factors *did*, in reality, contribute to given programs' success. This type of situation, and ultimate limitation, could exist even though the given results may rather adequately account for the oucome in a practical sense and although they may thus be useful in various respects.

Moreover, the limitation in question may exist even if one's conclusions were based on a series of studies that were well planned and implemented—a series that, say, might have included partial replications and purposive variations. To be sure, such a series would probably go a long way toward identifying all substantial contributors and perhaps several minor ones. In that respect it would likely provide well-rounded answers, ones that might often account for the preponderance of outcome variance; this might even apply to interventions whose structure and daily operations are rather complex. Nevertheless, even if somewhat simpler but still multifeature interventions are involved, one should not expect to account for literally all outcome variance, even via a well-planned research strategy.

Given adequate research designs and data, multifeatures analyses may produce reasonable insights even without the above series: they may often provide well-rounded and relevant results, ones that are of good quality and may account for most of the variance. Yet, because those results or insights *are* partial—partial in the sense of incomplete, not erroneous or inaccurate per se—they should perhaps be described as "accurate, but only up to a point"; that is, they move in the right, not wrong, direction but do not go all the way. Depending on just where that "point" is or on how far they move, their value could vary considerably, as may their potential for misinterpretation.

Though findings based on multiple-features analyses may not account for all known *variance*, they could, collectively, still make it clear that *multiple*, not single, inputs contribute to the outcome. That is, one need not identify every possible contributor in order to demonstrate that more than one is involved. Basic though it may be, this demonstration could play an important role itself. It could reduce the chances of drawing overly generalized and inappropriately simplified conclusions about the impact of any one feature, whether or not that feature is salient. Thus, for example, multifeatures analyses could reduce the likelihood that researchers, practitioners, policy makers, or others would inappropriately extoll or, in contrast, summarily dismiss, a given component or approach.

Portions of Reality

As implied, various present-day limitations were generated by analytic emphasis on only one program component (the "A-component"). More specifically, they were triggered by the exclusive or nearly exclusive use of a component which—though perhaps indeed salient, and possibly quite influential—had been separated, for analytic reasons, from the remaining components ("B-components"). In fact, no B-components might have been analyzed at all, as opposed to being examined separately—superficially or not. Moreover, B's might not even have been differentiated and recorded in the first place.

In any event, if no feature other than the A-component was used when studying the relationship between program input and program outcome, the following might have occurred: That particular feature may subsequently have been presented and/or interpreted—implicitly, inadvertently, or not—as if it *(a)* was the *entire* program (say, the one labeled "educational training"), *(b)* adequately *reflected* that program (without being the whole thing), or *(c)* otherwise represented all that *mattered* in the program. In reality, however, that feature might have been—or done—none of the above. At any rate, it might or might not have been decisive or perhaps even predominant; and had it been combined with any or all B-components its effect on outcome might have differed in degree and occasionally direction.

Thus, the findings summarized in chapter 4 regarding features that have seemed the most and least successful are, indeed, accurate, but in a restricted sense: They correctly identify individual *portions* of programs often associated with recidivism reduction or an absence thereof—portions, that is, features, which were commonly abstracted as generic categories. Yet, except for truly unimodal operations—whose representation in the totality of correctional programming is unknown but may be moderate at best—those identified features are indeed only *portions* of the respective, overall programs in which they appear. As such, they comprise slices of reality, but ones that are not necessarily *(a)* representative albeit abridged versions of actual programs, *(b)* isomorphic miniatures or capsule versions of such programs, or, in a sense, *(c)* broadly based samples thereof.

In short, we believe these slices or portions often may not adequately distill, convey, and represent various details or patterns—that is, B-component "realities" (aspects)—of the programs they help comprise.[5] In particular, those portions or features may not sufficiently, let alone entirely, reflect certain aspects that happen to be important or even critical. In these respects, for example, a given portion (an A-component) might not come close to representing a particular program's "essence," and/or to reflecting all its important features.

At any rate, the A-component may not fully or even largely account for given *outcomes*, because B-components—that is, other portions of the respective programs—may themselves contribute to those outcomes, individually or collectively.[6] In addition, unless B-components are present and analyzed in a given study or group of studies, A's importance (actually, its relative contribution), will very likely seem larger than it really is; and the B-components,' in any event, will have no chance to be known. This would apply even if A may often *have* been important and possibly even essential with regard to the outcomes, whether or not it was decisive per se.

Thus, the conclusions drawn in chapter *4* about the most and least promising approaches could themselves be misleading unless carefully qualified in light of the possible or probable role of *(a)* multiple features (each acting rather independently) and/or *(b)* combinations of individual features (in considerable interaction). This danger exists even though the chapter's conclusions contain important kernels of truth, integrate considerable information and widen perspectives, and provide leads for future research and programming. As such, they constitute information about correctional effectiveness that is more broadly based or reliable than before, though far from complete. (Note: Here, "information" is an outcome—a product of various inputs and processes. Elsewhere, it is used in the sense of "data"—thus, as an analytic input rather than an outcome or integration.)

DATA PROCESSING TOOLS

Meta-analysis

Thus far we have discussed content. We now emphasize tools—specifically, ways of processing that content in order to identify important elements of success. These are elements that make substantial or even key contributions to program outcome, and together they will be called "major elements" or "major features." "Tools" and "methods" will be synonymous.

As indicated, further progress in identifying major elements of success calls for broader and more integrative analytic methods than have been used to date, for instance, ones that take fuller account of programs as composites and often-complex wholes. However, the two methods used thus far to help predict and understand success have not focused on programs as composites; these tools are meta-analysis and literature review. Since the former has been widely and increasingly considered the method of choice in assessing effectiveness and in singling out generic approaches often associated with success, its role in (and its prospects with respect to) identifying major elements of success will be briefly reviewed in the context of three specific questions that follow. Many of the comments that appear also apply to most literature reviews. (It should be kept in mind that identifying elements or features which may *contribute* to success is different than determining whether given programs or types of programs *are* successful. Meta-analysis has succeeded on the latter score.)

Is meta-analysis essential? Meta-analysis is not *required* in order to identify major elements of success. Instead, what is crucial—besides having potentially relevant content to process—is the use of well-designed studies and well-described programs, ones that are also differentially analyzed. Meta-analysis can nevertheless contribute at various stages of knowledge building. In particular, it can tease out elements that might be called "initial possibilities," that is, "leads" or "suspects," and it can later close in on both them and others.

Yet, in developing accurate insights, meta-analysis is still not a sina qua non. This is because alternative approaches, such as the global and building-block, may achieve those ends and may certainly promote them. Moreover, even apart from such alternatives (say that none exist), a general question would arise: How well can meta-analysis itself develop accurate insights as to why intervention works? Insofar as these insights must, by definition, help explain the frequent complexities of actual program operations—and must help account for the relationship between inputs and oucomes—those insights must rest on the ability of meta-analysis to identify features and combinations of features that contribute to those complexities and outcomes.

The general question (which is stated more specifically, below) would therefore bear on this tool's present and future ability to identify single and—we hypothesize—especially *multiple* features that are empirically related to success (positive outcome). The latter features consist of elements that, in theory, jointly contribute to the effectiveness of a given program or set of programs, whether they do so simultaneously or successively. The question of whether meta-analysis—or any tool—can identify these features or combinations is one that could arise even if every study and constitutent program were well designed and thus contained explanatory potential and data that ranged from adequate to excellent.

Can meta-analysis examine and identify program complexity? To date, meta-analysis has excelled when used to determine the effectiveness of programs it collectively analyzed in terms of a *single*, salient feature— or at least one that was labeled and discussed as a unitary factor even though it was often rather obviously compound. Among these were the "cognitive" and "behavioral" approaches and diversion as well

(Gensheimer et al., 1986; Gottschalk et al., 1987; Izzo and Ross, 1990; Lipsey, 1992; Whitehead and Lab, 1989). However, meta-analysis has not been well positioned to collectively analyze those programs as, in most cases, they actually *are* (individually): either *(a)* combinations of interacting features or *(b)* composites of several features. (Both *[a]* and *[b]* involve substance, not just labeling and presentation. Point *[b]* features operate more or less independent of each other, and their respective effects on outcome are therefore largely additive.[7])

Though this situation partly springs from widespread data-inadequacies that could affect any method, it also reflects the particular way meta-analysis has been statistically focused and generally applied. At any rate, neither the data-inadequacies nor this particular focus is intrinsic to the basic concept of meta-analysis. As a result, if no other relevant restrictions exist, technical advances and different applications that involve this tool could theoretically reduce the positioning problem regarding combinations and/or composites and could thereby allow meta-analysis to better reflect more, perhaps considerably more, of intervention's reality—in particular, more of its complexity. (To be sure, before meta-analysis or any other tool could *in fact* reflect that reality, broader and/or more detailed data would be needed.) At least, there would be no a priori reason why meta-analysis could not "identify a set or group of major elements."

Have relevant advances recently occurred in meta-analysis? Relevant technical advances and different applications have, indeed, recently begun to appear in connection with meta-analysis, albeit mostly outside corrections. (The recent advance within corrections involves Lipsey's [1992] analysis.) These bear not only on identifying multiple features but on breadth of focus as well. Specifically, three meta-analyses have recently gone beyond examining intervention as a single feature, that is, beyond studying the input side of the input/output (outcome) relationship as an undifferentiated entity or a unitary factor—quantitatively dominant or otherwise. (In the corrections context, "input" can include intervention approaches [programs], staff, and so on, and it is considered a contributor to outcome/effectiveness.)

For instance, in one meta-analysis, a specified intervention-process (namely, "cognitive reappraisal of events")—that is, a black-box feature or technique—was singled out *within* the generic "psychoeducational" area in which it was found (namely, "skills teaching"). This analysis focused on adult surgical patients (Devine, 1992). Similarly, in a separate meta-analysis, several dimensions of marital and family psychotherapy, not just the therapy as an undifferentiated entity, were studied. Again, these dimensions or features were examined as possible contributors to outcome (Shadish, 1992).

Though neither of these analyses studied the input (intervention) in terms of its possibly containing specified combinations of mutually *interacting* features, the second one did study it as a composite of individual features, for example, ones that might hardly have interacted with each other but may nevertheless have each contributed to outcome. Nor did these analyses examine outcome as a function of any combinations of input that might have been hypothesized to exist *across* major areas, such as staff, setting, and client. Still, the analyses did study areas over and beyond that of program content and/or process, per se: In one meta-analysis, several staff characteristics were examined; in the other, clients and setting were each studied.

The third meta-analysis examined interactions per se. Though these were entirely within the client area and centered on two-feature combinations, they showed (as did Lipsey) that meta-analysis can accommodate interactions. More to the immediate point, they and various noninteracting features reflected the concept of multiple contributors (Becker, 1992). (In this study, meta-analysis was used to develop correlations that became links—in effect, bases for inferring possible causation—in a path analysis that modeled the genesis of differences between boys and girls in math and science achivement.)

Given these studies, there is no question as to whether meta-analysis can identify multiple features, certainly within a single content-area; more specifically, it can identify composites or combinations of outcome-relevant inputs. Yet, even when this tool *is* technically advanced, as in the above, and even when it does identify such features or composites, it might still not reach the goal of *(a)* largely identifying and then adequately describing the frequent complexities of actual program-operations and of thereby *(b)* largely accounting for outcome. In short, identification of features/composites would not guarantee the achievement of goals *(a)* and *(b)*. (Naturally, further technical advances, and resulting analytic gains, could substantially promote those goals.)

Moreover, even under that condition, the nonachievement of goals *(a)* and *(b)* would probably be *common*, and this could mainly reflect the following: Although that condition, namely, the identification of multiple features, may often be a necessary and major step toward achieving *(a)* and *(b)*, and in that respect toward developing accurate insights, it may not always be *sufficient* for accomplishing those goals—depending, for example, on the programs' degree of complexity. (Recall that insights may be accurate as far as they go—without, however, necessarily being complete. This also applies regardless of complexity.) Simply stated, additional factors may be needed. For instance, the meta-analysis might not have identified various individual features and/or combinations that may have been essential to program operations as well as outcome. Nor may it have identified and described broader combinations of features—some called "patterns"—that might themselves be integral to both. Finally, apart from the features themselves, that is, aside from content per se, the meta-analysis may not have identified certain important sequences in the program operation—specifically, various events or conditions that typically occur or emerge in a given order.

This entire situation, which involves unidentified or perhaps only unanalyzed features, combinations, and so forth, could of course apply to any tool, including the global and building block. In fact, it almost certainly would. Moreover, even if most such factors and conditions were identified and were analyzed in one way or another, there would remain the scientific and practical matter of the extent to which, or the manner in which, they are melded together and subsequently displayed. The latter would especially bear on the achivement of goal *(a)*, above.

The issue, then, boils down to the question of how well any given tool can identify and integrate features that may be described as follows: *(a)* the content of their input-contribution ranges from relatively simple to complex (e.g., from individual features to patterns); *(b)* they may involve not just content but "form" or "structure" (e.g., sequences of individual features or of combinations thereof); and *(c)* collectively, i.e., across programs, they may be quantitatively substantial, regardless of (a) and (b). (*Note*: Features that have been integrated may be called "information"—that is, *results* per se, as distinguished from the input basis of those results, e.g., from the individual features themselves. To be sure, if individual "input" features do not end up as part of a combination of features, they can still be considered information in the sense of *results*, that is, outcomes or findings.) This issue may be reflected, for instance, in how well or even adequately a given tool—say, meta-analysis—can interrelate and display (e.g., display without unduly simplifying or seriously curtailing) various combinations that seem important or essential to programs' often-complex operations and seem likely to bear on outcome.

On balance, the global approach would seem more likely than the others to "do well" in terms of identifying and integrating the above features, especially those whose collective input-contribution is substantively complex. That is, the features may involve lengthier combinations and patterns, and/or those which cover more content-areas, such as staff and setting rather than program alone. As to features which, collectively, are *quantitatively extensive*—but which, "individually" (and especially as combinations) are substantially less complex than the above—the building-block method might do at least as well, particularly in the long-run. And again regarding features that—collectively—are quantitatively extensive, the technically advanced meta-analyses may do well in both the short- and long-run.

We believe a tool can "do well"—can, say, produce a good deal of correct and useful information—even though its program descriptions may be far from perfect and although substantial variance remains unexplained. Restated, its correct—accurate—information need not always be complete. Similarly, although any *two (or more)* tools—say, the global and meta-analysis—may each help develop accurate insights, none of those insights need be complete; yet, although both tools' insights may be *accurate*—correct as far as they go—one tool's insights may be *more complete* than the other's. For instance, it may be broader and deeper, and may account for more outcome variance as well.

Given the above, although technically advanced meta-analyses could probably produce broader and more integrated results than their present-day counterparts, those analyses should—whenever possible—probably not be substituted for the suggested *new* approaches, especially the global. This is because the latter's results—compared to the former's—are likely to be more complete and, thus, are *(a)* likely to reflect a larger number and possibly a broader range of intervention's outcome-relevant aspects and *(b) more* likely to reflect any *given* outcome-relevant aspect. In our view, many such aspects are complex, and—under most conditions—the global approach could probably analyze and integrate them better than other approaches.

Basically, we believe the global approach could produce better integrated results because of the difference in type (complexity) and range of information that it and meta-analysis would process and the difference in how the global approach would process that data. This situation mainly reflects the two approaches' differing analytic frameworks and procedures: The global involves a broader and, in functional terms, a more flexible structure and data-handling process, one that lets it first accommodate and then analyze and integrate a wider range of individual and combined features. This difference in structure and process makes it possible for the global approach's results to reflect intervention in a more integrated and complete (albeit less strictly quantified) way, even though the difference in question cannot, by itself, actually ensure the outcome. (Regarding "integration" in general, see the next section, titled "Emphasizing Totalities.")

Fourth, both despite and because of their limited focus, meta-analyses of the 1980s—together with detailed literature reviews—shed new light on the effectiveness of intervention's various generic program-components, taken individually, and on intervention as a whole—meaning, those same components analyzed collectively.[8] However, meta-analysis neither spotlighted nor otherwise focused on *staff, setting, and clients* in the 1980s, though meta-analytic results were sometimes reported for setting (Andrews et al., 1990; Izzo and Ross, 1990; Lipsey, 1992; Whitehead and Lab, 1989) and also for clients (Andrews et al., 1990; Gensheimer et al., 1986; Gottschalk et al., 1987; Lipsey, 1992; Mayer et al., 1986; Whitehead and Lab, 1989). To be sure, these meta-analyses addressed setting and clients in terms of broad and quantitatively limited dimensions only: Regarding setting, these almost entirely involved the community versus institutional/residential distinction; as to clients, they centered almost wholly on gender, age, and, to a lesser extent, offense history or recidivism risk.

Nevertheless, the contribution of meta-analysis in assessing the impact of correctional programs was major, and it helped prepare for further progress.[9] This occurred despite the fact that this approach mainly focused on generic program components, not on "black-box" processes and other factors of a more specific nature.

EMPHASIZING TOTALITIES

Some of the progress that is needed in intervention research can occur, and will probably have to occur, independent of meta-analysis. For instance, the global approach can doubtlessly facilitate important advances regardless of meta-analysis, refined or otherwise. Moreover, the global and building-block can, by themselves, advance knowledge regarding the separate impacts of features that comprise the staff, setting, and other content areas, respectively.

Beyond that, the following is particularly important with respect to the combining, juxtaposing, or other interrelating of *(a)* descriptive information as well as *(b)* program findings *across* those content areas (together, "combining" and so on will be called "integrating"): The breadth, directness, and degree of *integration* with which the global approach can probably reflect real-life operations are needed in order to adequately understand and predict program success (see point 1, below); moreover, such understanding and ability to predict may be difficult to equal via other known or presently suggested techniques, individually or collectively.[10] This situation emphasizes the integration of information, particularly that of findings which do not just focus on staff, setting, clients, and so forth *individually* but which cut across any two or more such areas. The specific features that comprise those areas may interact with each other and may contribute to outcome on the basis of combinations within as well as across areas.

Programs as Totalities

For the following interrelated reasons, programs should be examined as totalities or composites:

1. Features. Understanding and predicting program success may often require not just the identification of any one or two features but that of various combinations, broad conditions, and interactions among the program's *several* features.
2. Areas. The combinations, conditions, and so on include not just the traditional *programmatic* components, that is, not just "generic program categories" (such as individual counseling), but—collectively—widely differing nonprogrammatic aspects of the overall operation (such as staff and setting).
3. Prominence. Often, promising combinations and interactions can best or perhaps only be delineated and then hypothesized by first reviewing all known aspects of a program, not just certain prominent features—whether or not the latter are centered on the program, staff, setting, *or* client.

Together, these points imply that intervention research should emphasize the roles of and interactions among individual features that comprise the staff, setting, client, *and* programmatic areas, including those of "black-box" processes and techniques.[11] They suggest that the individual features will often have to be studied in combination with each other, whether within or across areas. Such multifeature, multiarea analyses would thus draw from all parts of a program (hence the "totalities" or "composites" designation, depending on whether those parts are mutually interacting or largely independent, respectively). This widely inclusive approach would thereby provide the framework or elbow room for the analytic integration of various features within and/or across several possible areas. That is, the framework would make this integration possible by allowing for the given variety and range to enter the analysis in the first place.

Though this prescription for multifeature, multiarea research is easier to write than fill, emphasis on such detail and breadth seems unavoidable if one is to realistically describe intervention and adequately identify the ingredients, combinations, and interactions that are important or even critical to its success. Progress in this direction can be achieved not only via the suggested new approaches—the global and building-block—but also, quite probably, by technically advanced or differently focused meta-analyses and literature reviews.[12] However, despite this probability, the best overall way to begin serious, direct movement toward a broad and detailed understanding of the relationship between program inputs and program outcomes would be to emphasize the new approaches. The global, in particular, could better reflect intervention's scope, patterns, broad conditions, and dynamics—in effect, its actual, integrated operation.

Differing Types of Progress

Certain types of progress can be made without these new approaches and even with no change in current methods. For instance, in the latter case, one could test and possibly increase *reliability* by *(a)* first replicating or partly replicating already existing programs, *(b)* then adding the new programs to those already analyzed, and *(c)* subsequently applying the present day meta-analytic and literature review approaches to that expanded sample. Similarly, one could test and possibly increase *generalizability* by *(a)* first conducting purposive variations—that is, applying existing types of programs to somewhat different targets—and by *(b)* then analyzing those variations via present-day methods. (Here, in fact, one would not need a full-blown meta-analysis or literature review, though a focused review could be useful and efficient.)

Testing reliability and generalizability, and increasing them if the results warrant it, is quite important in itself. As a result, it could justify additional analyses that use present-day, "unmodified/unrefined" tools. This would be especially true in content areas for which the sample size, that is, the number of programs, has been small, or for which the targets have been narrow.

Nevertheless, despite their importance, these advances would not move intervention research in a major direction we believe it should go, namely, that of developing more accurate, in-depth insights as to *how* effective programs are generated and maintained in real-life situations. Insofar as these insights require broader and more detailed data than are common today, they are not, for instance, likely to occur to a substantial degree by simply expanding the sample size of present-day programs or by widening given targets. This would apply whether one uses newer or older tools in order to analyze the given data. Nor are such insights likely to occur simply because one analyzes fairly *different* types of programs, that is, relatively new approaches, while still using the same limited breadth and detail.

In short, without studies of staff, setting, clients, and black-box features per se—including their combinations and interactions where possible—progress toward the goal of developing more accurate, in-depth insights may be modest at best. The importance, even centrality, of this goal does not detract from the independent value of testing/increasing reliability and/or generalizability and from that of assessing the basic effectiveness as well as power of given approaches and techniques, particularly those which are relatively new or different. Still, without knowing why a program works (for instance, which of its ingredients are particularly important or essential), one cannot systematically increase its power and efficiency; nor can one efficiently reproduce it, improve similar ones, and generate effective, well-focused new ones. To be sure, without knowing *for whom* the program works, one might target it inefficiently or inappropriately in any event. The importance of under-standing why programs work has been recently discussed at length by Cook et al. (1992), albeit in the context of meta-analysis and not only with regard to corrections.

A NEW PRIORITY

From "Whether" to "Why"

Insights as to *why* intervention works, that is, knowledge about its key ingredients, can help develop effective new programs and improve exist-ing ones. We believe the need and desire for such programs has substan-tially increased in recent years and that their development/improvement should therefore be given higher priority. Given this priority, knowledge building regarding intervention's key ingredients should itself receive higher priority, since such knowledge can help produce better programs and could conceivably become their main source.

If the suggested new tools, for example, the global, are applied to numerous, well-described experimental programs in the next several years, considerable progress could be made toward identifying key ingre-dients and combinations within ten or so years.[13] Progress could be made even if technically advanced meta-analyses and literature reviews, rather than the new tools, were applied to such programs. However, we believe the latter progress would be considerably less than the former and that, in any event, it would involve knowledge which is less integrated in nature.

This hypothesized, lesser integration and therefore insight would occur mainly because of the following: Even the advanced present-day tools would be less able than the suggested new ones—at least the global—to reflect the various combinations and patterns that help comprise real-life opeations. This would apply within and especially across the major content-areas, such as program and staff. At any rate, whether the above-mentioned difference in knowledge would in fact exist is an empirical question. At this point the logic of the matter would seem to make its existence likely, or at least a strong possibility. (Again, at issue is the quantity and quality of complex knowledge that would be associated with the differing types of tools.)

Whether new tools or advanced present-day ones are used, intervention research in the 1990s and perhaps beyond should no longer give top priority to the question of *whether* intervention works. The question, Does it work? should be de-emphasized especially, but not only, in relation to "generic program approaches"—these being operations that are analyzed as undifferentiated entities and/or interpreted as chiefly driven by a single component.

Replication Studies   De-emphasizing Does it work? or even Does generic approach X work? does not mean replications or partial replications of already completed studies should not be conducted, even if those studies *did* focus on those questions and their E-programs *were* analyzed as generic approaches. However, when replications are conducted, two interrelated principles might be considered:

1. For any program or type of program that has shown promise, for example, at $p < .05$, even a very few well done replications either can justifiably and substantially increase confidence in the original study's findings or can clearly challenge those findings and perhaps necessitate sizable qualifications.[14]
2. If one then conducts further replication studies that cover fairly similar ground, rapidly diminishing returns will likely occur and, for example, unneeded confirmation ("overkill") will exist.[15]

These principles apply whether or not one wishes to de-emphasize or, for that matter, emphasize any particular question and whether or not "generic program approaches" are involved. Parallel principles apply to purposive variations as well—thus, to the issue of generalizability. Replications, of course, address reliability.

Emphasizing "Why"   If the question, Does it work? were to dominate intervention research during the next several years, this would unnecessarily divert attention from the question that should now be emphasized: *Why* does it work? To be sure, studies that focus on "why" (Why is it effective?) must do so in connection with programs that evidently *are* effective (based on p-levels or effect sizes). Therefore Does it work? or Is it effective? must still be asked. Moreover, if that question is answered affirmatively for a given study, an answer to How effective is it? is needed for the guide-programs procedure in particular.

Though "whether effective" and "how effective" questions will remain essential, the main emphasis in data collection and analysis should and theoretically could now shift to "why." Once in place, this priority should continue for at least several years, or, quite possibly, for well over a decade if the situation so warrants. The new emphasis would be concretely reflected in the type and amount of data that are needed. That is, the priority would be operationalized in terms of the breadth and detail of required program-description—more specifically, in the greater substantive complexity that is needed to address the "why" question than the "whether and how."

The suggested new tools are designed to accommodate this descriptive complexity. Their structures, particularly that of the global approach, makes it possible to combine and otherwise integrate data in ways that can reflect either the overall program or various major patterns and interactions that characterize the program and may be integral to its operation. The resulting, comparatively rich data base can then comprise the "units," or ingredients, that are used in the final stage of the analysis: the relating of ingredients (now "inputs") to outcome (effectiveness) for an overall sample of studies. Based on this analysis, some ingredients (including combinations) will be found to contribute to success; and of *these*, some may contribute in a large portion of all programs studied and can be called "key ingredients" or major contributors.

Thus, without ignoring or devaluing such goals as the identification of effective interventions and the testing/increasing of reliability and generalizability, we venture to say it is time to place primary emphasis on the challenge of directly and systematically determining what makes intervention work. We believe this challenge can best be met by applying new tools, such as the global and building-block, to a wide range of detailed features. These tools should be given a strong and sustained opportunity to demonstrate their utility, whether or not advanced meta-analyses and/or literature reviews are used at the same time as, but independently of, them, and are sometimes even substituted for them.

Tools and Raw Material   To give these tools the opportunity in question, they should be applied to a type of content—in effect, to raw material—that has not usually been provided in intervention research: a detailed description of each program as a whole, that is, of its various facets. (Examples of specific descriptors comprise chapter 7's data-item list.) Such descriptions would not occur just in the one area that has received almost all the attention to date—namely, the programmatic (where, however, most descriptions have been rather general and quantitatively limited, not specific and extensive[16]). Instead, the descriptions would include greatly increased emphasis on the staff, setting, client, and intervention-process (black-box) areas and subarea, ones that have received little attention even at a general level.[17]

The suggested new tools could facilitate analyses of all such areas, whether in relation to general descriptors or to features that are more "detailed," for instance, more specific and quantitatively extensive. Such tools could also help focus on *combinations* of those specific, individual features—thus, on "multiple features"—that are delineated within and across areas. Individual and multiple features constitute relevant subject matter for research and practice insofar as they substantially describe and represent intervention's reality and may help generate its outcomes. They are also relevant insofar as they accurately, though not necessarily *fully*, describe intervention's targets, particularly its clients and perhaps various intermediaries.

These particular tools, the global and building block, should be used in close conjunction with such detailed content. In fact, to bring out the fuller value and power of both the tools and the content, an interdependence would have to exist between them, for the following reason: On the one hand, the potential utility of the suggested new tools would remain largely untapped if they were not used to bring out and process this relevant and often complex content; on the other hand, even the most relevant content, especially that which is complex or multiple, would largely lie fallow and unintegrated if it remains untapped and unprocessed by these or other sufficiently accommodating tools.

Part III
Technical and Conceptual Issues

Chapter 11

Success Criteria and Positive-outcome Studies

This chapter discusses two technical subjects that pertain to single- and multiple-features analysis alike. It first addresses the general subject of success criteria—indices of program effectiveness that may be reflected in such questions as, When and why are specified criteria appropriate? and, Are some criteria better than others? This topic is of basic theoretical and practical importance in studies and applications of intervention research. The chapter then presents the rationale for averaging the results from several positive-outcome studies when addressing—as in chapter 4—the question, How effective—say, in reducing recidivism—*are* programs that seem to have worked?

ISSUES AND DIRECTIONS REGARDING SUCCESS-CRITERIA

The Two-thirds Criterion

For two main reasons, the two-thirds criterion might be a useful supplement to $p < .05$, especially for policy makers and administrators (PMAs); however, it would not substitute for it. First, $p < .05$ may be difficult for many PMAs to translate into usable, everyday terms, since its meaning and concrete implications may be unclear to them. Second, and no less important, many PMAs may believe that a given approach should show a recidivism reduction in at least two-thirds of its individual programs before they can feel justified in—albeit far from comfortable about—investing substantial resources in it, that is, justified in taking a chance on it.

Such a belief might well be common and would be especially understandable if resources were difficult to obtain or divert. It could occur even if the meaning and implications of $p < .05$ *were* apparent to those policy makers and administrators and if $p < .05$ *had* been obtained for the generic category in question, that is, for the intervention approach or type of program as a whole. (For simplicity, we will assume that other factors, such as costs and operational feasibility, are considered roughly equal to those in traditional programs.) At the same time, other PMAs might want that same intervention approach to reduce recidivism at least 75–80% of the time, rather than two times out of three. In this connection they might, for example, point out that this higher frequency of past reductions, while still not a virtual guarantee of future success, would substantially reduce the risk of future failure. Like the two-thirds criterion, this somewhat stricter view might also be common, albeit equally implicit.

Pragmatic Factors

However, if either group of PMAs considers its existing approaches obvious or possible *failures* or even rather inadequate, and especially if it receives considerable external pressure to change those approaches, it might modify its above-mentioned beliefs, preferences, or requirements. More specifically, though it may not change its underlying views or assumptions about what constitutes "reasonable" or even minimum success/achievement with regard to past performance, it might still alter its views about whether and when certain approaches might prove useful in the immediate *future*, and may therefore be worth a try. For example, under the above conditions the PMAs may believe that an approach which they might otherwise have ignored *would* perhaps be worth a try, even if its individual programs, taken together, had thus far reduced recidivism no more than half or even one-third of the time, and even if, in those instances, the average reduction was modest. (We will assume that no better alternative is known or available to those PMAs and that they are not specifically concerned about whether $p < .05$ was reached for the approach as a whole, that is, for all programs combined.)

　　This suggests that what many policy makers and administrators may consider a "usable" degree of past success or achievement, that is, a degree which they believe might reasonably justify continued exploration of the given approach, may depend—often and/or largely—on factors such as the following ("continued exploration" will mean pilot-testing or full-scale use in a new or similar setting, often accompanied by experimental studies or other careful research): *(a)* the performance level of the PMAs *existing* programs; *(b)* the amount of external pressure for change; *(c)* the performance level, by the proposed *new* approach, that the PMAs would consider a significant improvement over existing programs; *(d)* the overall nature and amount of the PMAs' existing and anticipated resources; and, *(e)* the PMAs' general views regarding not only the consequences of taking and not taking small, medium, or large risks but also the nature of such risks in the first place.

Contextual judgments Such factors—even *(a)* and *(c)* alone—complicate the assessment of correctional programs, both individually and as approaches. (*Approaches, types,* and *categories* will be used synonymously, in connection with programs.) More specifically, they render it highly conditional or situational, and seldom, or in few respects, absolute. For instance, judgments about an intervention's utility, particularly in the sense of its *future promise or potential,* may vary as a function not only of the particular roles played by the assessors and of their related perspectives and needs but also of the difference or differences that the intervention seems able to make at a given time and place. (As suggested, the difference[s] may relate not only to level of program performance itself, but to degree of external pressure for change. Reducing such pressure may, in fact, sometimes be considered at least as important in the short run as producing, say, a *large* improvement in program performance. Thus, e.g., depending on the degree of pressure, many policy makers may consider the frequency of a recidivism reduction, i.e., its likelihood, more important than its amount, provided the latter is at least moderate.) Such contextual and role-related judgments would often occur even if generally accepted definitions of *reasonable success* or even *minimum success* already existed. Those definitions would have focused, not necessarily on success in connection with future promise or potential, but on *past achievements* or already existing products.

Such achievements/products may be described quantitatively, say, in terms of frequency of improvement brought about by new approaches as compared to traditional methods. One such description is reflected in the rather general two-thirds criterion or definition. There, as indicated, at least two of every three programs that were studied should have reduced recidivism when compared to their controls. Many policy makers and administrators might consider two-thirds—in and of itself, for instance, apart from the *amount* of reduction—a minimally acceptable level of past achievement. That is, based on their experiences as PMAs they might consider it a practical, generally "saleable," minimum success criterion, one that, in effect, would also provide a general guide to risk taking regarding possible future utilization. This criterion, which centers on *frequency* of improvement, would of course, be stronger if, say, at least half of the reductions in question had also reached $p < .05$ and were, in any event, other than slight. (The latter dimension, which includes such benchmarks as "slight," "moderate," and "large," involves *amount* or degree of improvement, as distinct from its frequency.)

Near-absolute judgments Though judgments about future utility may often be situational, and although assessments of future needs may even retrospectively color one's view regarding the significance or implications of an intervention's past achievements, some commonly held perspectives or "near absolutes" could exist. For instance, if a given approach had *infrequently* reduced recidivism, say, 15–20 percent of the time (and seldom to a large degree with any subpopulation), few PMAs would probably consider it successful in any major respect and therefore worth taking a chance on in their particular jurisdiction, except under unusual circumstances or pressures. In that regard, considerable agreement would exist not just on the assessment of the intervention's past achievements but regarding its future value as well.

Similarly, if an approach *almost always* reduced recidivism, say, in 85–90 percent of its individual programs, few PMAs and others would probably question its achievements or seriously challenge its potential utility as a substitute for or supplement to various existing programs. Their judgments in this regard would at least apply *(a)* if the reductions that were already obtained had often been substantial (in which case they would also have commonly reached $p < .05$) and *(b)* in connection with jurisdictions whose programs were not already considered excellent and seemingly open to little improvement. (Their judgments regarding past achievements, as distinguished from those involving potential utility, would generally not involve programs considered excellent.) Moreover, policy makers and administrators might also show considerable agreement in their assessments of the past success and potential utility of a given approach whose programs had *rather commonly* reduced recidivism, for instance, at least 75 percent of the time—if, collectively, those programs often produced fairly large reductions as well, for example, those of at least 25 percent.

Thus, as certain lower- and higher-end performance levels are approached—whether in terms of frequency of improvement, amount of improvement, or both—many people would probably make rather similar assessments. In that respect, and to that extent, "standards" of success and utility—even if implicit—would seem rather firm or reliable.

Yet, when assessing approaches that have performed anywhere *between* those relatively low and high levels, many individuals would probably disagree on where to draw the lines among *(a)* the successful, possibly successful, and unsuccessful (these distinctions involve past achievements), or at least between *(b)* approaches that "should be given a try" and those which should not (these involve potential utility). Implicitly or explicitly, such disagreements would often center on the following question: What frequency and amount of past recidivism-reduction should be required before a given approach should be considered promising or potentially useful enough to try—and, especially from the PMAs' perspective, not overly risky? (These two criteria, of course, are generally interrelated though not entirely equivalent. Frequency and amount, however, are more easily separated from each other.) However, as implied earlier, other factors, such as costs, also would typically be considered. Often of equal importance would be information regarding the possible relevance—on the part of the earlier studies—to the particular jurisdictions and organizational structures in which the given approach might be tried, and to the likely offender population as well. But in any event, recidivism—being a widely understood measure of public protection—would often remain central.

Research and Policy-maker Perspectives

The fact that judgments and resulting actions would often be situational does not preclude the development and utilization of broad guidelines. These might include, for example, a set of relevant factors and considerations—or, as it were, minimum, approximate, somewhat flexible "standards"—for jointly assessing past achievement and future value. But whatever factors might be involved, such guidelines should support a range and variety of interests and needs on the part of major contributors to intervention.

For instance, *researchers* might be mainly interested in developing new or better intervention per se, in both the short run and long run. Toward this end, they would need to test various empirically and theoretically based leads as to *why* given methods have reduced recidivism. As a result, they may sometimes wish to explore particular approaches whose majority of programs might *not* have reduced recidivism for their target populations as a whole but which nevertheless contained possibly important dimensions or techniques, say, those which seemed effective with given categories of offenders. (These considerations would also apply to, but would naturally have to be modified for, not only untried approaches but those which have rarely been studied yet which theory suggests would work. Obviously, the former could not have satisfied a two-thirds-success criterion and the latter could not have done so to a reliable degree.)

Policy makers and administrators, however, will usually be more interested in immediate or near-future utility, preferably for the preponderance of offenders. As a result, they would want guidelines to place considerably more weight on approaches that already contain programs which, collectively (say, based on a two-thirds-success criterion), seem likely to improve the PMAs current operations. That is, they would generally prefer to adopt and develop such approaches—if, in fact, they exist—than, say, to refine and otherwise explore those which, while containing positive leads regarding many offenders, have *not* already shown frequent reductions for their overall populations. Moreover, in this regard, even a relatively large average *amount* of recidivism reduction for various portions of the overall population might only partially compensate for a *frequency* of reduction that is not sizable (e.g., one that occurs fewer than two times out of every three).

Certainly from a *research* perspective, given programs may well be worth modifying, refining, and then further exploring if they or similar ones have been found to work even half the time, at least for a considerable portion of their population, or with delineated subpopulations. This would apply even if those programs had not yet been tested under a sizable range of conditions. For one thing, such programs, especially if and when refined, *may* often prove useful for a substantially broader range of offenders, circumstances, and jurisdictions than before. Yet even then, they should not have to make a relatively large or major difference for the *preponderance* in order to justify their further use and exploration. (This would apply to their earlier, that is, "first-generation" refinement and exploration as well.) In fact, to successfully address a preponderance of offenders, circumstances, and so on, a combination of approaches may be required, since few if any single approaches may be sufficiently powerful, flexible, and/or cost effective to do so. This does not mean it may not be possible, in the near or intermediate future, to achieve at least *moderate* recidivism reductions with most offenders who have comprised typical, heterogeneous—that is, unselected—populations.

Common Interests At any rate, although many policy makers and administrators may be far more interested in approaches they can already consider successful (for instance, using the two-thirds criterion) and that already seem applicable to jurisdictions and situations such as their own, this interest need not sharply or usually conflict with the above-mentioned research perspective; nevertheless, it often would produce different recommendations. Our belief that such a degree and frequency of conflict need not occur reflects at least the following fact: "Success," for one thing, does literally refer to achievements that have already occurred (again, using the two-thirds criterion). More specifically, from the perspective of many PMAs and others, "success" refers to such achievements more than to those which have thus far only shown *promise* of occurring (e.g., "promise" based on a somewhat lower but still not *low* frequency of past recidivism reduction for overall, heterogeneous populations). For instance, on the one hand, most PMAs are mainly interested in already existing achievements or at least in approaches they can consider good prospects, that is, approaches they can feel justified in using right away. Yet, on the other hand—this being a second perspective—both they and others, recognize that "potential" and "promise" are important, too—even if, for example, the approach in question may not have satisfied the two-thirds criterion of past achievement, not to mention that of 75–80 percent.

Indeed, bearing on both perspectives is the further fact that corrections presently *contains* more promise than success—at least unquestioned, certainly widespread success (e.g., "success" at, and especially beyond, the two-thirds level for overall approaches). At the same time, corrections does contain several good prospects both with respect to overall approaches as well as individual programs. These, in particular, constitute an important area of common interest for PMAs and researchers, one they can generally agree should be further developed and tested, especially regarding applicability to somewhat different offenders or settings. Moreover, such agreement would occur not just when PMAs are experiencing above-average external pressure to change various aspects of their operations and may be more willing than usual to modify their typical and preferred bases for action, and perhaps their views on risk taking.

Guideline for Decision making

At any rate, "already existing achievements," in the sense described above, need not and should not be the sole basis for determining whether to further utilize a given program or approach, let alone refine and scientifically explore it at the same time. In this connection, three items might be considered major components of a broad and flexible guideline for present-day decision making regarding the further utilization, refinement, and exploration of intervention. As will be seen, the first component would emphasize many policy makers' and administrators' fairly immediate interests, without essentially ignoring the chief concerns of most researchers. The second component would emphasize researchers' interest in knowledge building for eventual practical application, while not ignoring PMAs more immediate concerns. These components, together with the third, can be largely complementary, certainly within corrections as a whole and not just through time; this is despite the first two components' differing emphases and their respective, internal tensions.

First, if prior studies suggest that a given approach has at least a two to one chance of improving fairly typical jurisdictions' existing operations by roughly 15 percent or more in terms of reducing recidivism, that approach would definitely warrant further utilization, refinement, and exploration on grounds of past achievement as well as potential utility. This would apply *(a)* even if factors other than recidivism were equal, *(b)* whether or not the approach seemed unusually effective with given offender-groups, and *(c)* whether or not, but especially if, one-third or more—certainly half or more—of the approach's individual recidivism-reducing studies had reached $p < .05$ as well.

Second, if even one-third or possibly one-half of a given approach's prior experimental programs had fairly substantial recidivism reductions for specified *offender-groups* ("subpopulations") only (for instance, had E/C reductions averaging some 20 percent or more within those programs collectively), new or modified programs that could contain several features similar to those in the one-third or one-half would be worth establishing and exploring. In other words, the original one-third or more would merit further utilization, development, and testing—in the form of new or modified programs—even if that same group of original programs, taken together, had made little or no apparent difference with its *remaining* offenders and even if its average recidivism reduction for all offenders combined was only slight. (If the reduction for all offenders combined had been more than slight, that same one-third or more would of course be even worthier of future exploration. "All offenders combined" refers to the above-mentioned, successful offender-groups plus all remaining offenders or offender groups, analyzed as a single entity. Together, they would therefore obtain a single, average recidivism rate.)

Still more specifically, new or modified programs that could have several features similar to those in the original one-third or more should be used and researched if the new/modified programs would contain offender groups similar to those for whom recidivism was substantially reduced in the original programs, that is, in the original one-third or more. This would especially apply if those offender groups comprised a sizable portion of the overall offender population in either the prior or the new/modified programs—preferably in both. (If possible, those offender groups should receive more than their usual representation in the new/modified programs. Hopefully, they would be common in other correctional populations as well.)

The present strategy would be relevant even if one-third or more of a given approach's prior programs showed the above recidivism reductions, not for any particular offender-groups, but for specified *settings* only. It would also apply to offender/setting *combinations* that were associated with the above reductions, even if offender and setting, taken individually, were not.

Third, neither of the above components should prevent one from carefully examining certain *individual programs*, especially if they have been partly replicated at least once. The programs in question—not the overall category or categories in which they may have appeared—would be those which show substantial and reasonably reliable recidivism reduction, say, 20 percent or more, at $p < .05$. These programs may or may not have appeared in an overall category that reduced recidivism at least two-thirds of the time. This strategy may be at least as useful in both the short run and long run as that for which positive outcome was obtained in two-thirds or more of the *several* but—collectively—far more varied and, on average, probably less well replicated programs that comprise the overall category or categories in which they may have appeared. The following would be among this strategy's or suggestion's primary goals for both research and utilization: *(a)* determine whether key elements and combinations of elements in the original and replication programs are transferable to new settings and/or new offender-groups and *(b)* determine what those elements/combinations might be, in the first place. Though systematic, cumulative research is needed to essentially achieve goal *(b)* and, to a lesser extent, *(a)*, substantial and usable progress can occur with each study along the way.

Independent of the above, individual programs that have shown unusually large reductions—say, 40 percent or more (with $p < .05$) when compared to their controls—should be further explored even if replications have not yet occurred and regardless of various outcomes involving "their" overall category.

The preceding discussion suggests there is probably no universally or unconditionally "best" method or strategy (for example, no such set of steps and/or criteria) for evaluating the collective results from any given category of programs. Nor is any single, all-purpose criterion (see below) likely to be best—perhaps even sufficient—under all or most conditions. What can exist, instead, is a variety of interrelated yet separable strategies, for instance, the three components just discussed. Individually and especially collectively, such strategies, we believe, can provide useful direction and suggestions regarding the further utilization and exploration of given categories. (By themselves, these strategies are not designed to systematically *compare* categories with each other, say, along each of several dimensions.) Accompanying such strategies is the assumption that, wherever possible, evaluations of given categories should not only reflect researchers', administrators', and other individuals' specified goals regarding intervention but should also support the steps needed to implement those goals. This differentiated means/ends framework could help these strategies promote theoretically as well as pragmatically relevant assessments and decisions.

Evaluating Individual Categories

Technical Criteria   Whether independently of or in conjunction with such strategies, specific *technical criteria* could be used to evaluate the strength of individual categories; that is, they could be used separately from or in conjunction with those strategies. By themselves, they could also be used to systematically compare given categories with each other, that is, to compare them in terms of any one or more criteria. These criteria or factors would include, for instance, the *(a)* percentage of a category's studies that involve random assignment, *(b)* percentage of studies that demonstrate adequate matching, *(c)* category's breadth of coverage (thus, e.g., its generalizability and potential applicability to various offenders and settings), *(d)* quality and extent of replication among the category's studies, and *(e)* number of studies that comprise the category. For any given category, and depending on one's main goal, these criteria could be applied to all studies combined or to just those with positive outcomes. In either case, some or all such criteria could be used in various combinations; if desired, they could also be used in conjunction with the "outcome criteria" mentioned below. Together, those criteria could be developed into a *scale*, one that could be used to assess the average or overall strength of the respective categories' findings. For instance, each criterion or factor—say, factors *(a)* through *(e)*, above—could first be assigned a given weight; each category, after then being scored on each such factor, would end up with an overall scale-score. A priori cutoff points could be used to establish such designations as "strong," "acceptable," "borderline," and "weak."

   Outcome Criteria   If desired, results involving specific *outcome criteria* could be added to those from the technical criteria. For instance, additional points could be given for the *(f)* percentage of a category's studies that involve positive outcomes ($p < .05$ or not), *(g)* percentage that reach $p < .05$, *(h)* mean effect size, *(i)* average recidivism reduction, and *(j)* extent of support from other outcome measures, for instance, psychological change and community adjustment. (Since these five factors are often closely related, some may substitute for others, though different weights may be appropriate.) Other types of criteria, such as costs and operational feasibility, could be considered as well—say, to better focus on the category's prospects for immediate utilization.

   If one does wish to reflect and emphasize specific goals mentioned above, for example, short-term goals of various administrators, the relative weights of given technical criteria, say, factor *(c)*, can be increased from those which they would have received if the given criteria had *not* specifically been used to reflect those goals or if the criteria were otherwise used independently of the differentiated means/ends framework. For example, generalizability might be considered a more important goal or subgoal in some contexts than in others, particularly if immediate utilization of given approaches/programs is a key concern. To reflect or emphasize this goal, factor *(c)* might therefore be given added weight. In other contexts, however, long-term knowledge building may be considered central; here, factors *(a)* and *(b)* might therefore receive extra weight. In any event, technical criteria may often make a more discriminating and perhaps more meaningful contribution if used in conjunction with the differentiated means/ends framework than if used on their own.

Regardless of how one uses individual scores and scales that may be developed in connection with technical and outcome criteria, utilization of the three components/strategies mentioned above need not preclude certain alternative assessments that might seem more "absolute" and uncomplicated, as, for example, when either a relatively low (15–20 percent) or very high (85–90 percent) proportion of a category's programs yields positive results. Nevertheless, those components, especially when used together, can be particularly useful in all remaining situations— today's large majority—where the category's positive results, collectively, are neither that infrequent nor common.

Caution Versus Risk

One last point. For any given set of studies, say, those involving educational or vocational training, one can simply define its positive-outcome programs as those in which E outperforms C on recidivism by any amount (designation: E > C). However, to increase one's confidence that this E > C subset consists of programs in which E truly outperforms C, that is, in which chance or measurement errors do not make the difference, a more discriminating, less inclusive criterion is needed.

Exclusion Versus Inclusion To establish this criterion, the basic question is, Where should the line be drawn between including and excluding given E > C programs? Here, the goal—at least, the ideal—is not just to include all the "right" programs (truly positive programs) and *only* those programs but also to exclude all the "wrong" ones (false positives and true negatives) and *only* those programs. The underlying issues are How confident does one want to be? and, What price must be paid for that confidence? Since no universal answer exists to these questions, some pull and tug will occur regarding the desired level of caution/strictness (and its resulting exclusiveness), on the one hand, and that of risk/lenience (and its resulting inclusiveness), on the other. Moreover, wherever the line is drawn, one will still occasionally exclude some "right" programs and include some "wrong" ones.

For instance, if one makes $p < .05$ the criterion for classifying a program as truly positive (E >> C), one will still inadvertently, unavoidably, and unknowingly *exclude (a)* some programs that are indeed true positives but which, nevertheless, do not quite reach .05 because of measurement error. In addition, one will inadvertently *include* the following: *(b)* some programs in which the true recidivism rates for E's and C's are essentially the same yet whose measurement errors help E's reach .05; and, *(c)* an occasional program that is in fact truly negative (C >> E) but which still reaches .05. (Naturally, if one's minimum cutoff-point were more inclusive, say, $p < .10$, misclassifications—specifically, erroneous inclusions—of the *(b)*- and *(c)*-programs would increase.)

Yet, if one sets one's minimum inclusion-level for positive programs much *beyond* $p < .05$, say, at or especially beyond .01, one might be viewed as overly cautious, stringent, or unduly demanding. (Such an inclusion level, that is, cutoff point, may be chosen in order to exclude virtually all false positives, even at the recognized price of probably excluding some true positives.) Specifically, one might be considered too prone to exclude, not just true positives that happen to *miss $p < .05$* due to measurement error, as in the erroneously excluded programs mentioned above, but too likely to exclude still other positive-outcome programs as well, namely those which *attain* .05 and do so validly—but do not go much beyond it. These could be called "*(d)*-programs." Moreover, the number of likely exclusions may be considered sizable, not small.

Naturally, researchers or policy makers who might be viewed as overly strict may regard those who make that judgment as unduly lenient, and vice versa. Of course, individuals considered "overly strict" may be chiefly interested in not including any false positives and/or programs that they think make little difference; meanwhile, those called "overly lenient" might be much more concerned with not excluding true positives, that is, even at the price of probably including some false positives and/ or programs in which E's and C's are, in fact, *not* strikingly different from each other. In any event, when making a dichotomous judgment, more specifically, a decision to either include or exclude a given program, any change at one end of the caution/risk continuum requires some change at the other. That is, increased caution necessitates decreased risk, and vice versa. This applies whether or not one emphasizes any group of outcomes—false positives, true positives, and so on—and irrespective of one's preferred cutoff point, if any.

The p < .05 Criterion   Though one cannot simultaneously increase strictness and leniency, or, for that matter, simultaneously decrease both, a general balance seems possible. Specifically, we believe $p < .05$ is a sensible place to draw the line—a line, or criterion, that seems neither overly strict nor overly lenient (in fact, not really lenient at all). While even this criterion would not preclude all possible misclassification, it would especially reduce the number of potentially larger-scale misclassifications at *both* ends of the caution/risk (or *p*-level) continuum and would be reasonably accurate in itself, at least in adequately designed studies. (Using .05 as the cutoff, *(c)*- and *(d)*-programs, above, would exemplify larger-scale misclassifications at each end of the continuum, respectively; *(a)*- and *(b)*-programs would represent the smaller-scale ones.)

For instance, regarding accuracy and its related reduction of larger-scale misclassifications, if E's and C's have been fairly well matched in a given study, especially via randomization, an .05 outcome should be taken quite seriously and not considered very likely to be misclassified if one uses an .05 cutoff, even with a modest-size sample. To be sure, if matching but not randomization exists, .05 would probably involve more risk; and if neither matching nor randomization exists, no *p*-level can provide substantial assurance. This would apply in theoretical and practical contexts alike.

Finally, understandable concerns over whether one has erroneously included a false-positive program, even one that has reached .05, should decrease considerably under either of the following conditions: *(a)* a replication or partial replication study has produced similar results (E > C, at $p < .05$); *(b)* an .05 outcome has already been obtained for at least one other program (e.g., within the same broad category) that has several features in common with the program in question. These concerns may have reflected, not necessarily or primarily the research design itself, say, matching and randomization, but the nature of the outcome measure and data instead.

THE AVERAGING OF POSITIVE-OUTCOME STUDIES

Balancing of Distortions

The analysis of an otherwise unselected group of *positive*-outcome studies (POSs) that have been obtained from a broader population comprising all available POSs *and* negative-outcome studies (NOSs) combined—that is, from all eligible experimental studies grouped together—is not likely to produce a distorted estimate of the POS group's average recidivism reduction; nor is an analysis of the POS plus NOS group itself. Basically, this is because of the following: When any group of individual studies is analyzed *collectively*, especially if it is large, the probabilistic nature of the measurements that are analyzed (here, these are the effectiveness results) is likely to result in a general balancing-out of any upward or downward distortions that may have occurred in the measurements that were obtained for the *individual* studies which comprise that group.

Details of the preceding explanation are presented below. They focus on any group of otherwise unselected POSs for which a single outcome measurement, such as an overall recidivism rate, has been computed by averaging the results obtained from that group's individual studies, that is, by combining the separate outcome measurements reported in the respective studies. Each study has one outcome measurement, that is, one result—based on a comparison between an experimental (E) program and its control (C).

True Versus Observed Performance The possibility of distortion in the average recidivism rate of a *group* of studies that is analyzed collectively springs from the fact that the recidivism rate which is obtained for any individual program which is part of that group may not quite be that program's "true" rate, that is, the rate which, theoretically, would be obtained if one could average the results from numerous replications of the study. (*True* and *actual* will be used synonymously.) The fact that an *individual* program's *obtained* ("observed") rate may deviate from this theoretically "true" rate springs from the basic fact that any program's statistical measurement of effectiveness, such as its recidivism rate, contains "noise" (i.e., error variance, random fluctuations, etc.). This noise can and often does produce an upward or downward distortion in the measurement of that program's "true" performance level and can thereby result in the program's degree of effectiveness being misrepresented and in the program itself being erroneously categorized as successful or unsuccessful. In short, noise can produce an inflated or deflated picture of a program's *actual* effectiveness; in the present context, this involves an E-program's effectiveness as measured against the performance of its C-program. ("Successful" means E outperforms C; "unsuccessful" means C outperforms E.)

Erroneous Inclusion and Exclusion

Thus, when analyzing a *group* of E-programs that each have positive outcomes—that is, when analyzing a group of positive-outcome studies whose overall degree of recidivism is determined by averaging the differences in recidivism rates between the E- and C-programs in each of that POS group's individual studies—distortion *may* occur in the POS group's overall, average degree of recidivism reduction. Though this problem can ultimately be traced to noise that exists in *individual* programs, its immediate trigger and essential precondition centers on the erroneous categorization of individual studies—more specifically, on either their erroneous inclusion within or their erroneous exclusion from the group of positive-outcome studies (i.e., "successful" E-programs) that is being analyzed collectively. These conditions are illustrated in cases A and B, below. As will be seen, although distortion may and often does occur in the outcome measurement of individual programs and *may* therefore occur in the average recidivism rate of the POS group which those programs comprise, the chances are that the individual distortions will not in fact affect the average recidivism rate of the POS group itself— due to those distortions' balancing out, which is also discussed below.

Case A   Here, distortion may occur in the average recidivism rate of a POS group because of the erroneous *inclusion* of individual E-programs whose *true* performance levels would not have turned out to be positive if those levels could have been determined. For instance, any group of unselected positive-outcome studies (i.e., all available POS's) is likely to contain an unknown percentage of erroneously included programs— specifically, the following type of individual E-programs (here, an E- program's categorization as "positive" is based solely on its observed, that is, obtained, recidivism rate or related index, since its "true" rate/ index is, of course, unknown): those whose *observed* (known, reported) level of performance was—due to noise alone—slightly to substantially better than their *actual* (true) performance-level would have been if that level could have been determined.

In case A, for instance, an individual E-program that is included in the "POS group" may have had an *observed* recidivism rate that was 8 percentage points *lower* than—thus making its performance apparently better than—that of the C-program with which it was compared (e.g., E = 22 percent and C = 30 percent on one-year follow-up). However, if that E-program's *actual* recidivism rate (i.e., the rate that might be described as "noiseless," "theoretical," and/or "an average of many replications") had in fact been found to be *higher* than that of its C-program (e.g., if it turned out that noise had previously *decreased* the E-program's recidivism rate by 10 percentage points—from an actual 32 percent to the observed 22 percent—and if, say, that noise had not affected the C-program's rate), then the E-program would not have qualified for inclusion in the POS group—again, if that rate had been known.

Case B   However, regarding that same group of positive-outcome studies, the following would also be true: An unknown percentage of individual E-programs—but, in any event, the same percentage as in case A—is likely to have been erroneously *excluded* from the group of POSs in question. In contrast to the erroneously included programs involved in case A, these are the ones whose *actual* level of performance would have been slightly-to-substantially better than their *observed* level—again, due to noise alone.

Here, for example, an individual E-program would have been erroneously *excluded* from the POS group because it may have had an *observed* recidivism rate that was 8 percentage-points *higher* than—thus making its performance apparently worse than—that of the C-program with which it was compared (e.g., E = 30 percent and C = 22 percent). However, if that E-program's *actual* recidivism rate had in fact been found to be *lower* than that of its C-program (e.g., if it turned out that noise had previously *increased* the E-program's recidivism rate by 10 percentage points—from an actual *20 percent* to the observed 30 percent—and if, say, that noise had not affected the C-program's rate), the E-program would then have qualified for inclusion in the POS group—once again, if that actual rate had been known.

In short, although noise may and often does exist among the individual programs that comprise a given subpopulation of programs, for example, among a group of E-programs that have each been categorized as positive, the *overall* degree of noise—that is, the total measurement-error which bears on that POS group's average recidivism rate—is likely to reflect essentially the same percentage of erroneously included as erroneously excluded programs; in that connection it is likely to reflect a statistically similar or identical frequency of upward-tending and downward-tending noise, as well. In addition, the erroneously included and excluded programs are likely to be equally strong, that is, if one were to compare the performance levels of the given E-programs, collectively, with those of their C's, also collectively. (This applies to obtained levels, actual levels, or both.)

Thus, insofar as the direction and extent of noise is randomly and in effect equally distributed among programs that are erroneously included and erroneously excluded, upward-tending noise that may exist in those individual programs is likely to be counterbalanced and statistically cancelled by downward-tending noise, when findings from those programs are examined collectively. As a result, when analyzing a group of programs that report positive outcomes there is no a priori likelihood that either upward or downward bias, that is, distortion, *will* occur in the average amount of recidivism reduction that is calculated for those studies as a group, even though it *may* occur. (In case A, if the erroneously included E-programs had *not* been present, the average recidivism rate for the group of positive-outcome studies would have been *higher* than it was. This is because most such individual E-programs—by statistical chance alone—would have been those which perform only *slightly* better than their C's, thereby leaving a higher percentage of the E-programs that performed *substantially* better [these being programs that were less likely to have been *erroneously* included] to be used as a basis for computing the group average [i.e., the latter programs would have comprised a higher percentage of the total group of programs than before]. In case B, the opposite would have occurred—thereby counterbalancing the effects of A.)

Appropriate Inclusion

Equally relevant to the issue of potential distortion in an overall group's average recidivism rate are the following facts regarding any individual E-program that has been *appropriately* included among the POSs that are examined—specifically, any program whose *inclusion* was not due to upward-tending noise: *(a)* the recidivism rate of each program is just as likely to have been decreased as increased by noise alone, and *(b)* the *extent* of any noise-based decrease in recidivism rate is likely to have statistically equaled that of any increase; for instance, if the *true* recidivism rate is 25 percent, the *observed* rate—if one assumes the presence of moderate noise—is just as likely to have been 20 percent as 30 percent. (In either case, the given program would still have been appropriately included among the positive-outcome studies if the observed recidivism rate of its C-program [and, absent any evidence to the contrary, the presumed *actual* recidivism rate of that program as well] had been, say, 35 percent.) Thus, no upward or downward bias in the average recidivism rate is—a priori—likely to have occurred with respect to appropriately included programs either.

Issues of potential and actual distortion in an average recidivism rate do not just apply to POSs. Instead, each context reviewed above—erroneous inclusion, erroneous exclusion, and appropriate inclusion—pertains to negative-outcome studies as well, that is, to studies in which E's, based on their observed recidivism rates, are apparently outperformed by C's.

In sum, though noise-based upward or downward distortion *may* occur in the average recidivism rate of any subpopulation of programs that is analyzed collectively, it is unlikely to do so in any given instance. This is mainly because the lowered average that results from the erroneous inclusion—in that subpopulation—of programs that seem better than they really are is counterbalanced by the erroneous exclusion of programs that seem worse than they really are. In the first case, the program's observed recidivism rate is lower than its true recidivism rate; in the second, it is higher.

This situation would remain essentially unchanged even if one focused on median rather than mean (literally average) recidivism rates. That, in turn, would be true not just if (a) *numerous* programs were involved but even if (b) a not inconsequential percentage of those programs (say, 5–10%) happened to have *extremely large E/C recidivism differences*—ones which, moreover, were usually in the *same direction* (thereby involving effect sizes that were at least +1.00 or +1.50), and which were therefore not counterbalanced by other extreme (and usually just as uncommon or rare) E/C differences.

Chapter 12

Deciding Factors and Dimensions of Change

This chapter presents two subjects that have seldom if ever been systematically conceptualized in connection with intervention research: *(a)* the nature of "decisive" or "deciding" factors, and *(b)* the descriptive dimensions of change. The first topic bears on such research, especially multiple-features research, not only because many factors may contribute to outcome, whereas only some may make *sizable* contributions, but also because any one or more factors may be essential without actually being *sufficient*. The second subject is important mainly because of the often dynamic, interactional, and phased nature of many real-life interventions.

CONCEPTUALIZING THE DECIDING FACTOR

Among all factors that affect outcome, the "deciding factor" is the one that makes the final, essential difference. Broadly stated, it is the one that puts a situation or entity "over the top" or completes it, and without which that specific outcome, condition, or difference would not occur or be reached.

To be sure, other factors may make important, even essential contributions along the way, even to the very end.[1] They may promote, elicit, shape, or otherwise produce, assemble, and consolidate significant aspects or elements of the overall outcome, and this applies to the outcome's initial, intermediate, and later stages alike. However, the *deciding* factor is the one needed to generate the *final* stage, insofar as that stage or step can and should be distinguished at all. ("To generate" this stage includes completing it, not just initiating or subsequently supporting it, or helping to do so. A stage that "should be" distinguished is one which is substantive and in that sense legitimate; that is, it is one that apparently reflects real-life processes or phenomena and is therefore more than just an analytic

199

construction which is substantively ungrounded and in that respect artificial.)

Thus, if the deciding factor is absent, inactive, or deficient close to the end[2] (that is, if it is not operating adequately when the final stage can theoretically begin), one cannot generate that stage. This applies even if one has adequately approached or reached it and although other factors may influence it to some degree, for instance, may help initiate and/or subsequently support it. In short, the decisive factor is needed in order to elicit, shape, or otherwise produce and consolidate *the specific—that is, the distinctive*—outcome, condition, or difference. It is needed to "pull it together," "to activate it," to "help—or make—it break through," or to otherwise give it that which results in its being viewed as final, finished, or having met a criterion.[3] In that regard, only the deciding factor is "sufficient"—beyond being necessary.

Though sufficient in the above sense, the decisive factor, as implied, may interact with other factors when it is producing and consolidating the final stage or step; and some of the latter factors may themselves be performing a critical function at that point. In other words, although the deciding factor is a sina qua non with respect to generating the specific, final outcome—more precisely, though it is the only one whose presence and adequate operation is needed to complete the job, and that is not exchangeable with others—it need not be the sole factor or condition that is operating during that stage. (See the section entitled "Further Theoretical Observations," below, for more details.) To be sure, the deciding factor *may* generally be the largest contributor at that point.

In sum, though the decisive factor may interact at any stage or stages with one or more of the remaining process-factors and even with other contributors, the specific outcome or condition in question requires its presence and adequate operation at some point or points during the final stage. Though the deciding factor may or may not be the most powerful factor during that stage, it is the only sufficient one in the above-described sense. In addition, it may make significant, even essential contributions at *various* stages/steps, and these may occur by one or more of the following means (the deciding factor would of course generate the *final* stage/step in particular, by such means): broadly pressing; pointedly forcing; triggering; catalyzing; integrating; synthesizing; permissively guiding or directing; and so on. Other factors may contribute in these ways, as well.

Broader Applications

Given the assumption mentioned next, most of the discussion thus far can apply not just to the final stage but to any one. That is, each stage—

assuming it *is* in fact distinct or relatively distinct—may conceivably have its own decisive factor; and insofar as the deciding-factor concept is widely applicable, that concept would be generic. This applies even though a generic deciding factor would not, of course, produce and consolidate the distinctive, *final*-stage outcome, condition, or difference in connection with any *pre*-final stage. (All stages together, i.e., their totality, can be termed "the overall process" or—simply—"the phenomenon.")

As indicated, the discussion thus far assumes the existence of distinguishable, substantive stages. While many phenomena doubtlessly can be divided into such stages or steps, others—whether brief or lengthy—seem to occur as relatively seamless flows or continuities. In other words, these overall processes or phenomena do not appear to have natural or otherwise unforced stages/steps. This is not just a reflection of how the phenomena are measured and/or analytically represented. Nor is it an instance of "default," for instance, the product of an inability (temporary or not) to reliably distinguish and/or adequately represent any stages that actually exist. Instead, it mainly reflects the existence of little apparent change through time in a program's generic approaches, general emphasis and strategy, interaction techniques, target areas, and goals. (See below, regarding change through time.) Obviously, there is no series or sequence of goals, either.

A different and broader way of defining "decisive factor" would involve the question, Which factor has the most influence on the *overall* process of bringing about the outcome? Here, focus is on neither the final stage nor any other stage, and the factor in question need not be able to give an outcome its (the outcome's) specific or distinctive character. Basically, this perspective would equate "decisive" with overall strength, that is, quantitative dominance. This alternative view—yet, in some contexts, supplementary view—is meaningful and potentially valuable in itself.

Added Considerations

In practice, it would be difficult and time consuming to definitively, that is, experimentally, identify a deciding factor. Indeed, several interrelated experiments might be needed, whether the "final stage" or the "entire process" is involved. This would be particularly true for the more complex multimodal programs, whether they are of short duration—and perhaps intensive—or fairly long—and perhaps multitargeted as to areas of impact. Yet, the task of identifying a deciding factor is not necessarily tortuous per se; and the achievement of that goal would likely be helpful in practical (e.g., program development) and theoretical contexts alike.

Beyond that, although the challenge of identifying a decisive factor may be mostly technical, procedural, and resource based—and these are formidable on their own—it would be partly conceptual and definitional as well. Thus, insofar as it is important to know *what* one is looking for, in the first place, the above discussions and distinctions may be useful.

Nevertheless, if either *(a)* the conceptual complexities and subtleties or *(b)* their related methodological and practical challenges prevent the decisive factor from being identified, it would still be possible—and certainly valuable—to single out a number of main *contributors* to both the final stage and the overall process. Pinpointing such contributors— some of which may at least be identified as *essential*—might in fact be the likeliest outcome of even long-term, carefully coordinated experiments and observations of good quality.

Further Theoretical Observations

Thus, the decisive factor is necessary ("essential") and sufficient during the final stage despite possible contributions during that stage by any or all other factors, individually or jointly. Unlike the deciding factor, those factors—some of which may be essential themselves—could, conceivably, each be exchanged for other factors that were not previously present during the final stage; moreover, they *might* be exchangeable without any resulting loss of effectiveness. In short, even an "essential" factor (excluding the deciding factor itself) might be exchanged without reducing impact ("workably exchanged"), during the final stage, for a new factor or factors; and if that occurs, the new factor, that is, the substitute, would itself be essential. (Note: Loss of—or reduction in—effectiveness should be distinguished from loss of "specific, distinctive character," even though the two can be identical in the case of failure to reach a statistical cutoff. A loss of specific, distinctive character may or may not result in, or otherwise be associated with, a loss of or reduction in effectiveness.[4])

What are the immediately preceding statements or ideas based on? More specifically, What is their scientific—their empirical—status? and What makes them even plausible (though not necessarily likely)? First, the idea that "the substitute [factor] would itself be essential" is theoretical only; it is a logical possibility (logical in the sense of conceivable, and conceivable in not being self-contradictory). Moreover, it is plausible (in terms of adding logically consistent cognitive content to the broader context in which it appears)—but not ipso facto probable—because the "exchange" has already been defined as workable. At any rate, the idea rests on neither experimental evidence nor other systematic—especially, quantitative—observations.

Second, the earlier, more basic idea is itself theoretical. Moreover, even this concept would be *(a)* consistent with the definition of a *decisive* factor and *(b)* plausible, in the first place (given consistency [a]), only if the following situation had existed, prior to any possible exchange:[5] The factor to be exchanged ("exchange factor") would have to have been essential, not by itself, but contextually. That is, it would have to have been essential only within an overall configuration, namely, a set of factors that includes one or more "nondeciding factors" that were operating at the time—in this case, during the final stage. Logically, this would be necessary because the exchange factor would have been a *decisive* factor, not just an ordinary essential one, if it had been essential by itself rather than contextually, during the final stage. (An "ordinary" essential factor is contextually essential. In the discussion thus far, it is the only type of essential factor—other than the deciding factor—that exists during the final stage.) This would have applied whether or not the subsequent factor, that is, the substitute rather than the exchange factor, turned out to be essential itself, contextually or otherwise.

However, if studies that were of adequate quality were to show that the first such factor—an ordinary essential one—*(a)* could *not* be exchanged, and, especially, *(b)* was needed in conjunction with the deciding factor in order to give the outcome its distinctive character, then that factor would have been functioning as a decisive factor itself, and the theoretical situation would thus be as follows: The present definition of a "decisive factor" would itself have to be changed—basically, broadened—since more than one such factor (specifically, more than one nonexchangeable factor that is needed to produce/consolidate the distinctive character of the outcome) could apparently operate during the final stage. (No less important would be the possibility that two or more decisive factors—that is, jointly decisive factors—could operate at *any* stage, whether or not one such deciding factor would be stronger than another.) However, if above-mentioned condition *(a)*, but not condition *(b)*, applied, the definition of a deciding factor could remain unchanged, though if that were the case, a second category of essential factors (excluding the deciding factor itself) would be needed, one that was other than ordinary.

DESCRIPTIVE DIMENSIONS OF CHANGE

Change requires time, and it involves form as well as content. Form can be unidirectional, cyclic, and so on. Content—on which we will focus—may be based on mutually independent or mutually interacting contributors. Particularly important, the latter dimensions also bear on certain *effects* of change. To help conceptualize these and other dimensions, some basic change-sequences and types of effect will be outlined and compared below. In this regard, three major "analytic units" ("features") will be used, namely, generic approaches, interactional techniques, and target areas. A unidirectional framework will be assumed.

Change-Sequences

Successive Additions   Say that a probationer was in a program that consisted almost entirely of educational training (plus standard supervision) during its first two months. Next, say that a second generic approach—group counseling—was added to the first, in month three. In other words, "G.2" (generic approach 2) was added to "G.1" (educational training) after the latter had been used for some time and while it was still in use. This sequence of program features illustrates change that occurs via successive additions. The underlying concept would remain the same even if a third generic approach (G.3), and then a fourth (G.4), and so on were subsequently added.[6]

The same type of sequence—namely, a succession of added features—can occur with *interactional techniques* (e.g., I.2, I.3) rather than generic approaches. Or, it may occur with *target areas* (e.g., T.2, T.3) instead of either G's or I's. Alternatively, rather than just having an unbroken succession of the *same* type of features (e.g., instead of adding I.2 and then I.3 to *I.1* or adding T.2 and then T.3 to *T.1*), more than one type can be added to the original feature or, say, to the original *set* of features (namely, G.1, I.1, and T.1). Collectively, this may be done in an interspersed way, e.g., in the sequence I.2, G.2, I.3, T.2, G.3. But each addition would still be successive.

Simultaneous Additions   Here, two or more features are added more or less simultaneously. For instance, G.2 and G.3 may be added to G.1 at essentially the same time; or G.1 and G.2 (or perhaps G.2 and G.3) may be introduced together. Alternatively, simultaneous additions ("temporal coupling") may involve other types of features only (for instance, interactional techniques alone or target areas alone, rather than generic approaches alone).

Further, temporal coupling may occur across two or more types of features and may therein resemble the above-mentioned interspersion, but with more than one new feature as a time. For example, when a new generic approach (G.2) is added to an existing one (G.1), one or more interactional techniques (I.2, I.3) and/or new targets (T.2, T.3) may be added as well; simultaneously, of course, the I.2 (etc.) and/or T.2 (etc.)

would also have been added to the *I.1* and/or *T.1* that coexisted with G.1.[7] (This would apply whether or not the particular I's and T's were mutually independent.) Such interspersed, simultaneous additions may be common—perhaps modal—particularly in somewhat complex programs.

Finally, combinations of simultaneous and *successive* additions can occur during the course of a program, with or without the successive substitutions mentioned in endnote 6 of this chapter.

Types of Effect

Independent Effects   When a G.2 is added to a G.1, the direct and indirect impact of G.2 on client behavior may be minimally related to the impact of G.1. That is, G.2 may neither increase nor decrease *G.1's* effect per se; instead, its effect on client behavior may simply add *to* G.1's. If, at the same time, G.1 has minimal impact on *G.2*, these two features can be said to hardly interact with each other in terms of altering the amount of impact that each would have had on clients if the other had not been used. In that regard, G.2's quantity of impact would be separate from—that is, in addition to—that of G.1 (and vice versa).[8] This would also apply if G.2 (or, say, G.2 and G.3) had been added to the program at the *same* time as G.1, not subsequent to it. Thus, unless G.1 and G.2 had influenced behavior in opposite directions, their combined impact on the client would have been essentially the sum—not a multiple—of each.[9] This would have also applied to *(a)* combined effects of mutually independent *interaction techniques* (I's) and *(b)* mixtures of G's and I's.

Regarding this overall process, these accumulating/accreting effects of change may often occur at a fairly steady ("linear") rate, that is, at a comparatively even or at least nonescalating pace. Moreover, the separate effects in question—specifically, the respective *independent* impacts, on clients, of various features—may be no less important than the *interaction-based* effects described next. This hypothesis regarding importance applies whether noninteracting features, on the one hand, and interacting ones, on the other, exert their influence directly or indirectly and produce their effects at a fairly linear or nonlinear rate.

Interaction-based Effects   Some or all of a program's features may substantially interact with each other and may thereby have a positive, negative, or neutral influence on one another. For instance, when G.2 interacts with G.1, it may enhance (+) G.1's ability to affect clients; alternatively, it may either diminish (−) or hardly affect (0) G.1's power. (Zero influence would also occur if the features did not interact with each other; and +, −, and 0 would apply to G.1's possible effect on G.2, as well.) Still other features, such as G.3, may also play a role; and different *types* of features, for example, interactional techniques (I's), may be involved as well. In the following, we will review positive (enhanced) interactions only and discuss just two features at a time; also, generic approaches (G's) will serve as the examples. This selectivity will make it possible to avoid unnecessary complexity while still illustrating basic interactions and their effects on clients. *Enhance* and *augment* will be synonymous.

We first focus on interactions among the features themselves. Interacting features either enhance or do not enhance each other's ability (power) to affect clients, and the source as well as scope of this augmented power can be represented by two broad scenarios. In the first, *one* feature—say, G.2—enhances the other's (G.1's) power when the two features interact; however, the latter feature neither augments nor diminishes the former's power. In the second scenario, each feature enhances the other's power, and a two-way effect is therefore involved. (See the section entitled "Hypothesized Relationships," below, for more details.)

We now examine the joint impact those features may have on *clients*. This impact encompasses the total, that is, the overall, effect of those feature's combined power—in this case, their combined augmented power.[10] *Joint impact, joint effect,* and *combined impact* will be used synonymously.

To begin with, when focusing on the combined impact that features may have on clients, one can define any two such features as a "set" if one or both of them had first been enhanced via their mutual interaction, per scenario one or two above. We hypothesize that such a set—say, G.1/ G.2—can have a joint effect on clients which exceeds the overall effect that its *individual* features would have had. This can even occur under the following conditions: *(a)* if those individual features' mutual interaction resulted in neither scenario one nor two, that is, in essentially no *enhancement* of *either* feature, or *(b)* if those individual features hardly *interacted* with each other, in the first place.

Individual features that interact with each other but do not enhance *one another*—whether in terms of scenario one or two—each have what may be called a "separate, independent" influence on *clients*; that is, the impact of each feature on clients is distinct from (but many still *enhance*) that of the other. (Separate, independent effects on clients are, of course, also associated with features that hardly interact with each other in the first place.) Nevertheless, we hypothesize that, other things being equal, features that positively *interact* with each other can *better* help clients address their major social and/or personal needs than those which either do not mutually interact or that interact but produce neither a one- nor a two-way enhancement of each other.

As can be inferred, the term *joint effect* is used to signify the overall impact that two features (here, G.1 and G.2) may have on clients, not on each other. They may have this effect under the following conditions: *(a)* when they operate on clients together, that is, as a set rather than independently; *(b)* whether or not their impact on *each other* involved scenario one or two;[11] and *(c)* regardless of whether one feature had been successively added to the other, rather than simultaneously joined. At any rate a joint effect on clients is a product of features that not only operate as a set and interact with each other, but one or both of which have been enhanced via their mutual interaction.

Enhanced features do not operate jointly in just a temporal sense, that is, in simply affecting clients at the same time or at partly overlapping times. Instead, they may affect them in relation to their specific behaviors, attitudes, feelings, and so on—that is, in terms of *content* ("substance")— whether simultaneously or not. In this respect, substantive impact has a major qualitative (content-centered) dimension, though, as seen below, we will highlight the quantitative.

The joint effect of G.2 and G.1 on clients should not be considered only qualitatively different than the overall effect (impact) of the separate impacts that those same features would have had if little or no interaction had occurred between them.[12] For instance, regarding qual-ity—used descriptively, not evaluatively—interaction (I)-based impact can differ from little-or-no-interaction (no-I)-based impact with regard to more than just content. (Say that the impact in question partly results from such input-features as group counseling [G.2] and educational training [G.1]. Also say that the impact includes not just improvements in the clients' skill levels, environmental situations, and/or personal difficulties but related or resulting reductions in illegal behavior.) Specifically, and of importance here, I-based impact—say, impact on illegal behavior—may also be significantly *stronger*. That is, such an effect can be stronger/larger than that which would have resulted if no-I had been involved instead. It may also be more extensive with regard to clients' skills, environment, and personal problems. At any rate, I-based impact can be more intense, more widespread, and/or longer lasting than if G.2 and G.1 had each made only a separate contribution, one that might be called "additive only" rather than "enhancement related." A joint, enhancement-related (thus, interaction-based) impact on clients that is stronger than the no-interaction-based impact may be described as "heightened," "expanded," or "magnified" in amount— heightened and so forth in comparison to no-I. ("Amount" mainly includes number, intensity, and extent.)

The following summarizes and then further characterizes our main hypotheses about heightened impact on clients:

1. The foundation or content basis of such impact is a combination of input features, for instance, generic approaches and interactional techniques. (Here, a *combination* is a product—something already established and operating. *Combining*, in contrast, centers on the process of establishing.)

2. To actually generate such impact, that combination must allow for, encourage, and/or require client activities and responses (A/Rs) which, by definition, differ from A/Rs that would have occurred if those same input-features had been combined differently or had hardly interacted with each other. More specifically, the A/Rs differ in type, degree, or both.

3. Besides being somewhat different, those activities/responses would sometimes have been difficult or impossible to generate if the combination of features, or the nature of those features' mutual interactions, had been different than it was. At least, the A/Rs would often have been *more* difficult for clients—and staff—to bring about.

4. The particular combination helps open up or expand possibilities and opportunities—for clients—which would not otherwise have existed or existed to the same degree. It may, of course, also help curtail, divert, and exclude other possibilities, external pressures, and so on.

5. Given these new or expanded possibilities and opportunities the clients' resulting activities and responses directly pave the way for— and soon afterwards reflect—heightened impact. That impact, in turn, can help reduce recidivism.

The preceding hypotheses and remarks do not indicate that only one combination can lead to increased impact; yet they strongly imply that many cannot. Nor do those points mean that all activities and responses associated with such impact are difficult—difficult to initiate and maintain, particularly by clients. (Also involved may be activities by staff.) This applies even with clients who cannot be called "lightweight." Nevertheless, many activities and responses *are* often difficult.

The *(a)* combination of enhanced input-features and the *(b)* different kinds of activities/responses that this combination makes possible and helps generate on the part of clients may each be called a "synthesis" or "integration." In that respect, *(a)* and *(b)* can each be considered a new "reality" (i.e., a new or different set of conditions, which then has an organizing force of its own), or at least a different type/"level" of functioning. As such, each synthesis can in turn lead to or at least provide a basis for further syntheses.

In any event, synthesis *(a)* simply refers to the jointly operating—in that sense, the integrated and functioning—individual features. Synthesis *(b)*, on the other hand, involves client activities/responses that not only are made possible by the given combination but that also occur partly because of it. This synthesis thus involves activities/responses that would have been rather different, or might not have even occurred, if the combination or its functional equivalent had been absent.

Theoretically, the structural and substantive relationship that any given synthesis has with its constituent features (elements) can be described as "emergent." As such, it parallels that which, say, *water* (regarded as a product) has to its own elements (viewed as inputs). Here, the specific synthesis or compound—H_2O—differs radically from that which would have been the simple "sum" of its individual elements, if the latter had remained unintegrated or unsynthesized (thus, water is a fluid, but its constituents were previously gases; and those constituents, viz., hydrogen and oxygen, could only have been combined into water under certain conditions).[13] Similarly, in the present context, client activities/responses that result from a particular combination of features are structurally and substantively "more than" or at least different than A/Rs which might have resulted from those same features, if the latter had not been synthesized/combined. Theoretically, albeit at a structurally more complex level, the same type of relationship can exist between a product and its constituents even if those individual features (constituents) *have* been joined together—but under different conditions.

On a somewhat different but related track, the mere temporal and even spatial juxtaposing of various features does not automatically and necessarily produce or promote either of the following: *(a)* enhanced power among those features; *(b)* different behavior by clients, especially improved behavior. Even the fact that those juxtaposed features may be *interacting* with each other need not, by itself, lead to *(a)* and *(b)* above.[14]

In short, the combining of two or more G's, I's, and so forth, does not, for example, ipso facto guarantee heightened impact on clients and a related, subsequent increase in public protection. To achieve that impact and outcome, conditions such as the following may be jointly required:[15] First, the G.2s, I.2s, and so on—that is, the features which are successively or simultaneously added/joined to G.1s, I.1s, and so on—must be relevant to various content-issues and must bear on them substantially. These issues especially include major needs of clients and perhaps even skills/interests of staff. Second, the features must also be operationally compatible and coordinated with each other.[16] This would especially apply to programs that are not unimodal and it could be particularly important with the more troubled, lacking, and/or troublesome clients.

Finally, and whatever the validity of the above hypotheses may be, increased impact that results from interacting features can occur more rapidly than impact from noninteracting features.[17] Though such acceleration *may* in fact be typical it is probably far from guaranteed. In any event, increased rate should be distinguished from greater strength, that is, from heightened impact as reflected in increased intensity, extent, and duration of effect.

Hypothesized Relationships

In the above presentation of enhancements, interactions, and the successive or simultaneous introduction of features, the type and scope of relationship that existed among those dimensions was neither fully nor directly stated; instead, it usually remained implicit. Several of these hypothesized relationships will now be made explicit or, in some cases, more specific. They center on the features themselves, not on the impact of those features upon clients.

I. *Enhancement as a Product, and Interaction as Its Input*

A. The enhancement of one or both features, for example, G.1 and/or G.2, is based on an interaction among those features. More specifically, the existence of enhancement always requires the preexistence of interaction. (In general, enhancement may also require the continued but not necessarily the constant existence of interaction.) In short, enhancement never occurs if interaction has not first occurred or does not presently occur. In that respect, interaction, by itself, is an essential condition.

B. However, enhancement does not *always* occur when interaction has occurred or is occurring. (In this regard, interaction, per se, is not a decisive condition.) That is, some interacting features do not invariably lead to or otherwise help produce an enhancement of one or both features.

II. *Successively Introduced Features as Input, and Interaction as Product*

A. Successively introduced features, for example, G.1 followed by G.2, can interact with each other. However, they do not *always* interact with one another, and when interaction occurs, *successive* introduction is not invariably its basis.

B. Specifically, for interaction to occur among features, the successive introduction of those features is not always required. Interaction can sometimes be partly or entirely based on simultaneous introduction, instead.

III. *Successively Introduced Features as Input, and Enhancement as Product*

A. Successively introduced features can enhance each other. However, they do not always do so, and succession is not always the basis of enhancement that does occur. This applies whether one feature (G.1 or G.2) or both features are enhanced.

B. Specifically, for enhancement to occur, the successive introduction of features is not always required. Enhancement can, at times, partly or entirely reflect simultaneous introduction, instead.

IV. *Simultaneously Introduced Features as Input, and Interaction as Product*

A. Simultaneously introduced features, for example, G.1 together with G.2, can interact with each other. However, they do not *always* interact; and when interaction occurs, simultaneity is not always its basis.

B. Specifically, for interaction to occur among features, the simultaneous introduction of those features is not always required. Interaction can sometimes be partly or entirely based on *successive* introduction, instead.

V. *Simultaneously Introduced Features as Input, and Enhancement as Product*

A. Simultaneously introduced features can enhance each other. However, they do not always do so, and simultaneity is not always the basis of whatever enhancement occurs. This applies whether one feature or both features are enhanced.

B. Specifically, for enhancement to occur, simultaneous introduction is not always required. Enhancement can, at times, partly or entirely reflect successive introduction, instead.

Thus, successively as well as simultaneously introduced features can, but do not invariably, interact with—and enhance—each other. Also, interaction among features and the enhancement of one or both such features can each reflect the successive as well as simultaneous introduction of those features.

#601 Thu Nov 09 2000 08:58PM Item(s) c
hecked out to SANCHEZ MARTHA PATRICIA.

TITLE
BARCODE   DUEDATE
A profile of correctional effectivenes
A1504177616   Dec 09 2000
Community corrections : probation, par
A1501556925A   Dec 09 2000

Appendix A. The Risk, Need, and Responsivity Principles, and Appropriate Versus Inappropriate Services

In "Does Correctional Treatment Work?" Andrews et al. described the risk, need, and responsivity principles as follows:

> The risk principle suggests that higher levels of service are best reserved for higher risk cases and that low-risk cases are best assigned to minimal service . . . The need principle [refers to the importance of addressing crime-related or crime-producing factors via the] selection of appropriate intermediate targets . . . The most promising intermediate targets include changing antisocial attitudes, feelings, and peer associations; promoting familial affection [etc.] . . . The responsivity principle [involves] the selection of styles and modes of service that are (a) capable of influencing the specific types of intermediate targets that are set with offenders and (b) appropriately matched to the learning styles of offenders . . . [A]ppropriate types of service typically, but not exclusively, involve the use of behavioral and social learning principles of interpersonal influence, skill enhancement, and cognitive change. Specifically, they include modeling, graduated practice, rehearsal, role playing, resource provision, and detailed verbal guidance and explanation [etc.]. (Andrews et al., 1990b, pp. 374–75).

Given that framework, Andrews et al. used the following definitions to classify "correctional services"—as distinct from "criminal sanctions"—as either appropriate or inappropriate (the remaining services were called "unspecified," mainly due to insufficient information):

> Appropriate service included (1) service delivery to higher risk cases, (2) all behavioral programs (except those involving delivery of service to lower risk cases), (3) comparisons reflecting specific responsivity-treatment comparisons, and (4) nonbehavioral programs that clearly stated that criminogenic need was targeted and that structured intervention was employed . . . (379).
>
> Inappropriate service included (1) service delivery to lower risk cases and/or mismatching according to a need/responsivity system, (2) nondirective relationship-dependent and/or unstructured psychodynamic counseling, (3) all milieu and group approaches with an emphasis on within-group communica-

tion and without a clear plan for gaining control over procriminal modeling and reinforcement, (4) nondirective or poorly targeted academic and vocational approaches, and (5) "scared straight" . . . (379).

Criminal sanctions . . . involved variation in judicial disposition, imposed at the front end of the correctional process and not involving deliberate variation in rehabilitative service (e.g., restitution, police cautioning versus regular processing, less versus more probation, and probation versus custody). (379)

Appendix B. Repetition Versus Convergence of Evidence

Before turning to chapter 4's discussion of findings presented thus far, the following might be noted. Each generic approach reviewed in chapter 3 was examined by a number of authors (meta-analysts and literature reviewers)—often many. For any approach, two or more authors may have examined some of the *same* studies ("identical studies") that comprised the approach. More broadly and precisely, those and/or other authors—collectively—may have examined not just identical studies but also several *different* ones; in fact, that is what almost always occurred among the authors who had studied any given approach. (Regarding terminology, "identical studies"—studies examined by two or more authors—are also called "overlapping studies," and they overlap some though not necessarily all authors. "Different studies"—studies that two or more authors do *not* both [or all] examine and in that sense do not share—are also called "nonoverlapping"; at least, they do not overlap those particular authors. Finally, the following combination illustrates "two or more authors": (a) Gendreau and Ross and (b) Whitehead and Lab. Another example is (c) Romig and (d) Lipsey; and an example of more than two [specifically, three] reviewers/analysts would involve authors (a) plus (d) plus (e)—the latter one being, say Gottschalk et al.)

To quantitatively illustrate this identity and difference, say that three authors—A, B, and C, respectively—examined 10, 15, and 17 vocational training (VT) studies each. For purposes of simplicity, say that no other authors had analyzed/reviewed this approach. Of the 10 VT studies examined by A, #5, 6, and 7 may also have been included among the 15 examined by B, whereas A's #1, 2, 3, 4, 8, 9, and 10 may not have been. The former studies (#5, 6, and 7) would thus have overlapped (being "shared by") authors A and B whereas the latter (#1, 2, . . . 10) would not have overlapped those authors. Nor would B's #11, 12, 13, 14, and 15 have overlapped any A-studies. (Since B had 15 studies and A had 10, at least 5—any 5—of the former's could not have overlapped any of the latter's. For purposes of simplicity we illustrate this point by choosing numbers 11 through 15.) Similarly, author C's review/analysis of VT— an examination which, as indicated, involved 17 studies—may have

215

overlapped A's examination of #1, 2, 5, 6, 9, and 10, and B's #5, 6, 13, 14, and 15, but did not overlap the remaining studies reviewed/analyzed by either A or B. Naturally, author C's #16 and 17 would have overlapped none of A's and B's studies, and this absence of overlap would have applied to several other C-studies, as well.

In that particular example, authors A, B, and C—collectively— examined a total of 30 individual studies, studies that differed from each other despite their shared "vocational training" label. *Twenty* of these studies were reviewed/analyzed no more than once; that is, they were examined by a *single* author only (e.g., by Romig, or by Gottschalk et al.)—either A, B, or C. Since "overlap" across authors logically requires at least two authors, those 20 studies were nonoverlapping; that is, they were shared by no two or more authors who had examined VT. In that respect, they—67% of the 30 studies (20 ÷ 30)—were "unique" (entirely unshared) in connection with the entire VT analysis and review. *Eight* other studies were shared by one or more combinations of two authors— authors A and B, A and C, and/or B and C. Those eight shared studied (i.e., shared with respect to their analysts/reviewers) were A's #1, 2, 7, 9, and 10, and B's #13, 14, and 15, and they constituted 27% of the 30 VT studies (8 ÷ 30). The remaining *two* studies—A's #5 and 6—were shared by all three authors. This small set of overlapping studies therefore comprised the final 7% of the 30 (2 ÷ 30). (Percentages presented here are rounded to the nearest whole number.)

In short, most studies in this example—specifically, the first 20 (67% of all VTs)—were unique, that is, nonoverlapping across *any* authors, not just nonoverlapping across some (e.g., A and B) but not others (namely, A and C, or B and C). The 10 remaining studies (33% of all VTs)— overlapped either two authors or all three. Obviously, far more than 33% overlap would have existed if, in a different example, authors A, B, and C had each examined, say, 12 studies—involving VT or any other generic approach—and a sizable majority of their respective studies turned out to be the *same* ones (i.e., a large majority overlapped A and B, A and C, and B and C alike).

Now, the question arises: How much overlap and nonoverlap— identity and difference—existed across the studies that were in fact examined by the authors who reviewed any given generic approach that appeared in chapter 3? More specifically, for each approach whose effectiveness was indicated in that chapter,[1] what *percentage of all studies* that were examined by all the authors collectively[2] had been reviewed by each of the following *percentages of authors,* respectively: *0%; 1–19%; 20–39%; 40–59%; 60–79%;* and *80% or more?*[3] Here, "0%"

means no overlap among *any* authors. (Thus, all studies are "unique" if 100% of them overlap 0% of the authors; similarly, half of the studies are unique if 50% of them overlap 0% of the authors.) "1–19%" therefore refers to overlap among very-few-to-few authors. (Thus, if 100% of all studies are found within this category-range, it means that all studies had no more than a slight degree of overlap, in the following sense: They were shared by fewer than one author out of every five who reviewed the given generic approach.) "20–39%" refers to overlap among a substantial-to-large minority of authors; "40–59%" refers to roughly half; "60–79%" means a clear-to-large majority; and "80% or more" means a preponderance—or more.

The above question is important for a reason that will now be illustrated, via a further hypothetical example: In scenario *one* of this new example, say that each of 10 authors (or even five-to-seven of them) who had examined the recidivism rates that were reported for a total of 40 group counseling studies (i.e., 40 studies across those authors collectively), concluded—in his/her individual review/analysis—that this generic approach was promising. These separate conclusions—when subsequently assembled and integrated across those authors collectively, i.e., when evaluated as a *set* of conclusions—might have been considered reasonable evidence or even strong evidence that group counseling has promise. Indeed, such evidence definitely *would* have supported that evaluation if at least two conditions existed: (a) a sizable percentage of the individual studies that comprised many or most of the respective reviews/analyses had significantly or substantially reduced recidivism; (b) most of the remaining authors (e.g., those other than the five-to-seven above) had not drawn a contrary conclusion—especially a sharply opposing one—based on evidence whose strength and quality was comparable. (In the following discussion of this example, we will assume conditions (a) and (b) remain satisfied.)

Yet, if the conclusion that group counseling is "promising' had been based on reviews/analyses that, collectively (i.e., across authors), had mainly involved studies which *overlapped* across authors—(one example of such substantial overlap would be if roughly 70–75% of the 40 studies had been shared by some 65–80% of the authors)—that conclusion, while useful in itself, would carry less scientific and practical weight than one which might have instead resulted from either of the following (called scenario *two*): (a) the same 10 authors—still viewed collectively—had mainly examined *different* individual studies; (b) the studies that those respective authors examined had not, on average, been reviewed/analyzed by the *majority* of those authors, collectively. In both instances, a large degree of overlap did not exist across most authors, with respect to the studies they examined. Thus, an example of (a), above, would be if no more than approximately *25–30%* rather than the previously mentioned 70–75% of the 40 *studies* had overlapped the 65–80% of authors. An example of (b) would be if approximately 70–75% (not to mention only 25–30%) of the 40 studies had overlapped some *20–35%* rather than the above-mentioned 65–80% of the *authors*, that is, if they were shared by about one-fifth to one-third of the authors. Again, in both cases, *most* studies would not have overlapped *most* reviewers/analysts, and in that respect a contrast would exist with scenario one.

As is clear, scenario one's overall conclusion that group counseling is promising depended heavily on what, for the most part, were repeated studies—in a sense, repetitious evidence (i.e., the same evidence, only found in different authors): In that scenario, almost 75% of all group counseling studies were shared by up to 80% of the authors. (Considerable repetition would also have existed—and the point would have been essentially the same—even if 60% of the studies had overlapped 60% of the authors.) In contrast, scenario two's conclusion regarding group counseling's promise rested largely on a substantially higher—in fact, a sizable—percentage of *non*overlapping (i.e., unique or nonrepetitious) studies. This scenario's conclusion thus involved more cross-validation that was based on new/different/independent evidence; and if other factors were roughly equal, the conclusion would thus be stronger—certainly broader-based—than that derived from scenario one.[4] Collectively, these broader-based findings might have had wider practical and even theoretical applicability, as well.

Answers to the question of how much overlap (and, conversely, nonoverlap) actually existed can be obtained from Table B-1. For various generic approaches in turn, the table indicates the percentage of studies (within each given approach) that had specified degrees of overlap across the authors who reviewed those respective approaches. For instance, regarding the group counseling/therapy studies (N = 56), *36%* (i.e., 20 of the studies) had 0% overlap among the authors who reviewed/analyzed this approach (i.e., each of those 8 studies was examined by only one author); another *14%* (i.e., 8 studies) overlapped only a small percentage of authors (1–19%); an additional *39%* of the studies overlapped a moderate percentage of authors (20–39%); and the remaining *11%* overlapped roughly half (40–59%). Thus, on average, the group counseling/therapy studies that were examined overlapped no more than a moderate percentage (i.e., between "none" and a "large minority") of the authors who, collectively, had examined this approach.[5, 6]

Table B-1

Percentage of Overlapping Studies, by Percentage-category of Authors, for Seventeen Generic Approaches

| | | | Percentage of Overlapping Studies | | | | | |
| | | | Percentage-category of Authors | | | | | |
Generic Approach[a]	No. of Studies[b]	No. of Authors[b]	0	1–19	20–39	40–59	60–79	80+
Confrontation	9	7	33	0	11	33	0	22
Delinq. Prevent. (Area-wide . . .)	5	4	60	0	0	40	0	0
Delinq. Prevent. (Casework . . .)	15	6	40	0	27	20	7	7
Diversion	67	11	46	13	39	1	0	0
Physical Challenge	2	3	0	0	0	0	100	0
Restitution	13	4	69	0	0	15	8	8
Group Counseling/Therapy	56	12	36	14	39	11	0	0
Individual Counseling/Therapy	44	10	32	0	48	20	0	0
Family Intervention	45	12	16	42	36	7	0	0
Vocational Training	20	5	50	0	0	10	15	25
Employment	15	3	67	0	0	0	20	13
Educational Training	14	5	14	0	0	57	29	0
Behavioral	57	14	0	46	37	18	0	0
Cognitive-Behavioral	46	6	83	0	13	2	0	2
Life Skills	32	3	72	0	0	0	25	3
Multimodal	22	3	59	0	0	0	32	9
Probation/Parole Enhancement	41	10	44	0	34	10	12	0
Average (Unweighted)	29.6	6.9	42.4	6.8	16.7	14.4	14.6	5.2

[a]Excludes three of the 20 generic approaches described in chapter 3. (See Appendix B, note 6, regarding reasons for exclusion.)
[b]Excludes Genevie, Margolies, and Muhlin (1986), due to the difficulty of determining or estimating which specific studies they included.

For most of the 17 generic approaches shown in Table B-1, the majority of studies that comprised those respective approaches over-lapped—on average—no more than a moderate percentage of authors (20–39%). Specifically, the 0% through 20–39% categories, collectively, contained 65.9% of all studies, whereas the remaining categories (mainly those involving 40–59% and 60–79% of the authors) encompassed 34.1% (rounded). This indicates that many cross-author trends and conclusions that appear in chapter 4 regarding chapter 3's generic approaches reflect a substantial convergence of evidence (studies) and are not mainly based on overlapping—repetitious—evidence. The latter evidence would have existed, for example, in the form of a sizable core of studies that *most* reviewers/analysts—certainly more than 40–59% of them—shared in common. To be sure, considerable overlap did sometimes exist. Specifically, with confrontation, physical challenge, vocational training, and educational training, 50% or more of the studies (collectively) overlapped *at least* 40–59% of the authors. Nevertheless, only physical challenge had a *high* degree of overlap across authors, and, as indicated, a large majority of the 17 generic approaches shown in Table B-1 had considerably more converging than repetitious evidence.

The analyses described above centered on the question, What percentage of all *studies* that were examined by all the authors collectively had been reviewed by specified percentages of *authors*? However, overlap and nonoverlap can be analyzed relative to a different question as well—thus, from a differing angle: For each approach whose effectiveness was assessed in chapter 3, what percentage of all *authors* had examined each of the following percentages of all *studies* that were reviewed in connection with that approach: *1–19%; 20–39%; 40–59%; 60–79%;* and *80% or more*? Answers are seen in Table B-2.

For instance, regarding the group counseling/therapy approach (56 studies; 12 authors), *67%* of the authors had examined between 1% and 19% of *all* the studies that were reviewed. (Specifically, 8 of the *12 authors* [67%] had each examined between 1 and 10 studies [i.e., between 1.8% and 17.9% of the *56 studies* that the 12 authors had examined collectively].) Similarly, an additional *17%* of the authors had examined between 20% and 39% of all studies that had been reviewed. (That is, 2 of the 12 authors [17%] had each examined between 11 and 22 studies [i.e., between 19.6% and 39.3% of the 56 studies which that group of 12 authors had reviewed].) An additional *8%* of the 12 authors had examined between 40% and 59% of the 56 studies; *0%* examined between 60% and 79%; and *8%* had examined 80% or more. Thus, the individual authors who reviewed the group counseling/therapy approach had examined, on average, no more than a moderate percentage—that is, between a "slight" amount and a "large minority"—of all the studies that were reviewed by all the authors collectively. In that respect, only moderate overlap (repetition) existed across authors.

Table B-2

Percentage of All Possible Studies Examined by Authors, by Percentage-category of Studies, for Seventeen Generic Approaches

| | | | Percentage of Studies Examined | | | | |
| | | | Percentage-category of Studies | | | | |
Generic Approach[a]	No. of Studies[b]	No. of Authors[b]	1–19[c]	20–39	40–59	60–79	80+
Confrontation	9	7	0	57	0	0	43
Delinq. Prevent. (Area-wide . . .)	5	4	0	25	75	0	0
Delinq. Prevent. (Casework . . .)	15	6	17	33	33	17	0
Diversion	67	11	64	18	18	0	0
Physical Challenge	2	3	0	0	67	0	33
Restitution	13	4	25	50	0	0	25
Group Counseling/Therapy	56	12	67	17	8	0	8
Individual Counseling/Therapy	44	10	80	10	0	0	10
Family Intervention	45	12	58	25	8	8	0
Vocational Training	20	5	40	20	0	20	20
Employment	15	3	0	67	0	0	33
Educational Training	14	5	20	60	0	0	20
Behavioral	57	14	64	7	21	7	0
Cognitive-Behavioral	46	6	83	0	0	0	17
Life Skills	32	3	67	0	0	0	33
Multimodal	22	3	33	33	0	0	33
Probation/Parole Enhancement	41	10	30	50	20	0	0
Average (Unweighted)	29.6	6.9	38.1	27.8	14.7	3.1	16.2

[a]See Table B-1, note a.
[b]See Table B-1, note b.
[c]For each generic approach, each author examined at least one study. Therefore, no "0" (zero) percentage-category exists.

What about *all* generic approaches, not just group counseling/therapy? In a clear majority of the 17 approaches shown in Table B-2, most authors had reviewed no more than a moderate percentage of all the studies that had been examined by the authors collectively. In that respect, the findings resembled those in Table B-1. More specifically, the overall overlap—the average degree for all five percentage-categories combined—was slight-to-moderate. To be sure, considerably more overlap—though never a high degree, overall—was found for confrontation, for area-wide approaches to delinquency prevention, for social casework (and other) approaches to delinquency prevention, for physical challenge, and for vocational training. In this regard, their results are less well-anchored than those involving generic categories (approaches) whose studies—collectively—were less repetitious and more often converging.

Less Promising and More Promising
Approaches

Less promising approaches. As seen in chapter 4, five generic approaches were substantially less likely than others to have been associated with reduced recidivism. More precisely, the individual studies that comprised these respective approaches either had—collectively, but within each approach—(a) the lowest percentage of recidivism reduction (and in that respect were the least successful or promising) or, in some cases, (b) an average effect size that was relatively low. These approaches were:

Table B-3

Percentage of Overlapping Studies, by Percentage-category of Authors, for Five Generic Categories Least Often Considered Successful or Promising

			Percentage of Overlapping Studies					
			Percentage-category of Authors					
Generic Approach	No. of Studies[a]	No. of Authors[a]	0	1–19	20–39	40–59	60–79	80+
Confrontation	9	6	44	0	0	33	0	22
Delinq. Prevent. (Area-wide . . .)	5	4	60	0	0	40	0	0
Diversion	52	6	83	0	12	2	2	2
Group Counseling/Therapy	56	7	61	0	18	21	0	0
Individual Counseling/Therapy	30	4	80	0	0	13	7	0
Average (Unweighted)	30.4	5.4	65.6	0.0	6.0	21.8	1.8	4.8

*Number of studies, number of authors, and percentages-of-overlap are those for all studies examined by authors who considered the given approach unsuccessful or non-promising.
[a]See Table B-1, note b.

Table B-4

Percentage of Overlapping Studies, by Percentage-category of Authors for Five Generic Approaches Most Often Considered Successful or Promising

| | | | Percentage of Overlapping Studies | | | | | |
| | | | Percentage-category of Authors | | | | | |
Generic Approach	No. of Studies[a]	No. of Authors[a]	0	1–19	20–39	40–59	60–79	80+
Family Intervention	44	9	70	0	25	2	2	0
Behavioral	54	7	19	0	31	37	7	6
Cognitive-Behavioral	46	4	89	0	0	9	2	0
Life Skills	32	3	72	0	0	0	25	3
Multimodal	22	3	59	0	0	0	32	9
Average (Unweighted)	39.6	5.2	61.8	0.0	11.2	9.6	13.6	3.6

*Number of studies, number of authors, and percentages-of-overlap are those for all studies examined by authors who considered the given approach successful or promising.
[a]See Table B-1, note b.

confrontation; area-wide strategies of delinquency prevention; diversion (at least "nonsystem"); group counseling/therapy; individual counseling/therapy. In that connection, the question arises: Did the specific meta-analyses and/or literature reviews that evaluated those approaches as not being particularly promising utilize mainly repetitive (mutually overlapping) or mainly converging (mutually nonoverlapping) evidence (individual studies)? (That is, did they utilize such evidence collectively, i.e., *across* those analyses/reviews?) As derived from Table B-3, the answer is that converging evidence clearly dominated. This, at least applied to four of the five approaches in question—the exception being confrontation.

More promising approaches.   Chapter 4 also lists the five generic approaches that were most often, or proportionately most often, considered successful or promising from an E-better-than-C perspective, and/or those which seemed, on balance, to have the strongest positive results (e.g., the highest average effect sizes or the largest recidivism reductions). These were: family intervention; behavioral; cognitive-behavioral or cognitive; life skills or skill oriented; and multimodal. Again, Did the specific analyses/reviews that evaluated those approaches as being successful or promising mainly use (collectively) repetitive or converging evidence? As with the less successful/promising approaches, mentioned above, convergence was by far the rule—the one exception being the behavioral approach. (Table B-4.)

Appendix C. The Percentage of Statistically Significant Studies

These fourteen analyses and reviews are among those whose results were presented in Chapter 3. The percentage of studies described by the individual analysts/reviewers as being significantly ($p < .05$) positive and negative, respectively, is *underlined* in parentheses. For example, Lab and Whitehead's findings are shown as "*27/13*, 48"—meaning 27 percent positive and 13 percent negative studies, out of forty-eight usable studies in all. The analyses and reviews are thus as follows: Andrews et al., 1990 (*33/6*, 80); Geismar and Wood, 1986 (—, 15); Gendreau and Ross, 1979 (—, 14); Gendreau and Ross, 1987 (*50/0*, 26); Gordon and Arbuthnot, 1987 (*46/4*, 26); Greenberg, 1977 (*26/2*, 47); Johns and Wallach, 1981 (*47/20*, 15); Lab and Whitehead, 1988 (*27/13*, 48); Lipton, Martinson, and Wilks, 1975 (*30/7*, 61); Romig, 1978 (*19/14*, 95); Rutter and Giller, 1983 (*35/6*, 52); Schneider, 1986 plus Ervin and Schneider, 1990 (*43/0*, 7); Whitehead and Lab, 1989 (*40/10*, 50); Wright and Dixon, 1977 (*41/7*, 27).

Further details, and a number of technical points, will now be mentioned. First, for the total of 90 studies that were examined by Whitehead and Lab, Lab and Whitehead, and Andrews et al., collectively, the percentage of significantly positive and negative studies was 34 and 7, respectively. Second, for Geismar and Wood's (1986) and Gendreau and Ross' (1979) reviews, we derived almost all probability estimates from the numbers presented for individual studies in either the respective reviews or in combination with numbers from one or more of the remaining thirteen analyses/reviews. Third, all findings are based on recidivism only—one such measure for each of the 270 studies, centering on the study's total sample wherever possible. If analysts/reviewers presented more than one type of recidivism outcome—and they usually did not—we gave priority, whether for prevalence or incidence, to arrests, convictions, detentions/incarcerations, suspensions, revocations, and unfavorable discharge or termination, in essentially that order. (The presence of any *three* or more measures, including those mentioned next, was rather uncommon in any one study.) Other, not infrequent outcome measures were complaints filed, court petitions, and so on. Each study received equal weight and was counted only once, even if it appeared in more than one analysis/

review. Fourth, of all 270 studies that appeared in one or more of the fourteen analyses/reviews, 54 percent were reported in two or more of them, 31 percent were reported in three or more, and 12 percent were reported in four of more. These percentages—reflections of overlap across studies, and of related convergence of findings—would have been higher if *(a)* the remaining eighteen analyses/reviews were included in this analysis, and, of course, if *(b)* the time period covered by the given collection of studies (whether fourteen or thirty-two) was more similar than it was. For instance, regarding *(a)*, if Gottschalk et al. (1987) and Panizzon, Olson-Raymer, and Guerra (1991) were included, 68% of the 270 studies (thus, an added 14 percentage points) would have been reported by two or more analysts/reviewers. (This and the preceding percentages exclude Lipsey [1992]—whose analysis would probably have encompassed nearly all of the 270 studies by itself.)

When *all* E/C comparisons ("tests") are included from the studies that comprised the fourteen analyses/reviews—that is, not necessarily just one test per study, as discussed in the third point above—the following are representative of the positive and negative percentages of statistically significant studies, respectively: Andrews et al. (*38/9*, 154); Gendreau and Ross (1987) (*48/4,* 27); Gordon and Arbuthnot (*50/4*, 27); Greenberg (*30/2*, 53); Lipton, Martinson, and Wilks (*35/11*, 80); Romig (*23/13*, 114); Rutter and Giller (*40/10*, 67); Wright and Dixon (*45/7*, 29). These added tests occurred, for example, in studies that used two different recidivism measures and obtained differing results for each.

Finally, Lipsey's (1992) indicated that a positive, $p < .05$ finding was obtained in 35 percent of his several hundred studies in which statistical significance had been presented. Similarly, the report indicated that 32 percent of his total sample of studies had an effect size of +.26 or higher and that 10 percent had one of −.25 or lower. Adjusted for the 10.4 percent of studies for which no ES could be derived, the portions of his sample with those ESs were 36 percent and 11 percent, respectively. A preponderance of studies whose effect sizes are ±.25 are likely to attain $p < .05$, unless the individual sample sizes are fairly small. (In Lipsey's meta-analysis, the median sample size was approximately 60 "in each experimental group." Unless the control or comparison group's size was considerably smaller, this number generally provided enough statistical power to allow an individual study whose ES was ±.25 to reach $p < .05$.)

Appendix D. Implications of Differential Representation

If most approaches that were involved in given meta-analyses and literature reviews were in fact combinations, the following would probably have applied, even if those combinations had no more recidivism-reducing power than unimodal approaches: E/C reductions that were found for given categories of experimental studies were more likely to have been products of mixes or combinations than of unimodal approaches or inputs, simply because the former were more numerous. That simple mathematical reality would have applied even apart from an earlier-mentioned fact that was logically independent of whether or not most categories mainly consisted of multi- rather than unimodal programs: Since only some E programs within a given category provided *major* reductions with most offenders (but most such programs did not), the category as a whole, that is, all its programs combined, obviously could not have routinely produced such reductions. That, in turn, would have applied *(a)* whether or not *unimodal* approaches, when they did exist, often lacked the scope to adequately address many offenders' difficult or complex situations and needs, and *(b)* whether or not most unimodal programs—even if, say, they were *not* a minority of all E programs—usually did reduce recidivism but seldom by more than moderate amounts. (We assume that difficult situations and so on very often existed, and that uni- as well as multimodal approaches were used with them.)

Appendix E. Effectiveness of Differing Combinations of Program Components

BACKGROUND

In a detailed study of all fifty-three county juvenile probation camps that existed in California in 1984, it was found that almost all camps used at least six program components during any given week—especially educational training, vocational training, counseling, recreational activities, structured offgrounds activities, and work details. Other components were outside contacts, for example, visits from parents, and religious activities. (*Components* and *features* are used synonymously.) In a typical week, nearly all youths participated in at least three or four of these activities a number of times, for a total of several hours per activity—usually ten or more. However, since considerably more hours were spent on classroom education than on any other activity, and given the fact that virtually everyone attended, this could have been considered the dominant feature in the preponderance of camps; as a result, meta-analysts and literature reviewers might understandably have grouped and analyzed camp programs under the heading "educational training"—even though, as indicated, many hours were also spent on certain other activities and nearly everyone participated in them as well (Palmer and Wedge, 1989a, 1989b; Wedge and Palmer, 1989).

The camps in this study housed juveniles who were considered serious or troublesome enough to be removed from their communities but not sufficiently serious to be committed to the state for longer and heavier incarceration. Almost all individuals were males aged thirteen to seventeen at intake.

FINDINGS

Before we examine the findings themselves, it would be useful to note the following points. First, as indicated, educational training was—quantitatively—the most salient feature. (In this specific respect, it may also have been called the "dominant" feature.) It might thus have been considered the most likely "generic category," and this feature was therefore held constant across all camp-groups discussed below. Second, the key observation, mentioned below, centers on the *difference in relative effectiveness of group A camps compared to group B camps,* with the effectiveness of each such group having been separately assessed in relation to its own comparison camps. Third, all groups, that is, "sets," of camps mentioned below were identified via multiple regression. Regarding the hypothesis that only *some* combinations within a given generic category reduce recidivism, the following was observed when all camps from the several counties other than Los Angeles County were analyzed together:

1. One set of camps—group A camps—was identified that, besides providing an average (therefore, a nondistinctive) amount of *educational training*, had a particular combination of distinguishing program features: an above-average amount of vocational training, work details, and religious activities, and a below-average amount of counseling. On 24-month post-camp follow-up, the group A camps were found to have the *same* recidivism rate as *other* camps that also provided an average amount of educational training but clearly differed from group A with respect to the four distinguishing features mentioned above, that is, substantially differed from A in degree of activity. Thus, group A's particular combination of features made no difference in terms of recidivism.

2. However, another set of camps—group B camps—was identified which, besides providing an average amount of educational training, had a *different combination* of distinguishing program features than that found in group A. Specifically, B had a below-average amount of vocational training and an above-average weekly frequency (but a below average number of weekly hours) of work details. *Like* A, it also had an above-average amount of religious activity. On 24-month post-camp follow-up, group B camps were found to have a significantly *lower* recidivism rate than other camps that also provided an average amount of educational training but clearly differed from group B on B's distinguishing features. (Almost no overlap existed with regard to the individual camps that comprised Group A and group B, respectively, and little overlap existed between their respective comparison camps as well.)

Thus, although group *A*—which had its own combination of distinguishing features—might *not* have been considered successful in terms of recidivism reduction when compared to other camps, group *B*—which had a different combination of distinguishing features than A but which, like A, might still have been called "educational training"—*could* have been considered successful. In short, not all combinations within a given category—in this case, the educational training category—made a difference.

The same type of finding was obtained for education-salient camps whose populations mainly came from a very large, urban area; here, still other combinations of program features were involved. Specifically, the following was observed when all fourteen camps from Los Angeles County were analyzed together:

1. One set of camps—group C camps—was identified that, besides providing an average and therefore nondistinctive amount of *educational training*, had a given combination of distinguishing program features: a below-average amount of recreational activities and vocational training as well as an above-average amount of outside contacts. On 24-month post-camp follow-up, group C camps were found to have essentially the *same* recidivism rate as other camps that also provided an average amount of educational training but clearly differed from group C on those three distinguishing features. In other words, group C's combination made little or no difference in recidivism.

2. However, a different set of camps—group D camps—was identified that, besides providing an average amount of educational training, had a *different combination* of distinguishing program features than that found in group C: group D had an above-average amount of counseling and a below-average amount of offgrounds activities. On 24-month post-camp follow-up, group D camps had a significantly *lower* recidivism rate than other camps that also provided an average amount of educational training but clearly differed from group D on D's two distinguishing features.

(In each of the above comparisons the risk-level of youths in the respective sets of camps was statistically controlled.)

Though the above findings, like those of any other single study, were by no means definitive, they illustrate certain facts regarding "combinations." They also suggest that an individual program's feature—educational training, in this case—can have different outcomes (sometimes even *opposite* outcomes) with respect to recidivism, depending on other features with which it is combined. In fact, in the probation camps study this was observed often, not just with educational training.

Contextual differences were also obtained by Wooldredge (1988).[1] For instance, he observed that when longer supervision was combined with community treatment, it was associated with lower recidivism rates than those seen with shorter supervision by itself; yet, longer supervision, also by itself, correlated positively with *higher* recidivism rates. Wooldredge's study also supported the idea that a combined-feature approach was not automatically better than a single feature. Specifically, he found that some combined probation dispositions were no more effective than some singles.

The fact that a combined-features approach does not invariably produce better recidivism results than a single-feature approach may sometimes occur for the following, hypothesized set of reasons: Not only is a particular component (i.e., part) of the combined-features approach largely irrelevant to or unable to adequately address certain needs of the given population but also, at the same time, staff's involvement with that component may absorb resources and energies that are needed elsewhere—resources/energies that perhaps *are* applied elsewhere in some single-feature approaches. (Both the single- and the combined-feature approaches may, of course, still be considered effective—or ineffective—just equally so.)

Yet, the outcome in question—say, equal results for single- and combined-feature approaches—may have occurred for somewhat different reasons. For example, a component might have been inappropriate in itself for a large part of the population, used too often, and/or used at the wrong time. As a result, it may have weakened, diluted, or blocked the positive or potentially positive impact of other components. Such possibilities, it might be added, suggest that the potential advantages of combined-feature approaches are inevitably accompanied by at least one potential drawback: In certain combinations or under given conditions, some components can weaken or negate others, not reinforce or complement them. This possibility, of course, is greatly reduced or eliminated in single-feature approaches; but there, the question of variety, breadth, or scope of coverage emerges.

Appendix F. Selected Issues Regarding Control Programs

Some issues that have been rarely if ever examined will now be reviewed. The first stems from the relationship between possible jurisdiction (or agency) differences and types of control programs. The second focuses on implications of intra- and interjurisdiction changes or developments in control programs. Individually and especially together, these and other issues discussed here reinforce the importance of describing and analyzing control programs more closely than before, not just their outcomes, but their individual and combined features. Such descriptions, and so on, can help interpret results from E-programs themselves. This, in turn, can help develop more effective new programs and improve existing ones.

As will be seen, control programs—individually and collectively—should not be considered simply a neutral, passive, background operation, one that can hardly make specific, independent contributions to knowledge building and program development. Nor should all C-programs be regarded as fairly simple or even unimodal, whether structurally or operationally.

JURISDICTION DIFFERENCES

Say that a fairly typical E/C study was conducted in jurisdiction one and that a second, similarly designed and comparably implemented study was carried out in jurisdiction two—that is, in a different city, county, and/or state—at about the same time. Further, say that the first study obtained an 18-month recidivism rate of 30 percent for its E-program (E_1) and a 30 percent rate for its C-program (C_1). Based on those rates, no E/C outcome difference existed.

Next, however, say that a study of a second jurisdiction obtained an E-program (E_2) rate of 30 percent and a C-program (C_2) rate of 20 percent, again at 18-month post-program follow-up and using the same outcome measure. If this study's sample size was at least moderate, E performed significantly worse than C. This difference from the first study existed despite the obvious fact that the second E-program—jurisdiction two's—

233

had the same absolute recidivism rate as the E in jurisdiction one, namely 30 percent. (In a third jurisdiction's or agency's study, yet another E-program [E_3] could have recidivated at 30 percent; but this one would have performed *better* than its C if, say, the latter's rate was 40 percent.) In any event, E_1 was neither effective nor ineffective relative to C_1, whereas E_2 was less effective than C_2.

Such differences in the relative effectiveness or ineffectiveness of E_1 and E_2 could have occurred even if the features of those E-programs—that is, the programs' characteristics and operations—were nearly identical to each other and even if the E_1, E_2, C_1, and C_2 client groups were quite similar as well. (For present purposes we will assume that arrest and conviction practices were also sufficiently similar across both programs—thus, across both jurisdictions.)

Given that E/E program similarity, given the E/E, E/C, and C/C client similarity, and given perhaps other essentially equivalent factors and conditions, the difference between the E/C outcome obtained in the first study (E = 30 percent, C = 30 percent) and that observed in the second (E = 30 percent, C = 20 percent) may have largely reflected the following: Jurisdiction one's traditional programs—one of which was used as the control in the first study—were routinely less effective than jurisdiction two's, one of which was the control in the second study. That possibility or hypothesis (to which, of course, there could be alternatives) would have meant the following: Two or more comparable and adequately designed and implemented E/C studies, *across which* various other key factors and conditions are fairly to highly equivalent, may nevertheless produce mutually different—even contradictory—pictures as to the relative "effectiveness" of particular E-programs. More specifically, it would have suggested that jurisdiction differences in the absolute power of *C*-programs may sometimes make the decisive difference.

This example tacitly but not unreasonably assumes that one jurisdiction's or agency's traditional or otherwise standard programs *(a)* may be less developed than those of another's and that *(b)* this difference, if reflected in the particular C-programs that are used, *may* sometimes determine the relative effectiveness or ineffectiveness of the former jurisdiction's *E*-program as compared to that of the latter. As seen next, this situation could have substantial implications for program evaluation in general, not just for comparisons across a *small* number of individual programs and their particular jurisdictions.

Specifically, if one accepts assumption *(a)* and applies it collectively to the numerous programs/jurisdictions involved in the following example, a general hypothesis could emerge (the example involves a completed, hypothetical meta-analysis of eighty E/C studies; collectively, the studies cover, say, eight generic program-approaches that each contain about ten individual studies; and again collectively, they would occur in many jurisdictions). The general hypothesis could be as follows: Differences in the *absolute* recidivism rates of control programs that exist in one jurisdiction as opposed to another may affect the extent to which various *types* of E-programs either outperform or do not outperform their respective C's. (The types in question—for example, the cognitive behavioral, family counseling, multimodal, and/or confrontation—would come from the eight generic program-approaches.) Restated, the jurisdiction differences in absolute rates may, for given reasons, affect some kinds of programs more than others. That is, they may substantially influence the degree to which various types of E's are considered effective.

Thus, for example, if it happened that the *C* (standard) programs which were used in the approximately ten studies of family counseling turning out to be relatively weak in terms of recidivism rates, this would have made it easier for that type of *E* (experimental) program to appear more promising than would otherwise have been the case. Based on the general hypothesis, much of that weakness might have been associated with jurisdictions whose standard (C) programs were below par—this, regardless of the type of *E*-program with which those C's were compared. Thus, the jurisdictions could also have used generally weak C-programs in studies whose E emphasized, not family counseling, but, say, the cognitive-behavioral approach. To be sure, the E/C outcome difference might have been smaller or perhaps nonexistent with other approaches, such as confrontation, in those same jurisdictions.

(Two points before continuing. First, in the above context, "relatively weak" may, for instance, refer to either or both of the following: An absolute recidivism rate whose mean and/or median is substantially higher than that of the C-programs in many or most remaining generic approaches, taken individually, and/or [still using the family counseling example] one that clearly exceeds that of approximately seventy other programs, collectively. Second, the advantage that one generic E-approach—say, approach A—may have over another (B) because of A's weaker C-programs does not have to be produced by *jurisdiction* differences in particular, whether primarily or at all. It may reflect other sources, instead or in addition. Yet regardless of the specific factors or conditions that might produce those weaker controls, generic approach A's advantage over B would be no less "real" and should therefore still be addressed.)

Though some variations in the recidivism rates of control programs will always exist across jurisdictions, *random* variations in those rates would likely cancel each others' effects—at least for the most part and if the number of control programs (thus, the number of E/C studies) is sizable. As a result, cross-jurisdiction variations would probably have an impact on the collective E versus C comparisons—an impact that is "*un*cancelled" and not infrequently substantial—only under other conditions. Two main conditions are probably as follows: *(a)* as indicated earlier, a *systematic* relationship, that is, a nonrandom interaction, exists between jurisdiction differences (or any alternative differences), on the one hand, and certain types of programs, on the other; and *(b)* the number of E/C studies is relatively small. Both *(a)* and *(b)* would apply whether or not the E-programs are fairly new to corrections. In addition, condition *(a)* would pertain even if the E-programs involved in any single analysis are, collectively, a *mixture* of generic types, for instance, not just individual counseling but perhaps that and vocational training. Both conditions, especially *(b)*, can often exist when one uses strategies described in chapters 8 and 9.

The outcomes and features of one jurisdiction's control program may affect other jurisdictions' views of and decisions about their own standard (C) programs. For instance, in connection with the original example, jurisdiction two's C-program (C_2), whose recidivism rate was 20 percent, may have had features that jurisdiction one considers much better than those in its own traditional program (C_1). As a result—and certainly in light of the 20 percent rate compared to its own C's 30 percent—jurisdiction one might wish to quickly incorporate such a C_2 program or substantial parts of it into its own operation. More specifically, it might wish to either substitute it for or add it to its own repertoire of programs, in each case without first testing it scientifically against an existing standard program. Alternatively, the jurisdiction might first wish to examine a C_2-type operation as an *experimental* program in a future E/C study it might undertake. (This is apart from whether jurisdiction one might choose to compare the effectiveness of that future "C-turned-E" with that of its *present* control-program—C_1—in particular.)

Though the form of these wishes, and the jurisdiction's level of interest in an alternative or substitute program, parallels (albeit is the converse of) the program developments next mentioned, the previously noted wishes can be implemented independent of them. The developments in question focus on a jurisdiction's responses to its own *experimental* program, not to another's control program and on how the latter compares with its own *C*-program. Changes that have been triggered by the performance of a jurisdiction's own experimental program have probably been more common than those springing from the jurisdiction's responses to another's control—that is, standard—program, even when many details of that C-program have been known.

PROGRAM EVOLUTION

E's-turned-C's

In any given jurisdiction, the experimental program that was part of an original E/C study can—after having demonstrated its feasibility and promise—be incorporated in whole or part by that jurisdiction as a full-fledged component of its overall, standard operation. From that point on, this then-former E could be used as a *control*, that is, a standard program. In short, other programs, including new ones that the jurisdiction or agency would consider *E's*, could then be scientifically compared with *it*—the E-turned-C.

Such incorporations are a form of program evolution, and they have likely occurred in several jurisdictions during recent decades. Often, the incorporation of these E's-turned-C's probably helped the given agencies equal or outdistance others and/or improve their own operations in any event. To be sure, such developments or improvements could in turn pose a sizable challenge to practitioners and others who, for instance, might later wish to develop an even *newer* program within the jurisdiction. (The newer program, which might address the same types of clients as before, would be designed to have a lower recidivism rate or at least be more cost-effective than the jurisdiction's "control"—that is, the now-former E which was incorporated by that jurisdiction.) A similar challenge could exist in any setting that had adopted and adapted an apparently successful E- and/or C-program from any *other* jurisdiction—a program that, say, had a low absolute recidivism rate for the types of clients in question. In either case, the incorporation of former E-programs necessarily complicates matters for cumulative research. (See the next section, entitled "Selected Implications for Research.") Nevertheless, such evolution is important.

(Developments regarding *individual* programs should be distinguished from those which may involve *types* of programs. For instance, reasonable evidence exists that both family counseling and the behavioral approach generally improved during the 1980s. It should be noted, however, that these improvements probably did not just reflect—or did not primarily or even necessarily reflect—substantial changes in the *salient* feature per se [say, in "family counseling"] and/or in how that feature was implemented. Instead, it likely reflected changes in *other features/combinations [F/Cs] as well,* that is, in F/Cs which were part of the same type of program. Improvements in family counseling and the behavioral approach involved several jurisdictions and did not seem to simply be an artifact of below-average C-programs.)

Selected Implications for Research

The preceding discussion indicates that the content ("substance") of some jurisdictions' E-programs may substantially resemble that of some other jurisdictions' *C's,* or, in some cases, that of the first jurisdictions' prior C's. Such content resemblance ("overlap," or "similarly") can encompass *(a)* not just one or two features and perhaps combinations of features but several features/combinations instead—programmatic and/or nonprogrammatic in nature. The resemblance might also involve *(b)* several interactions among those features and/or combinations. The existence of such overlap—even item *(a)* alone—would mean that study samples which were examined in meta-analyses and literature reviews to date may have included—and probably did include—some E-programs that were similar or rather similar to C's. (These E's and C's would have been from differing studies.) *Collectively,* some inadvertent mixing of E's and C's would thus have occurred.

Also, this substantive overlap would help explain why the performance of various *individual* C's at least equaled that of their E's, including E's that were probably relevant to the client population and had been adequately implemented. Such overlap—assuming it exists—will be increasingly important in future research, at least if a rising number or percentage of jurisdictions incorporate, into their current operations, former E's or sizable portions of E's that seem feasible and promising. (Any substantial amount of overlap will be important, whether or not it is *increasingly* so.) Moreover, the likely existence of content overlap reinforces the importance of carefully describing the features of C-programs, not just those of E's. By definition, such descriptions are needed in order to *(a)* systematically examine and specifically compare the prima facie substance of given programs and *(b)* relate actual details of those programs to outcome. (Substance or content includes not just items or entities but operations and dynamics, as well.)

Adding Control Programs   This use of and emphasis on detailed content can occur whether or not the programs under study are—technically—C's or E's. For instance, when using the earlier mentioned descriptive information, one can directly examine the relationship between given features/combinations (i.e., substance), on the one hand, and program effectiveness, on the other, irrespective of whether those F/Cs are found among E's or C's. In short, the F/Cs that are focused on can be drawn from a collection of studies that may include promising E- and C-programs alike. (Broadly conceived, promise or success may involve, for example, *(a)* low absolute recidivism rates, *(b)* E > C, or C > E, at *p* < .05, and/or *(c)* attainment of at least a given effect size. Elsewhere in this volume, it is defined somewhat differently (see the sections in chapter 9 entitled "Guide Programs" and "Prominent-programs Procedure").

This means that for purposes of grouped research, that is, multiple-study research, the following would apply: One could soften or even eliminate the boundaries between that which—in various *individual* E/C studies that constitute those *groups* of studies—comprises E- and C-programs, respectively. This flexible-boundaries approach could be used in supplementary analyses, in any event. (Chapters 8 and 9 describe analytic strategies and procedures designed to focus on substance per se, that is, on detailed F/Cs. Though these strategies and so on are presented in terms of standard E/C distinctions and fixed boundaries only, they can instead—or also—be viewed and reformulated as "E/C neutral" in any given instance.)

Obviously, even occasional content overlap between E- and C-programs would create analytic and interpretive complications that should be acknowledged and addressed in future intervention research. Yet, that same overlap might be used positively—in particular, to increase sample size. Even so, utilization of flexible boundaries would not mean that traditional analytic distinctions between E's and C's should be ignored. Instead, it would suggest that a F/C-centered analysis can provide an appropriate setting and opportunity for broadening one's analytic and interpretive perspectives. It can facilitate an increased emphasis on the substance and operations of given programs in any event, whether or not those programs are E's or C's. (It should go without saying that any C-programs which are included in an analysis should have been imple-mented no less adequately than were the E's.)

Review and Related Considerations

Regarding various generic approaches, some effectiveness results obtained to date may have partly reflected the following interrelated conditions (these conditions should be considered possibilities, not necessarily probabilities, since no systematic effort has yet made to assess a *wide* range of evidence one way or the other regarding their existence):

1. Analyzed collectively, a substantial portion of the E-programs that comprised these generic approaches had, on average, better or worse *C*-programs, respectively. The E-approaches might have em-

phasized, for example, confrontation, on the one hand, and the cognitive-behavioral, on the other. Again, these are just possibilities.

2. Greater or lesser effectiveness on the part of C-programs was, in turn, sometimes a partial function of the mean or median effectiveness of the typical standard program in the jurisdictions in which those respective C-programs were implemented. That is, effectiveness was influenced by the jurisdictions themselves, by virtue of those jurisdictions' impact on the content and implementation of the programs. (Also on this score, some jurisdictions may have had considerably more wherewithal than others for implementing given E-programs or types of E's.)

Condition *(2)* may be thought of as having reflected the position of those respective jurisdictions or agencies on, say, a hypothetical scale that represents a developmental/evolutionary track. This track would run from low effectiveness to high effectiveness, as judged by the absolute recidivism rate of the jurisdictions' standard programs, adjusted for client risk-level. In the present context, these respective jurisdictions would receive a collective average, and the adjustments in question would be based on their mean risk-level. (Apart from these collective analyses and averages, but using the same scale, any *one* jurisdiction could be compared with any other at a given time. Moreover, a jurisdiction's changes could be tracked through time.)

Though conditions *(1)* and *(2)* have not been systematically explored, the underlying issues should be carefully addressed in future research. Assuming the conditions exist, we hypothesize that they frequently exert a substantial, and occasionally a dominant, influence on the relative effectiveness of given E-programs, that is, on E versus C outcomes. However, that influence may *often* be major when the sample of studies is fairly small. These points are relevant not just to studies organized around generic program-categories but to those arranged in accordance with the suggested new procedures described in chapters 8 and 9. In these procedures, data are not organized around those program categories.

OTHER ISSUES

Using Absolute Rates

It is often said, in effect, that "This program was better than that one, because it significantly reduced recidivism (E > C; $p < .05$), whereas the second program did not (E = C)." This type of statement is based on a comparison of two E-programs with their respective C's. However, to better—more fully and more precisely—assess the strength of one program (say, an E) relative to another (also an E), it is important to compare those programs with *each other*, not just with different ones (C's). Moreover, that comparison should be done on as equal a basis as possible or feasible.

This direct, targeted comparison could involve two main steps. First, one would use the E-programs' respective recidivism rates—that is, their "raw" or "absolute" rates (e.g., 30 percent and 25 percent at 18-month follow-up) rather than, say, the amount of *difference* between the respective E-program and C-program rates. (The latter would involve the difference between the first E and C's rates minus the difference between the second E and C's rates.) Second, one would at least roughly adjust those rates for unequal follow-up periods and other relevant, preexisting inequalities. An alternative, albeit related way to define absolute recidivism rate would be in terms of the average number of offenses per client per month—standardized, say, over a 12- or preferably 18-month postprogram follow-up. However, for present purposes we will simply focus on recidivism rates per se and will assume equal or equalized followups, and so on.

As suggested and implied, the absolute-rates approach reflects two interrelated premises: *(a)* the strength or effectiveness of two E-programs cannot be adequately compared by examining only how each one performs relative to its C, however good or poor the latter's performance may appear; and (b) direct, E/E comparisons—that is, E versus E—would be more relevant than indirect ones— E versus C—with respect to the goal of assessing one E-program's strength relative to that of another.

Thus, for instance, it would certainly be helpful to know that the first E-program had outperformed its C—say, at .05—whereas the second did not outperform *its* C. However, that information would not be enough, and it would certainly not be optimal. (As suggested earlier, such "outperformance"-differences between two E/C outcomes could have mainly reflected the fact that the two C-programs in those studies had different recidivism rates—even after various adjustments—and that they therefore provided an unequal basis for comparison. Beyond that, even if both E-programs *had* outperformed their C's at .05, each of the four programs—the two E's and two C's—still could have had mutually different recidivism rates, that is, substantially different absolute rates.) Similarly, it would be useful, but again neither sufficient nor optimal, to know the *effect sizes* of the respective E's in relation to their C's—since, as before, one C's performance could have been rather different than the other C's, even if one *E's* recidivism rate may have equaled that of the second E. (This is independent of the fact that effect sizes—like *p*-levels themselves—can reflect substantial "noise," i.e., error, at the individual-program level.)

In the same vein, in order to better assess the performance and strengths of one *C*-program relative to that of a second C, one should directly compare those particular programs with each other; that is, one should not just compare them indirectly, via any other programs (whether E's or non-E's). This, too, should be done on as equal a basis as possible, starting with the respective programs' absolute rates (e.g., C_1 = 30 percent and C_2 = 20 percent, in the jurisdiction example). Like absolute-rate comparisons between E's and E's, those between C's and C's could provide key information over and beyond that supplied by C/E's—here, the same as E/C's. Direct, C/C comparisons—and, separately, direct E/E comparisons—could add breadth and accuracy to one's understanding of the reliability and possible generalizability of findings from C and E programs alike, individually and collectively.

The absolute-rates approach—here, the direct comparison of E and E recidivism rates and/or (separately) C and C rates—would be scientifically appropriate whether or not *(a)* the above-mentioned program evolution (growth/development) had occurred and *(b)* any jurisdiction differences were present. That is, the absolute-rates approach would be defensible, not to mention useful, independent of the existence—and degree—of any such evolution and differences. Among its useful products, this approach could spotlight the seldom discussed fact that an E-program may statistically outperform its C yet not be especially strong. This situation, which is further discussed below, could arise if the E-program's C is unusually weak in connection with the target at hand.

Further Use of Controls

As implied above, a fuller understanding of C-program strengths could help one better interpret and utilize E's themselves. Another, perhaps more direct contribution to knowledge on the part of C's will be discussed shortly (here, we must begin by first presenting background material that focuses on E's).

The fact that some statistically successful E-programs (E > C; $p < .05$) may not be strong in absolute terms* reinforces the potential value of

---

*For instance, though E may outperform C at .05, the actual recidivism rates might be 45 percent and 55 percent respectively—say, at 18-month followup—for generally moderate-risk individuals.

using the "guide programs" procedure or approach detailed in chapter 9. There, in what might be called the "basic" guide-programs analysis, one focuses on a sample of $E's$ (described shortly). For that sample, one tries to determine if any particular programmatic, staff, and so on, *features/ combinations* occur in a sizable portion of the programs (e.g., in four of the six programs) that comprise the sample, That is, one tries to see if any F/Cs are relatively common within that collection—sample—of guide programs. Separately, one tries to determine if any such F/Cs (that is, any F/Cs often found) are substantially *less often* found in programs that comprise a sample of *non*-guide E's.

To conduct this "basic" analysis one would examine only those E-programs which had rather clearly outperformed their respective C's, say, by at least 40 percent on recidivism;* in fact, only those particular programs would be included in the study sample itself and would be defined as "guides." (Subsequent steps in the analysis need not be specified here.) Given this eligibility requirement, most such E's would probably have a comparatively low, or no more than moderate, absolute recidivism rate as well.** (This rate differs from the "outperformance" rate, which, in the suggested eligibility requirement, would involve a 40+ percent E/C *difference*.) In this respect, E's that constituted the guide-programs sample would not likely be weak. This is despite the fact that the presence of statistical significance does not by itself guarantee strength, at least not in terms of absolute rather than outperformance rates.

Now then, it is possible to go beyond the "basic" analysis and to thereby bring C-programs into the picture. Specifically, by working from the premise that some C's can closely resemble some E's, one could justifiably add to the guide programs' study sample all C-programs that clearly outperform their E's. (Presumably, the latter would not be E's they might turn out to resemble.) This addition of C's would be part of an

---

*If an E's recidivism rate was, say, 30 percent whereas its C's was 50 percent, the reduction in recidivism would have been 40 percent, using the C rate as base: (50 percent – 30 percent) ÷ 50 percent = 40 percent. In that respect, E would have "outperformed" C by 40 percent, though the E/C percentage-*points* difference would have been 20.

**A moderate (medium) rate might range from about 25 percent through 39 percent, at approximately 18-month post-program follow-up, and this would generally involve unusually difficult clients. The "low-to-medium" estimate would apply to the full range of clients, combined—"lightweights" through "heavyweights." With a typical population-mix, most guide programs would probably have an absolute recidivism rate of roughly 17–30 percent.

"expanded" rather than a basic analysis. It could be important mainly because some of those C's might indeed turn out to have factors/combinations in common with various E's that would already be in the analysis. If that commonality did exist, it could enhance reliability and perhaps generalizability, essentially by increasing the sample size and, perhaps, the content-range, respectively. However, if it did not exist, knowledge of this fact could itself provide a more realistic picture of the extent to which given *features/combinations* are—or are not—associated with the more promising outcomes (specifically, those involving the outperformance criterion, in this case the suggested 40+ percent).

Such an expansion need neither eliminate the basic—the E's-only—approach nor devalue its possible products; for instance, if one wished to do so, one could still use that approach and the expanded one in parallel. Moreover, one could add or not add the specified C-programs to the *basic* approach even if one decided to use a rather different eligibility-criterion. Specifically, instead of using the 40+ percent outperformance criterion, one might wish to construct a study sample containing only those programs which have low *absolute* recidivism rates, or, alternatively, those with rates in the lower half—or perhaps third—of an overall distribution. (*Medium* absolute rates might be included if a sizable percentage of the studies focus on unusually difficult clients.) Each of these eligibility or inclusion criteria would be distinct from the above-mentioned 40+ percent recidivism-*difference* criterion. In other words, an absolute-rates criterion would substitute for one based on a percentage difference, such as the outperformance criterion. Or, it would be used in a parallel, independent analysis. Nevertheless, we believe the outperformance criterion would probably provide the best initial basis for a guide-programs analysis, assuming this criterion is operationally feasible.

In sum, in order to identify key contributors to success and to increase the reliability and generalizability of one's findings, it would be useful to address the following questions: *(a)* Which features/combinations—that is, what specific contents—are commonly found among C-programs that meet a preestablished outperformance criterion or that have low or low-to-medium recidivism rates? *(b)* Which of those F/Cs are, and which are not, generally found among C's with *higher* rates? Methodologically and structurally, analyses that address those questions for C-programs would parallel or be identical to the "basic" guide-programs procedure described in chapter 9 for E's alone. As to the F/Cs themselves, these would become an integral substantive part of those analyses—ones that would otherwise have reflected E-programs alone. That is, these control F/Cs would become full-fledged, qualitatively equal components of those analyses, even if they—the control F/Cs—were quantitatively less common than the E's. At any rate, they would not simply be supplements, even though one could, if one wished, analyze them on their own.

By identifying the common and perhaps most distinguishing features and combinations associated with specified C- and E-programs or with C's and E's combined, practitioners, researchers, and others could better develop or recommend effective new programs and improve existing ones. In particular, they could obtain and apply more and better information about what to emphasize and curtail, and about which components might work together in real-life operations. The "specified" programs in question would be those which meet a preestablished outperformance criterion or that have low or low-to-medium recidivism rates, as in item *(a)* above.

Appendix G. Offender Intervention Scales[1]

1. Enhancing/promoting a nondelinquent or noncriminal self-image

Involve client in activities and interests that show promise of reinforcing a nondelinquent or noncriminal self-image.

Try to extinguish, in client, the value of a delinquent or criminal self-image.

Expose client to adequate males/females who are neither impressed nor taken in by "tough" or "delinquent" mannerisms.

2. Modifying attitudes toward adults/establishment

Show client that there are many adults whom he can trust.

Show client that many adults are worthy of his respect—including genuine appreciation, positive regard, or esteem.[2]

Try to convince client that you represent more than "the man" or more than an extension of "the establishment."

3. Teaching values and internal controls

Try to get client to start "thinking twice" before he acts.

Teach client to cope with delayed gratification of his needs and wants.

Try to instill in client certain basic social values and standards.

Instruct client on basic do's and don'ts, as though he were a child.

4. Increasing self-awareness/self-acceptance

Help client understand some of the early sources of his present self-image.

Help client change some of his beliefs regarding what and who he "should" be or "ought" to be.

Help client resolve doubts about his basic adequacy and worthiness.

5. *Reducing apathy/indifference*

Try to get client to be more evaluative of and responsive to his social world.

Encourage client to more actively care about what happens to him.

Try to get client to be more reactive to the events in his life, to take a more active stance in determining what happens to him.

6. *Improving/altering family/parental relationships*

Help client become aware of how the personal problems of parental figures can interact with, or have interacted with, his own development.

Get client to see his parents in a realistic light—their strengths, weaknesses, and individual personalities.

Increase client's understanding of the role he has played in his family (as child and sibling), and of the particular ways this might have influenced his life.

Get client to see his present family (wife, children) in a realistic light— their strengths, weaknesses, and individual personalities.

Increase client's understanding of the role he has played in his present family (as father and husband), and of the particular ways this might have influenced his current behavior, especially illegal activities.

7. *Altering peer influence/pressure*

Explain to client specific ways in which peers may set him up to meet their own needs at his expense.

Discuss issues of "the price of loyalty" to, or "the price of going along with," peers in various situations.

Suggest to client alternatives to conforming behavior on his part when he is confronted with peer pressure, especially in relation to possible illegal activities.

Serve as a counterforce to negative effects of peer influence.

8. *Focusing on everyday practical adjustment*

Teach client how to take care of himself and meet his needs on a practical basis.

Work primarily with performance, for example, school, employment, and living arrangements, rather than with emotions and psychological issues.

Actively help client find job opportunities and obtain actual work.

9. *Utilizing/focusing on client/worker relationships*

Talk with client about how you and he are relating to one another, about the nature and quality of your relationship.

Encourage client to begin actively thinking about the nature of, and changes in, his relationship with you.

Use your relationship with client to illustrate themes and problems in the way he relates to others.

Emphasize to client that you expect him to relate to you on a personal basis.

10. *Gaining client's confidence in worker as being understanding/capable*

Gain client's confidence as someone who is skilled in understanding interpersonal problems.

Demonstrate to client that you can understand very personal feelings and needs on his part.

Gain client's confidence in you as a worker (person, intervener/treater) who can in fact help.

11. *Expressing personal concern for and acceptance of client*

Help client feel you really do care about him in more than a formal, "It's-my-job" fashion.

Help client feel that you accept and care for him as an individual, not only in terms of his uniqueness but also independent of his particular problems and behavior.

Help client feel that his personal happiness is quite important to you.

Help client feel that you do not see him as "sick," "weird," or undesirable.

12. *Exposing client to same sex adult-models*

Expose client to same-sex adult models whom he cannot regard as weak, incompetent, and so on.

For male workers with male clients, behave in a masculine manner that the client can recognize and accept or respect as such. For female workers with female clients, behave in a feminine manner that the client can recognize and accept or respect as such.

13. *"Programming"/rehearsing client for specified life situations*

Teach client how to handle specific difficulties he may experience when he's on his own and you're not available to him.

Review with client his ideas about or plans for handling difficult situations (e.g., temptations, pressures) that may arise when you're not around.

Teach client specific ways of "avoiding trouble" (e.g., fights or narcotics).

14. *Ego-bolstering via success experiences*

Expose client to situations in which he can "win."

Expose client to probable success experiences, even if they represent menial challenges.

Make sure client gets ego-bolstering recognition from others, even for menial successes or accomplishments.

15. *Using positive peer influence*

Encourage client to interact with nondelinquent or prosocial peers.

Encourage client to interact with delinquents or offenders who wish to communicate nondelinquent or prosocial views.

16. *Using authority (legitimate power or force)*

Give client a relatively specific set of terms or conditions that he must meet or live up to.

Make client responsible for failure to follow through on his agreements with you by taking privileges or freedom from him.

Provide support for those who live with client and/or are responsible for helping to control his behavior.

Keep "on top of" client; don't accept any "shining-on"; let him know you're usually around and interested in what he's doing.

Make sure client sees you as the main source of power with whom he must deal when making decisions and plans.

Make sure client does not succeed in "power plays," intimidation tactics, or manipulation efforts when interacting with you.

17. *Using internal stress as stimulus/motivator*

Capitalize on distress or anxiety in client as a stimulus for change.

Capitalize on internal pressures (e.g., anxiety or guilt) as stimuli for motivating client in the direction of treatment or change.

18. *Doing the unexpected*

Maintain an element of unpredictability in how you react to client under particular circumstances.

Intentionally relate to client in ways that will not readily fit into his usual manner of perceiving and interpreting others.

Try to prevent client from thinking he can predict, using simple formulas, your responses to his behavior.

19. *Involving client in case planning and decision making*

Discuss with client your intervention rationale, plans, and goals.

Involve client as an equal in case decisions.

Thoroughly discuss with client any challenges and objections he has to your decisions concerning his case.

Allow client to significantly determine the extent of your involvement in his life.

Allow client to make nearly all his own decisions, largely without your participation.

Allow client to pretty much run his own life.

Discuss and review the progress of intervention with client.

20. *Emphasizing concreteness versus abstractness of verbalizations and interpretations*

Avoid using adult-level concepts or explanations when talking with client.

Speak to client in very concrete terms, avoiding abstractions.

Repeat (more than once) any expectations you have of client, so that he will be less likely to forget them as soon as you're gone.

21. *Increasing interpersonal sensitivity*

Encourage client to perceive, appreciate, and respond appropriately to more individual differences among other people.

Encourage client to consider new ways of perceiving and interpreting the behavior of others and their motives and needs for acting as they do.

Give feedback and clarification to client about the reactions of others to him.

Teach client more mature ways of influencing others.

22. *Promoting the expression of feelings*

Help client verbalize and more adequately express his feelings and emotional reactions toward others.

Serve client as a source of catharsis, listening to expressions of pent-up needs, emotions, or fears.

Show client it is ok to verbally direct reasonable emotion and anger at their true source, rather than displace or suppress them.

Emphasize to client the importance of expressing his inner feelings directly to those whom they involve (e.g., parents, spouse, peers, yourself).

23. *Promoting self-understanding*

Try to get client to begin asking questions (at least of himself) regarding inner sources of his behavior.

Use review of early/earlier years and of social-history events to help client better understand his behavior and feelings.

Increase client's awareness of how such factors as guilt or feelings of inadequacy can be a destructive force in his life.

Discuss with client particular ways in which his unique needs and response style can manifest themselves in his interpersonal relationships.

Develop what may approach a professional counseling or therapy relationship with client.

24. *Emphasizing recreational/socializing experiences*

Encourage client to participate in any of several recreational activities (e.g., fishing, sports, or group field trips).

Involve client in group recreational activities.

25. *Establishing/maintaining frequent contact*

Make sure that you and client are in frequent contact.

Maintain a regular schedule of frequent contacts with client.

26. *Promoting informality—lack of social distance*

Minimize social or personal distance between yourself and client.

Talk with client about yourself and your feelings in order to let him know you on a fairly personal level.

Invite client to your home, much as you would a friend.

27. *Developing/maintaining client's commitment to intervention (treatment/control)*

Let client know he must meet you halfway in the sense of committing himself to intervention, for example, showing reasonable willingness to work on whatever main goals have been established for him.

Let client know that your support of him is largely contingent upon his making a reasonable commitment to intervention objectives and goals.

28. *Expressing warmth, friendliness, affection*

Relate to client in an interpersonally warm or affectionate manner.

Express, to client, positive affection that you may feel for him.

Give client warm, friendly, physical contact, for example, pat on back, arm, or shoulder.

29. *Protecting, minimizing demands and pressures*

Expose client to supportive, nonthreatening social situations.

Make only minimal demands on, and establish only minimal expectations for, client.

Allow client to be childish and immature, including expressing childish dependency.

Avoid exposing client to harsh, personal encounter-group situations.

Avoid exposing client to sophisticated, aggressive, or manipulative offenders.

30. *Being forceful, blunt*

Be willing to "tell off" client when you feel he needs it.

Be verbally forceful, even harsh, during necessary confrontations.

Be willing to yell at (but not be abusive toward) client during confrontations.

31. *Associating concern with control*

Try to convince client that controls, by you, reflect real concern for his well-being.

Make sure client understands that discipline of him, by you, is not a sign of personal rejection.

Emphasize to client that his being controlled by you is not the same as his being emasculated by you.

32. *Familiarizing client with authority figures*

Expose client to police, probation officers, and judges as individuals, by means of informal meetings and on-site tours.

Via meetings, lectures, and on-site tours, familiarize client with the goals, philosophies, and rules that underlie the thinking and govern the activities of police, probation officers, and judges.

33. *Involving client in the community*

Involve client in civic activities.

Involve client in community projects.

34. *Being an advocate for client*

Present client's side and help him obtain his rights with school officials.

Present client's side and help him obtain his rights with police, the court, and so on.

35. *Being personally available during crises*

Use crisis-intervention techniques to help client during emergencies.

Use 24-hour availability and/or "hot lines" to help client during emergencies.

Appendix H. Staff Characteristics Scales[1]

1. *Socially desired qualities*

pleasant (vs. unpleasant)

unaffected (vs. affected)

friendly (vs. unfriendly)

patient (vs. impatient)

sensitive (vs. misses meanings)

interesting (vs. uninteresting)

self-confident (vs. lacks self-confidence)

comfortable with youths (vs. ill at ease)

resourceful (vs. "helpless")

2. *Attributes that most adolescents would probably like*

has a sense of humor

is "one-of-the-boys" (girls)

has "been around" (vs. rather sheltered)

enjoys youths' activities (vs. not interested in them)

is enthusiastic (vs. bored)

has quick, sharp mentality (intuitive)

is understanding of youths' world; can talk their language

is "up" on things

3. *Sharpness/alertness*

is intelligent

is intellectually flexible

is inquisitive

is original (conceptually . . . vs. unoriginal, imitative)

has a broad perspective

4. *Bold/forward/direct/outspoken*

is outspoken

is blunt

is candid

is direct

in intervention (treatment/control), would "shoot the works" if he/she thought it was needed

5. *Strength of feelings/expressions/opinions*

typically makes "absolute" statements (vs. relative ones)

overdramatizes (vs. underplays)

displays emotional ups and downs (vs. displays stable mood)

has a rapid pace of speech (if extreme)

conveys quality of force, ardor (vs. passivity, lethargy)

conveys sense of haste, urgency, impatience (vs. ease, leisure, calm)

6. *Moralistic orientation*

staff member's own view of role: policeman

coder(s)' view of staff member's role: policeman

moralistic approach to job (vs. pragmatic, expedient approach)

moralistic personality structure (vs. expedient structure)

positive effect of religious upbringing (of supernatural precepts/ obligations)

strong concern with theme/concept of right versus wrong

interest in protecting society (vs. protecting youths), if this interest is extreme or clearly emphasized

7. *Socially undesirable qualities*

is quarrelsome

is stubborn

is unpleasant

is impatient

is immodest

tries to "snow" interviewer

is tactless

displays his temper

8. *Covert or overt aggression/hostility*

manipulates

deprives

is vindictive

is threatening

is unfriendly

is competitive

is aggressive (vs. assertive)

"asks for" submission from others

"asks for" conflict with others

9. *Past personal difficulties, felt as such*

stresses own difficulties in growing up

indicates own adolescence was not happy

feels he has gone through much personal struggle, conflict

feels he has overcome much personal struggle, conflict

10. *Current personal "troubles," often unrecognized as such*

is frightened

takes things personally

feels anxiety about his own life

is self-depreciating

uses defense of projection

11. *Personal satisfaction with work, with accomplishments*

enjoys his work

is satisfied with work accomplishments

believes his work is of value

feels he is competent in his work

12. *Satisfaction with the world about him*

is basically satisfied with own society

is critical of middle-class standards (vs. accepting of those standards)

is alarmed about issues, problems

indicates life in general is basically happy (vs. sad)

is optimistic (vs. pessimistic)

13. *Personal involvement with youngsters*

important for him to feel youth is improving

wants to protect youngster from society (if this stance is extreme or clearly emphasized)

voluntarily spends extra time working with, doing things for, youths

14. *"Social distance" : familiarity versus formality*

treats youths in a familiar manner (vs. in a professionally dignified manner)

staff member's own view of role: friend

coder(s)' view of staff member's role: friend

staff member's own view of role: big brother (or big sister)

coder(s)' view of staff member's role: big brother (or big sister)

emotionally demonstrative (vs. emotionally distant)

overly familiar during interview (vs. stands on professional dignity)

allows youths to set the pace, or 50/50

15. *Lack of professional sophistication, self-discipline*

believes youths need goals, experiences, emotional satisfactions similar to one's own believes youths need to conquer inner problems similar to one's own

does not differentiate between behavioral and emotional changes in youths

is unaware of own emotional responses to youths

believes people, including youths, can be taken at face value (almost exclusively)

16. *Use of self (past experience) as a frame of reference for understanding/working with youths*

indicates that he considers it important to recall, draw upon one's own adolescence (in his work)

considers own adolescence similar to youths'

draws examples from his own adolescence (in the interview)

motivation for working with others: giving known (felt) pleasures, inner triumphs

motivation for working with others: vicariously correcting own past

17. *Concern with establishing/maintaining atmosphere for working relationship, and mutual communication*

is concerned with creating a proper atmosphere for the relationship

tries to build youths' trust in him

values confidentiality

accepts youths' feelings

attempts to establish adequate communication

explains why things are done or not done

values consistency

values sincerity

indicates a strong concern with theme/concept of poor communication

18. *Concern with "negative reactions relating to self and others": Impulses and needs associated with guilt, hostility, aggression, rejection*

works with anger

believes guilt is important or essential to work with

believes aggression is important or essential to work with

believes sex is important or essential to work with

strong concern with theme/concept of 'contempt'

strong concern with theme/concept of 'hostility'

strong concern with theme/concept of 'defiance'

19. *"Inner" focus (techniques and aims)*

believes anxiety is important or essential to work with

focuses on youths' thinking about things (vs. youths' doing things)

tries to clarify youths' strivings, needs

tries to work with youths' inner, emotional needs or desires

tries to build youths' self-confidence

tries to develop strong dependency relationships

20. *Expressive of dissatisfaction; critical*

is relatively critical of the department/agency

believes things are getting worse in the department/agency

is a complainer

is self-critical

criticizes peers

21. *Orientation toward change and activity*

tries to change things in the department/agency (vs. "resigned" to working conditions)

expresses strong concern with theme/concept of 'eagerness'

expects *rapid*, major (relatively permanent) changes in youths

believes youths' "will power" is sufficient to overcome problems

considers adventure/excitement an important personal reward, goal in his work prefers to proceed quickly with youths

does not consider security an important personal reward, goal in his work

does not regard "a good deal of time" as being important in developing a desirable working relationship

focuses on youths' doing things (vs. thinking about things)

22. *Firmness/finality (tough-minded, exacting)*

exacting (vs. easygoing)

demands certainty (vs. tolerates ambiguity)

tough-minded (vs. tender-minded)

is strict

23. *Controls, limits*

sees too little control by others as cause of delinquency

uses his authority with youngsters

tells youngsters what to do and what not to do

indicates strong concern with theme/concept of 'obedience' (during interview)

indicates strong concern with theme/concept of 'domination' (during interview)

indicates strong concern with theme/concept of 'punishment' (during interview)

indicates concern with laws and rules (vs. with youth as individual) (during interview)

Appendix I. Selected Issues Involving Sample Size

Two issues might be noted regarding the sample size in any one E/C study. The first involves relatively large samples, for example, those comprising more than three hundred cases. The second relates to very small samples, for example, those involving fewer than twenty or twenty-five:

1. When $p < .05$ has been reached and the E + C sample is relatively large, the E/C percentage-difference in recidivism rates will sometimes be too small—say, 5 percent— for much practical use. This does not mean it always *is* too small—just that it sometimes will be.

2. If the E + C sample is quite small, any E/C percentage-difference in recidivism rates may be somewhat unstable; certainly, a potential for this exists. This potential refers to the fact that an originally obtained E/C percentage-difference—say, one of 20 percent—can vary substantially if just a few individual cases, that is, clients, are added or subtracted. To be sure, substantial—as opposed to fairly modest— variation is not highly likely. To all intents and purposes, it will occur if the rates for those few individual cases *(a)* differ *considerably* from the average rates of the remaining cases (the "original" cases) combined, and if *(b)* all or almost all the rates for those individual cases differ in the *same direction*, for example, are above the average of the original cases.[1] Nevertheless, the potential does remain, and —while not likely—it is by no means remote. This potential and sometimes actual instability goes beyond the usual level of "noise" that is caused by unreliability in dependent—and independent— measures. (The issue of potential instability, or sensitivity, can also apply to the *effect sizes* that are derived from very small samples, and the cause of this sensitivity is the same as that described above.)

When the E + C sample size in any individual study is in the *middle (typical) range* rather than the relatively high or very low regions mentioned above, issues 1 and 2 are largely precluded. Specifically, under the "middle range" condition a study that reaches the .05 level will seldom be associated with an inconsequential, impractical E/C difference. Its difference will commonly be at least 15 percent (issue 1). Similarly, the original E/C percentage-difference in recidivism rates will not be rather sensitive to quantitatively minor sample-size changes (issue 2).

The present discussion, of course, does not center on the individual E/C study; it involves the collective results from several at a time, that is, from studies as a group. Any E/C percentage-difference in recidivism that is obtained for a *group* of studies is more reliable—in fact, far more—than the difference observed in any *single* study. Basically, this is because reliability increases as the number of instances rises—a principle that applies to small, medium, and large samples alike, whatever the field. (In this discussion, "studies as a group" is any collection of individual E/C studies that is included in an analysis by virtue of the fact that each of its E-programs has satisfied the 15 percent criterion of success.)

Given these definitions and considerations, the following would also apply to any group of studies whose E/C outcome-difference is at least 15 percent in each of its individual studies: That group—*as* a group—would be distinguished fairly reliably from any *other* group whose individual studies never reached that level.[2] This, at least, would be true if each of those groups contained more than just a handful of studies, and it would apply despite the presence of error variance ("noise") in the outcomes of each study.

Also, in this discussion, the $p < .05$ level does not just apply to results from individual studies whose E + C sample is relatively *large*. Instead, it pertains to results from those whose respective samples are small, medium, *or* large—with a clear majority being medium and the rest more or less divided between small and large. Under these conditions, and given a significance level of at least $p < .05$ for every individual study regardless of its sample size, the average E/C difference in recidivism rates across those studies would be medium, not small, and the overall E/C difference would therefore not be inconsequential as to practical import.[3]

Appendix J. Selected Issues Involving Parts and Wholes

Under given conditions, some parts—perhaps many—can doubtlessly be separated from their current, respective wholes. Any such whole or entity will be called "program A" or "combination A" (see below). These parts, or features, may include vocational training, group counseling, and so on. Following their separation from a given program, some parts may be used elsewhere. In particular, they may be transferred and added to other existing entities, for example, different programs within an agency. Any such alternate program or operation, or even a newly created one, will be called "program B" or "combination B." Within B, the transferred features may or may not be operated in much the same way as in A, and they might or might not make a comparable contribution to B's outcome. At any rate, those are some of the events and possibilities that can unfold when various features (parts) are separated from the combinations or programs (wholes) that encompass those features prior to their separation. The same types of events, and so on, can also unfold if only *one* feature (rather than two or more) is separated.

(As may be deduced, combination A can also include parts other than those which are removed. In fact, some combinations may be so inclusive that they comprise virtually an entire program, that is, encompass or otherwise substantively involve themselves in almost all its known operations and apparent interactions. Hence the general interchangeability of "program" and "combination" in the present discussion. In the following text, "separation" and "removal" will be functionally equivalent.)

Whatever "fate" may befall the removed features—for instance, however they may operate and contribute in the context of program B, or whether they are even transferred to B in the first place—the program or combination that *remains behind* after those features are removed may perform better or worse than before their removal. This applies irrespective of whether the remaining program/combination is then *modified*, that is, after the removal of those features. For instance, performance of the remaining program may be better or worse, or even essentially the same, whether or not any restructuring and/or programmatic expansion takes place that is designed to restore, maintain, or improve its preremoval performance level. The same would apply whether or not any changes and reductions occur in the type and range of clients worked with, or in the relative amount of effort expended on various types of preremoval clients. (In a program expansion, such features as educational training, restitution, and/or others may be substituted for those which were removed, though this will not necessarily restore, maintain, or improve program A's preremoval performance. If one [or more] of those features already existed in A, it [or they] may be given different overall emphasis or relative priority, whether or not client-shifts occur.)

Moreover, the removal of given features may differentially affect programs that remain. For instance, it may ordinarily have a larger negative impact on those which are among the most effective, prior to any separation. This hypothesis, which would also apply to model programs, would be reasonable if, say, many such preremoval programs *(a)* depend a good deal on particular interactions between—and close operational coordination of—their parts, and if they *(b)* contain relatively few superfluous parts.

Separately, the removal of given features may cause some programs that had *barely* reached $p < .05$ to no longer attain that level. That loss of effectiveness, in turn, could perhaps result in those programs' exclusion from certain samples, analyses, or conclusions, or in their being part of a different conclusion.[1] This loss may occur even if considerable restructuring and perhaps program expansion takes place. At any rate, removal of given features may have a larger practical effect on such programs than on those which are not borderline with respect to statistical significance. If such a drop in effectiveness proves difficult to reverse, this may sometimes reflect the challenge of working with the borderline programs' particular set of clients—that is, effectively working with them under almost any conditions or, perhaps, within given settings and/or in the face of certain staff limitations. Differentiated analyses, of course, may indicate that the statistical drop in effectiveness does not apply to all client-groups, but that it is rather conspicuous with some.

Appendix K. Definitional Issues Regarding Similarity

Presently, different individuals might often describe the *degree* of similarity that exists between any two "similar programs" in different ways. For instance, they might often use different terms, such as *highly*, *substantially*, *moderately*, or *slightly* to convey comparable meanings—say, comparable ratios of similarities to dissimilarities. As a result, one person's *substantially* might be another's *moderately*, and a third individual's *moderately* may be a fourth's *slightly*. Also, even if two people used an identical term, such as *substantially*, that word could often have a different quantitative not to mention qualitative and/or evaluative meaning to each. These two situations would apply even if the respective individuals observed and recorded essentially the same features/combinations when focusing on each given program and when comparing one program with another.

This situation partly reflects the fact that no standardized or widely used set of descriptive categories exists regarding the similarity dimension. To our knowledge, no quantitative or even qualitative similarity-scale has been explored, either. Absent such terminology and/or scale, degrees of similarity cannot yet be distinguished from each other in any widely recognized and consistent—let alone statistically reliable—way, and, perhaps, in other than very broad terms. This situation (and its consequences) also exists in other fields and sciences. It applies to "adjacent targets" as well, if and when the latter partly overlap each other in real-life operations and in that respect are actually somewhat similar.[1] (See chap. 9 n. 27.)

Though the degree of similarity might not, at present, be described consistently, similarity itself can be defined. For instance, broadly speaking, two or more programs may be considered similar if any content overlap—major or minor—exists between them. (Such overlap would mainly focus on operations but could also involve setting as well as staff and offenders. See the data-item list in chap. 7.) However, for "similar" programs to resemble or overlap each other to a degree that might have practical and perhaps theoretical import, their similarity should probably be at least moderate to substantial.

267

As indicated, however, terms such as *moderate* and *substantial* are currently undefined in any specifically agreed-upon sense, relative to the present subject area. Therefore, to create some initial consistency, broad, provisional distinctions might be considered. For example, the term *moderate similarity* could indicate that the programs or sets of programs being compared do not seem to mostly overlap each other with regard to their respective individual features/combinations, and/or their operations as a whole. That is, the term could be used to describe the programs or sets that seem more different than similar yet are not just slightly or sparingly the same. *Substantial similarity* could mean that the programs seem more alike than dissimilar as to their F/Cs and/or overall operations—without, however, even approaching identity.[2] Though these and other possible distinctions would not resolve all the above-mentioned problems and eliminate all individual preferences as to usage, they could reduce them to an important degree.

Glossary of Abbreviations, Symbols, and Terms

a/r:	Analyses/reviews (meta-analyses/literature reviews)
A/Rs:	Activities and responses
C:	Control (C case, C group, or C sample)
C's:	Controls (C cases, C groups, or C samples)
C-program:	Control program
E:	Experimental (E case, E group, or E sample)
E's:	Experimentals (E cases, E groups, or E samples)
E/C:	Experimental/Control (Experimental and Control)
E/F/L:	Emphasis/framework/level
EPC:	E-program combination
E-program:	Experimental program
ES:	Effect size
ET:	Educational training
F/C:	Features/combinations
GC:	Group counseling
GU-AC:	Generically unrestricted, across-categories
IST:	Interaction strategy and/or technique
NS:	Not statistically significant at or beyond $p < .05$
PMA:	Policy makers and administrators
P/R:	Programming/rehearsing
S:	Successful (Successful program)
SCI:	Staff/client interaction
SES:	Socioeconomic status
U:	Unsuccessful (Unsuccessful program)
VT:	Vocational training

Notes

INTRODUCTION

1. Lipsey's (1992) analysis, which includes more than four hundred individual studies, is the broadest and most systematic to date.

2. Such an overview would also contain less by way of average "measurement error" regarding program effectiveness. In any given literature review, this measurement problem would reflect, for example, an accumulation of (a) errors whose size is often small to moderate, and/or (b) random fluctuations. These inevitably occur when researchers try to measure or estimate the "true" recidivism rate associated with any individual program. To some degree, this problem even exists in large-scale meta-analyses, each of which focuses on many such programs.

3. In any one analysis or review, the limitations (regarding conclusions or generalizations) that reflected or should have reflected various emphases or even exclusions were sometimes large. This applied not just to (*a*) individual studies that comprised the analysis/review but also to (*b*) certain characteristics of the offenders who comprised those studies. The latter emphases or exclusions generally resulted from responses by decision makers—for instance agency administrators, program planners, or managers—to the nature and seriousness of given individuals' offenses, or to the apparent extent of their social/psychological difficulties. Nevertheless, in most reviews and analyses, the approximately forty-five to ninety studies that were examined contained a wide range of offenders *collectively*, that is, when all individual studies were combined. As a result, most types of offenders seemed to be reasonably well represented in most reviews and analyses, even though the less-common individuals may still have been quite infrequent or virtually absent, particularly in connection with certain interventions (approaches). The limitations in question existed whether the given review or analysis focused on a range of interventions— say, counseling, vocational training, and cognitive-behavioral, together—or on one intervention alone.

CHAPTER 1

1. One correctional meta-analysis we knowingly excluded happened to be conducted in Western Europe (Losel and Koferl, 1989). It was excluded because it involved only 16 studies and only adults as well. The only other meta-analysis not included in our review of results involved 20 studies of preadjudicated, at-risk youths only (Kaufman, 1985).

CHAPTER 2

1. Garrett's meta-analysis used not only a variety of *outcome measures*, say, recidivism, psychological adjustment, and institutional adjustment, but also a range of *study designs*, say, random allocation, matching, convenience sampling, and pre/post only. Individually and together, this variety and range, by itself, helped produce rather different pictures of or perspectives on treatment-efficacy in the differing categories of studies that were examined, for instance, categories such as cognitive-behavioral and family therapy. This occurred partly because the various categories did not contain identical varieties and ranges. Besides simply providing *different* pictures/perspectives, the variety and range can be said to have "distorted" particular conclusions that might have been reached regarding the treatment efficacy of any given category—for example, changed those conclusions from what they might have been if only one outcome measure, such as recidivism, or only one study design, such as random allocation, had been used. Yet at the same time, this variety and range helped provide a realistic, composite picture of the types and amounts of impact one could in fact expect to find in a representative cross section of studies. Along another dimension—one that was secondary in Garrett's analysis—utilization of these several outcome measures and designs made it difficult to closely *compare* the various categories with each other in terms of treatment efficacy. (The *design-based* part of this problem has existed in all meta-analyses to date.) In any event, the combined outcome-measure-and-design-based problem was somewhat reduced when Garrett focused on any *one* outcome measure at a time, for example, recidivism. (Of the thirty-four studies that used recidivism, nineteen had a "more rigorous" design and fifteen had a "less rigorous" design (Garrett, 1985).)

2. An earlier account stated that "probation and parole enhancements had no positive impact, *nor did broadly labeled approaches such as counseling and skill-oriented programs*" (Palmer, 1991a, p. 335; emphasis added.) However, the italicized statement is incorrect. It was based on preliminary information only (Lipsey, 1989) and does not reflect findings in the final report (Lipsey, 1992). This report indicates that (*a*) skill-oriented programs were, on average, successful and that (*b*) particular forms of counseling produced—again, on average—slight to moderate recidivism reductions. Both (*a*) and (*b*) applied to justice and nonjustice system programs combined.

3. This may have partly reflected (*a*) the wide variability in effect sizes from one individual study to the next, *within* the Davidson et al. analysis as a whole, and (*b*) the fact that the modest sample-size that existed in many individual studies yielded insufficient power to produce statistical significance for the more *typical* effect sizes that were obtained. (Such statistical limitations are discussed in Lipsey, 1992.) Though analyses of the present studies are found in several publications, the most comprehensive report may be that of Gottschalk et al. (1987). Though neither Davidson, Gottschalk, Gensheimer, and Mayer's (1984) nor Gottschalk et al.'s E/C difference reached statistical significance, the effect size that was obtained (cf. Gottschalk's weighted mean ES of .22) was,

according to Lipsey (1992), similar to that obtained by others—for example, Garrett (.24) and Andrews, Zinger, Hoge, Bonta, Gendreau, and Cullen (1990) (.21)—"for the better-designed studies, averaged over studies and outcome-measures."

4. The remaining—fifth—category that was included was called "specialty pro-grams" and had only three studies. (Based on an average phi coefficient computed from Whitehead and Lab's summary table, Lipsey (1992, p. 86) concluded that their analysis "yielded a positive mean effect [size] of about the same order of magnitude" [as that found in Garrett, 1985, Kaufman, 1985, and Andrews et al., 1990—the three main studies he reviewed]).

5. Classification as appropriate or inappropriate was based entirely on individual-program status with respect to risk, need, and responsivity. This, at least, was true for behavioral programs, and possibly for most or all nonbehaviorals.

6. The programs that—together—comprised the a priori content of "appropriate correctional services" fell within the following collection of general categories: "short-term behavioral/systems family counseling"; "structured one-on-one paraprofessional/peer program"; "specialized academics/vocational services"; "intensive structured skill training"; "introduction of individualized rehabilitative regime"; "individual/group counseling"; and, "appropriately matched according to risk or responsivity/needs systems."

7. In all likelihood, statistically significant advantages would not easily have emerged even if large *percentage*-differences had been found in the respective recidivism rates associated with any two or more conceptualizations. This is because of the very small cell-sizes that existed for most or all conceptualizations. Such sizes existed because the eight primary conceptualizations were distributed across a total of forty-six studies, thus producing an average cell-size of about six studies per conceptualization. In addition, a low numerical ratio of mean recidivism rate to overall variance rate may have existed for many or most individual conceptualizations, thus further contributing to the lack of statistical significance.

CHAPTER 3

1. An additional review—that of Martinson (1974)—discussed data later presented in Lipton, Martinson, and Wilks (1975), as did Palmer's (1975, 1978) reviews. In the present chapter, each of these reviews will be mentioned only as needed. Gottschalk et al.'s (1987) review will be used instead of Davidson et al.'s (1984), since the two are very similar as to the studies they examined and the methods they used, while Gottschalk et al.'s was more detailed in some respects and Davidson et al's was discussed in chapter 2. Johns and Wallach's (1981) review updated, that is, expanded on, that of Wright and Dixon (1977)—which covered the period 1969–74.

2. Though shock probation is often called "split sentence," these categories sometimes differ from each other. In addition, both categories can be distinguished from "shock incarceration"—this being a somewhat newer approach, to which the above findings do not refer (Parisi, 1980; Vito, 1984; Parent, 1989).

3. Lipsey, 1992 analyzed "reduced caseload" programs and "intensive supervision" programs together, and referred to them generically as "probation/parole reduced caseloads."

CHAPTER 4

1. The total number of meta-analyses and literature reviews that were examined regarding the above-mentioned approaches, respectively, is as follows (analyses are shown first, reviews second): confrontation (3, 5); diversion (3, 9); individual counseling/therapy (3, 8); group counseling/therapy (9, 4); area-wide strategies for delinquency prevention (0, 4). Thus, the generally negative assessments for *confrontation* were found in 6 out of a total of *8* analyses/reviews (specifically, they were found in 3 meta-analyses and 3 literature reviews, out of all 3 meta-analyses and 5 literature reviews), and the generally negative findings for the remaining approaches were found in the following: *diversion*—6 out of 12 analyses/reviews (a/r's); *individual counseling/therapy*—5 out of 11 a/r's; *group counseling/therapy*—7 out of 13 a/r's; *area-wide strategies of delinquency prevention*—4 out of 4 a/r's. Apparently, out of the five generic approaches under consideration, (a) area-wide strategies of delinquency prevention and (b) confrontation received negative assessments most uniformly, across the total group of analysts/reviewers. The remaining three approaches received an even or essentially even mix of analyses/reviews.

2. Absence of absolute certainty reflects the fact that "noise"—say, measurement error in a success-index such as mean recidivism-rate—can distort given programs' *actual* ("true") performance upward or downward in varying degrees and can thereby lead to "false positives" as well as "false negatives." Since the statistical distribution of noise around any given mean or group of means is most likely to be random—say, as often upward as downward, and approximately equal in amount—the following can generally be assumed: For any set of false positives, that is, programs which were not actually successful but nevertheless *seemed* successful (e.g., in terms of their having reached $p < .05$) because of upward-distorting noise, there is an equal-sized set of false negatives, namely, programs that were in fact successful but nevertheless seemed *un*successful (e.g., not having reached .05) due to downward-distorting noise. Given such potential errors and the absence of absolute certainty, the main point of using probability-level cutoffs, such as $p < .05$, is to indicate, nevertheless, how likely it is that (*a*) a given E/C difference is not simply due to random errors, and so on, either upwards or downwards, and that (*b*) a given program has been correctly rather than erroneously classified.

3. Although an earlier analysis (Palmer, 1991a) included vocational training (VT) among the "most successful approaches," it would have been much more accurate to use

the "life skills or skill oriented" category instead. Though VT had usually been included *within* the skills category—this being a considerably broader and, indeed, a relatively successful or promising category (p. 42)—VT was not, by itself, among the generally successful let alone most successful approaches (p. 38).

4. The total number of meta-analyses and literature reviews that were examined regarding the above-mentioned approaches, respectively, is as follows (analyses are shown first, reviews second): behavioral (6, 8); cognitive-behavioral or cognitive (4, 2); life skills (2, 1); multi-modal (1, 2); family intervention (3, 9).

For the remaining approaches (excluding those in note 1), the total number of analyses and reviews is as follows (analyses first, reviews second): social casework, social agency, or societal institution approaches to delinquency prevention (1, 6); physical challenge (1, 4); restitution (0, 3); vocational training (2, 4); employment (2, 2); educational training (3, 3); probation enhancement and parole enhancement (3, 7); intensive probation supervision (0, 2); intensive aftercare (parole) supervision (0, 1); community-based vs. institutional (4, 6).

5. Lipsey's average of 64 percent positive-outcome studies was comparable to the 58 percent obtained by combining the results from literature reviews by Bailey (1966), Logan (1972), Palmer (1975), Gendreau and Ross (1979), and Lab and Whitehead (1988). Each review contained far fewer studies than Lipsey's analysis, and the average percentage of positive-outcome studies (POSs) was 59, 50, 48, 86, and 47, respectively. The fourth review, of course, intentionally highlighted POSs, while the others neither emphasized nor partly selected for such studies. In Gensheimer et al.'s (1986) analysis of diversion studies there were 47 percent POSs; in Mayer et al.'s (1986) analysis of behavioral studies there were 63 percent.

6. Since these reductions apply to the overall target sample, they are doubtlessly larger for some types of offenders than others. Future studies should try to determine which "types" are most and least responsive to the methods and techniques used in given programs.

CHAPTER 5

1. This applies whether or not those samples contain primarily serious and/or repeat offenders ("multiple offenders," especially those with three or more sustained petitions—or else convictions, which is their equivalent in *adult* courts).

2. "Amenability was defined generally as a perceived capacity to respond to treatment by changing in a positive or constructive direction. . . . In [determining] amenability, the clinicians placed heavy emphasis on the factor of anxiety. Other [factors were] . . . (1) intelligence, (2) verbal ability, (3) readiness to accept therapy, (4) insight, (5) awareness of personal problems, and (6) a desire to change" (Adams, 1961, pp. 1–2).

3. The Borstal and Highfields studies (Mannheim and Wilkins, 1955; Weeks, 1958) showed differential impact of open versus closed institutions on more as well as less

amenable youths (or higher- and lower-risk youths). Reiss, 1951 showed differential impact of assignment to home and community placement versus closed institutions on youths with "relatively strong personal controls," "relatively weak personal controls," and "marked social deterioration or very immature personalities." Mueller, 1960 showed differential impact of assignment to institutional, to noninstitutional or open institutional, and to direct parole settings on "conforming and over-inhibited," "aggressive or insecure," and "emotionally-disturbed" youths. Palmer, 1974 found differential impact of initial institutionalization versus initial community programming to be a function of youths' subgroup or personality type combined with their degree of problems/vulnerability. Sealy and Banks found that "the difference in success rate between open and closed institutions is greatest for boys of the lowest levels of maturity and is negligible for boys of higher maturity" (1971, p. 257). Brill, 1978 found differential impact of lower-structured versus higher-structured residential treatment programs to be a function of the youths' preprogram conceptual level.

4. Some complexities associated with "risk level" findings may involve not just differential relevance but the relative, contextual, and thereby shifting manner in which that term has been applied. For instance, in one type of sample (an institutional sample), individuals who have been called "high risks" "middle risks" and "low risks" may *all* have had substantially longer prior records than all individuals who were called "*high* risks" in a different sample (an in lieu sample of intensively supervised probationers). The latter individuals may have been viewed as high risks because they were compared, not with an institutional sample, but with a standard, nonintensive probation sample that averaged, say, one or two prior arrests per person. Thus, even the institutionalized individuals who had been called "low risks" (that is, low with respect to the institutional sample as a whole) may have been worse risks than most or all offenders from the community-based sample—including offenders with, say, an average of three or four priors. The above is independent of the fact that differing recidivism rates may exist among individuals who fall within any *one* risk-level as well, whatever the definition of "level" may be and whatever its justice system context. Thus, some "high risks," for instance, individuals with five or more prior arrests (and other risk-related factors), may still be more responsive to given interventions than other high risks, whether in institutional or community settings. This was seen, for example, in an intensive, in lieu program in which almost all offenders would have been called "high risks" from the perspective of most standard definitions (Palmer, 1974).

5. Thus, for example, more contacts and months may generally be needed to complete a vocational training plus counseling program than one that centers mainly or exclusively on either nonsystem diversion, on confrontation, on physical challenge (e.g., Outward Bound), or on probation/parole enhancement. At the same time, however, many skill-oriented and behavioral programs may require only intermediate amounts.

6. Nontraditional or experimental programs have no monopoly on talent, quality leadership, and even charisma, and C's should not be stereotyped as almost always

mediocre. Researchers might wish to pay increased attention to standard programs in the 1990s, in order to discover whether, why, and for whom selected C programs outperform other C's, not just given E's. C versus C comparisons, that is, research on standard programs per se, could have practical benefits independent of those resulting from E/C studies.

7. Multiple inputs, say, combinations of educational training, individual counseling, recreation, and external controls, can occur either essentially simultaneously (at least for several consecutive months) or mainly one after another. The simultaneous approach may be better for some individuals; the successive, for others.

8. Though "combinations" in the above sense were common—very likely the rule—they often seemed to differ in part from programs described in some meta-analyses as "multimodal" and presented in one review as "combined therapeutic approaches." For instance, multimodals generally seemed to utilize a second (or third) component, not just to a small or moderate degree, but about as often as a "first"; moreover, program managers apparently considered these components indispensable (or at least major contributors) to the operation as a whole. In these respects they explicitly supported and intentionally highlighted each such component, and they tried to rely on it heavily. Nevertheless, despite these distinctions and efforts, the net difference between multimodals and the above-mentioned combinations was probably one of degree as often as one of "type." When a substantial difference did exist, it seemed to center on the relatively equal status given to the components in question by multimodals and on the large, integral role that they then played. (This, of course, did not mean those components were simply considered "extras," in the case of combinations.) Again, however, shortcomings in available program accounts prevent one from routinely being sure of this.

9. It is often believed that certain unimodal (literally unimodal) methods that are sometimes used in given countries or have been used in the past may, by themselves, "sharply" curtail recidivism. Among them are mutilation or dismemberment, sterilization or castration, physical stigmatization (e.g., by branding), and flogging. However, we are not examining such drastic approaches; instead, we are focusing on ones that mainly rely on positive incentives and rewards in order to utilize, develop, or redirect the powers and mechanisms of the mind and body, so as to enhance the individual's ability to cope and grow.

10. The hypothesized contributions of multicomponent inputs are apart from those of staff and setting, for instance, the community-based versus the institutional setting.

11. A paucity of knowledge also exists not only regarding the particular emphasis that has been given to any one feature, say, any one component, compared to others, but also regarding the sequencing of various features in relation to each other. Such a paucity also exists with respect to the relative contributions those features have made to success.

12. And still *other* combinations that consisted of the salient feature plus nonsalient features.

13. Though positive-outcome studies constituted a clear majority of all experimental studies—about 65 percent—the subgroup of POSs that reached $p < .05$ was well under half of all experimental studies. Nevertheless, both the POSs and their subgroup that attained $p < .05$ were numerous (particularly the POSs). Their absolute numbers, of course, were basically independent of the fact that there were also four or more times as many $p < .05$ studies per se, that is, a clear majority of those particular studies, in which E's outperformed C's as those in which C's outdid E's.

CHAPTER 6

1. To be sure, it is not known if the effectiveness of any given program, for instance, that of Lee and Haynes (1980), was largely accounted for by (*a*) a particular *subset* of the various features mentioned above or by (*b*) either that same subset or a different one in combination with other *types* of factors, namely, staff characteristics, staff/client interactions, and/or intervention strategies/techniques. We believe case (*b*) applies and that, in addition, the content of the given combination varied somewhat for different types of clients, as did the relative weight of its components.

2. We assume that more than one effective combination exists in connection with the many E-programs studied to date.

3. This situation would not necessarily reflect, or substantially reflect, the following, in particular: Though two or more components (here, generic approaches) may each have shown considerable promise with respective target populations or types of clients, those components may not work well or equally well with the *same* types of clients. That aside, various combinations of components may sometimes be operationally incompatible with each other or largely unfeasible in given settings. At any rate, one either should not, need not, or, in some cases, cannot combine or necessarily combine given components with each other simply on grounds that each one—taken individually—showed promise in several studies in which it was considered the distinguishing or salient feature. As a result, although such combining of any two or more individually promising components is not, a priori, unreasonable and logically unfounded in itself, the following would seem appropriate regarding this approach: Wherever possible, the linking of individually promising components into a hypothetically effective overall combination should first be checked against practical realities and direct field experiences, not to mention statistical information that might exist regarding the joint effectiveness of any two or more components of that combination. This suggestion especially applies to individual components and to combinations of such components that each show promise based on a cross-programs, "building block" analysis (Chapter 8). It also applies, but to a lesser degree, to components that appear in a number of "guide programs" (Chapter 9).

4. Further research is needed to validate, refine, augment, qualify, and/or oppose these and other leads. This research might show, for example, that some program elements and types of relationships which seem critical for certain individuals, such as the very

seriously delinquent, are substantially less important with others, or with different goals. To test these and related ideas, separate analyses would be needed for the different types of offenders in the overall population, and these individuals would have to be delineated in the first place (not just by risk level). Other important leads could be obtained even without categorizing offenders.

5. This is independent of the fact that any of the four factors may have more or less impact than any other factor, within any given combination. That, in turn, is separable from the fact that any given factor may have a different weight or ranking when it appears in some *other* combination, that is, a different weight in relation to the remaining factors that are found in both the "original" and the "other" combination.

6. "Client type" refers not just or not necessarily to individuals of differing risk levels but to those with specified personality features, even though level and feature may sometimes interact.

CHAPTER 7

1. This applies to whichever E's and C's—groups or subgroups—are being compared: everyone who entered the respective programs; everyone who completed them; or both. Also, E's and C's should not be poorly matched on any of those variables or, for that matter, on other crucial variables.

2. In any given program, differing methods/techniques may or may not be used for the respective subgroups. If such differences exist, separate descriptions could provide a more realistic picture of the program and could help avoid masking. (Masking typically occurs when positive results for one or more subgroups are counterbalanced by negative outcomes for others—with the overall results therefore showing no substantial or significant difference between E's and C's. This can occur across studies as well—with positive-outcome studies being counterbalanced by negatives. Even in the context of meta-analysis, the counterbalancing of positive-outcome studies by negative-outcome studies can lead to an overall effect size that reflects "no significant overall difference" between E's and C's—that is, for the entire set of studies combined.)

3. Meta-analyses conducted to date did not focus on the techniques, strategies, and various related conditions—for instance, the techniques and strategies that were present in more than one approach (e.g., those which existed in the group counseling, behavioral, and vocational training approaches alike)—that may have contributed to positive outcomes. This was partly because the necessary data seldom existed.

4. Area III-B contains four subsidiary classes of items: developmental level, classification or personality type, trait clusters, and specific factors or generic variables. For each of the first two classes, researchers would categorize offenders with respect to at least one developmental level or classification system, say, the interpersonal and/or

moral level system. For each of the remaining classes, researchers would make separate ratings on all dimensions that are listed, that is, on communicative-alert, passive-uncertain, and so on. (The latter approach, namely, the one that involves separate ratings on all dimensions, also applies to areas I-C, II-B, and the second section of II-C. It applies to the "social climate dimensions" item in area IV-B as well.) For the first section of area II-C, researchers would focus on at least one orientation set, say, A type vs. B type. Relative to that set, they would choose the specific orientation (e.g., A type) that best describes the staff or staff member in question. This approach, namely, selecting the most descriptive characteristic, also applies to the last two items of area IV-B.

5. Each item in this subdivision represents a separate scale. This also applies to the last two items in area II-C. For details regarding these scales, see Palmer, 1967.

6. This would include (*a*) absolute number of arrests and/or convictions and (*b*) number of arrests and/or convictions, categorized as above average, average, or below average relative to offenders of the same age group. Other components could be added to this item, for example, dominant type of offense history (against other persons, property, other). As an alternative approach, this and/or other components could be used as independent items.

7. The interpersonal, psychosocial, moral, ego, and conceptual-level systems are described in Warren, 1971; Palmer, 1969; Kohlberg, 1976; Loevinger, 1976; and Hunt, 1971, respectively.

8. In this regard, researchers might reflect on a thought expressed almost four centuries ago. Writing soon after the epoch-making discoveries by Kepler, Galileo, and Brahe, Francis Bacon remarked that the advancement of knowledge seems to involve a type of investigation that is "laborious to search, ignoble to meditate, harsh to deliver . . . and minute in subtlety" (Bacon, [1620] 1960, p. 80). Thus, even at the dawn of observational science and at the moment of its early triumphs, the painstaking aspects of progress had already emerged. Bacon's insight into the problems of knowledge building provided a lesson that was eventually accepted by the now-established sciences.

9. The preceding and subsequent discussion of purposive variations involves two main assumptions about operations, for instance, about types of program components—particularly generic approaches. First, it assumes that the main or major operations would be fairly similar from one E-program to the next *within* any given *setting*, say, intensive probation. Second, it assumes that those respective operations would have important commonalities *across* different settings, say, intensive probation and probation camps. Existence of the latter commonalities would not be crucial to achieving the goals of purposive variation if one mainly emphasized gender and age. However, if one's interest centered on setting, the commonalities would be essential.

10. In referring to offenders from either a more practical or more theoretical perspective, a theory need not reflect only one "end" of any given spectrum, or, perhaps,

descriptive scale. Thus, for example, a given theory-based combination may refer to any or all data items within the following, hypothetical combinations: (*a*) young, nonstatus offenders,with longer, nonviolent histories; and (*b*) older, status offenders, with short, nonviolent histories. Some theories, of course, are not broad enough to encompass such a range of items.

11. No combination of data items (i.e., no target combination) that is used in a purposive variation study conducted subsequent to the original E/C study may be entirely consistent with or central to the original theory, specifically, the one that led to the first combination of data items. Nevertheless, in addition to performing its basic function with respect to the *purposive variation series*, each such combination that is examined subsequent to the original study could serve as a way of partly testing the original *theory's* breadth of applicability. More precisely, it could serve this function by addressing the impact of interactions between itself, on the one hand, and any given subsequent program (i.e., program that follows the original study), on the other. Of course, a theory's applicability—like that of a program itself—could be meaningfully tested only if, among other things, the program in question is adequately implemented.

12. Included might be specific motivations, environmental/situational pressures or opportunities, level of interpersonal development, and so on.

13. This applies even though—and partly because—any factor (item) within any area may later be refined, redefined, and/or substantively merged with parts of other items. Such modifications may, for instance, result from new information or clearer insights regarding (*a*) item X's overall relationship to and possible overlap with other items at any one point in time, and (*b*) X's change or growth through time, as, for example, in the case of any given personality type that may eventually develop into a somewhat different type, with various individuals.

14. Moreover, process factors 1, 2, and 3 often substantially help achieve an implementation that is qualitatively appropriate and quantitatively sufficient, from the standpoint of theoretical or actual program models or individual standards. To be sure, these factors are not the only inputs or conditions that may bear on appropriate and sufficient implementation (or lack thereof), whether directly or indirectly. Available resources, organizational factors, and broader political support or pressure can also contribute (or detract).

15. "Otherwise" refers to situations in which process factors, say, certain staff/client interactions or staff characteristics, did not occur in their usual manner or were not expressed to a substantial degree. This, for example, may occur if a program happens to place heavy reliance on methods, such as electronic monitoring and restitution, which—individually or collectively—may sharply delimit various types of staff/client contact. (In this particular scenario, the given methods—whatever they may be—do not intrinsically *have to* constitute virtually the entire program. As a result, the program—under various conditions—can allow or even ensure substantial opportunity for the staff/client contact to occur, that is, even if the given methods are used. However, in a different scenario,

certain programs, say, given unimodals, may almost invariably—perhaps even intrinsi-cally—preclude such contacts in the first place.)

16. This analogy relates to the previously mentioned aspects of process, respec-tively: (*a*) address/use(s) would relate to *objectives and general thrust*; (*b*) compartments or structure would bear on *content areas*; (*c*) outward features (size, perimeter, design) would pertain to *overall scope (and, in some respects, general thrust again).*

17. In this regard a direct means-ends relationship can exist between areas, on the one hand, and goals, on the other. This relationship differs in content but not form from that between program components and those same areas and goals (this time collectively).

18. Though various features (individually or collectively) may influence clients by more passive *means* than many type 1 items, the features themselves (collectively) may range from what are often considered fairly active to fairly passive. This is apart from whether their contributions are mostly direct or indirect, in common contexts.

19. These bases would apply whether or not the studies involved combinations-research per se.

CHAPTER 8

1. Also synonymous with those terms are *generic category, broad generic cat-egory*, and *program category.*

2. Here, "grouping" (or group) refers to any collection of programs to which an individual program may be said to belong, if the grounds for belonging are as follows: Operationally, the latter program's salient or quantitatively dominant generic program-matic feature seems quite similar to that of the former, that is, the remaining programs in the collection. (Though the individual program and the remaining programs may also have a similar or even identical programmatic *label* prior to the grouping, this compara-bility is not an essential condition.) In other contexts, "grouping" may simply refer to the overall collection itself, for instance, one based on a salient/ dominant feature that is operationally, but not necessarily nominally, shared by every individual program. Here, the nature or status of each such program in relation to that of the remaining programs is already a settled issue.

3. Given this absence of interactions, results obtained for the given program would simply be added to those from any other program in the same study sample. More specifically, in the building-block approach one would aggregate findings from the sample's individual studies in an essentially linear way. (Both the aggregation process and its linear character are substantively and procedurally separate from statistical adjustments that one could later make for small sample-size, sample-size differences between E's and C's—and across studies—etc.) This additive process would apply to the global method as well, though somewhat differently or to a different degree.

4. If the study meets these conditions, it should be included unconditionally and from the start; it should also be considered "in good standing" throughout the analysis. For various analytic and postanalytic purposes—say, when subsequently evaluating the operational utility of the collective findings, or even of individual programs—studies with excellent designs, and with sophisticated as well as differentiated statistical analyses, may nevertheless receive more weight than others. Other things being equal, this could also apply to studies whose results largely replicate those of other investigations.

5. Thus, for example, a given vocational training program should not be excluded on grounds that the VT programs—collectively—did not consistently or almost always reduce recidivism, or perhaps achieve some other goal.

6. Theoretically, studies that focus heavily or exclusively on the given target-population/setting may be given more weight in an analysis (and/or in certain postanalysis decisions) than studies that have given them somewhat less, but still substantial, consideration.

7. For exploratory purposes, $p < .10$ could be used instead. In all remaining contexts, $p < .05$ would be the level of choice.

8. As indicated, these programs—collectively—can include various generic approaches, say, vocational training and group counseling. Nevertheless, the many individual programs would be analyzed together. Specifically, they would be analyzed as if these differences in approach did not exist, and however many approaches there are.

9. In other contexts, we might examine the *degree of difference* between E's and C's, for instance, more versus less programming/rehearsing. Basically, we would examine the degree of presence rather than *presence versus absence*. With still other items, such as physical condition (age, upkeep, space) of the intervention setting, dichotomies such as above average versus average plus below average (combined) could be used instead of more versus less. In nondichotomous analyses, degree of difference could involve three or more categories, for example, low, medium, and high, or 1–2, 3–5, and 6 or more.

10. Ideally, the definitions of those variables would be rather comparable across programs, as well.

11. An analysis might be called "partly dichotomous" if either its independent or dependent variable is bipartite. A fully dichotomous approach would not be possible for item (c), that is, for all S's and U's combined. This is because the dichotomous approach would require a bipartite dependent variable, but the combining of S and U that would occur in item (c) would preclude or eliminate that partition.

12. Similar distinctions might be found regarding level of cognitive development, moral development, and so on. (As with interpersonal development, these features would be used as independent variables.) Ideally, one would organize a developmental-level

analysis around *each client's individual level*, irrespective of the level of other clients within his/her program. One would thus group clients by level, whatever program they might be in (this being a cross-programs analysis). One would not organize the analysis around *each program's general or typical level*. (Such an organization would have occurred if, say, one had dichotomized those levels—in terms, for instance, of the clients' modal [thus, collective] level within each respective program.) Ideally, then, clients would be combined across programs, not, in effect, subdivided within them. (If one subdivided clients within programs, the program—not the client—would be the basic analytic unit.) In short, the modal, the median, and the mean developmental-level would not be used as an independent variable—by program. Nor would any other collective results be used that way.

13. Beyond that, if replication studies are conducted, differentiated analyses may indicate that the findings regarding lower- and middle-level clients (combined) either apply to or "wash out" with *different* targets, for example, clients ages 16 to 18, whatever their setting. Alternatively, those or other analyses may reveal that the findings regarding lower- and middle-level clients only apply in *specified settings*, such as institutions, irrespective of the individuals' age. (Conceivably, an age *x* setting interaction might be found, instead.)

14. These standards, which constitute key requirements for a study's inclusion in an analysis, are twofold: (*a*) the presence of an experimental or quasi-experimental design; (*b*) reasonable equivalence between E's and C's on a number of variables known to correlate with the principal or sole outcome-measure. Equivalence should exist not only at point of program entry but also, if possible, immediately after the program, that is, subsequent to sample shrinkage.

15. The differential weighting-scale could be applied to all studies that are included in an analysis. Based on their resulting scale-scores, those studies could then be ranked rather than treated equally. That is, they could be arrayed from highest to lowest on overall design-quality, even though they are equal in having satisfied the minimum—the lowest acceptable—standards for inclusion in the analysis. (Equality with respect to satisfying minimum standards of inclusion is independent from equality in terms of having satisfied the success criterion of 15 percent with regard to *program impact*, and from possibly being analyzed homogeneously in that respect.) The factor of sample size might be included on the scale.

16. When fewer than twenty programs are involved, the Fisher exact-probability test might be substituted for Chi-square, regardless of the Yates correction.

17. This is distinct from their having remained *present*—but present to a lesser or greater degree.

18. In all likelihood, that portion of the outcome for which the given *part* might have been essential would often be smaller than the portion for which the overall *combination*

might have been essential. At any rate, the latter portion might often encompass the former; and the reverse would never occur.

19. In any of the four content-areas—say, operations—two or more features could be examined simultaneously, in connection with a given hypothesis. Also, any feature could be studied individually within a given area. Across any *two or more* areas that may be studied jointly—say, offender and setting—two or more features could again be examined together. Here, each area would provide at least one such feature, and any area could provide several.

20. If one used the building-block approach, one *might* find it easier to substantially improve existing programs than to develop effective new ones. (We believe this is the case.) If one used the global approach (discussed later), the opposite might be true.

21. Here, the overall set would thus contain not only ingredients derived via the building-block method but also those obtained by other means. However, it is conceivable that these other means *could* sometimes provide an adequate set by themselves. In any event, it may often be very difficult to obtain an adequate set via the building-block method alone, that is, a set which is sufficiently powerful and complete.

22. This does not mean they may have insufficient power/flexibility to produce pre-to-post improvements within the E-program itself.

23. The same situation would have existed if only one unidentified factor, rather than two or more, were involved.

24. In addition, though these factors missed with the target at hand, they need not miss with every target.

25. If an individual factor were linked with an *individual* feature for purposes of an analysis, those two components—jointly—would then be called a "combination," that is, an analytic combination. However, if one or more factors were analytically linked with what was already a *combination* of features, those linked analytic components—jointly—would then be part of a "still broader combination." Note that all the above factors and features were linked for *analytic* purposes. Prior to and apart from that analysis they did not necessarily coexist in any actual program, let alone interact compatibly with each other in such a program.

26. The importance of the unidentified factors could be reasonably inferred if the jointly analyzed items were statistically stronger than either factors or features alone.

27. This impact might have occurred when developing new programs, not just when improving existing operations.

28. Some researchers and practitioners would regard these as having some specific scientific support and as therefore being more than first-cut, untested hypotheses.

29. Naturally, since these mixed, neutral, or positive factors were unknown, they could not be "measured"—in this case, quantified and statistically analyzed. This would apply to the unidentified *negative* factors, as well. As a matter of passing interest, the following might be noted: Though all the above factors were unmeasured at the time, they nevertheless did exist. They may often have interacted with various features and, in so doing, they had particular impact on those features (even though that impact may not be measurable precisely). They may also have interacted with *other* unknown factors. This perspective that "nevertheless they do exist" (i.e., philosophical realism) differs from one generally found in quantum physics and associated with microlevel systems. There, it is asserted that "entities" (cf. factors) literally do not "exist" until "theys" (in other words, "they"—"somethings"—which nevertheless do not *exist* [in that sense are not ordinary entities], at least not in the reality we ordinarily experience) are somehow "measured" (again without absolute precision). In that contingent-reality or dual (floating)-existence view it would appear to follow that the entities would literally have neither any definite nor any single impact on "their" surroundings (momentary or otherwise) until they are measured—more specifically, until their measurement has, in some sense, been *completed*. This is because entities/factors that do not literally exist presumably would not, in that view, have any effects—definite, single, or otherwise.

30. This may involve either a narrow, medium, or wide range of features/combinations.

31. Negative effects might also occur if already operating—albeit unidentified—factors whose impact had been relatively *neutral* during a program's early and middle stages were substantially changed in degree, for instance, were considerably intensified or diminished. This is separate from the possibility that identified as well as unidentified factors which had *positive* effects during early and/or middle stages may undergo changes which—from that point on—neutralize or reverse those effects.

32. This applies whether the content of those negatives is fairly simple or complex.

CHAPTER 9

1. Though ingredients—collectively—may have worked, not all of them—individually—may have made an important contribution, particularly one that would have reached .05 if a separate analysis had occurred. Nevertheless, absent such information about significance level, each feature would justifiably be viewed, at the start, as having *possibly* made an important contribution.

2. This does not mean that all parts necessarily interact with each other to an equal degree and/or equally well.

3. As seen later, various parts do nevertheless drop out in a subsequent step.

4. In a building-block analysis, still other ingredients may have appeared neutral or superfluous with respect to outcome. Yet even these ingredients, when functioning as part of a *totality* (as they presumably would, in a real-life program), might have played an important role. They may have played this role largely through their interactions with other features. However, the building-block method might not have reflected these interactions unless particular analyses had been used, especially those involving combined ingredients.

5. Rejection of this position would at least apply to all but the fairly "lightweight" clients—individuals to whom the formal justice system often pays little attention.

6. Both hypotheses would be reasonable possibilities particularly if some or all of the features that are identified via the building-block approach were seldom if ever joined together in various real-life programs. To be sure, there is no a priori reason why those features might *not* have operated adequately or perhaps even excellently if they were joined. Yet, the fact remains that if indeed they *had* seldom if ever been operationally joined, there would be no clear experience-based reason to believe they generally *would* be mutually compatible in an actual, new program.

Naturally, if some of those features already *had* operated together in numerous programs, the odds could reasonably be considered higher than otherwise that the features *could* also operate together in a new program that focused on the same or similar targets. Indeed, program descriptions available to date suggest that various individual features often have been joined together in previous programs. Given this, it is not far-fetched to assume that at least many of those features have also been *mutually compatible* and could thus function together in a new program as well. The preceding remarks are independent of the fact that identified *combinations* of features must, by definition, have been compatible if they were jointly associated with positive outcome. At least, they were compatible enough, and were compatible often enough, to contribute significantly. Yet ever here, the following possibility remains: Even if those combinations often existed together in real-life programs and were largely compatible as well, they might not have been strong enough to produce the given outcomes by themselves.

7. In addition, the issue of administrative/organizational support should remind one that operations, staff, offender, and setting are not the sole factors and conditions that contribute to success, whether directly or indirectly. Indeed, without such support or at least acceptance relatively little can usually be achieved or sustained by way of substantial recidivism reduction, and so on. In turn, administrative and organizational support or even tolerance is often largely shaped by the general sociopolitical situation and atmosphere— local and even beyond. The latter circumstances reflect not only historical realities and long-standing philosophies or ideologies but also prevailing economic conditions and more immediate pressures and events. Though administrative and organizational support are not focused on in this book, they—especially collectively—probably play a critical role with respect to adequate implementation. This, we believe, applies in most contexts

and particularly with fairly complex or costly programs. At any rate, those factors should be considered important, even integral, components or dimensions of any holistic framework. Administrative, organizational, and sociopolitical factors were recently discussed in Duffee and McGarrell (1990). (Also see Coates, Miller, and Ohlin, 1978.)

8. These programs, one may hypothesize, helped generate those outcomes via their overall combination or combinations of operations, staff, offender, and setting features and activities, and also via particular interactions among some or all of those components. The same, of course, could be hypothesized of any program, however effective or ineffective. Organizational/administrative factors may also contribute to outcome.

9. In this context, "outperformed" therefore means that E's had a lower recidivism rate, a larger effect-size, and so on, than C's, whether or not the E/C difference was statistically significant.

10. Obviously, these shared features need not be the very same ones across all combinations of programs. Nor need all such programs contain the same specific features, or even the same number of features, in the first place.

11. In the guide-programs procedure, results—for any given percentage of sharing (say, 67 percent)—merit increased consideration as the absolute number of programs rise. Thus, features shared by two of three (i.e., 67 percent), by four of six, and by six of nine guide programs, respectively, would be considered increasingly reliable, even though the percentage remains constant. Basically, this positive relationship between level of consideration and sample-size reflects standard replication or reliability principles, but without specific confidence levels and, thus, significance tests per se.

12. A related example is as follows. Say that most guide programs are found to share comparatively few positive individual features with each other, for instance, an average of one or two out of the approximately eight (again an average) recorded per program. Also say that most _non_guide programs are found to share those same types of positive features with each other and that they do so to about the same degree that was observed for guides, namely, one or two out of eight. In this scenario the *guide* programs, collectively, would therefore not seem to have any unique or even relatively distinguishing individual features compared to nonguides, also collectively. Yet since guides did outperform nonguides, the former may have contained combinations of features that distinguished them from the latter. (Other explanations are of course possible.) These combinations may have involved, e.g., the one or two shared features plus others that were unshared.

Differences among programs may emerge in other ways, some of which do not require the concept of guide programs. For instance, if one used effect-sizes to rank all forty programs (those which might otherwise be called "all guide plus all nonguide programs, combined") from most positive to least positive, one might still find distinguishing features/ combinations among those programs ranked in the upper half. Yet the programs that contained those F/Cs need not be thought of as "guides" or, for that matter, as particularly prominent. (See the "Prominent-programs Procedure" discussion later in this chapter, at the end of the section titled "Global Approach Compared to Building-Block Approach.")

13. Though the common-elements product of the guide-programs procedure might filter out or reduce possible negative, neutral, and superfluous features, that procedure, by itself, would not specifically identify them. To help identify possible negative features, one might, for instance, have to separately focus on "negative guides." These would be programs that were associated, say, with a 20 percent or more increase in recidivism or had an effect size of at least -.15. Here, the task would be to identify any factors that these poorly performing E-programs shared in common or that usually distinguished those programs from ones with positive outcome (not just from positives that comprised the *guide*-programs group). Information about detrimental factors could be useful, since any newly constructed program would probably be more efficient, less costly, and perhaps more effective if such factors were identified and eliminated. (Neutral and superfluous features may be harder to pinpoint than negative features.)

14. Given this definition, yet allowing for "noise" or error variance, one could say—more precisely and realistically—that positive features which are identified via this approach are much more *likely* to be significant contributors than are neutral or superfluous features.

15. Besides effectiveness, one would hope for or might even insist upon humaneness and comparative efficiency.

16. This hypothesized difference in success partly reflects the further hypothesis that building-block features will often not function as well together in real-life programs as will global-approach features.

17. This could occur even if the guide programs were excluded from the building-block sample. Such exclusion would make the respective analyses mutually independent.

18. By the same token, if *guide programs* contained features or combinations that had previously been identified as positive via the *building-block* method, this would substantially strengthen the operational implications—including the reliability and generalizability— of the building-block's findings. (This would especially apply if the guide programs had been set aside or otherwise excluded from the building-block analysis, as mentioned in n. 17.) This interpretation seems reasonable on grounds that if any programs can be said to have worked in real life and to have operational significance in that respect, they would be the guide programs.

19. Increased support, but not priority itself, would also be obtained for less-often-shared features, if convergence occurred for them as well. "Priority," as used in this discussion, applies only to often-shared features.

20. The possibility that some features are more important than others is neither contradicted nor weakened by the fact that a program's various features may be interrelated—some more closely than others. "Various features" also includes the instant ones.

21. Point 3 is independent of the minor technical fact that since the guide-programs procedure centers on the identification of items *shared across programs*, no effort that focuses on only one program can reflect that procedure as such. This would be true even if that program were a guide and were described holistically.

22. Even if no shared features are linked with any other such features, any one or more of these unlinked features might still help improve *existing* programs, by being added to and/or substituted for some of those programs' components.

23. Though a program may be unique, it will not, however, *necessarily* succeed let alone be outstanding, say, in terms of recidivism reduction. At the same time, even if a program is *not* unique it may reduce recidivism and may, in any event, lead to useful insights.

24. "Prominent" could of course be defined somewhat differently than in this discussion. One could, for instance, define it as the upper 25 percent of all programs in which E outperformed C by at least 10 percentage points on recidivism. Or, one might define it as the upper one-third of all programs that satisfied the earlier-mentioned 15 percent criterion cutoff. Under a wide range of conditions, all such definitions would probably produce roughly comparable results as to type and amount of programs. At any rate, the differences among those results might hardly matter for present purposes.

25. Since the added programs will not be precisely the same as the original, there will be grounds for somewhat greater generalization as well.

26. By increasing the sample, one would obtain a higher reliability than that which applied to just the original sample of guide programs, collectively. This higher reliability, that is, the new result, would be based on the expanded sample, namely, all original plus all added programs combined.

27. To be sure, in real-life operations some overlap may often be found in the age groupings of two "adjacent" targets. This overlap may exist *(a)* from point of program-intake, *(b)* starting during the respective programs but after intake, or *(c)* beginning during the post-program follow-ups. Other things being equal, the shorter the respective programs and/or follow-ups, the less the overlap—and vice-versa, for longer programs/followups. For example, under condition *(b)*, the previously adjacent client-samples that comprise each of two fairly short programs (one an E, the other a C) may end up with relatively little by way of mutual age-overlap, even if no overlap existed at intake. This also applies to samples with comparatively short post-program follow-ups.

28. This hypothesis assumes that other factors or conditions would be equal or essentially equal—for instance, that the number of similar-program replications would equal that of adjacent-target replications.

29. Though "more points or areas" can refer to a larger absolute number of individual features, combinations, and so on, it can also or instead signify a higher *proportion* of all known or measured content, for instance, all known F/Cs. The use of proportions would be particularly appropriate—in fact, preferred over absolute amounts— if the two sets of programs being compared have an unequal number of F/Cs—in that sense, a dissimilar quantity of distinguishable content-units. (In this example, the programs being compared with each other would be the adjacent-target set and the similar-program set.) This inequality regarding number of F/Cs could exist even if the number of individual *programs* that comprise those respective sets were equal, as in n. 28.

30. Not to mention more operationally feasible.

31. In effect, this support involves at least three partial replications ("replications"): If the original target contains only one study (though it may well have more), that study is separately replicated via each of the two adjacent-target studies; and the latter replicate each other. Two further examples illustrate how small increases in the number of original and/or adjacent-target studies produce larger increases in the number of replications (this reflects the rise in number of combinations). First, if both the original and adjacent targets contain *two* studies, there are six replications. This also includes not only the originals replicating each other, but the adjacents doing so as well. Second, if there are two originals and three adjacents, the replications total ten.

32. This substantive connection (i.e., empirical relationship)—namely, the similar *outcomes*—differs from any relationship based on possible *content*-similarity, say, age overlap, between the original and adjacent targets.

33. Regarding risk, two points might be noted: *(a)* Though widespread, *noise* may vary widely as to magnitude, say, from slight to marked. *(b)* We will exclude errors of *logic* and will assume they are minimal.

34. One that is not counterbalanced by a negative finding.

35. Similar factors would probably operate in various other contemporary societies, even if the particular age-groupings varied.

36. Naturally, in this circumstance, no findings of any type—supportive or other— would exist in the adjacent-target area.

37. Increased risk would probably occur with relatively large samples as well, though to a lesser degree. Implicit, in any case, is the view that distance and similarity are inversely related.

38. Here, as elsewhere, the ratio of supportive to nonsupportive plus oppositional findings can be more important than the absolute number of supportives alone.

39. What might be called "pure hypotheses" would have been supported by no adjacent and no original studies, simply because no studies of any type existed. In some contrast, "extrapolations"—which may also be called "first-level hypotheses" or "first-level generalizations"—would have been supported by at least one original-target study, though no adjacent studies yet existed.

40. Besides raising the average number of similarities per program, new studies may also increase the ratio of similarities to dissimilarities. To be sure, new studies could instead *lower* the average number of similarities and/or decrease the ratio in question.

41. Though the logical possibility of having *any* ampliative generalization in the first place requires the presence of differing targets (namely, at least two), the validity of any such generalization itself—that is, the accuracy of the assertion that is made about the relationship between those targets—depends on the similarities that exist between the *programs* that comprise those targets. That is, it depends on actual content. (Here, "programs" includes operations, staff, settings, etc.)

42. They may or may not apply this view to the *preponderance* of clients (at least clients who are "nonlightweights")—whether juveniles or adults and whether in institutional or community programs.

43. It goes without saying that terms such as *enough* and *considerable* can often have rather different meanings to different individuals, depending, for example, on their particular standards and/or expectations.

CHAPTER 10

1. As noted earlier, these analyses focused on such a feature for understandable reasons. While some reasons were mainly pragmatic, others may have ultimately reflected a limited awareness of the qualitative challenges involved in intervention. (See n. 2.)

2. In part, the single-feature strategy predominated because it seemed straightforward and because each feature seemed relevant and worth exploring, in any event. However, the strategy also seemed straightforward and realistic for purposes of analyzing any *sizable collection* of programs, say, via meta-analysis or literature review. This situation mainly reflected the limited breadth and detail of information available regarding most *individual* program's features. That information often consisted mainly or exclusively of the salient or seemingly dominant feature; and it was this particular feature which provided a conceptually simple basis for grouping various programs—that is, for analytically equalizing them, as it were—and for thus making it logically acceptable to

explore them as a set. (It was this feature to which the "single-feature strategy" referred.) Though some programs also contained descriptive information about staff, setting, and so on, this information did not routinely accompany that which existed regarding any *one* salient/dominant programmatic feature. As a result, the former information was not used in combination with the programmatic data. (It could, of course, have been used either *across* programmatic features, *instead of* them, or in connection with a relatively *small* number of programs that were characterized by a given, individual program-feature.) At any rate, this lack of a routine or frequent copresence of programmatic, black-box, staff, setting, and client data—together with the fact that only the programmatic information commonly existed—left only the "single feature" (the salient/dominant programmatic feature) as a basis for analytically unifying, and thus uniformly analyzing, any sizable group of programs. Again, however, this would not have had to occur if one chose to organize the analysis across programmatic features.

At the original, *program-development stage*, the fact that the breadth and detail of information about individual programs was relatively limited in the first place partly reflected the long-standing, widespread practice of seeking single-factor interventions that were comparatively easy to implement. (This goal will be called "A.") At the *research-design stage*—insofar as this differed from the other—the limitation in question also reflected a desire for relatively simple and straightforward analyses as well as interpretations. This goal—called "B"—existed separately and apart from the fact that it may already have been known, during this design stage, that limited data would probably be available regarding the individual program.

At any rate, goal A—the principal one in this discussion—may often have reflected a limited awareness or acceptance of the frequent difficulties and complexities involved in working with "nonlightweight" clients, especially for purposes beyond short-term behavior control. While this presumed awareness/acceptance mainly involved practitioners and policy makers, a similar one may often have existed among researchers and may even have borne on goal B. To be sure, goal B would primarily have had other, methodology-centered sources as well.

3. One should, where possible, also ask, Why? and, For whom?

4. Two views are implicit in these responses or are easily read into them. First, "working" or "not working" is essentially an all-or-none matter, not something that, say, varies in degree and/or by type of client. Second, the named-approach accounts for the outcome largely or entirely by itself.

5. Here, "adequately" relates to "largely" or "fairly realistically," not to "fully." "Adequate representation" does not require complete isomorphism, for example, one-to-one correspondence at every relevant "point"—that is, a reflection of *all* such points.

6. This point would also apply if the A contribution were relatively modest.

7. Though mutually independent, any two or more point *(b)* features may operate simultaneously. They and/or others may also—or instead—operate successively.

8. With some individual programs, a generic component was equated with the *entire* operation; with other such programs, that same component was seen as *representing* the operation but not coextensive with it. In both situations, this generic component—which was not only the salient feature but also the central unit in the respective programs' analysis—may have involved the cognitive approach, the behavioral approach, educational training, or others.

9. In general, the staff, setting, and offender areas were addressed to a greater degree by literature reviews than by meta-analyses. However, neither method examined them often, let alone systematically, and rarely were such areas studied in detail.

10. This hypothesized advantage should not obscure the fact that the global approach would have problems and challenges of its own, for instance, those centering around the small samples involved in the guide-programs procedure.

11. Where feasible, such research should examine administrative/organizational features and other broad inputs as well.

12. Progress toward describing and identifying the stated factors and dimensions can be made despite the fact that no single program which is part of the study sample may itself contain or even adequately represent most, let alone all, of intervention's many complexities. This especially applies to the combinations, patterns, and interactions included in all programs *combined.*

13. "Well-described" programs would contain not only a wider range of information than exists in most programs studied thus far but also more information of a detailed nature.

14. Other factors being equal, the stronger the design of and findings from an original study and/or a replication study, the less need there is for continued replication. However, even with strong designs and findings, some need remains. Both considerations apply to purposive variations as well.

15. Other things being equal, reliability keeps rising as the number of replications or partial replications increase. However, after a very few replications, the *rate* at which it rises is no longer rapid.

16. These descriptions—and certainly the related analyses—mainly focused on generic program approaches, seldom on operational details.

17. Since administrative/organizational factors can involve process as well as structure, they should—collectively—perhaps constitute a general area of their own

rather than be included, say, within "setting." The suggested new area should itself receive much-expanded attention.

CHAPTER 12

1. Theoretically, these factors may even pave the way for the one that—as described in the text—will perform the *decisive* function during the final stage.

2. Irrespective of whether it was previously present, active, and adequate.

3. Satisfying a criterion may also include reaching a statistical cutoff, for example, a minimum significance level or effect size.

4. When a new factor is substituted for the original one during the final stage, appreciable change may or may not occur in the specific, distinctive character (SDC) of what—to that point—could have been labeled "entity (or situation) X." (Here, change and no change may be called "SDC-case 1" and "SDC-case 2," respectively.) When X does change under those circumstances, partial or total loss of program effectiveness either will or will not take place. (Loss, and no loss, may be termed "outcome-type A" and "outcome-type B," respectively.) To illustrate various theoretical and definitional issues while also minimizing any *further* complexity, the next section of this (text) discussion will focus only on instances in which no loss results from appreciable change in X's SDC. It thus centers on SDC outcome-type 1B—that is, those case-1 SDC's (namely, ones that involve *change*) which also involve no loss (thus, outcome-type *B*).

5. The concept in question is that of exchanging an essential factor (i.e., an otherwise essential one) for a different factor, namely, one that was previously absent during at least the final stage. The essential factor, that is, the exchanged one, is sometimes called the "original." The different or new one is sometimes called the "substitute."

6. If an approach (e.g., G.1) that has been used hitherto is *eliminated* when a new one (e.g., G.2) is added, this could be called a "successive substitution" or "subtraction."

7. The *further* addition of I's and/or T's (e.g., I.4 [or I.3] or T.4 [or T.3]) requires no further addition of G's (e.g., G.3).

8. Though the present examples focus on enhancements, some features (inputs) may work against and even cancel each other, whether immediately or later. For instance, it is possible and plausible that G.2 and/or I.2 (and their sequels) can interfere with and thereby diminish the effects of G.1 and/or I.1, respectively and/or collectively. This may be likelier to occur if the inputs are not mutually coordinated.

9. This is apart from the fact that, when tracked through time, a given feature's *own* impact on clients, that is, its separate impact, may increase—at least for a while. This increase may be steady ("linear"), accelerating ("nonlinear"), or a combination of both.

10. Strictly speaking, this total reflects the cumulative impact that the features have on clients, starting from the first interaction those features have with each other—whether in terms of scenario one or two. The total also reflects the fact that impact on clients can be indirect; for instance, it can occur via prior input to other persons in the clients' lives.

11. Again: In the first scenario, G.2 enhances G.1 but G.1 does not augment G.2; *or*, G.1 turns out to enhance G.2 (even if the latter is introduced later rather than simultaneously), but G.2 does not augment G.1. This would also apply to interactional techniques (I's).

12. This would also apply if the two features *interacted* with, but did not enhance, each other. It would further apply if little or no *outcome-relevant* interaction occurred between them. However, for present purposes, and to illustrate the concepts in question, it is only necessary to focus on the noninteraction condition.

13. In philosophical contexts the relationship between water and its constituents is often used as a prime example of a whole that is "more" than the sum of its parts—the latter being hydrogen and oxygen alone. Such a whole is sometimes called an "emergent new reality" or a "higher level of integration." Even if this reality or condition is not considered "higher" or "better" (e.g., closer to some ideal, or more resilient/adaptable), it is acknowledged to be *(a)* palpably different and *(b)* generally more complex in a structural sense.

14. Juxtaposition, in the sense of simple or formal copresence only, may occur in some programs that—technically—could therefore be called "multimodal."

15. The concept of 'joint conditions' need not be limited to *pre*conditions, especially in a strictly literal, temporal sense. Rather, it may also include *co*conditions. In the latter, relevant conditions would operate beyond the point at which the given impact and outcome began to take shape, that is, the point at which *temporal preconditions* (in the strict literal sense) may be said to have completed their input. In that respect, those coconditions might largely support, reinforce, or help augment certain impacts/outcomes—that is, changes—which the preconditions triggered or otherwise made possible.

16. This is apart from the fact that *combinations* of features (e.g., G.1/G.2) probably interact with other types of combinations (e.g., I.1/I.2) and that those combinations (sets of features) may interact individually and collectively with still other combinations (e.g., T.1/T.2). Given this complexity, it is virtually certain that no one or two studies—however large and sophisticated—will, by themselves, adequately test the several hypotheses mentioned in the text, or will largely unravel intervention's processes. To achieve this goal, long-term, systematic, cumulative research is needed.

17. This could apply to given portions of a program or to the program as a whole. That aside, one need not assume that the more rapid change is always appropriate,

preferable, or even feasible. For some clients and circumstances, slower-paced change may be not only appropriate, adequate, and preferable but also the *only* type that is feasible, particularly for given goals and subgoals. At any rate, its potential benefits may outweigh its likely drawbacks.

APPENDIX B

1. Judgments regarding effectiveness or ineffectiveness directly reflected the assertions, the implied views or logical implications, and/or the data displays of the authors in question.

2. In the vocational training *example*, this involved 30 studies and three authors.

3. These percentage-categories were chosen mainly for ease of interpretation and for relative uniformity as to category-width.

4. "Other factors" would include, for instance, the number of studies that were examined and their average recidivism rates or effect size.

5. The figures shown in Table B-1 (and in B-2, below) for group counseling/therapy do not greatly change when one excludes Lipsey's meta-analysis—an analysis whose several hundred studies included those of most other authors, individually and collectively. With Lipsey excluded, the percentage-of-studies becomes *22%*, *33%*, *39%*, and *6%*, for the 0%, the 1–19%, the 20–39%, and the 40–59% categories, respectively. That is, the general thrust still involves no more than moderate overlap. Much the same applies when Lipsey's meta-analysis is added to most other generic approaches he focused on as such: The general thrust remains unchanged, even though individual percentages may shift substantially from one percentage-category to the next. Thus, for example, such changes as the following are typical: *Confrontation*: from 33%, 0%, 11%, 33%, 0%, and 22% (for the six percentage-categories, respectively) to 17%, 0%, 33%, 17%, 0%, and 33%. *Multimodal*: from 59%, 0%, 0%, 0%, 32%, and 9%, to 78%, 0%, 0%, 0%, 0%, and 22%. *Life skills*: from 72%, 0%, 0%, 0%, 25%, and 3%, to 89%, 0%, 0%, 0%, 0% and 11%. *Employment*: from 67%, 0%, 0%, 0%, 20%, and 13%, to 60%, 0%, 0%, 0%, 0%, and 40%. *Probation/Parole Enhancements*: from 44%, 0%, 34%, 10%, 12%, and 0%, to 51%, 0%, 32%, 10%, 7%, and 0%. Other generic approaches also remained much the same regarding their general degree of overlap, albeit at a slightly broader level. For instance, when one combines percentage-categories 0 with 1–19, combines 20–39 with 40–59, and combines 60–79 with 80+— that is, when one reduces the original six categories to three somewhat broader ones— the following occurs: *Behavioral* changes from 46%, 55%, and 0%, respectively, to 56%, 44%, and 0%. When the original six categories are combined into *two*—namely, 0% plus 1–19% plus 20–39% (no more than moderate overlap), on the one hand, and 40–59% plus 60–79% plus 80% or more (i.e., substantial to very high overlap), on the other—the following is observed: *Delinquency Prevention (Social Casework, etc.)* changes from 67% and 34% to 60% and 40%; *Individual Counseling/Therapy* changes

from 80% and 20% to 93% and 7%. (Regarding *Family Intervention*, the following occurs when those same two categories are involved: 94% and 7% changes to 98% and 2%. When the above-mentioned three categories are involved, 58%, 43%, and 0% changes to 82%, 18%, and 0%.) When Lipsey's analysis was excluded, three approaches underwent a change that could be characterized—collectively—as ranging between "rather substantial" to "quite large," even if one had combined the percentages into two or more adjacent categories. Thus, *Restitution* changes from 69%, 0%, 0%, 15%, 8%, and 8% to 0%, 0%, 0%, 0%, 75%, and 25%. *Vocational Training* changes from 50%, 0%, 0%, 10%, 15%, and 25%, to 20%, 0%, 0%, 30%, 50%, and 0%; and *Educational Training* changes from 14%, 0%, 0%, 57%, 29%, and 0%, to 67%, 0%, 0%, 33%, 0%, and 0%. Finally, the four remaining generic approaches underwent no change because Lipsey had not broken down his study-sample in terms of those categories. That is, *Delinquency Prevention (Area-wide. . .)*, *Physical Challenge*, *Cognitive-Behavioral (or Cognitive)*, and *Diversion* did not appear in his analysis as such, in the first place. With Lipsey's massive analysis excluded, most studies that comprised Table B-1's 17 generic approaches still overlapped—on average—no more than a moderate percentage of authors: The percentage of studies that fell within the 0%, 1–19%, 20–39%, 40–59%, 60–79%, and 80% or more categories was *47.4, 5.4, 13.9, 10.6, 14.4*, and *8.2*, respectively. (As before, the categories were unweighted by sample-size.) This set of percentages was rather similar to the one in which Lipsey's analysis had been included, namely, *42.4, 6.8, 16.7, 14.4 14.6*, and *5.2*.

Since Lipsey had not yet presented the list of studies he utilized in his metanalysis, the following approach was used in the present analysis (note that the *number* of studies which comprised Lipsey's respective analytic categories, e.g., the multimodal category and that of family intervention, was known): (1) Whenever Lipsey's sample-size for a given generic category *exceeded* that of all other authors collectively, his sample was assumed to have encompassed all the individual studies examined by those other authors. (This applied unless—as was rare—given studies examined by those authors were known to have violated Lipsey's inclusion criteria or had occurred outside his time-frame.) The Lipsey studies that were assumed to have duplicated those of other authors contributed to overlap, whereas the "excess" studies added to nonoverlap. (Of the 17 generic categories shown in Table B-1 [and B-2], Lipsey's sample exceeded that of all other authors—collectively—in nine categories: Confrontation [or "deterrence" and "deterrence/shock"]; restitution; multimodal; life skills; vocational training; employment; educational training; individual counseling/therapy; and group counseling/therapy. In four instances the excess was between 40% and 60%, and in four others it was at least 100%.)

(2) Whenever Lipsey's sample-size for a given generic category (approach) was *less* than that of all other authors collectively, his studies were distributed on what amounted to a stratified random basis; that is, they were thusly distributed among the remaining authors' collective studies for the given category. (There were four such "deficit" categories: social casework [and other] approaches to delinquency prevention; family intervention; behavioral; and probation/parole enhancements ["reduced caseloads" plus "other enhancements"]. More specifically, as a first step, Lipsey's studies were distrib-

uted among those (of the remaining authors) which were the most often observed. As before, Lipsey's inclusion criteria had to be met and the time-frame had to be appropriate. Any studies that remained undistributed after that first step were then allocated randomly across those other authors' remaining studies—these being their collectively-less-common ones.

Since this entire procedure—both its excess and deficit aspects—added a degree of uncertainty to the estimates of overlap and nonoverlap (Table B-1), a supplementary analysis was conducted in which Lipsey's meta-analysis was excluded. The differing results that were obtained between the original and supplementary analysis, that is, with and without Lipsey's studies, are specified in the earlier part of this footnote.

6. Three of the 20 approaches described in chapter 3 were excluded from the analysis: (a) "intensive probation supervision," (b) "intensive aftercare (parole) supervision," and (c) "community approaches versus institutional intervention." *Approach (a)* was excluded because only two authors existed—a factor which would have markedly limited the significance of any cross-author comparisons. (These authors, it might be noted, had examined generally different, i.e., nonoverlapping, studies.) *Approach (b)* was excluded since it contained only one review/analysis, thus precluding any cross-author comparisons at all. *Approach (c)* was excluded because the "community" and "institutional" categories each constituted a composite of many or most of the remaining 19 approaches. Thus, for example, with a number of authors—such as Lipsey (1992), Whitehead and Lab (1989), and Izzo and Ross (1990)—"community" and "institutional" (collectively) had encompassed all the individual studies that had already been analyzed in terms of individual generic approaches, for instance, vocational training, diversion, and/or cognitive-behavioral. This time, however, those studies had been recombined (*across* the above [and perhaps other] generic categories), based on the type of *setting* in which the programs occurred.

APPENDIX E

1. Wooldredge analyzed the relative impact of twelve court dispositions on the recidivism of an unselected, consecutive sample of 2,036 offenders who had been processed in four Illinois jurisdictions over a four-year period. Dispositions ranged from "doing nothing" (case dismissed, with legal guilt supported) through "supervision" (weekly reporting to officer to update current events), "community treatment" (exposure to individual or group counseling), or "detention" (incarceration in state detention center), in specified combinations and lengths. Logit and life-table analyses statistically controlled, insofar as possible, the effects of different follow-up lengths, differing arrest policies across jurisdictions, seriousness of instant offense, offense history, age, gender, ethnicity, and even factors such as grade point average and learning difficulties. In this study, *recidivism* meant one or more arrests during the follow-up (a minimum of three years and maximum of seven) from the point of case closure.

APPENDIX G

1. The following scales represent a slight modification of an instrument developed in California's CTP for studying intervention methods used with adolescent and young adult parolees in the early 1970s (Palmer, 1974). The original instrument was subsequently used in connection with individuals from juvenile diversion programs (Palmer and Lewis, 1980). In the Palmer and Lewis study, each content scale was assessed via a four-point rating scale ("slight or none," "moderate," "much," "very much") that was applied to each of the following questions in turn: "In your work with most youths, to what extent did you focus on this area (or use this method . . . or work toward this goal)?" "When you did focus on this area (etc.), how much positive impact did it seem to have?" The statements that appeared in any given content scale were used as examples, to give respondents a clearer and more standardized picture of the factor reflected in the scale title. These statements were not rated individually; as implied above, only the overall scale was rated.

2. Throughout these scales, the masculine pronoun should be read as referring to females as well as males.

APPENDIX H

1. The following scales were developed in the Santa Monica study of juvenile probationers. They were later used to help match staff and clients in California's CTP and in other correctional programs within the USA and Canada (Palmer, 1967, 1973, 1974).

APPENDIX I

1. Any individual client's rate may be expressed in terms of offenses per month, for example, 0.80 offenses per 12 months of post-program, community followup. Rates for one or more *groups* of individuals may be similarly expressed—for example, as an average of 0.40 offenses for, say, 100 E's and 0.50 offenses for 100 C's—again, per 12 month followup. Since a hypothetical, average E had 0.40 offenses while each such C had 0.50 offenses during the followup, the group of 100 E's and 100 C's would have accumulated 40 and 50 offenses respectively, during that followup. The E's rate would therefore be 20 percent lower than the C's, since ([50 - 40] $\div$ 50) $\times$ 100 = 20.

2. It should be kept in mind that only the first group contains the individual studies called "successfuls"—studies which satisfied the 15 percent criterion. Only the second contains "unsuccessfuls"—the studies which missed that criterion. In this example, there are no additional groups; nor are there any categories other than successfuls and unsuccessfuls.

3. As indicated in chapter 4, Palmer (1978) found that, of all studies with at least a 15 percent recidivism reduction, 81 percent had also reached .05. (The sample-sizes in these studies were small, medium, and large—mostly medium.) A 15 percent reduction means that for every 1,000 offenses committed by C's, the E's committed some 850, that is, 1,000 minus 150. A decrease of 150 offenses per 1,000 is not inconsequential.

APPENDIX J

1. Some of these consequences could be precluded or rendered less likely to occur if effect sizes instead of significance-levels per se, were used. However, preclusion, and so on would essentially depend on whether an effect-size cutoff were itself used and on exactly where any such cutoff would be.

APPENDIX K

1. As indicated above, even some adjacent targets may overlap—say, regarding age or, for example, age and ethnicity combined. Moreover, the degree of overlap with respect to socioeconomic status, ethnicity, and, of course, gender, can often be about as high or low as one wishes—though sometimes the approximate level is a given. This can apply to *setting* and other factors as well—not that one always needs to or is able to control them, as to type or amount.

2. In general, "operations as a whole" refers to the program in toto—this usually being an integrated or generally integrated entity. More concretely, however, it refers— at a minimum—to the program's various components operating collectively and doing so at least in general concert, though not necessarily in considerable harmony, for example, "harmony" in the case of each and every major feature.

References

Adams, S. 1959. "Effectiveness of the Youth Authority Special Treatment Program: First Interim Report." Research Report no. 5. Sacramento: California Youth Authority.

————. 1961. "Effectiveness of Interview Therapy with Older Youth Authority Wards: An Interim Evaluation of the PICO Project." Research Report no. 20. Sacramento: California Youth Authority.

Aichorn, A. 1935. *Wayward Youth*. New York: Viking Press.

Akers, R. 1977. *Deviant Behavior: A Social Learning Perspective*. Belmont, Calif.: Wadsworth.

Alexander, J., and B. Parsons, 1982. *Functional Family Therapy*. Monterey, Calif.: Brooks/Cole.

Altschuler, D., and T. Armstrong. 1990. Intensive Community-Based Aftercare Programs: Assessment Report. Washington, D.C.: Office of Juvenile Justice and Delinquency Prevention.

Andrews, D., J. Bonta, and R. Hoge. 1990. "Classification for Effective Rehabilitation: Rediscovering Psychology." *Criminal Justice and Behavior* 17(1): 19–52.

Andrews, D., and J. Kiessling. 1980. "Program Structure and Effective Correctional Practices: A Summary of the CaVIC Research." In *Effective Correctional Treatment*, edited by R. Ross and P. Gendreau. Toronto: Butterworths.

Andrews, D., J. Kiessling, D. Robinson, and S. Mickus. 1986. "The Risk Principle of Case Classification: An Outcome Evaluation with Young Adult Probationers." *Canadian Journal of Criminology* 26(4): 377–84.

Andrews, D., D. Robinson, and M. Balla. 1986. "Risk Principle of Case Classification and the Prevention of Residential Placements: An Outcome Evaluation of the Share The Parenting Program." *Journal of Consulting and Clinical Psychology* 54(2): 203–7.

Andrews, D., I. Zinger, R. Hoge, J. Bonta, P. Gendreau, and F. Cullen. 1990. "Does Correctional Treatment Work? A Clinically Relevant and Psychologically Informed Meta-analysis." *Criminology* 28: 369–404.

Annis, H., and D. Chan. 1983. "The Differential Treatment Model: Empirical Evidence from a Personality Typology of Adult Offenders." *Criminal Justice and Behavior* 10(2): 159–73.

Armstrong, T. 1988. "National survey of juvenile intensive probation supervision." Parts 1 and 2. *Criminal Justice Abstracts* 20(2,3): 342–48, 497–523.

Bacon, F. [1620] 1960. *The New Organum.* Indianapolis: Bobbs-Merrill.

Bailey, W. 1966. "Correctional Outcome: An Evaluation of 100 reports." *Journal of Crime, Law, Criminology, and Police Science* 57: 153–60.

Barkwell, L. 1980. "Differential Probation Treatment and Delinquency." In *Effective Correctional Treatment*, edited by R. Ross, and P. Gendreau. Toronto: Butterworths.

Bartollas, C. 1985. *Correctional Treatment: Theory and Practice.* New York: Prentice Hall.

Barton, W., and J. Butts. 1990. "Viable Options: Intensive Supervision Programs for Juvenile Delinquents." *Crime and Delinquency* 36: 238–56.

Becker, B. 1992. "Models of Science Achievement: Forces Affecting Male and Female Performance in School Science." In *Meta-analysis for Explanation: A Casebook.* See Cook et al., 1992.

Becker, H. 1974. "Labelling theory reconsidered." In *The Aldine Crime and Justice Annual*, edited by S. Messinger et al. Chicago: Aldine.

Brill, R. 1978. "Implications of the Conceptual Level Matching Model for treatment of delinquents." *Journal of Research in Crime and Delinquency* 15(2): 229–46.

Brody, S. 1976. "The Effectiveness of Sentencing: A Review of the Literature." Home Office Research report no. 35. London: Her Majesty's Stationery Office.

Byrne, J., A. Lurigio, and C. Baird. 1989. "The effectiveness of the new intensive supervision programs." *Research in Corrections.* 2(2): 1–75.

Camp, B., and M. Bush. 1981. *Think Aloud: Increasing Social and Cognitive Skills—A Problem Solving Program for Children.* Champaign, Ill.: Research Press.

Clear, T., and G. Cole. 1990. *American Corrections.* Pacific Grove, Calif.: Brooks/Cole Publishing Co.

Cloward, R., and L. Ohlin. 1960. *Delinquency and Opportunity.* New York: Free Press.

Coates, R., A. Miller, and L. Ohlin. 1978. *Diversity in a Youth Correctional System.* Cambridge, Mass.: Ballinger.

Cohen, A. 1966. *Deviance and Control.* Englewood Cliffs, N.J.: Prentice-Hall.

Cohen, J. 1988. *Statistical Power Analysis for the Behavioral Sciences.* Hillsdale, N.J.: Lawrence Erlbaum.

Collingwood, T., and R. Genthner. 1980. "Skills Training as Treatment for Juvenile Delinquents." *Professional Psychology* 11: 591–98.

Cook, T., H. Cooper, D. Cordray, H. Hartman, L. Hedges, R. Light, T. Louis, and F. Mosteller eds. 1992. *Meta-analysis for Explanation: A Casebook.* New York: Russell Sage Foundation.

Cullen, F., and P. Gendreau. 1989. "The Effectiveness of Correctional Rehabilitation." In *The American Prison: Issues in Research Policy*, edited by L. Goodstein and D. MacKenzie. New York: Plenum.

Cullen, F., and K. Gilbert. 1982. *Reaffirming Rehabilitation.* Cincinnati: Anderson Publishing Co.

Davidson, W., R. Gottschalk, L. Gensheimer, and J. Mayer. 1984. "Interventions with Juvenile Delinquents: A Meta-analysis of Treatment Efficacy." Washington, D.C.: National Institute of Juvenile Justice and Delinquency Prevention.

Davidson, W., R. Redner, C. Blakely, C. Mitchell, and J. Emshoff. 1987. "Diversion of Juvenile Offenders: An Experimental Comparison." *Journal of Consulting and Clinical Psychology.* 55: 68–75.

Devine, E. 1992. "Effects of Psychoeducational Care with Adult Surgical Patients: A Theory Probing Meta-analysis of Intervention Studies." In *Meta-analysis for Explanation: A Casebook.* See Cook et al., 1992.

Duffee, D., and E. McGarrell. 1990. *Community Corrections: A Community Field Approach.* Cincinnati: Anderson Publishing Co.

Dunford, F., D. Osgood, and H. Weichselbaum. 1981. National Evaluation of Diversion Projects. Final report. Washington, D.C.: National Institute of Juvenile Justice and Delinquency Prevention.

Elliot, D., S. Ageton, and R. Canter, 1979. "An Integrated Theoretical Perspective on Delinquent Behavior." *Journal of Research in Crime and Delinquency* 16(1): 3–27.

Empey, L. 1978. *American Delinquency: Its Meaning and Construction.* Homewood, Ill.: Dorsey.

Empey, L., and M. Stafford. 1991. *American Delinquency: Its Meaning and Construction*. 3d ed. Belmont, Calif.: Wadsworth.

Ervin, L., and A. Schneider. 1990. "Explaining the Effects of Restitution on Offenders: Results from a National Experiment in Juvenile Courts." In *Criminal Justice, Restitution, and Reconcilation*, edited by B. Galaway and J. Hudson. Monsey, NY: Criminal Justice Press.

Fagan, J., M. Forst, and T. Vivona. 1988. Treatment and Reintegration of Violent Juvenile Offenders. San Francisco: URSA Institute.

Fiske, D. 1983. "The Meta-analytic Revolution in Outcome Research." *Journal of Consulting and Clinical Psychology* 51(1): 65–70.

Folkard, M., D. E. Smith, and D. D. Smith. 1976. *IMPACT: Intensive Matched Probation and After-care Treatment*. Vol. 2, *The Results of the Experiment*. Home Office Research Study no. 36. London: Her Majesty's Stationery Office.

Galaway, B. 1988. "Restitution as Innovation or Unfulfilled Promise?" *Federal Probation* 52(3): 3–14.

Garrett, C. 1985. "Effects of Residential Treatment on Adjudicated Delinquents: A Meta-analysis." *Journal of Research in Crime and Delinquency* 22: 287–308.

Geismar, L., and K. Wood. 1986. *Family and Delinquency: Resocializing the Young Offender*. New York: Human Sciences Press.

Gendreau, P., and D. Andrews. 1989. "What the Meta-analysis of the Offender Treatment Literature Tells Us about 'What Works.'" Laboratory for Research on Assessment and Evaluation in the Human Services, University of Ottawa.

Gendreau, P. and R. Ross. 1979. "Effective Correctional Treatment: Bibliotherapy for Cynics." *Crime and Delinquency*. 25: 463–89.

———. 1987. "Revivification of rehabilitation: evidence from the 1980s." *Justice Quarterly* 4(3): 349–407.

Genevie, L., E. Margolies, and G. Muhlin. 1986. "How Effective is Correctional Intervention?" *Social Policy* 17: 52–57.

Gensheimer, L., J. Mayer, R. Gottschalk, and W. Davidson. 1986. "Diverting Youth from the Juvenile Justice System: A Meta-analysis of Intervention Efficacy." In *Youth Violence: Program and Prospects*, edited by S. Apter and A. Goldstein. New York: Pergamon.

Gibbons, D. 1965. *Changing the Lawbreaker*. Englewood Cliffs, NJ: Prentice-Hall.

Gibbons, D. and G. Blake. 1976. "Evaluating the Impact of Juvenile Diversion Programs." *Crime and Delinquency* 22: 411–20.

Gibbs, J., K. Arnold, H. Ahlborn, and F. Chessman. 1984. "Facilitation of Socio-moral Reasoning in Delinquents." *Journal of Consulting and Clinical Psychology* 52: 37–45.

Glaser, D. 1971. *Social Deviance*. Chicago: Markham.

———. 1975. "Achieving Better Questions: A Half Century's Progress in Correctional Research." *Federal Probation* 39: 3–9.

Glass, G., B. McGaw, and M. Smith. 1981. *Meta-analysis in Social Research.* Beverly Hills, Calif.: Sage Publications.

Goldstein, A. 1986. "Psychological Skill Training and the Aggressive Adolescent." In *Youth Violence: Programs and Prospects*, edited by S. Apter and A. Goldstein. New York: Pergamon.

Gordon, D., and J. Arbuthnot. 1987. "Individual, Group, and Family Interventions." In *Handbook of Juvenile Delinquency*, edited by H. Quay. New York: Wiley.

Gottfredson, G. 1987. "Peer Group Interventions to Reduce the Risk of Delinquent Behavior: A Selective Review and Evaluation." *Criminology* 25: 671–714.

Gottfredson, M., and T. Hirschi. 1990. *A General Theory of Crime*. Stanford, Calif.: Stanford University Press.

Gottfredson, S., and D. Gottfredson. 1986. "Accuracy of Prediction Models." In *Criminal Careers and Career Criminals, vol. 2*, edited by A. Blumstein. Washington, D.C.: National Academy Press.

Gottschalk, R., W. Davidson, L. Gensheimer, and J. Mayer. 1987. "Community-based Interventions." In *Handbook of Juvenile Delinquency*, edited by H. Quay. New York: Wiley.

Graziano, A., and K. Mooney. 1984. *Children and Behavior Therapy.* Chicago: Aldine.

Greenberg, D. 1977. "The Correctional Effects of Corrections: A Survey of Evaluations." In *Corrections and Punishment*, edited by D. Greenberg. Beverly Hills, CA: Sage Publications.

Gruenewald, P., S. Laurence, and B. West. 1985. "National Evaluation of the New Pride Replication Program: Executive Summary." Walnut Creek, CA: Pacific Institute for Research and Evaluation.

Guttman, E. 1963. "Effects of Short-term Psychiatric Treatment on Boys in Two California Youth Authority Institutions." Research Report No. 36. Sacramento: California Youth Authority.

Harrison, R., and P. Mueller. 1964. "Clue Hunting about Group Counseling and Parole Outcome." Research Report No. 11. Sacramento: California Department of Corrections.

Havel, J., and E. Sulka. 1962. "Special Investigative Parole Unit: Phase III." Research Report no. 3. Sacramento: California Department of Corrections.

Hazel, J., J. Schumaker, J. Sherman, and J. Sheldon-Wildgen. 1981. *ASSET: A Social Skills Program for Adolescents.* Champaign, Ill.: Research Press.

Hedges, L., and I. Olkin. 1985. *Statistical Methods for Meta-analysis.* New York: Academic Press.

Heinz, J., B. Galaway, and J. Hudson. 1976. "Restitution or Parole: A Follow-up Study of Adult Offenders." *Social Service Review* 50: 148–56.

Hirschi, T. 1972. *Causes of Delinquency.* Berkeley and Los Angeles: University of California Press.

Hunt, D. 1971. *Matching Models in Education.* Toronto: Ontario Institute for Studies in Education.

Izzo, R., and R. Ross. 1990. "Meta-analysis of Rehabilitation Programs for Juvenile Delinquents." *Criminal Justice and Behavior* 17(1): 134–42.

Jeffrey, R., and S. Woolpert. 1974. "Work Furlough as an Alternative to Incarceration: An Assessment of its Effect on Recidivism and Social Cost." *The Journal of Criminal Law and Criminology* 65(3): 405–15.

Jesness, C. 1971–72. "Comparative Effectiveness of Two Institutional Treatment Programs for Delinquents." *Child Care Quarterly* 1(2): 119–39.

————. 1975. "Comparative Effectiveness of Behavior Modification and Transactional Analysis Programs for Delinquents." *Journal of Consulting and Clinical Psychology* 43(6): 758–79.

Jesness, C., T. Allison, P. McCormick, R. Wedge and M. Young. 1975. *"Cooperative Behavior Demonstration Project: Final Report."* Sacramento: Office of Criminal Justice Planning.

Johns, D., and J. Wallach. 1981. "Juvenile Delinquency Prevention: A Review of Evaluation Studies, 1974–1979." Sacramento: California Youth Authority.

Kaufman, P. 1985. "Meta-analysis of Juvenile Delinquency Prevention Programs." Master's thesis, Claremont Graduate School. Claremont, Calif.

Kelley, F., and D. Baer. 1971. "Physical Challenge as a Treatment for Delinquency." *Crime and Delinquency* 17: 437–45.

Kiessling, J., and D. Andrews. 1980. "Behavior Analysis Systems in Corrections: A New Approach to the Synthesis of Correctional Theory, Practice, Management and Research." *Canadian Journal of Criminology* 22(4): 412–27.

Klein, M. 1979. "Deinstitutionalization and Diversion of Juvenile Offenders: A Litany of Impediments." In *Crime and Justice: An Annual Review of Research*, vol. 1, edited by N. Morris and M. Tonry. Chicago: University of Chicago Press.

Klockars, C. 1975. "The True Limits of Correctional Effectiveness." *The Prison Journal* 55: 53–64.

Kohlberg, L. 1976. "Moral Stages and Moralization." In *Development and Behavior*, edited by T. Lickona. New York: Holt, Rinehart, and Winston.

Krisberg, B., O. Rodriguez, A. Baake, D. Neuenfeldt, and P. Steele. 1989. "Demonstration of Post-adjudication, Non-residential Intensive Supervision Programs: Assessment Report." San Francisco: National Council on Crime and Delinquency.

Lab, S., and J. Whitehead. 1988. "An Analysis of Juvenile Correctional Treatment." *Crime and Delinquency* 34: 60–85.

Lee, R., and N. Haynes. 1980. "Project CREST and the Dual-treatment Approach to Delinquency: Methods and Research Summarized." In *Effective Correctional Treatment*, edited by R. Ross and P. Gendreau. Toronto: Butterworths.

Lemert, E. 1972. *Human Deviance, Social Problems and Social Control.* Englewood Cliffs, N.J.: Prentice-Hall.

Lerner, K., G. Arling, and C. Baird. 1986. "Client Management Classification Strategies for Case Supervision." *Crime and Delinquency* 32: 254–71.

Leviton, L., and T. Cook. 1986. "What Differentiates Meta-analysis from Other Forms of Review?" *Journal of Personality* 49: 231–36.

Light, R., and D. Pillemer. 1984. *Summing Up: The Science of Reviewing Research.* Cambridge, Mass.: Harvard University Press.

Lillyquist, M. 1980. *Understanding and Changing Criminal Behavior.* Englewood Cliffs, N.J.: Prentice-Hall, Inc.

Lipsey, M. 1989. "The Efficacy of Intervention for Juvenile Delinquency." Paper presented at the American Society of Criminology annual meeting, Reno, November.

————. 1992. "Juvenile Delinquency Treatment: A Meta-analytic Inquiry into the Viability of Effects." In *Meta-Analysis for Explanation: A Casebook.* See Cook et al., 1992.

Lipton, D., R. Martinson, and J. Wilks. 1975. *The Effectiveness of Correctional Intervention: A Survey of Treatment Evaluation Studies.* New York: Praeger.

Loevinger, J. 1976. *Ego Development.* San Francisco: Jossey-Bass Publishers.

Logan, C. 1972. "Evaluation Research in Crime and Delinquency: A Reappraisal." *Journal of Criminal Law, Criminology, and Police Science.* 63: 378–87.

Losel, F. and P. Koferl. 1989. "Evaluation research on correctional treatment in West Germany: a meta-analysis." In *Criminal Behavior and the Justice System: Psychological Perspectives*, edited by H. Wegener, F. Losel, and J. Haisch. New York: Springer-Verlag.

Lundman, R. 1984. *Prevention and Control of Juvenile Delinquency.* New York: Oxford University Press.

McCord, W. 1968. "Delinquency: Psychological Aspects." In *International Encyclopedia of the Social Sciences*, New York: Macmillan and Free Press.

McDonald, C. 1989. "The Cost of Corrections: In Search of the Bottom Line." *Research in Corrections* 2(1): 1–40.

McShane, M., and F. Williams. 1989. "Running on Empty: Creativity and the Correctional Agenda." *Crime and Delinquency* 35: 562–76.

Maltz, M. 1984. *Recidivism.* Orlando, Fla.: Academic Press.

Mannheim, H., and L. Wilkins. 1955. *Prediction Methods in Relation to Borstal Training.* London: Her Majesty's Stationery Office.

Martin, S., L. Sechrest, and R. Redner. 1981. *New Directions in the Rehabilitation of Criminal Offenders*. Washington, D.C.: National Academy Press.

Martinson, R. 1974. "What Works?—Questions and Answers about Prison Reform." *The Public Interest* 35: 22–54.

———. 1976. "California Research at the Crossroads." *Crime and Delinquency* 22: 180–91.

———. 1979. "Symposium on Sentencing." Pt. 2. *Hofstra Law Review.* 7(2): 243–58.

Masten, A. 1979. "Family Therapy as a Treatment for Children: A Critical Review of the Outcome Research." *Family Process* 18: 323–35.

Matza, D. 1964. *Delinquency and Drift.* New York: Wiley.

Mayer, J., L. Gensheimer, W. Davidson, and R. Gottschalk. 1986. "Social Learning Treatment within Juvenile Justice: A Meta-analysis of Impact in the Natural Environment." In *Youth Violence: Program and Prospects*, edited by S. Apter and A. Goldstein. New York: Pergamon.

Megargee, E., M. Bohn, Jr., and F. Sink. 1979. *Classifying Criminal Offenders: A New System Based on the MMPI.* Beverly Hills, Calif.: Sage Publications.

Merton, R. 1968. *Social Theory and Social Structure.* New York: Free Press.

Miller, W. 1958. "Lower Class Culture as a Generating Milieu of Gang Delinquency." *Journal of Social Issues* 14(3): 5–19.

Moos, R. 1975. *Evaluating Correctional and Community Settings.* New York: Wiley.

Mueller, P. 1960. "Success Rates as a Function of Treatment Assignment and Juvenile Delinquency Classification Interaction." California State Board of Corrections Monograph 1: 7–14.

Nye, F. 1958. *Family Relationships and Delinquent Behavior.* New York: Wiley.

O'Donnell, C., T. Lydgate, and W. Fo. 1979. "The Buddy System: Review and Follow-up." *Child Behavior Therapy* 1: 161–69.

Olson, D., C. Russell, and D. Sprenkle. 1980. "Marital and Family Therapy: A Decade of Review." *Journal of Marriage and the Family* 42: 973–93.

Palmer, T. 1965. "Types of Treaters and Types of Juvenile Offenders." *Youth Authority Quarterly* 18: 14–23.

———. 1967. *Personality Characteristics and Professional Orientations of Five Groups of Community Treatment Project Workers: A Preliminary Report on Differences among Treaters.* Sacramento: California Youth Authority.

———. 1969. "A developmental-adaptation theory of youthful personality." Pt. 1. Sacramento: California Youth Authority.

———. 1973. "Matching Worker and Client in Corrections." *Social Work* 18(2): 95–103.

———. 1974. "The Youth Authority's Community Treatment Project." *Federal Probation* 38(1): 3–14.

———. 1975. "Martinson Revisited." *Journal of Research in Crime and Delinquency* 12: 133–52.

———. 1978. *Correctional Intervention and Research: Current Issues and Future Prospects.* Lexington, Mass.: Lexington Books.

———. 1983. "The 'effectiveness' Issue Today: An Overview." *Federal Probation* 47(2): 3–10.

———. 1984. "Treatment and the Role of Classification: A Review of Basics." *Crime and Delinquency* 30: 245–67.

———. 1991a. "The Effectiveness of Intervention: Recent Trends and Current Issues." *Crime and Delinquency* 37: 330–46.

———. 1991b. "The Habilitation/Developmental Perspective: Missing Link in Corrections." *Federal Probation* 55(1): 55–65.

———. 1992. *The Re-emergence of Correctional Intervention.* Newbury Park, Calif.: Sage Publications.

Palmer, T., and R. Lewis. 1980. "A Differentiated Approach to Juvenile Diversion." *Journal of Research in Crime and Delinquency* 17(2): 209–29.

Palmer, T., V. Neto, D. Johns, J. Turner, and J. Pearson. 1968. "The Sacramento-Stockton and the San Francisco Experiments." Report no. 9, pt. 1. Sacramento: California Youth Authority.

Palmer, T. and R. Wedge. 1989a. "California's Juvenile Probation Camps: Findings and Implications." *Crime and Delinquency* 35: 234–53.

————. 1989b. "California's juvenile probation camps: summary." Sacramento: California Youth Authority.

Panizzon, A. G. Olson-Raymer, and N. Guerra. 1991. "Delinquency Prevention: What Works/What Doesn't." Sacramento: Office of Criminal Justice Planning.

Parent, D. 1989. "Shock Incarceration: An Overview of Existing Programs." Washington, D.C.: National Institute of Justice.

Parisi, N. 1980. "Combining Incarceration and Probation." *Federal Probation* 44: 3–12.

Patterson, G. 1986. "Performance Models for Antisocial Boys." *American Psychologist* 41: 432–444.

Patterson, G., and M. Fleischman. 1979. "Maintenance of Treatment Effects: Some Considerations Concerning Family Systems and Follow-up data." *Behavior Therapy* 10: 168–85.

President's Commission on Law Enforcement and Administration of Justice. 1967. *The Challenge of Crime in a Free Society.* Washington, D.C.: U. S. Government Printing Office.

Quay, H. 1984. *Managing Adult Inmates.* Washington, D.C.: American Correctional Association.

Quinney, R. 1977. *Class, State, and Crime.* New York: Longman.

Reckless, W. 1967. *The Crime Problem.* New York: Appleton-Century-Crofts.

Reiss, A. 1951. "Delinquency as a Failure of Personal and Social Controls." *American Sociological Review* 15: 196–207.

Romig, D. 1978. *Justice for Our Children.* Lexington, Mass.: Lexington Books.

Ross, R., and E. Fabiano. 1985. *Time to Think: A Cognitive Model of Delinquency Prevention and Offender Rehabilitation.* Johnson City, Tenn.: Institute of Social Science and Art.

Rutter, M., and H. Giller. 1983. *Juvenile Delinquency: Trends and Perspectives.* New York: Pergamon.

Schneider, A. 1986. "Restitution and Recidivism Rates of Juvenile Offenders: Results from Four Experimental Studies." *Criminology* 24: 533–52.

Schneider, A., and L. Ervin. 1990. "Specific Deterrence, Rational Choice, and Decision Heuristics: Applications in Juvenile Justice." *Social Science Quarterly* 71(3): 585–601.

Schneider, A., and P. Schneider. 1985. "The Impact of Restitution on Recidivism of Juvenile Offenders: An Experiment in Clayton County, Georgia." *Criminal Justice Review* 10: 1–10.

Schrag, C. 1971. *Crime and Justice: American Style.* Washington, D.C.: National Institute of Mental Health, Crime and Delinquency Issues.

Sealy, A., and C. Banks. 1971. "Social Maturity, Training, Experience and Recidivism amongst British Borstal Boys." *British Journal of Criminology* 11(3): 245–64.

Sechrest, L., S. White, and E. Brown. 1979. "The Rehabilitation of Criminal Offenders: Problems and Prospects." Washington, D.C.: The National Academy of Sciences.

Selke, W. 1982. "Diversion and Crime Prevention: A Time Series Analysis." *Criminology* 20: 395–406.

Shadish, W., Jr. 1992. "Do Family and Marital Psychotherapies Change What People Do? A Meta-analysis of Behavioral Outcomes." In *Meta-analysis for Explanation: A Casebook.* See Cook et al., 1992.

Shaw, C., and H. McKay. 1972. *Juvenile Delinquency and Urban Areas.* Chicago: University of Chicago Press.

Shore, M., and J. Massimo. 1979. "Fifteen Years after Treatment: A Follow-up Study of Comprehensive Vocationally Oriented Psychotherapy" *American Journal of Orthopsychiatry* 49: 240–45.

Siegal, L., and J. Senna. 1985. *Juvenile Delinquency: Theory, Practice, and Law.* St. Paul, Minn.: West Publishing Co.

Strube, M., and D. Hartmann. 1983. "Meta-analysis: Techniques, Applications, and Functions." *Journal of Consulting and Clinical Psychology* 51(1): 14–27.

Sutherland, E., and D. Cressey. 1970. *Principles of Criminology.* New York: Lippencott.

Sykes, G. 1974. "The Rise of Critical Criminology." *Journal of Criminal Law and Criminology* 65: 211–17.

The Staff of the Computation Laboratory. 1955. *Tables of the Cumulative Binomial Probability Distribution.* Cambridge, Mass.: Harvard University Press.

U. S. Department of Justice. 1992. "Bureau of Justice Statistics, National Update." Washington, D.C.: U. S. Department of Justice, Office of Justice Programs.

Van Voorhis, P. 1987. "Correctional Effectiveness: The High Cost of Ignoring Success." *Federal Probation* 51(1): 56–62.

Van Voorhis, P. 1994. *Psychological Classification of the Adult, Male Prison Inmate*. Albany, NY: State University of New York Press.

Vito, G. 1984. "Developments in Shock Probation: A Review of Research Findings and Policy Implications." *Federal Probation* 48: 22–27.

von Wright, G. 1972. "Induction." In *Encyclopedia Britannica*. 12th ed. Chicago: Encyclopedia Britannica.

Warren, M. 1971. "Classification of Offenders as an Aid to Efficient Management and Effective Treatment." *Journal of Crime, Law, Criminology, and Police Science* 62: 239–58.

———. 1972. "Classification for Treatment." Paper presented at the National Institute of Law Enforcement and Criminal Justice Conference on the State of Research, Washington, D.C.

Wax, M. 1977. "Effects of Symbolic Restitution and Presence of Victim on Delinquent Shoplifters." Doctoral diss., Washington State University, Pullman, Wash.

Wedge, R., and T. Palmer. 1989. "California's Juvenile Probation Camps: A Technical Analysis of Outcomes for a 1982 Release Cohort." Camps, Ranches, and Schools Study, report no. 4. Sacramento: California Youth Authority.

Weeks, H. 1958. *Youthful Offenders at Highfields*. Ann Arbor, Mich.: University of Michigan Press.

West, D., and D. Farrington. 1977. *The Delinquent Way of Life*. London: Heinemann.

Whitehead, J., and S. Lab. 1989. "A Meta-analysis of Juvenile Correctional Treatment." *Journal of Research in Crime and Delinquency* 26(3): 276–95.

Wilson, J. 1980. " 'What Works' Revisited: New Findings on Criminal Rehabilitation." *The Public Interest* 61: 3–17.

Winterdyk, J., and R. Roesch. 1982. "A Wilderness Experimental Program as an Alternative for Probationers: An Evaluation." *Canadian Journal of Criminology* 23: 39–49.

Wolf, F. 1986. *Meta-analysis: Quantitative Methods for Research Synthesis.* Beverly Hills, Calif.: Sage Publications.

Wooldredge, J. 1988. "Differentiating the Effects of Juvenile Court Sentences on Eliminating Recidivism." *Journal of Research in Crime and Delinquency* 25(3): 264–300.

Wright, W., and M. Dixon. 1977. "Juvenile Delinquency Prevention: A Review of Evaluation Studies." *Journal of Research in Crime and Delinquency* 14(1): 35–67.

Index

About the Author

Ted Palmer is a Senior Researcher at the California Youth Authority. He received a Ph.D. in Psychology from the University of Southern California in 1963. He was coinvestigator of California's Community Treatment Project from 1963 to 1967 and principal investigator from 1967 to 1974. In addition to writing articles and monographs on treatment effectiveness, worker-client matching, and developmental change, he has authored *Correctional Intervention and Research* and, recently, *The Re-emergence of Correctional Intervention*. Palmer researched group homes, was principal author of *An Evaluation of Juvenile Diversion*, directed a statewide study of juvenile probation camps (1984–89), and coordinated statewide needs-assessments of youth centers, youth shelters, juvenile detention facilities, and Native-American youth. He has also been a consulting editor of various correctional journals.